Talk Radio's
AMERICA

Talk Radio's
AMERICA

How an Industry Took Over a Political Party

That Took Over the United States

Brian Rosenwald

Harvard University Press

Cambridge, Massachusetts
London, England

2019

Library of Congress Cataloging-in-Publication Data

Names: Rosenwald, Brian, author.
Title: Talk radio's America : how an industry took over a political party
    that took over the United States / Brian Rosenwald.
Description: Cambridge, Massachusetts : Harvard University Press, 2019. |
    Includes bibliographical references and index.
Identifiers: LCCN 2019014146 | ISBN 9780674185012 (alk. paper)
Subjects: LCSH: Radio talk shows—Political aspects—United States. |
    Radio talk show hosts—United States. | Radio in politics—United States. |
    Conservatism—United States. | Right-wing extremists—United States. |
    Political parties—United States. | United States—Politics and
    government—1989– | Republican Party (U.S. : 1854–)
Classification: LCC PN1991.8.T35 R67 2019 | DDC 384.54/430973—dc23
    LC record available at https://lccn.loc.gov/2019014146

To my parents, without whose love, support, and sacrifices this book wouldn't be possible.

Contents

Talk Radio's
AMERICA

Introduction

AUGUST 1, 1988, marked the beginning of the long road to President Donald Trump. But even political junkies took little notice of the fateful event that unfolded on that day, as a failed disc jockey and former Kansas City Royals executive named Rush Hudson Limbaugh III made his national radio debut. Only a small audience tuned in. So poorly commemorated was the moment that we don't even know how many stations broadcast day one of Limbaugh's syndicated program. Limbaugh claims the show began on fifty-six affiliates, while other counts range between fifty-seven and eighty-seven.[1]

From the beginning the show was brash, entertaining, controversial, and boundary-pushing. Before Limbaugh this sort of programming did not exist outside major cities. In 1983 there were just fifty-nine talk radio stations nationwide, and the programming on many of those stations consisted of advice shows, staid interviews, and caller-driven discussions of everything from neighborhood schools to abominable snowmen.[2] Most talk radio programming focused on local concerns, and most of the industry's stars, such as Larry King and Sally Jessy Raphael, had left-of-center views but rarely shared them.

At the time of Limbaugh's national debut, talk radio had negligible political impact. In talk radio hotbeds such as Boston, hosts might influence local and statewide policy debates, especially on visceral issues such as seat belt laws. But talk radio was not a partisan force, and it had no role in national politics. In fact the wall-to-wall conservative political talk stations that dominate the AM airwaves today were impossible until 1987, thanks to a regulation called the fairness doctrine. That year, however, the Federal Communications Commission (FCC) eliminated the policy, which required broadcasters of opinionated programming on controversial issues to offer an array of viewpoints.

In this more permissive environment, Limbaugh would go on to revolutionize the radio business. In doing so he helped unintentionally to spawn a major new political player. Within a decade the broadcast format he inaugurated aired on more than a thousand stations and kept millions company as they commuted, worked, and shouted back at their radios. It took just a few years before conservative talk radio began to influence national politics and public policy. That influence only grew throughout the decade as the business changed. Over the course of the 1990s and early 2000s, the number of nationally syndicated talk shows rose dramatically, and the content of talk radio programs became increasingly political and conservative.

Liberal pundits and some scholars agree on the broad outlines of the story: conservative station executives, conspiring with their Republican allies, built a format modeled on Limbaugh's program, and thousands of Limbaugh-wannabes cropped up all over the country.[3] Executives, hosts, and politicians turned talk radio into an appendage of the Republican Party, using the platform to get Republicans elected and advance the party's agenda. The success of talk radio led to the development of partisan and ideological cable news networks, and some hosts complemented their radio shows with primetime cable programs. Eventually this content found a home in the new digital sphere, with equally strident cheerleaders proliferating on blogs and other online publications.

This narrative makes sense, especially to liberals. After all, many conservative-media executives—and their corporate political action committees—donate to Republican candidates, and most hosts champion conservative candidates and causes. But this narrative is wrong. In reality the story of talk radio's emergence as a popular conservative format, and the impact it had on American politics, weaves together two distinct, complex tales. Neither has anything to do with a conspiracy to create a media servant of the Republican Party.

The first describes how talk radio spread across America, in the process saving AM radio from financial ruin. Limbaugh had no intention of affecting elections or legislation, and no inkling that he could. Nor did any of his early successors. The executives who gave these hosts a chance also had no interest in political outcomes. Hosts and their bosses were in business. They wanted to captivate listeners and make money, and they discovered, essentially by accident, that conservative political talk—in the mouth of an entertaining personality—achieved this. Conservative hosts had strong opinions, but their primary goal was, and still is, financial gain. And it is because they realized financial gain that more and more stations invested in their style and content, while divesting from competing formats.

The second story concerns talk radio's transformation, after 1995, into an almost entirely conservative and doctrinaire medium that eventually spawned successors in other media, took over the Republican Party, and reshaped it in hosts' and listeners' image.[4] Limbaugh was a great innovator, but he didn't change American media and politics all at once or on his own. In conservative talk radio's early days, hosts shared stations with liberal talkers and apolitical programs. There was not an immediate sense that conservative radio was the future, either. But gradually its success snowballed thanks to trial and error in the radio business, regulatory changes, political events, happenstance, and most importantly, listener behavior.

Hosts also got a boost from marginalized conservative Republican politicians, who realized that talk radio would enable them to circumnavigate the mainstream media and deliver their message directly to voters. Before talk radio came along, these politicians had trouble attracting media attention. So they invested their own credibility in the burgeoning medium, and they got lucky. It turned out that talk radio hit a nerve with a segment of the public that was disgusted by what they perceived as the mainstream media's liberal bias. In partnership with talk radio, Republicans secured an extraordinary victory in the 1994 midterm elections, capturing the House of Representatives for the first time in forty years. This unlikely outcome cemented the bond between Republicans and talk radio.

Over time the GOP would become more and more reliant on radio entertainers, until those entertainers became essential to Republicans' electoral hopes. Talk radio and its successors thereby became a more powerful force than the party that cultivated them. Limbaugh, Fox News, and eventually Breitbart News proceeded to hollow out the Republican Party, replacing its moderate and pragmatic factions with hard-right ideologues who promised to pursue the priorities conservative media personalities and their audience had long demanded. But these promises were never achievable, and as they were repeatedly broken, conservative media and activists

3

became that much angrier. They doubled down, broaching no dissent and severely constraining Republicans' freedom of action.

The consequences are plain to see. Today's Republican Party is incapable of bipartisan governance. And it is led by Donald Trump, a figure who resembles less a president from central casting than a talk radio host. Trump owes his political career to the likes of Sean Hannity and Laura Ingraham and to conservative social media. They gave him a platform and, if his rhetoric is any indication, trained him in political oratory. His election is the purest product of the revolution Limbaugh began.

The faulty notion that talk radio is and has always been a puppet of the Republican Party is popular in part because scholars have not delved deeply into this topic. They have explored the broadest consequences of the development of talk radio and cable news: the echo chambers that reinforce Americans' partisan and philosophical convictions and skew their understanding of policy debates and political opponents.[5] These echo chambers in turn produce a more polarized political arena in which it is hard to get the public's business done.[6] Early research on the rise of talk radio also examined who listened to talk radio; whether the medium affected electoral outcomes, especially in presidential races; and listeners' attitudes toward political figures, furthering our understanding of who is in the echo chamber and what are its effects.[7]

Yet, while we now have valuable knowledge about how ideological media enable echo chambers, scholars have neglected the critically important impact of these media on the nuts and bolts of politics and policymaking. The two parties use these media differently. A close look at their histories with ideological media clarifies the power dynamics between the parties and the media and shows how those dynamics have reshaped the Republican Party and affected which bills become law. Scholars, pundits, and politicians tend only to see one element of the relationship between ideological media and Republicans. They see the very public alliance, exemplified by hosts cheerleading on behalf of Republicans, but less so the contest for power within the GOP itself, which talk radio has won at the expense of party moderates and even pragmatic conservatives.

Further, few observers have addressed the fact that talk radio is a business driven by the need to entertain and engage. Even those who do recognize that talk radio is a business rarely appreciate how commercial imperatives dictate the medium's content, tone and, accordingly, political impact. For example, Sarah Sobieraj and Jeffrey M. Berry, in *The Outrage*

Industry, position talk radio as a businesses in which decision-making is influenced by desire for profit. But they don't take the next step and point out that entertaining, more than informing or articulating the views of the audience, is talk radio's goal.[8] Nor have many scholars focused on the historical development of talk radio and the critical question of why it came to be dominated by conservatives.[9]

The pages that follow provide this history, chronicling how talk radio blazed a path that would later be followed by cable news and digital media with dramatic consequences for the media in general. Talk radio became the first of a new wave of ideologically driven niche media that revised how Americans consumed information and how they viewed journalism, in some respects returning us to the partisan press of the nineteenth century, albeit one more focused on entertaining than informing. When hosts spotlighted salacious, often-unverified stories that made for great radio, they forced the mainstream media to address these same stories, thereby damaging journalists' capacity to serve as gatekeepers who determined newsworthiness. The newsworthiness standard would crumble further with the rise of digital and social media, helping to blur the line between fact and fiction and spread mistruths, exaggerations, and distortions. At the same time, conservative media's relentless denigration of the mainstream press discredited journalism itself in the eyes of a large segment of the population.

With the traditional media no longer an arbiter of truth, extremist politicians were free to make outlandish claims that no one could effectively dispute. These claims were music to the ears of a scorned segment of the population that felt like its values were under siege. The lure of conservative media stardom pushed politicians down this path. When they followed it, they found their power augmented. They didn't have to be backbenchers in Congress, on the party fringe. The backing of conservative media protected them from Republican leaders trying to maintain party discipline, inverting traditional political and congressional power structures.

Limbaugh occupies center stage in this story. His meteoric national rise was the most important catalyst in the development of talk radio during the 1990s. The combination of his success and his political views triggered some of the programming decisions that helped to transform the medium into an almost entirely conservative and political megaphone. Politically, Limbaugh had a larger impact on the national consciousness than any other host by virtue of his near-universal name recognition and his ability to draw headlines. Limbaugh has long had the largest audience in the business; as of this writing, in February 2019, trade publication *Talkers Magazine* estimated Limbaugh's audience at 15.5 million listeners per week. This reach has enabled Limbaugh to throw his weight around in politics and in the broader media environment.[10] When Limbaugh rips an elected Republican, especially a party leader, he creates news, and the victim knows it from the phones ringing off the hook in his or her office.[11]

Limbaugh is a highly divisive figure, a hero to those who view him as a champion for their beliefs and a villain to those who loathe his ideas, his style, and his impact on society. Yet he is unquestionably a broadcasting visionary and master showman. He belongs in the pantheon of innovators alongside Edward R. Murrow, Chet Huntley, David Brinkley, Walter Cronkite, Tim Russert, David Letterman, Jon Stewart, and sportscaster John Madden. Regardless of how one judges Limbaugh's contributions to politics, public policy, broadcasting, and punditry, one must appreciate the magnitude of his impact and strive better to understand it.

Though business necessity and Limbaugh's success—not ideological or political goals—drove the development of talk radio, the medium would nonetheless emerge as a powerful political actor, upending electoral politics, the legislative process, and the fortunes of policy proposals. Most importantly talk radio contributed to the transformation of the Republican Party. It is in this respect that the narrative of talk radio as a GOP water carrier is most flawed. This conception fundamentally misunderstands the relationship between hosts and the political party that they generally support.

To be sure, hosts have aided Republicans greatly over the years. Although hosts were not typically elected officials, nor elected or appointed party dignitaries, they came to fulfill many traditional party leadership functions such as raising money, energizing voters, and framing events in a manner beneficial to the party and its politicians. Hosts' platform also enabled them to assume unique party leadership functions. They could promote incendiary stories that the mainstream media didn't consider newsworthy or didn't feel comfortable addressing, ginning up the conservative base without offending moderate voters who weren't paying attention. Hosts then channeled the ensuing conservative fury into political or legislative campaigns. Finally, hosts' pummeling of the mainstream media handed Republicans a means of escaping negative stories or charges. Rather than grapple with the charges, politicians could simply decry media bias or, later, fake news.

Yet dismissing hosts as mere Republican boosters ignores the influence they came to accumulate over the party. Indeed such a dismissal inverts the power relationship that emerged over three decades between hosts and elected Republicans and mistakes the source of hosts' clout. Hosts were never simply mindless partisan automata who blessed whatever elected Republicans did. Even dating to the early 1990s, they blasted Republican maneuvers with which they disagreed. During the 1990s and early 2000s, they gave Republicans a major lift, but by President George W. Bush's second term, hosts were drifting away. While they continued to aid Republican candidates and officials, especially at election time, they often proved more hindrance than help when it came to Republican efforts to govern and win majorities. Hosts frequently turned against Republican officials and candidates whose principles contradicted their own or who were insufficiently willing to wage war on behalf of the principles they shared.

Hosts' political power stemmed from the tight bond they shared with listeners—not from official party power structures. This bond, formed through hours spent together every day, gave hosts enormous influence with precisely the sort of people who voted in primaries: politically engaged partisans. These listeners took their favorite hosts' advice seriously in matters of politics and policy, candidates and issue positions. In turn Republicans were forced to take hosts' proclamations and threats with equal seriousness. Ignoring hosts' demands risked a primary challenge from a farther-right candidate who could rely on hosts for support. Even moderate Republicans treaded lightly lest they incite hosts' wrath.

Hosts were free to scold or eviscerate Republicans because, unlike traditional party leaders, their primary goal wasn't the well-being of the party. Instead their primary goals were commercial. Whereas elected officials and political operatives seek to win votes and affect the shape of government, radio hosts seek the largest possible audience for the greatest amount of time. Hosts experimented with their style and issue focus and, as the years progressed, discovered that pummeling Republicans, especially Republican leaders, boosted their bottom line. Conservatives frustrated by the officials they elected—in particular, by their perceived failure to fulfill promises and their ineffectual pursuit of a right-leaning agenda—were compelled to tune in.

Hosts' successful pursuit of their commercial goals had the effect of narrowing the contours of the GOP, constraining the range of acceptable ideology within the party. Talk radio's influence also reinforced a new type of party leadership that emerged over the last half century from two major changes in electoral dynamics: first, the decentralization, amid shifting campaign-finance rules and technological change, of control over electoral resources; second, the rise, due to increased gerrymandering and partisan population sorting, of primary elections as the most important locus of electoral competition in many states and districts. These changes empowered nonofficials—donors, think-tankers, grassroots organizers, pressure groups, and, above all, conservative media personalities. Hosts and other media impresarios could sometimes sway enough base voters to affect a congressional primary outcome.

The relationship between talk radio and the Republican Party was a Faustian bargain. Hosts provided substantial aid to Republican candidates and frequently labored to advance the Republican agenda. But, with time, the synergy of purpose between conservative media personalities and Republicans waned. As hosts and outlets proliferated, competition stiffened, and many conservative media figures guarded their flanks by lacerating Republicans. Hosts demanded from elected Republicans a level of ideological purity—and a warfare mentality—that made it far more difficult to be a nationally competitive party and to advance an agenda that would attract broad support.[12] These demands increasingly imperiled moderate Republicans and hamstrung governance.

Vulnerability to talk radio's favored primary challengers left Republicans more hesitant to compromise. During the 2010s the Republican leadership developed into villains in talk radio's soap opera, while backbenchers who specialized in incendiary soundbites and ideological purity became heroes. Talk radio joined with these elected hard-liners and new digital outlets such as Breitbart to thwart Speaker John Boehner and other leaders who would brook the compromises demanded by divided government. This coalition of right-wing media and rank-and-file House members often forced Boehner to seek Democratic votes just to pass basic appropriations bills that kept the government operational or to raise the debt ceiling and avoid economic catastrophe.

The result was a negative feedback loop: by expelling party moderates, the inflamed conservative airwaves forced Republicans to reach farther across the aisle for compromise during divided government, leading to still more inflamed conservative airwaves. Conservative media responded by calling for even more combative Republicans willing to fight for listeners' values at any cost.

This helps explain what may be the most stunning outcome in modern American political history: the election of President Donald Trump. Republican voters' attraction to Trump baffled many, especially during a highly competitive Republican primary. His past positions on issues such as abortion and guns had been outright heretical—disqualifying to primary voters, according to most observers. But Trump was the ideal candidate for the political world unleashed by talk radio and its progeny. His pugnacious style—constantly lashing out at liberals, the GOP establishment, and the mainstream media—was exactly what talk radio had offered for almost three decades. Trump supporters, many of whom cherished their favorite hosts for giving voice to what they felt but could not express publicly, at last had what they had craved for years: a candidate who sounded like their champions on the air, who didn't care about establishment approval or the politically correct press and wouldn't cave in the name of governance.

Even though Trump failed conservative purity tests, talk radio and eventually Fox News recognized their scion in him. Hosts went to bat for him, their diatribes against journalists encouraging Trump's fans to reject reporting on his many foibles, ideological heresies, boorish behaviors, and bigoted comments. What else could one expect from the awful liberal media? To conservative media consumers, negative press only confirmed Trump's qualifications for office.

Trump's debt to talk radio is apparent not only in his rhetorical style but also in his taste for conspiracy theories. Building on a long tradition in conservative circles, talk radio spread such theories and grew their political potency. For decades hosts fed their audiences a steady diet of salacious and outrageous charges against Democrats and liberals. In response the conservative base pressed Republicans to treat conspiracy theories as legitimate and take action. Republicans were forced to choose between their base and more moderate voters skeptical of the controversies peddled in conservative media. When Republicans attempted to chart a middle course, many conservative base voters fumed. To these voters Trump's penchant for slinging conspiracy theories and hyperbole was a refreshing bit of political courage. They cheered as he questioned whether President Barack Obama had been born in the United States and called for summary imprisonment of Hillary Clinton on the basis of unproven claims.

Trump's election exposed a truth that will be explored in the pages that follow: by 2016 talk radio had reshaped the American political landscape. No one had set out to weaponize the airwaves. But even though hosts' only goals were to create compelling radio and reap the financial rewards, talk radio had grown into a powerful political force. While many elected Republicans didn't notice until it was too late, under the influence of conservative media, their party gradually became a rigid far-right collection of politicians who had to lob rhetorical grenades and eschew compromise if they wanted to survive. The result was gridlock, hyperpartisanship, disdain for the political opposition and the establishment broadly construed, and a Republican Party transformed. In short, it is thanks to the commercial imperatives driving talk radio that the Republican Party was ripe for Trump's takeover.

1

The Colossus Rises

As a HIGHPOINT of the culture wars, the mid-1980s offered an auspicious moment for someone to develop a new, conservative-leaning media product. Yet no visionary appeared. Instead the growth of modern talk radio came about almost by accident. It was an unplanned byproduct of conservative disillusionment, financial crisis within the radio business, and Rush Limbaugh's talent.[1] Other factors, such as regulatory and technological changes, laid the foundation.[2] But these constituted preconditions for talk radio's rise more than causes.

At every turn the bottom line, not political calculations or ideological fervor, drove decision-making and shaped the talk radio product. The result, which reached full flower after the election of President Bill Clinton, was a curious creature: a political colossus for which commercial, not political, goals were of primary importance.

The culture wars that began in the second half of the 1960s alarmed and infuriated conservatives.[3] Over the course of the next two decades, they came to understand that the values they assumed all Americans embraced were anything but universal. In the realms of race, gender, and sexuality, conservatives were losing skirmishes, and they sensed that the war was slipping away. Nonwhites were winning greater legal equality and cultural recognition, while pressing claims to political power. The feminist movement scorned the notion of a male breadwinner married to a woman whose proper place was tending to the home and raising their children.[4] Although

11

LGBTQ equality was nowhere in sight, being publicly gay was increasingly common.

Conservatives' indignation also stemmed from an increasingly vulgar world of entertainment. From the 1988 film *The Last Temptation of Christ* to songs such as 2 Live Crew's "Me So Horny" and Madonna's "Like a Prayer," popular culture joined the ranks assaulting American beliefs and American greatness. What is more, conservatives were enraged that public money was funding profane art, revisionist textbooks, and colleges perceived as cultivating attitudes antithetical to capitalism, Christianity, and tradition. During the 1980s the costs and consequences of this moral degradation seemed ubiquitous and terrifying: AIDS, the crack epidemic, a 10 percent teenage pregnancy rate, and rampant divorce.[5]

In response conservative Americans directed their rage toward the liberal intellectuals, politicians, and media executives driving this invidious cultural permissiveness by supporting promiscuity (e.g., legalized abortion) and opposing moral guardrails (e.g., prayer in schools). Progressives claimed to care about equal rights, yet, from the perspective of conservatives, they cared only for the rights and priorities of minority groups—everyone imaginable—not those of good, God-fearing, law-abiding Americans. Hence liberals backed affirmative action and bilingual and multicultural education, and foisted offensive, obscene, unpatriotic textbooks on impressionable youth, but they rejected the rights of Christian parents to control what their kids learned about sex.[6]

Indeed, progressives seemed bent on undoing hard-working people for the sake of the slovenly, an economic argument that was linked to the culture wars through the language of "welfare queens" and opposition to "big government" social programs that benefited poor minorities, among others. Enough was enough. Attorney Augustus Agate spoke for aggrieved American conservatives when he told a *Boston Globe* reporter in 1987 that welfare programs were "bankrupting the country. . . . I'm giving up a third to 40 percent of my salary, and I'm living one step better than people who aren't working."[7]

It seemed to conservatives that the government and the political process were failing to address—or were even aggravating—the ills of violence, sex, and drugs to which they, their children, and their grandchildren were exposed.[8] And yet there was nothing these voters could do about it, so estranged were they from their country's politics. Lowell Henderson, a Louisiana architect quoted in a 1988 *Washington Post* story on the political potency of born-again Christians, summarized conservatives' alienation: "You look around at a country where they've got four-letter words on bumper stickers and you can't take your children to a movie and you're scared to send them to the school. . . . And it comes to you that the government shouldn't let those things happen to our country."[9]

If it wasn't awful enough that the "liberal establishment"—the news media, Hollywood, feminists, the NAACP, the academy, and the Democratic Party—was undermining American values, it did so while deliberately ridiculing and scorning conservatives. As Beverly Shelton of the Traditional Values Coalition complained, television executives called LGBTQ groups to determine the acceptability of a program, but religious groups received no such respect.[10]

Even after Ronald Reagan's rise in 1980 gave them a champion in the White House, conservatives lacked a widespread medium through which to vent against the derision they felt from the liberal establishment. Many also felt isolated in their opinions, or ashamed to express them. Doing so risked the opprobrium of the politically correct establishment, which labeled conservatives bigoted, heartless, or foolish.[11] As one consumer of "outrage media" told scholars Jeffrey Berry and Sarah Sobieraj in 2010, "It's just harder to be conservative because it's easy to call someone a racist. . . . I can tell you exactly what [my views] are, and some people will sit there and go, 'You're just wrong, you're conservative, you just hate people. You just hate Black people or poor people or gay people, or whatever.'"[12]

By the late 1980s, a bipartisan swath of Americans thought the news lacked conservative perspectives—indeed, that such perspectives were subject to subtle and unconscious bias, even contempt, in nominally objective reporting. A 1987 Pew poll found that 62 percent of Republicans and 48 percent of Democrats thought the press demonstrated bias in favor of liberals.[13] The news was reported through a much more progressive lens than the one through which conservatives saw the world.[14] Conservative talk radio host and former San Diego Mayor Roger Hedgecock explained that newsmen of the 1950s–1970s all exemplified a certain mindset: they opposed Richard Nixon and Ronald Reagan, supported President Kennedy and civil rights, and generally believed their worldview to be correct.[15] Journalist Howard Kurtz summarized the view of conservatives he spoke with, writing that mainstream journalists shared "the same assumptions about government, abortion, religion and just about everything else." Infuriatingly, in making these assumptions they failed "to realize how out of step

13

they are with the country."[16] Conservatives saw themselves as a majority being condescended to by a minority.

Conservative radio hosts Hugh Hewitt and Lars Larson, a Peabody Award–winning journalist, experienced this liberal groupthink during their time in television newsrooms.[17] Neither Larson nor Hewitt believed that journalists intentionally biased or distorted their reporting. Rather, they had a common orientation, a worldview stemming from the selection and training processes that underlay their profession. Journalists came from elite four-year universities that shared a similar liberal cultural background and ideology. They socialized with likeminded people, who all had the same notions about guns, women's roles in society, and other hot-button issues. Journalism schools taught reporters to put aside these views when working. But, inevitably, the values bred by their homogeneous experiences and learning environments affected journalists' story selection, assessments of newsworthiness, and the questions they posed while reporting.[18]

The push toward more investigative and advocacy journalism during the 1970s further fueled the perception of anti-conservative bias.[19] In the eyes of conservatives, investigative reporting forswore evenhanded coverage: instead of telling both sides of a story, journalists sought out stories that could be covered in a manner benefiting their preferred side. Thus veteran radio talker Dave Elswick felt that the mainstream media only presented conservative arguments when the journalist or host wished to explain conservative fallacies. For instance, in a perfect recent example of the journalistic practices that so rankled conservatives, host and former Congressman J. D. Hayworth argued that reporters allowed the left to set the terms, frames, and definitions of debate surrounding voter identification. The press, he said, discusses voter-identification laws in the context of conservative-led voter suppression, even though in 2005 the bipartisan Baker-Carter committee recommended that voters show photo IDs.[20]

Conservatives also detected condescension in this bias. In an interview Hayworth recalled overhearing a reporter tell another reporter that he had gone to a meeting of the conservative Republican Study Committee to see "what the wingnuts are up to."[21] Limbaugh has spent much of his career reminding listeners—and, between 1992 and 1996, TV viewers—that liberals consider them stupid and ignorant. "Liberal Democrats assign all of their defeats to the fact that you're stupid," he explained on one representative occasion. "You just don't understand what's good for you, and when you vote for Republicans or like what Republicans want to do, somehow you've been tricked—slick marketing and packaging."[22]

Finally, conservative culture warriors came to believe that the news media held them to different standards than they did liberals. For example the press ignored liberals' off-color humor, but the same kind of joke might land a conservative in hot water. Limbaugh pointed to one such case in 1995, when Ohio Democrat Sherrod Brown jokingly suggested reopening Pennsylvania Avenue, which had been closed to increase President Clinton's security. At the time Democrats were in "open revolt": Clinton had given an unexpected speech recommending a balanced budget, after his party had spent months savaging proposed Republican cuts. Limbaugh compared Brown's joke to Republican Senator Jesse Helms's quip that if President Clinton came to his state, North Carolina, he would need bodyguards. Unlike Brown, Helms was pilloried.[23] Similarly the press was said to judge ethical lapses on a sliding scale. Conservatives envisioned themselves in what Pat Buchanan branded "a war for the soul of America," and, in this war, journalists were cheerleaders for the opposition.[24]

Republican consultant Greg Stevens summarized the link between rising perceptions of media bias and the growth of talk radio. The latter took off, he said, "as the American people got tired of yelling back at talking heads on the evening television news."[25] Conservatives yearned for a voice that could speak truth to what they believed was the real power in America, without fear of reprisals. They were tired of tiptoeing through jobs, schools, and, increasingly, living rooms dominated by the liberal, politically correct establishment.

A Match Made in Heaven

AM radio faced dire straits in the late 1980s. The major culprit in its decline was the FM band, introduced in 1961. FM could carry a stereo signal, making it a better choice for music. And thanks to a unique culture, FM developed path-breaking, innovative stations that stood in stark contrast with the tightly programmed AM formats.[26] Soon enough FM stereos were standard in homes and cars, driving down AM's share of the radio audience from 75 percent in 1972 to 25 percent in 1988.[27] As listeners migrated to FM, advertising dollars followed; AM's share of radio ad revenue dropped from 90 percent in 1970 to around half in 1985.[28] By 1987 three out of four big-city AM stations, and about half of those in smaller markets, made no profit.[29]

During much of this period, the talk format was what star New York host Barry Farber called a "radio ghetto." Most talk shows aired late at night, as a way for music stations to fulfill the FCC requirement that they broadcast public-interest programming. As Farber recounted, in New York—outside of WOR, which blended music with shows about books, animals, and cooking—no mainstream 50,000-watt station would air talk radio before ten o'clock at night.[30]

It was desperation that drove many AM stations to discover the news-talk format in the 1980s and after. The format offered the potential for survival. Unlike music, talk sounded fine without a stereo medium. And, critically, FM did not carry news-talk, allowing AM a niche to exploit.[31] It didn't take long before the strategy paid dividends.[32] AM stations that switched from music to talk often enjoyed explosive ratings growth: WOL in Washington saw its audience increase by 48 percent after switching in 1981, and it was not alone.[33] Talk would not restore AM to the dominant position of its heyday, but the AM band would thrive into the twenty-first century thanks to interactive talk formats.

One factor that contributed to this success was the changing regulatory environment. In 1987 the FCC repealed the fairness doctrine, which for thirty-eight years had required that broadcast television and radio stations provide balanced coverage of controversial issues.[34] President Reagan's veto—issued out of ideological conviction, not a clairvoyant sense that the move would be politically beneficial—squelched bipartisan legislation that would have resurrected the doctrine.[35] While not the driving force behind the rise of talk radio, the elimination of the doctrine was an enabler and an accelerant. It had been possible under the terms of the doctrine to air edgy, opinionated talk shows, as Limbaugh had when he started on KFBK in Sacramento.[36] Two other acerbic and controversial conservative hosts, Bob Grant and Neal Boortz, provoked listeners for more than fifteen years with the fairness doctrine in place.[37] But with the fairness doctrine gone, they could do so without their bosses worrying that a lack of balance might land them in hot water with the FCC.

Technological innovations were more crucial to talk radio's rise. In particular the introduction of cheap satellite technology made it financially feasible to syndicate a radio program nationally, overcoming both distribution problems and the challenges small stations faced producing their own talk shows. Local talk was always scarce because it cost too much for many stations. Hosts needed to have better radio skills than the average DJ and thus demanded higher pay. And while a DJ could get by with just a producer, talk also required an engineer, a programmer, and a call screener. Syndication was no simple fix for stations facing these costs. A syndicator had to distribute programming over phone lines, which limited networks to transmitting one show at a time and forced stations to use expensive specialty lines. Satellite technology changed all that.

The advent of cellular phones was another major advance, allowing listeners to call talk stations from their cars. Bored drivers could engage their favorite hosts, boosting the popularity of talk radio. When veteran radio executive Gary Burns programmed WWRC in Washington, D.C., in the early 1990s, he cut a deal with two leading cellular providers to allow listeners to call the station for free.[38]

With the technological and regulatory ground prepared, talk radio was positioned to flourish in the cultural moment of the late 1980s. But it is important to keep in mind that talk radio thrived not only because of demand from disgruntled conservatives. Talk radio did speak to angry conservatives, but it also connected with alienated Americans more broadly, a fact that speaks to talk radio's forgotten origins as a purely commercial enterprise, innocent of any overarching ideology or partisan leaning.

The format blossomed at a time when American society had become more isolating: suburban sprawl drew neighbors farther apart and ensured more time spent alone in cars; new home-based forms of entertainment, such as cable television and VHS movies, also kept people to themselves. In his discussion of the "glorious, but terrifying isolation" of the 1980s, Gil Troy observes, "Talk radio would create an illusion of community and foster a surprisingly strong sense of identity at a time when anonymous shopping malls replaced intimate main streets, and political debate was exiled from the interactive town square to the passive TV studio."[39] Americans, especially older ones, yearned for connection and community, and talk radio provided it—a virtual replacement for the front stoop, through which they could discuss current affairs with people like themselves. Talk radio even allowed for the delicious experience of hearing others' intimate conversations.[40] As host Imhotep Gary Byrd put it, talk radio is "the one medium left where people can interact with each other with a sense of immediacy."[41]

It struck many hosts that talk radio's intimacy was an ideal means of filling voids in people's lives.[42] As liberal host Thom Hartmann explained, radio was a voyeuristic, personal, "hot medium," unlike the "cold medium" of TV, which offered no opportunities for interaction and no sense of a conversation between producer and consumer.[43] Boortz, an Atlanta libertarian host who rose to national stardom, said, "I'm in the bathroom with these people. . . . I'm in bed with them, taking showers, eating breakfast. This personal relationship gets built up. They think I'm talking to them one-on-one."[44] When Hayworth joined the talk radio ranks, he too fostered this intimacy. For example he might introduce a segment with the phrase, "as you and I discussed the other day," underscoring the illusion of an intimate conversation with each listener.[45] Once television surpassed the console radio as the family gathering point, this intimacy became radio's niche in people's lives. People listened individually on transistor and car radios, and they started forging individual relationships with favorite hosts.[46] Over the years comedian and political talker Tom Becka experienced this closeness repeatedly. For instance, listeners brought him cookies and flowers as thanks for taking their minds off of personal hardships such as cancer.[47] One avid fan of Ray Briem even left her home to the longtime Los Angeles host after she died.[48]

Radio hosts also had community impact. If a caller revealed that his brother's house burned down, the host could start a collection drive.[49] Los Angeles host Bill Handel helped to save a half-century-old local toy store from bankruptcy by staging a "cash mob": he encouraged listeners to shop at the store on a specific day and then spent hours signing autographs and greeting listeners who had heeded his call.[50] This ability to rally listeners would form the foundation of talk radio's political power.

In the early days of its ascent, talk radio was a safe harbor in a rapidly changing world—for listeners of any political persuasion. Talk radio was a "place" where one could be entertained and chat with friends. For conservatives alienated by the mainstream press, beginning in the late 1980s, talk radio offered a critical additional benefit: hearing one's views valorized. While the jokes and topics might change from day to day, conservative listeners gradually came to know that their values would guide most talk radio discussions and that their favorite hosts would punch back against the forces they saw dragging society down: liberals and the establishment media. The stations that pioneered political talk radio rarely shared that political agenda—their goal was to make money, and certainly they never took marching orders from Republicans. Broadcasters got lucky with the conservative audience. They stumbled upon an untapped market, and they capitalized on it.

2

With Talent on Loan from God

THE NEEDS OF FRUSTRATED conservatives and frantic AM radio executives might never have converged but for one man. Rush Limbaugh revealed the demand for conservative media programming and, according to many in the radio business, "single-handedly [kept] AM alive."[1] In the late 1980s and early 1990s, he exploded onto the scene with, as he cheekily put it, "talent on loan from God." Within a few years of his national debut, he had become a cultural phenomenon, catalyzing both the rise of talk radio and its eventual transformation into a predominantly conservative and political medium.[2]

If in 1984 one were trying to identify the next political-media star, or the guy who would save AM radio, odds are that Limbaugh's name would've been nowhere on the list of likely candidates. He was a college dropout who hadn't even registered to vote during his first twelve years of eligibility. He had gotten canned four times as a radio disc jockey, a job he performed under pseudonyms such as Jeff Christy and Rusty Sharpe. Years later at least one of the executives who fired Christy had no recollection of him, even when informed that the DJ actually was Limbaugh.[3]

With his radio career foundering, Limbaugh took a job with the Kansas City Royals in 1979. After a five-year stint doing group sales and special events for the team, Limbaugh was back on the air, reading the news for Kansas City's KMBZ. At first it seemed he was destined to get fired again, as he upset station management by adding commentary to the news. His beliefs—instilled by his father, who would have watched Fox News if it existed in the 1960s and 1970s—were affecting his story choices. Station management intended to let him go, but a consultant, Bill McMahon, asked to speak with him first. McMahon had discovered that radio executives often fired the most gifted people. He found himself mesmerized by Limbaugh's natural ability and offered to get him a slot doing commentary in exchange for reading the news straight. Limbaugh jumped at the deal. His short commentaries provoked massive response, largely negative at first. Over time the feedback became more mixed, though still visceral—people either loved or hated Limbaugh. Management liked the attention he drew in his new role and gave him his own talk program.

But some of Limbaugh's commentary ended up being too controversial for his bosses at KMBZ, which was owned by Bonneville, the radio arm of the Mormon Church. On one occasion, he got into hot water after ridiculing a gentrifying shopping development for replacing traditional Middle-American shops with tonier establishments. It was a reasonable protest against what he saw as a swipe at average people. Then, with tongue firmly planted in cheek, he suggested the management just prohibit ugly shoppers. Listeners complained, and management chastised Limbaugh. He eventually went too far when he ripped Kansas City Chiefs management at precisely the moment when the station was pursuing the Chiefs' radio contract. The team president complained to KMBZ's station manager, and once again Limbaugh was out of a job. Angry listeners could be good for business. Angry would-be sponsors or business partners—not so much.

As luck would have it, McMahon's business partner Norm Woodruff was programming KFBK in Sacramento, which had a vacancy after Morton Downey Jr.'s racist tirades cost him his job. Woodruff told Limbaugh that the station welcomed controversy and would support him so long as he believed what he said and treated callers politely. Limbaugh spent four years in Sacramento doing just that while he honed the program that would propel him to fame.

Pivotally, Bruce Marr, a consultant to KFBK who had also endorsed the station hiring Limbaugh, believed strongly in the host. Marr realized that Limbaugh had something special: he could reach through the radio and grab people, making them feel like he was their partner in an intimate conversation. Marr suggested to his friend, former ABC Radio President Ed McLaughlin, that Limbaugh had star written all over him. In 1988 McLaughlin checked out Limbaugh. After first listening in a hotel room, McLaughlin disagreed with Marr's assessment. But after enjoying dinner with the host and Marr, McLaughlin decided to give Limbaugh a second chance while listening from the car. It made all the difference. While driving, McLaughlin felt Limbaugh's special connection with his listeners. McLaughlin also liked the topical ideas, strong viewpoints, and show-biz elements of Limbaugh's broadcast.[4]

McLaughlin shrewdly brokered a deal for Limbaugh to broadcast a two-hour show in New York and a second two-hour nationally syndicated show. Access to the top radio market in the country was a must from the perspective of advertisers, but smaller markets wouldn't be left out—they could acquire the syndicated show through what was known as the barter method. A station would air Limbaugh's show for free, and in exchange McLaughlin's management company would be allowed to sell four minutes of advertising spots in each hour of Limbaugh's time on their airwaves. The barter method made Limbaugh attractive to many smaller stations that were struggling to survive.[5]

These stations were able to air talk radio thanks to the new satellite technology, but they still weren't exactly high-tech operations, as Limbaugh learned when he did a broadcast from one small-budget broadcaster. In 1989 he visited an early affiliate, WHKY in Hickory, North Carolina. The station charged just $8 per minute for advertising time. During his visit, Limbaugh used a jury-rigged mic stand and the station's only set of headphones. WHKY's sales manager, who also produced the show, listened on a Walkman he brought from home, and his wife, who screened calls, sprinted down the hall to hand Limbaugh a paper list of those dialing in. When Limbaugh started taking calls, feedback screamed in his earphones, and he and the callers could not hear each other. He resorted to talking into both his microphone and a telephone handset simultaneously. He even had to announce that the local Baptist church had canceled its pinto-bean dinner because of poor weather.

This arrangement was the polar opposite of Limbaugh's usual setup in New York, where he read caller information off a computer screen, and a glass wall separated him from his producer.[6] It also speaks volumes about the state of AM radio on the eve of its transformation.

The experience of KCNN in Grand Forks, North Dakota, another small, early Limbaugh affiliate, illustrates why the host proved so transformative for AM radio. Executive and host Scott Hennen turned KCNN into North Dakota's first talk station in 1986. The station initially had one hour of local programming, with the rest of the day featuring syndicated hosts.[7] After a convincing sell from McLaughlin and his affiliate-relations man Lee

Vanden Handel, Hennen became one of the first executives to add Limbaugh's program to his lineup. Within days Limbaugh had provoked reactions that no one had ever seen before. He generated similar reactions on stations throughout the country, revealing the potential audience for talk radio. Executives scrambled to hop on the bandwagon, and the format skyrocketed.[8]

Limbaugh's Allure

Limbaugh didn't just invigorate talk radio; he reimagined it, successfully fusing three distinct types of radio. One, interactive talk radio, dated back to the 1940s and 1950s and the first all-talk station, which launched in Los Angeles in 1960. Limbaugh joined interactive talk with the explicit conservative advocacy of radio sermonizers such as Dan Smoot and Clarence Manion and the fun stylings and sensibilities of rock-music radio.[9] Limbaugh was colorful, controversial, and highly entertaining, and as a consequence, he changed the direction of spoken-word radio.

The talk programming that flourished in a limited range of markets during the 1960s and 1970s sounded nothing like what Limbaugh would bring to the masses. Most talk stations aired diverse conversation spanning topics from pet advice to politics. One of Limbaugh's early affiliates that embodied this style of talk radio was San Diego's 690 XTRA. When XTRA adopted a talk format in 1988, the lineup included a local conservative morning host, followed by a local medical advice show, followed by Limbaugh, and finally a local psychologist.[10]

Before the revolution Limbaugh sparked, hosts came in all ideological stripes, and most kept their political views to themselves. New York star Barry Farber believed that most hosts in his era would "fly down to the Amazon and get our head shrunk before it would occur to attack the President." Farber, who was always gracious to guests and callers, sought out guests who were interesting and engrossing, regardless of the subject matter. Though himself a conservative, Farber wasn't trying to air a particular viewpoint. He just wanted to avoid one thing: a guest "so damn dull and inarticulate that he couldn't ad lib a belch after a Bulgarian wedding." When Limbaugh came along, Farber wondered, "Why didn't I think of that?"[11]

This isn't to say that Limbaugh was the first to do "PC-subversive" radio— opinionated programs incorporating stereotype-based humor and comments that many listeners found inappropriate, even outrageous. But if Limbaugh wasn't the first to put edgy content on the air, he was the one who flavored it conservative and took it national. Earlier shows in this vein had been limited primarily to select major markets, where competition among multiple talk stations drove hosts and executives to push boundaries in order to differentiate their stations.[12] Although none of these shows could be characterized as doctrinaire, their boisterous, norm-challenging hosts, such as Tom Leykis, tended to share a liberal perspective to the extent that they discussed politics at all.

If Limbaugh's show sounded different from those of older peers such as Farber, it was equally unlike the conservative lectures of earlier decades, broadcast by the likes of Manion and Smoot in the 1950s–1970s and Father Charles Coughlin in the 1930s.[13] In short weekly programs—Smoot and Manion had just fifteen minutes apiece—they preached conservatism to the masses. There was no opportunity for listeners to call in, and hosts' controversial political perspective precluded commercial support—a far cry from the interactivity and entrepreneurial quality of Limbaugh's show. Instead radio political preaching was essentially a nonprofit enterprise, with hosts sometimes paying stations for airtime. They stayed afloat thanks to conservative benefactors, such as the oil millionaire H. L. Hunt, who sponsored a series of shows beginning in 1951. Even Smoot, who sold advertising, largely relied on the beneficence of wealthy conservative businessmen, especially dog-food magnate D. B. Lewis. These businessmen cared primarily about promoting their ideology, not about ratings success.[14]

While Limbaugh shared many of his conservative predecessors' views— albeit with sunnier, more optimistic packaging—he maintained a fundamentally different goal: attracting commercial advertisers by generating good ratings. That meant entertaining listeners. By contrast, as Heather Hendershot describes, Smoot "wanted to inform people; people would tune in because they wanted the truth, not because the delivery of the truth was flashy or fun." Smoot's program was often "exceedingly dull." According to Nicole Hemmer, Manion's broadcasts could be similarly "cerebral, dense, and stultifying."[15]

While Smoot and Manion sternly educated about the dangers of Communism, Limbaugh humanized the threat. For instance, he coined the term "Gorbasm" to describe liberals' "expression of sheer delight" whenever Soviet leader Mikhail Gorbachev "was on the scene." News of a Gorbasm was accompanied by its own theme song—the "Imperial March" from

Star Wars, also known as Darth Vader's theme.[16] While it is tempting to draw a straight line from the old conservative crusaders to Limbaugh, stylistically, he is a study in contrast.

Limbaugh had more in common with the few outspoken talk radio hosts of the 1960s–1980s, such as Bob Grant, Joe Pyne, and Neal Boortz. All were first-rate showmen. Yet Limbaugh still differed from them stylistically. Grant and Pyne delighted audiences by abusing callers and focused their programs on callers and interviews.[17] Grant, though gentle and soft-spoken off the air, bellowed at callers to get off his phone.[18] Pyne urged callers to gargle with razor blades.[19] Don Page of the *Los Angeles Times* wrote that Pyne's "forte is the unadulterated insult, the sensational slap in the face."[20] Limbaugh, by contrast, treated callers politely—when he spoke with them. He took fewer calls than most hosts and conducted almost no interviews. His show's entertainment value came from his own scripted and extemporaneous humor—imitations, absurdity, parodies, and zaniness—not from berating callers and breathing fire. He was blunt but cheerful, leavening indignation with equal parts sarcasm and mockery.

In this regard Limbaugh's show contained echoes of the light-hearted antics of disc jockeys, reflecting the host's past spinning rock and pop records on music stations. Limbaugh was the first person to apply the DJ's performance art to politics.[21] His high-energy delivery changed minimally between his music-radio days and the 1988 debut of his national talk program. During a 1990 promotional appearance with Detroit host and former Cy Young Award–winning pitcher Denny McClain, Limbaugh confessed that he developed his "shtick" during his time as a DJ. He said he had always contemplated incorporating this style into a long-form talk show because he believed that a talk show, no less than music, could entertain young people.[22]

His humor and off-the-wall antics, not his conservatism, attracted radio executives such as WABC's John Mainelli, who made the fateful decision to bring Limbaugh to New York.[23] And it was Limbaugh's "outrageous behavior"—especially "caller abortions," in which he would drown out liberal callers with clips of screams and a vacuum-cleaner sound effect—that enticed Chattanooga programmer Bill Luckett. Luckett knew that this sort of thing would offend many Chattanoogans, but, believing he needed to shake things up, he welcomed the controversy and brought Limbaugh on.[24]

The caller abortions are pure Limbaugh: insulting and scornful, but also creative and funny. He took the same approach to the "updates" that dotted his show in its early days. Each update topic, ranging from condoms to homelessness, had its own theme music. For instance, Limbaugh signaled updates on animal-rights activism with a mix of Andy Williams's "Born Free," machine gun blasts, mortar explosions, and screeching animals.[25] Segments about openly gay Democratic Congressman Barney Frank began with a version of the 1950s song "My Boy Lollipop." In the first few years, Limbaugh created most of his parodies himself; in 1993 he brought on a writer, the conservative comedian Paul Shanklin, to help craft the sketches. Limbaugh also used material sent to him by fans. These included "The Philanderer," a popular bit targeting Massachusetts Democratic Senator Ted Kennedy, which featured a Kennedy impersonator crooning to the tune of Dion's 1961 hit "The Wanderer." The lyrics told the story: "Where pretty girls are, well you know that I'm around / I kiss 'em and I love 'em, cause to me they're all the same / I get so gosh-darn hammered, I don't even know their names / cause I'm a philanderer, yes a philanderer / I sleep around, around, around, around / / Well my views are on the left, got a bimbo on the right / Only God'll know where I'll be passing out tonight."[26]

Limbaugh's show even had its own vernacular. Alongside "Gorbasm," there was "safe talk." During the live stage show he took on the road in his early days on the national airwaves, he would cover his microphone with a condom, which he claimed protected listeners from any evil words he might speak.[27] People who died assumed "room temperature." Politicians received nicknames: Senator Alan Cranston, an old target from Limbaugh's Sacramento days, was "The Cadaver." Such brashness captivated even liberals, who laughed in spite of themselves or fumed at their radios.[28]

Limbaugh's edginess and engaging style represented one of the few commonalities between him and Howard Stern, the other transcendent spoken-word radio talent of their generation. For one thing, the content of their programs differed substantially. Stern only occasionally discussed politics, and he often explored crude and sexual topics that Limbaugh never touched. And while both targeted men, they played to vastly different audiences; Stern's program aired predominantly on FM rock stations. Yet, stylistically, both obliterated norms. They shared blunt opinions and used mockery and absurdity to their advantage. Listeners never knew quite what they would hear when tuning in.

Two of Limbaugh's early affiliates, KFI in Los Angeles and WLS in Chicago, discovered that he was demonstrating a new blueprint for radio success. These stations redesigned their formats in the Limbaugh mold. In doing so they challenged, respectively, KABC and WGN—popular but mellow talk stations. As KFI executive George Oliva explained in an interview, focus groups revealed KABC's sliver of vulnerability. There was an opening for a talk station whose hosts took clear stances, willingly stepped on toes, and used humor to the point of irreverence.[29]

Between 1988 and 1993, Limbaugh's audience swelled and the number of stations carrying his program exploded. His syndicated show launched on fewer than a hundred stations in 1988, with an average audience of 299,000 listeners per average quarter hour. By 1993 his program aired on 610 stations and had 17 million listeners per week.[30] Local restaurants even partnered with Limbaugh's affiliates to create hundreds of "Rush Rooms," where fans could eat lunch together while enjoying their favorite show.[31]

What Drove Limbaugh's Success?

Did ideology spawn Limbaugh's massive popularity, or was it his talent? No doubt ideology was critical in capturing the hearts and ears of alienated conservatives. Yet there is good reason to believe that the greater part of Limbaugh's stunning, sudden success rested on his radio abilities. Limbaugh possessed all the attributes radio executives look for in an ideal host. Outspoken and opinionated, he informed, entertained, inspired, and engaged. He grabbed listeners and held them riveted in their cars, idling in their driveways so they wouldn't miss a moment.[32] As radio-industry journalist Robert Unmacht described it, Limbaugh could "talk about trash can lids and make it a fun story."[33] Ideology was clearly the lesser factor in his success, according to McLaughlin and Kit Carson, Limbaugh's chief of staff. Two of the radio people who knew him best, they argued that Limbaugh was so entertaining that he would have been equally successful had he been a liberal.[34]

In the radio business, success and failure span the ideological spectrum, reinforcing the idea that Limbaugh's rise was propelled more by his skills than his conservatism. Hosts Stephanie Miller, Michael Smerconish, and Bill Handel present very different perspectives from Limbaugh, but all have thrived by doing what Limbaugh does best: they entertain. Conversely, boring hosts of all ideological stripes have flopped. Among these are big-name conservatives such as Downey, the late Senator Fred Thompson, and former Arkansas Governor Mike Huckabee.[35] In fact—as *Talkers Magazine* maven Michael Harrison, who knows talk radio as well as anyone, observed in 2004—many more conservatives have failed over the years than have liberals.[36] Granted, there were more opportunities; as time went on, conservatives found it easier to get on talk radio in the first place. But they still had to hold an audience.

There is little question that Limbaugh took entertaining at least as seriously as he did proselytizing. An ambitious 1991 spoof is a case in point. Limbaugh's satirical promotional trailer for a miniseries entitled "Gulf War Won" illustrates his pioneering combination of zany entertainment and political messaging.[37] The spot also demonstrates how much thought and effort he put into showmanship. He could have just railed against dovish liberals; instead he created a masterpiece of audio theater appealing to audiences seeking either conservative perspective or just entertainment.[38]

The trailer, set to old-fashioned Hollywood theme music, announced the miniseries' extensive "cast." Limbaugh picked his stars with an eye toward humor and real-life resemblance: James Earl Jones as General Colin Powell, Betty White as First Lady Barbara Bush, Ringo Starr as Palestinian leader Yasser Arafat.

Humorous though they were, many of the casting decisions also reflected Limbaugh's political slant: he chose suave, tough, manly actors to play major Republicans and conservatives. Clint Eastwood portrayed President Bush and Arnold Schwarzenegger played Colonel Oliver North, conservative hero and a future talk radio star himself. In a nod to traditional gender roles, a pre-credit sequence set in 1940 featured a man having his way with his wife after angrily thrusting aside a condom she asked him to use. The condom was stamped, "Provided by New York City School System."

Liberals and mainstream-media personalities fared poorly in the skit. Senator Kennedy portrayed "the luckiest man in Iraq because he knew what it was like to cross a bridge bombed"—a reference to the fatal accident at Chappaquiddick. Limbaugh assigned Star Wars character Jabba the Hut the role of Molly Yard, then the president of the National Organization for Women, and ET the extraterrestrial the role of House Majority Leader Richard Gephardt. Martin Sheen portrayed an anti-war activist who lost the lower half of his body trying to prevent the launch of a Patriot missile. The San Francisco chapter of Dykes on Bikes played the All-American First Cavalry Amazon Battalion, whose mission consisted of "taking out all future members of the Iraqi Republican Guard who were being maternally protected in intrauterine bunkers." Puppet Howdy Doody, Whoopi

Goldberg, and Jack Nicholson as the Joker portrayed prominent journalists Ted Koppel, Bernard Shaw, and Peter Arnett, respectively. These choices emasculated Shaw and impugned Koppel's and Arnett's integrity, morality, and independence.

In a surreal twist, Sylvester Stallone drew the role of Limbaugh. Finally, Limbaugh himself portrayed heroic General H. Norman Schwarzkopf—who did vaguely resemble the host—and attractive starlet Bo Derek portrayed Schwarzkopf's wife.

In spite of its consistent conservative slant, much of the vignette would have made a listener of any political persuasion laugh. The miniseries trailer epitomized the sort of fun Limbaugh had in his early days on air.[39] The best of Limbaugh's followers understood that he flourished on the basis of ideologically laden hijinks such as these, not just thundering conservatism. Other hosts mimicked his style, making their political agenda clear but prioritizing entertainment to the point where they sometimes provoked laughter even from ideological opponents. These followers also used popular music, usually either rock or country, ranging from Nirvana to Martina McBride. And they employed nicknames, sound effects, humorous imitations, and parodies to express scorn for liberals. Laura Ingraham, for example, dubbed Senator Kennedy the "Senior Balloon." On a 2005 show, she ran a montage of his comments on waterboarding and the country being "awash" in red ink, overlaid with sounds of splashing. The host recommended that Kennedy avoid water analogies—another obvious allusion to Chappaquiddick. This reference was routine on talk radio; other conservative talkers called Kennedy "the swimmer."[40]

Michael Medved, a former film critic, also followed Limbaugh's model. Consider one Limbaughesque 2006 program in which Medved asserted that Republicans liked gospel and country music, whereas Democrats liked rap stars such as DMX, who had just claimed that he had been raped. Medved suggested that Bill Clinton should have made the same accusation against Monica Lewinsky because "Monica's a big girl." This was followed by clips of Clinton saying "hot dog" and "just stop it."[41]

Ingraham, Medved, and thousands of other hosts owe their careers to Limbaugh. He blazed a trail and showed them how to push boundaries, avoid the staid and boring, and keep listeners rapt—all while conveying their conservative message.

3

Media That Sounds Like Us

IN THE LATE 1980s and early 1990s, no media executive plotted to reach
disillusioned conservatives. Most had no inkling that this potential audience existed. Even Limbaugh was flying blind in this regard—he launched
his show with no political goals. Rather, he argued that people "turn on
the radio for three things: entertainment, entertainment, entertainment."[1]
Yet caller after caller celebrated him for his views, so he adapted his show
to satisfy his fans and fulfill a newfound sense of duty to them. "As millions have tuned in," he explained, "there is now incumbent upon me a
responsibility to be honest, credible, believable, and to not do things that
are perceived to be outrageous, or off the wall just for the purpose of being
noticed or making a splash."[2] This meant sacrificing some of the irreverence that characterized his program in its early years and instead providing
more traditional political commentary.[3] While this change repelled some
liberal fans, it engendered even more loyalty from conservatives. They had
finally found their champion.

This was a crucial aspect of Limbaugh's appeal: he connected with alienated conservatives because he was one of them. In the words of the *Washington Post*'s Henry Allen, Limbaugh was "a lonely small-town guy who
was just as smart and funny as the people who sneered at lonely small-town
guys."[4] His massive success, and the trappings of it—he discussed on the
air cigars and rounds of golf and other luxuries he bought with his riches—
thrilled his conservative audience. Here was one of their own, striking
gold in hostile territory by strongly expressing their values and their anger
over the media's infuriating bias. Fan Nathan Willis told an interviewer

that he appreciated Limbaugh's morals, which Willis considered otherwise "dead in America."[5]

A 1992 discussion of youth violence epitomizes the unyielding approach to traditionally defined morality that captivated Limbaugh's conservative listeners. In one monologue, he embraced conservative values, pilloried the cultural forces challenging them, and amplified conservatives' sense of grievance by lamenting how the changes wrought by poisonous liberalism made it impossible to fix the problem. In this particular instance, Limbaugh blamed the constant barrage of sex and violence in music and movies for a dramatic increase in the number of teenage girls having multiple sex partners. To critics of this analysis, who might argue that every generation had "destructive" music, Limbaugh countered, "In my generation, the destructive music people thought was the Beatles. . . . The Beatles did get into psychedelic stuff and so forth, but you can't play Beatles music today and compare it to Ice T and 2 Live Crew and all these kinds of things." Worse still, liberal victories had ensured that nothing could be done to offset this destructive content:

> We can't teach 'em values except homosexual values in school in New York City. But you can't teach—you can't put the Ten Commandments in school even though it's great advice, it's remarkably instructive, and there are no better ten things to teach people how to live with one another than the Ten Commandments. You don't need the children of the rainbow curriculum. You don't need "Heather has two mommies" or "daddy has a roommate" to teach people how to live with each other. Ten Commandments does it. It's all right there. But you can't do that because it has a religious foundation and so it's not constitutional, it's not qualified. So when kids start hacking each other to death, the answers are plain and simple.[6]

This sort of blunt, full-throated defense of cherished values—replete with entertaining insults, winks, and nods—struck a chord with millions. As Jerry "Boogie" Gallant, a California oil-field worker, told a *Wall Street Journal* reporter, Limbaugh "is articulate to the common man like me. Most of us out there are working people, and we get tired of getting blamed for everything."[7] Garrett Headrick, a fifty-eight-year-old fan, described Limbaugh as "a man who expresses my sentiments, and does it with wit and humor. I appreciate the clarity of his thinking. And when he articulates my thoughts, I get a sense of not being alone. Now we have someone who can speak for us, against the mean-spirited nature and intolerance of the left."[8]

Boortz resonated in a similar way. He argued, "If I'm tapping anything . . . it's the frustration of people who have something to say at work or home or in some social setting and just can't do it. I do it for them. I don't take prisoners."[9] Even more gratifying, when liberals or the media pounced on these sentiments, hosts gleefully doubled down. After provoking outrage by questioning why none of the victims of the 2007 Virginia Tech massacre defended themselves, Boortz "started counting down the days until I once again said something that many people were thinking, but were afraid to express, and the howling dogs of the left-wing media would once again rise up in outrage."[10] This unwillingness to cave to the lords of political correctness reinforced hosts' almost heroic stature in listeners' eyes. One caller begged Bob Grant, the New York talker, "Please, please don't leave us. You are our only voice."[11]

Talk radio provided precisely the kind of anti-establishment medium through which conservatives could connect to the political process and freely express their views. Their favorite hosts discussed all the thorny issues—race, politics, religion, sex—that listeners believed they had to avoid in public for fear of offending people. As Susan Douglas explained, "So many white men came to feel that they were walking on eggshells, that they didn't know what was right and wrong to say anymore, that they wanted a place where they, too, could exhale. Talk radio gave them that refuge."[12] Callers could vent and voice their sentiments to likeminded, sympathetic people. And the virtual anonymity offered by the medium meant that callers and listeners need not worry about being identified and scorned by spouses, friends, bosses, customers, or neighbors who might disagree.[13]

Even at his most entertainment-focused, Limbaugh may have had an inkling that his brand of humor and fun had special resonance with a conservative audience. He sensed that he offered something liberals couldn't match because they took politics so seriously. On this point Limbaugh disagreed with those around him who thought he would have been equally successful as a liberal. He believed liberalism would have inhibited his success "for the simple reason that liberals don't laugh about things. I have a sense of humor."[14] While the rise of liberal comics on cable television in the 2000s and 2010s has proved this impression wrong, the connection Limbaugh drew between entertainment and ideology explained why he garnered such fervent adoration specifically from those on the right. His style of humor and entertainment was rooted in his decidedly conservative sensibilities. This electrified an audience that shared his values and his "Middle-American" upbringing.

These values pervaded the conversation on talk radio, even though hosts did not focus single-mindedly on spreading conservative political ideas. This sensibility made talk radio even more enticing: the conversation was not so different from the sort one might find at the dinner table in any conservative household. Hosts chatted about the news of the day. Local hosts spliced discussion of national politics with local stories; national and local hosts worked in the latest celebrity, sports, legal, or business news. Ingraham, for example, typically devoted her third hour each day to lifestyle topics.[15] Conversation on talk radio routinely included largely apolitical issues, from the best ways to handle mosquitoes to popular movies, hosts' travel woes, the proper location for new stoplights, and the perennial competition between lovers of white and dark meat. As Sacramento host Joe Getty explained, he and partner Jack Armstrong had a "human relationship with our audience." They considered their listeners "friends" to whom they could talk about many topics, including politics. Armstrong and Getty estimated that their show ranged from 70–75 percent political content on a heavy news day to less than half on a slower news day.[16]

Whatever the topic, the ethos of talk radio shined through. Hosts flaunted opposition to political correctness and sneered at the new norms promoted by the rights movements that inflamed conservative sensibilities. As radio executive David Hall put it, Limbaugh was "always looking to turn somebody's sacred cow into some delicious hamburgers and a couple of steaks." This style permeated the business.[17]

Economic developments during the 1980s, and the Democratic Party's response to them, made this ethos especially alluring to middle- and lower-middle-class white men.[18] Between 1982 and 1994, real earnings for white men with high school diplomas and white male high school dropouts declined 9.1 percent and 22 percent, respectively. By contrast mean earnings for white men with master's degrees rose by 24.3 percent. Minority men with low educational attainment experienced an even more severe earnings drop, but, as one writer argued in the *Washington Post*, minorities at least benefited from the care and sympathy of progressives. The "college educated, privileged and politically correct" population viewed declining minority earnings as the byproduct of systemic injustice, while reserving for blue-collar white men condescension and even contempt. Americans who shared this sense—themselves often blue-collar white men—found much to like in Limbaugh, who frequently railed against affirmative action, mocked Reverend Jesse Jackson, and highlighted what he perceived as extreme and hypocritical statements made by civil rights leaders.[19]

It was not just economic alienation—and its links to racial resentment—that made American men hunger for the sort of conversation that occurred on talk radio. Societal changes spurred by the women's movement also attracted men to conservative talkers. As host Jack Armstrong described, talk radio appealed to "angry white males" who were tired of being disrespected—by their children, who used them as ATMs, and by bosses and wives who were perpetually angry at them.[20] A 2004 Annenberg survey found that men comprised a full two-thirds of Limbaugh's audience.[21]

Hosts, who were also predominantly men, oozed testosterone and frequently objectified women. Talker G. Gordon Liddy, of Watergate infamy, described himself as virile, vigorous, and potent; after a three-day weekend he told his audience, "Ladies it has been a long dry period, three days, but we're back and the hour of free release is upon you." In the same episode, the former FBI agent amped up the masculinity by holding court about guns and bragging about the numerous ways he could kill a person.[22]

Boortz's show was similarly animated by an ethos that objectified women and appealed to men who found feminism stultifying, even as he venerated his wife and dubbed her "The Queen." For instance, during a 2005 discussion of a NASCAR race, Boortz's sidekick Royal Marshall thought female driver Danica Patrick had been lucky not to "bust her ass right there in front of God and everybody." That "sounds like a woman to me," he added. Boortz followed up by observing that Patrick was "hot." Later, a not particularly repentant Marshall issued an "apology" for criticizing Patrick, explaining, "Apparently that's a sacred cow." Boortz responded, "Oh she's not a cow."[23] When female guests appeared in studio, hosts often focused on their looks, not their ideas. For example, in 2005, when People for the Ethical Treatment of Animals sent a costumed "Santa's little helper" to debate Cincinnati host Bill Cunningham on the merits of Tofurkey vs. fried turkey, Cunningham and his sidekick spent most of the segment objectifying her. At one point Cunningham remarked, "Looking like you honey, I can see people buying whatever you're selling."[24]

Many hosts also tried to discredit feminist arguments, often by high-lighting what they saw as inconsistencies and double standards. For in-stance, in 1992 Limbaugh accused feminists of merely being partisans after they failed to come out behind a hairdresser who accused Democratic Sen-ator Daniel Inouye of sexual harassment. The same people, Limbaugh noted, had been all too ready to support Anita Hill the year before.[25] Then there was the time Liddy argued with a female veteran until she conceded that women were not fit for certain combat roles because they could not perform well enough to avoid getting themselves or members of their units killed. When the caller added that some men presented the same problem, Liddy replied that people accepted those men getting winnowed out, but that when the military winnowed women out, it faced accusations of sex discrimination.[26] In one fell swoop Liddy sought both to delegitimize gender-discrimination complaints and strike a blow for traditional gender roles.

Part of the political genius of talk radio was its promotion of a message that could comfortably resonate with two different, sometimes contradictory, flavors of conservatives. On the one hand, hosts appealed to the persistent rage of the Nixon-era "silent majority."[27] Diane from Los Angeles, a 2005 caller to Sean Hannity's program, observed that—in spite of Reagan, George H. W. Bush, and the 1994 revolution that delivered Republicans full control of Congress—for forty years the silent majority had no voice, until talk radio gave it one. Talk radio won over Diane and likeminded conservatives by championing the interests, opinions, and frustrations of blue-collar whites and anti-feminist traditionalists. Hosts had great appeal to so-called Reagan Democrats.[28] Limbaugh attracted many former Demo-crats, such as St. Louis listeners Patty O'Neill and Barbara Potzman. Potzman, the Catholic daughter of union member, came from a tradi-tional Democratic background.[29]

On the other hand, talk radio also offered up something for the new Sunbelt suburban conservatives and wealthier Americans more broadly. Hosts equated economic success with deregulation, low taxes, and per-sonal responsibility.[30] At times Limbaugh referred to the graduated in-come tax as "an assault on achievement." In his view tax cuts should benefit the wealthy because "there's nothing wrong with earning a lot of money—you do it the right way—hard work."[31] Limbaugh was so successful in pairing the fury of the dispossessed with the optimistic terms of "achievement" economics that, by the early 2000s, the majority of his audience were members of the middle and upper-middle class.[32]

This fusion of two strands of conservatism in Limbaugh's broadcasts makes sense when one considers his background: as David Remnick put it in 1994, Limbaugh's "conservatism is a mix of the traditional Republicanism of his father and grandfather and the fury of the pro–George Wallace forces that became so popular in his hometown" of Cape Girardeau, Missouri.[33] Limbaugh is a son of Missouri political royalty; his father even ushered vice presidential candidate Richard Nixon and his wife through town during a 1952 campaign stop. One in a long line of well-to-do lawyers, Limbaugh's father represented many corporations and appears to have imparted in his son a great deal of respect for the social value of unfettered profitmaking.[34]

Whether Limbaugh shaped his listeners' opinions, or simply voiced them, was difficult to discern.[35] He admitted that he liked "to try to persuade" but with the caveat that he wanted "it to happen genuinely. I don't want to be pointing fingers in people's face . . . and force them to agree. I want them to come to it on their own."[36] Limbaugh sensed that he thrived "because I validate what millions of Americans already think." But this didn't mean he was pandering to them; rather, he was espousing what he genuinely felt to be true. Early in his time in New York, he explained to McMahon that he refrained from covering certain newsworthy topics on his show because he hadn't decided what he thought about them; he would not discuss them until he had. He eschewed other hot topics because he didn't care about them, which was to his benefit: the intimacy of talk radio required authenticity from hosts; those who frequently changed positions or lied to listeners had ratings trouble.[37] Limbaugh's beliefs just happened "to fit what a certain number of Americans think who are not being satisfied by the mainstream press."[38]

Even if Limbaugh was not trying to tell listeners what to think, he undeniably advanced the Republican and conservative agendas. By applying his and listeners' worldview to issues and campaigns, Limbaugh helped his audience turn their values into votes and activism. Importantly, in the pre-Internet age, Limbaugh was a news source, directing his loyal audience to matters they otherwise would not be familiar with.[39] Limbaugh also had something of a clean slate to work with, as a portion of his audience knew little about politics or cared minimally about them. These listeners still tuned in because, as one put it, "Rush makes politics fun."[40] For millions who shared Limbaugh's values and were entertained by him, his show was the gateway to greater political awareness.

Overall the rise of talk radio was in many ways an accident; there was no conservative plot to build a right-leaning political medium. The new style of conservative talk was a byproduct of AM stations' financial straits and Limbaugh's discovery of an audience yearning for an in-your-face conservative media product. True, almost from day one, talk radio caught the eye of some in the political world, but only those who were most desperate to find a platform. Indeed, at the moment when those in politics began to experiment with talk radio, the medium wasn't conservative. It was diverse in topics and political orientations. The development of almost uniformly conservative political talk on the AM dial would come gradually over the next decade. In the late 1980s and early 1990s, there was still real uncertainty as to how talk radio would develop and what, if any, political impact it would have. Radio executives were still trying to figure out what would be the next step for the industry, and those in politics were slowly feeling their way along, wondering how to engage the medium.

4

Necessity, Mother of Invention

As the political world tuned into talk radio, it was less an ideological weapon and more the medium of the dispossessed. Political outsiders who couldn't get coverage from the mainstream media flocked to talk radio, while leaders in both parties ignored it. Political titans had no need for media upstarts, because they could spread their message using the three broadcast networks, CNN, and the elite newspapers that still dominated the media landscape. The first politicians to catch on to the potential of talk radio were therefore marginal figures—congressional backbenchers and state-level leaders, including one who wanted to be president: Arkansas Governor Bill Clinton.

On the Republican side, it was conservative castaways who turned earliest to talk radio, beginning in the late 1980s. Only in the mid-1990s did the top echelons of the Republican Party follow. That first motley band of House misfits included many colorful personalities, most of whom were associated with the Conservative Opportunity Society (COS) and the Republican Study Committee (RSC). Their number included Bob Walker of Pennsylvania, Vin Weber of Minnesota, and Newt Gingrich of Georgia, who founded the COS in 1984 to advance an agenda that did not always mesh with their leadership's goals.

As a rump faction of the typically irrelevant and seemingly permanent House minority—Republicans had last controlled the House in 1954—these strident, pugilistic conservatives had little influence. Accordingly the mainstream media paid them minimal attention. Talk radio was a weapon in their guerrilla war for coverage. Talk radio also offered the chance to get their message to activists beyond the Washington bubble. Walker began accepting requests from radio hosts in the late 1970s. When he joined the leadership in 1989 as chief deputy whip, he began pushing his leadership colleagues to engage talk radio more.[1]

Paul Morrell, by contrast, discovered the benefits of talk radio more accidentally. Morrell, the press secretary for California Republican Representative Bob Dornan, first noticed talk radio because hosts kept requesting interviews with his loquacious and flamboyant boss. Dornan, nicknamed B-1 Bob because of his unswerving devotion to the B-1 bomber, was a former media personality who made for a great guest. He was so good on the air that, in the early 1990s, he substituted for Limbaugh when the host was on vacation.[2] In fact, it was Dornan, not Limbaugh, who seems to have scored the first presidential interview on Limbaugh's show, when President Bush joined him on July 18, 1990.[3]

Morrell realized that talk radio not only fit Dornan's temperament but also served the GOP's political ends. The format presented an opportunity to draw attention and constituents to causes that major mainstream outlets thought too unimportant to warrant airtime. To realize that opportunity, Morrell launched the Talk Right initiative. First he collaborated with other staffers to compile a master list of talk radio hosts in each congressional district. Then the initiative produced one-pagers or member speeches explaining smaller issues that the mainstream media ignored. The RSC faxed these documents to hosts along with a list of members who had agreed to make radio appearances on the topics covered. The members loved the attention, and their staffers were thrilled to have a way to circumvent the mainstream press and get their bosses' message out.[4]

Republican leaders during this period may have shared backbenchers' disdain for the mainstream media's liberal cultural orientation, but they were satisfied with their access to the Sunday shows and the front pages. Epitomizing his generation of leadership, House Minority Leader Bob Michel, who led his caucus from 1980 to 1994, engaged talk radio sparingly. It simply wasn't part of his world; he didn't listen and he didn't call in. Former House Majority Leader Dick Armey recalled that Michel loathed Limbaugh, and, in general, put little store in newfangled ideas.[5] Nonetheless, as the penetration of talk radio grew in Michel's final years in office, the medium developed into a secondary tool to communicate House Republicans' message.[6]

Like Michel and his team, the George H. W. Bush White House did not fully understand or take advantage of talk radio. As Press Secretary Marlin Fitzwater ruefully acknowledged, "There was no sense of it as a tool. . . . We didn't recognize what was happening."[7] Paul Luthringer, the radio point person on the White House media relations team, conceded that he and his colleagues did not track what talk radio was saying about President Bush, nor did they work to disseminate talking points to hosts or arrange guests for them.[8] In an interview Dorrance Smith, who served as President Bush's assistant for media affairs, remembered no radio-specific strategy beyond the weekly Saturday radio address.[9]

Technology was a limiting factor. Tracking what was said on talk radio was far more difficult during the Bush presidency than it would be in later years, when stations streamed their programming online. Bush's aides had to settle for the programming available over the airwaves in Washington. So limited was the White House's technical capacity that only in 1990, when the media-affairs team built a new broadcast studio in the Old Executive Office Building, was the president able to make remote appearances.[10]

But design, more than technology, drove the Bush team's approach to radio. Bush's aides saw radio as a medium for delivering newscasts, not as a potential method for spreading their political message.[11] Luthringer did use radio to circumvent the White House press corps, but the hosts he brought to the White House to interview Bush included news anchors, disc jockeys, and black and Latino radio personalities, in addition to the occasional conservative talker.[12] More broadly Smith thought radio did not need special attention; a message skillfully delivered on television would make its way onto radio.[13] For example, if the White House placed a guest on *This Week with David Brinkley*, the media-affairs staff could reasonably expect that they had radio covered because top-of-the-hour ABC news reports on many stations would include soundbites from the interview.[14]

Talk radio would develop into a Republican tool and a conservative medium, but that wasn't the case in 1992. Instead, Bill Clinton was the first party-leading politician to grasp and capitalize upon talk radio's political potential. Clinton had joined the radio conversation as Arkansas governor and enjoyed the medium's immediacy.[15] He understood that talk radio provided access to voters unfiltered by the press, something rare at the time. And, as an adept retail politician, Clinton was poised to take advantage.[16]

Beginning with the New Hampshire primary, in January 1992, a former news radio reporter named Richard Strauss piloted radio outreach for Clinton's presidential campaign. Strauss and his boss, Jeff Eller, appreciated how valuable direct voter access was for a candidate with Clinton's skill set, so they invested substantial effort and energy into the operation. Early every morning, Strauss fed soundbites and actualities—recorded audio clips produced for radio—to local stations throughout New Hampshire and the surrounding states. While the campaign was not the first to produce its own audio for distribution, it was especially aggressive on this front.[17] Many of the stations Strauss targeted lacked access to a national network feed, which meant the campaign provided their only dose of audio from the candidate. Not only did this practice endear the campaign to stations, but it also allowed Clinton's media team to drive the discussion—on radio, in local newsrooms, and beyond—by tailoring the audio that reached voters. Strauss swatted aside requests for audio on the various scandals swirling around Clinton and instead offered stations soundbites on issues.[18]

After New Hampshire Strauss moved on to South Dakota, where he booked Clinton on talk radio for the first time. It proved to be a bumpy ride. The campaign bought airtime on stations throughout the state to stage a thirty-minute call-in show with Clinton. For twenty-five minutes or so the show went well. Then a caller asked Clinton about his purported mistress, Gennifer Flowers—just the sort of touchy subject a communications staffer would rather avoid. After the program ended, Clinton marched out with a stern look on his face and asked his aides who had set up the broadcast. Strauss's career flashed before his eyes. But instead of firing Strauss, Clinton declared that the experience had been fantastic. Direct contact with voters was unpredictable, but he relished it and wanted to do more radio.

A successful appearance on the popular *Imus in the Morning* program— after crusty, cantankerous, curmudgeony host Don Imus had spent months bashing Clinton—contributed to a crucial victory in the New York primary.[19] Along with other pop cultural forums—such as the late-night *Arsenio Hall Show*, where Clinton famously played saxophone—talk radio allowed the campaign to share its message in the spring of 1992. This might otherwise have been a dire moment: the campaign wanted to tell Clinton's inspiring life story, but its coffers were virtually empty, and the mainstream media had already been through the candidate's biography. To most journalists it was old news.[20] Although he was on his way to becoming his party's nominee, Clinton, like conservative House Republicans, latched onto talk radio in part because he lacked a better option.

During the general-election battle, Strauss built a system to pipe President Bush's speeches into Clinton headquarters in Little Rock. Immediately after Bush finished speaking, Strauss would hold a call with Clinton or his running mate, Tennessee Senator Al Gore, in which the candidates refuted and commented on the president's remarks. Strauss recorded the reaction and shared it with radio stations in the market in which the president had spoken.[21] Clinton and Gore also chatted with a fair number of radio hosts, although the medium was less practical for the principles during the general election campaign, when they each might be in five cities per day.[22] And, employing a novel strategy, the Clinton team arranged local television and radio interviews on days when the candidates *weren't* doing events in the broadcasters' markets. Other candidates chatted with local media primarily when they came to town. Clinton's tactic was another clever ploy to control the narrative: since Clinton and Gore didn't do interviews on event days, local media had to cover the events themselves, complete with careful staging designed to maximize the candidates' appeal. The campaign could then double back later to give the local media the one-on-one interviews they so desired, creating a second round of headlines.[23]

Bush's 1992 reelection campaign also tried to take advantage of talk radio, reaching out more aggressively than did either Bush's 1988 campaign or the Bush White House. Like Clinton, Bush distributed radio actualities and booked surrogates on radio.[24] But the Bush campaign's efforts were sluggish, less aware of the immense potential of talk radio. Whereas the Democrats' campaign courted the medium from the earliest primaries, Bush and his team were jolted to action in part after a political scare.

During the New Hampshire primary Limbaugh endorsed commentator Pat Buchanan over Bush, helping propel Buchanan to a surprisingly strong showing with 37.5 percent of the vote. (Bush had good reason to be worried: in 1968 Eugene McCarthy drove President Lyndon Johnson from the race after netting 42 percent in New Hampshire.)[25] Bush and his aides took notice, and, a few months later, on June 3, the president invited Limbaugh to Washington. There was a stop at the Kennedy Center and an overnight visit to the White House. Bush personally ferried Limbaugh's bag from the elevator of the White House residence to the Lincoln bedroom.[26] Limbaugh was in awe. In an interview with the *Today Show*, he described the experience: "It's about one in the morning, and I'm just sitting there at the desk where Abraham Lincoln wrote the Gettysburg Address. And there's a framed copy of it right there."[27] The visit spurred a correspondence between Limbaugh and the president. In one handwritten August letter, Bush noted hearing "some wonderful comments on your show" and gave Limbaugh insight into how he felt about the state of the race. "I just want you to know I am determined to get our positive message out—determined to win," the president wrote. "I will make it very clear why I should be re-elected and why the others would be a disaster. We've taken a lot of hits lately—many in my view grossly unfair, so it's nice to hear something positive. Come back to the White House." He concluded with "Good luck in the fall," an apparent reference to the television show Limbaugh would soon launch.[28]

Bush's former media strategist, Roger Ailes, catalyzed the relationship between Bush and Limbaugh. Ailes was friends with both men and had accompanied Limbaugh to the White House in June. He was producing Limbaugh's forthcoming television show even as he informally advised the president from time to time. At Ailes's behest the White House sent a letter from Bush congratulating the host a week before the television show launched, though Bush's staff rejected Ailes's request that the president tape a bit for a one-week anniversary spoof the show was planning.[29]

Limbaugh went to the Republican convention in Houston, where he spent time in the presidential and vice presidential boxes. This was but one of several ways that the convention served as talk radio's coming out party in Republican politics. The Republican National Committee's Scott Hogenson also accommodated a novel request from eight hosts to broadcast live from the convention site.

Throughout the fall, Limbaugh's support for Bush was unmistakable. As a National Journal article put it in September, Limbaugh's show "often sounds these days like a Bush campaign commercial."[30] When many were abandoning Bush's faltering campaign, Limbaugh fought on, advocating for the president with clarity and force.[31] Deputy Campaign Manager Mary Matalin, who was a Limbaugh fan, stayed in close touch with the host, often previewing the campaign's talking points for him. Campaign Communications Director Will Feltus tracked Limbaugh's show. Then, in the race's final months, Bush and Vice President Quayle appeared on Limbaugh's program. It was a special favor to the campaign; during this period, Limbaugh did not otherwise have guests on air.[32]

Even so, the lightbulb turned on slowly for Republicans in the fall of 1992. Although she believed that the campaign used talk radio as effectively as it could have at the time, Matalin conceded that the Bush team lacked the technical capacity to "leverage radio or posit it as an element of a horizontal communication strategy and force magnifier."[33] Put simply, the campaign did not have the tools, know-how, and vision to harness the power of talk radio to the degree that later campaigns would.

But there was more to it than a lack of technology or experience. After all, the Clinton campaign had the same technologies at its disposal, and it did not enjoy privileged access to radio expertise. The significant differences lay elsewhere. Talk radio was the medium of the political outsider, not the D.C. elite—most especially the president, the elite of the elite. Bush could grab the attention of any reporter or broadcaster in the country whenever he wanted it; he didn't need talk radio and therefore probably didn't take much notice of it. To the extent that he entered the talk radio arena, he did so grudgingly.

Bush's personality contributed to this half-hearted embrace. Unlike Clinton, the sober, patrician Bush, the scion of a family educated for generations at Andover and Yale, did not enjoy doing interviews. In particular he zealously guarded the dignity of the presidency by eschewing media appearances that he considered beneath the stature of the office. While Clinton was playing saxophone beside Arsenio Hall, Bush refused Feltus's suggestion that he and Mrs. Bush chat with morning-television yakkers Regis Philbin and Kathie Lee Gifford.[34] Bush's campaign also had to work to convince White House schedulers that any media appearances at all warranted a spot on the president's crowded schedule, presenting another obstacle to getting him on the air.

Even after Bush's loss, it took time before Republican leaders adopted a radio-friendly media strategy. A case in point is former Senate Republican leader Bob Dole. A quintessential insider, Dole, who aggressively courted media, was as slow to embrace talk radio as his contemporaries Michel and Bush. Before Clinton's election—but long after Limbaugh went national—Dole's radio appearances were limited to local talk shows and Larry King's nonpartisan national show.[35] Only after Clinton took office did Dole start to chat more frequently with talk radio hosts such as Limbaugh, Hedgecock, and Grant.[36] But, even then, he spread himself around; he was no creature of the right-wing media ecosystem. For instance he appeared regularly with Imus, who routinely took shots at politicians in both parties. Like Bush, Dole prioritized high-profile, established outlets, which helped him stand out against the background of less prominent politicians who lacked access to the heaviest hitters. In one year Dole appeared on at least one of the prized weekend talk shows on thirty-six of fifty-two weekends. At one point he also held the record for most appearances on CNN's *Larry King Live*.[37] Because of the mainstream media attention he attracted, Dole did not need talk radio to get his message out. And by focusing on King, the weekend shows, and the like, he ensured that the Senate Republican message reached the top echelon of the media world, leaving less glamorous outlets mostly to colleagues who couldn't reach these exalted heights.

The experiences of Bush, Michel, and Dole suggest that there also may have been a generation gap at work. The three men were all World War II veterans, born in 1923 or 1924. All three entered the political arena before the mid-1960s. By contrast the mid-1990s House Republican leaders who would use talk radio heavily were all children of the 1940s and 1950s, and all entered electoral office in the late 1970s or early 1980s. Another example: Bush's son, future president George W. Bush, who was born in 1946, was more eager about harnessing talk radio. At one point he urged his father to do an interview with Limbaugh about a proposed constitutional amendment requiring the federal government to balance its budget.[38]

The circumstances surrounding talk radio's entrance into the political arena are largely forgotten today. Most political observers assume that talk radio was always a Republican political tool and a deeply conservative force. But this is not so, and, although there are structural reasons for talk radio's eventual right-wing bent, its capture by conservatives wasn't foreordained. Ironically it was Clinton's 1992 victory, abetted by talk radio, that helped propel the medium in a conservative direction.

Talk Radio's Rightward Drift Begins

What Limbaugh demonstrated in his first years as a nationally syndicated host was the power of political talk radio to rescue AM stations—not the power of *conservative* talk radio, either financially or politically. As late as 1993, talk radio was fairly equally divided ideologically. That year David Bartlett, president of the Radio-Television News Directors Association, estimated that less than half of talk show hosts were conservative, although many of those hosting the most widely syndicated and popular programs were.[39] A 1993 Times Mirror survey of 112 talk radio hosts supported Bartlett's assertion, finding a "relatively even split" between liberal and conservative hosts, with a slight plurality leaning toward the Democratic Party. Thirty-nine percent of hosts had voted for Clinton, 23 percent for Bush, and 18 percent for Ross Perot.[40]

Even then, however, the balance was eroding. Radio executives were impressed by the ratings Limbaugh, Liddy, and other early conservative entertainers were garnering. (Liddy's show entered national syndication in 1993.[41]) It seemed conservative political talk was generating large numbers of devoted listeners, so programmers responded by hiring a steady stream of dogmatic conservatives of varying talent who pressed partisan talking points.[42] But this was just the beginning of a revolution that would culminate, a full decade later, in the transition to all-conservative syndicated stations.

Nineteen-ninety-one was an inflection point in this move toward all-conservative talk formats. To many conservatives the coverage of the Gulf War and Clarence Thomas's Supreme Court nomination fight—events Americans experienced in real time—exposed the press's bias. Viewers would watch General Norman Schwarzkopf's briefings, live war footage on CNN, or dramatic live proceedings from the Anita Hill–Clarence Thomas hearings. When those viewers later saw the synthesis and analysis presented on evening newscasts, they realized that the newscasts omitted everything they perceived to be important, while covering events in a manner that benefited liberals. As caller Phillip from Texas recalled to Liddy and the Media Resource Center's Rich Noyes in 2006, fifteen years earlier he had listened to the Pentagon briefing each day on the way home from work and then found himself baffled whenever he turned on the nightly news. Where, he wondered, did the newscasters get their information?[43] This disjuncture left many conservatives hungry for an alternative, expanding the potential audience for talk radio.

The Gulf War also compelled greater demand for news generally, leading people unintentionally to discover Limbaugh. At the time, his program aired on many full-service news-talk stations, and listeners would stumble upon Limbaugh while waiting for newscasts.[44] Some of them liked what they heard and added the program to their routines.[45]

In October 1991, against the backdrop of the hearings and impending presidential campaign, Seattle's KVI made a fateful hire that would eventually reveal the still-latent potential of conservative talk radio. Program director Brian Jennings joined the station and started migrating it from 1960s rock-and-roll to talk radio, including Limbaugh's program. In 1992 the station was broadcasting a mix of liberal and conservative talk when, during a meeting over cigars, Vanden Handel, Limbaugh's affiliate-relations manager, asked General Manager Shannon Sweatte a question: Why did KVI air liberal shows the audience didn't want to hear?

Sweatte and Jennings wanted to find out if there was any truth to Vanden Handel's assertion. So they did the research, studying ratings and fielding calls from listeners. As an experiment Jennings replaced one of the station's liberal hosts with a conservative. The result was higher ratings. Alongside other findings indicating the greater popularity of conservative shows, the experiment convinced KVI's executives. Station managers didn't suddenly discover their conservative souls, nor did they believe themselves accountable to the Republican Party. But they knew dollar signs when they saw them. By the end of 1992, under Jennings's direction, KVI became the country's first self-described all-conservative talk station. Others had programmed stations full of conservative chatter, but KVI was the first to advertise itself as all right-wing, all the time.

Within two years, KVI skyrocketed from twenty-third in the local market to first. The success of the unapologetic all-conservative format stunned not only Sweatte but also the station's advertisers. Listeners never went away, which allowed some advertisers to cut back from twenty or more commercials per week to three, while maintaining the same results. Advertisers flocked to the station, jolting ad rates upward. The miracle in Seattle captured the attention of radio executives nationwide.[46]

If KVI and its followers enjoyed good returns on their investments, they had Clinton to thank, at least in part. His candidacy and victory bolstered conservative hosts. The deeply polarizing Arkansas governor, with his checkered moral history and a Democratic agenda that had been absent from the White House for twelve years, gave hosts plenty to rail against.[47] To Limbaugh—who excelled at ridicule—and other conservative hosts, Clinton's presidency was a gift. As Taylor, the radio-industry journalist, put it, "It's a lot more fun to be outside on the lawn throwing rocks at the glass house."[48] In a 1993 interview with *Playboy*, of all outlets, Limbaugh himself admitted that his job was easier with Clinton in office.[49]

At this point the conservative-radio revolution was definitively under way. But the transformation of talk radio into an exclusively conservative medium would take years more to complete, precisely because radio executives were not the Republican puppets—or even conservative ideologues—that many presume. Station managers, driven by profits rather than politics, did not care about promoting a partisan message. They moved with the caution of businesspeople playing the percentages, not the urgency of activists facing a perceived crisis. It was only during the Clinton years that the ideological power of conservative talk radio at last came to the fore.

5

The New Republican King

PRESIDENT BUSH'S LOSS LEFT Republicans in the wilderness, confronting unified Democratic governance for the first time in twelve years. It also created a power vacuum in the GOP. *National Review* knew who should fill it: Rush Limbaugh. The intellectual center of the conservative movement anointed the radio host leader of the opposition.[1]

Limbaugh was an unusual choice for coronation, but also a natural one. He may not have been a politician, but he was a political rock star. By the time Clinton entered the White House, Limbaugh's growing footprint included a syndicated television show; millions watched and listened. A steady stream of gawking mainstream-media profiles during the early 1990s further elevated his stature. Bush may have been nominated at the convention, but buttons emblazoned "Limbaugh '96" were the hottest item among attendees.[2] A September 1992 *Providence Journal-Bulletin* cartoon illustrates just how powerful Limbaugh had become. The strip depicts Bush sitting in a classroom as the teacher tells her students, "Children, today we have a very special guest. Can anybody tell me who he is? He's a Republican . . . He's very influential . . . He's an expert on politics." The class asks in unison, "RUSH LIMBAUGH?"[3] Pollsters took Limbaugh's leadership seriously enough that they included his name in some Republican 1996 primary polls.[4]

Limbaugh's ascendancy was further cemented by the most important blessing in conservative politics. After the 1992 election, former President Reagan—Ronaldus Magnus to Limbaugh listeners—wrote:

Thanks, Rush, for all you're doing to promote Republican and conservative principles. Now that I've retired from active politics, I don't mind that you've become the number-one voice for conservatism in our country. I know the liberals call you the most dangerous man in America, but don't worry about it; they used to say the same thing about me. Keep up the good work. America needs to hear the way things ought to be. Sincerely, Ron.[5]

The Way Things Ought to Be was Limbaugh's best-selling 1992 book.

As the Clinton years went by, Limbaugh was joined on the podium by other hosts. At first his peers were largely local players with local political concerns. With increasing syndication after 1997, thanks to changes in the radio business prompted in part by the Telecommunications Act of 1996, other hosts followed Limbaugh onto the national stage.[6]

Scholars and political observers have often neglected hosts' impact because radio talkers don't line up with the traditional profile of a political power player.[7] But conservative hosts did just the sort of things party leaders do. They exercised influence over the party's operation, agenda, and nominating process and aided the party in elections and governance.[8] Hosts used their reach and name recognition to raise money, boost turnout, build support for candidates, and disseminate the party's message. Call-in hosts also were especially well positioned to take the pulse of the party's base and share what they learned with other party leaders.

In 1992 Limbaugh hosted a fundraiser for then–House Minority Whip Newt Gingrich, who had survived reelection by a razor thin margin in 1990.[9] In the campaign's final weeks, Limbaugh's WABC colleague Bob Grant energized the crowd at an event with President Bush.[10] Finally, in his only presidential campaign appearance ever, Limbaugh introduced Bush at an election-eve rally in New Jersey. The president made the most of the opportunity, proclaiming, "Last night, Governor Clinton was at the Meadowlands with Richard Gere and other Hollywood liberals. Well, here's a good deal for you. Let Governor Clinton have Richard Gere. I'll take Rush Limbaugh any day."[11] As radio executives tried to mimic Limbaugh's success, many copycat hosts, too, would openly support, campaign with, and fundraise for Republican candidates.

In addition to filling traditional party-leadership roles, hosts were pioneers in a kind of targeted leadership that is now far more commonplace in a digital age: they were uniquely capable of channeling national conservative sentiment toward local campaigns and, as the years passed and Republicans struggled with governance, of framing electoral contests in ways that kept disgruntled conservatives in the Republican camp. Today, with 24/7 political talk online and on cable news, and with the ease of information distribution across far-flung geographies, many other players—including the candidates themselves—can focus nationwide conservative attention on key races. In the early and mid-1990s, however, hosts were highly unusual in exercising these capacities.

But conservative hosts did not just join the ranks of the political elite, albeit from the edge of the party structure. They embodied a new type of party leadership.[12] Unlike the crusty party bosses of yore, they led from the bottom up. Politicians cut deals in the proverbial smoke-filled back room and then fed the voters options and opinions that would, the politicians hoped, enable them to win elections and govern. The power of talk radio hosts came from mobilizing voters' true beliefs—not telling them what to think, as some critics contend, but helping them apply their principles to sometimes-arcane policy matters and unfamiliar candidates. Most importantly, hosts told politicians what their base voters thought and demanded politicians' adherence to the base's preferences. The capacity to mobilize voters—especially primary voters—meant that politicians couldn't ignore the sentiments hosts expressed.

A final, critical divergence between hosts and typical American political leaders was the bottom line. Among hosts, the party didn't come first. Unlike the RNC chair or Republican congressional brass, hosts did not place the GOP's electoral and policy agendas over other goals. Their top priority was building and maintaining the largest possible audience. That meant creating entertaining, passionate radio that provoked emotional response. Sometimes that goal lined up with the party's electoral and policy aims, but talkers jettisoned the party's agenda and ignored its needs when these conflicted with what they had to do to generate ratings.

One consequence was that hosts might champion a primary candidate whose rhetoric and stances inspired listeners but who couldn't win in a general election. Or hosts might rally listeners against a bill proposed by a Republican president or rail against the Republican leadership for compromising with Democrats. Even when hosts built support for Republicans, they argued in the name of conservatism, not Republicanism.[13] As the years went by, and Republicans struggled to make the compromises necessary

53

to govern, this gap between the agendas of hosts and traditional party leaders would become a source of considerable tension.

But this didn't bother hosts. Most considered themselves entertainers first and conservatives second. The party was a distant third. But there were exceptions, such as future stars Sean Hannity and Hugh Hewitt. Hannity would sometimes declare his independence from the party, but he was for the most part a loyal team player. He usually took interviews when leading Republicans wanted them, and he queried campaigns as to how he could help. He routinely trumpeted Republican candidates.[14] By contrast the libertarian-leaning Boortz was more iconoclastic and rebellious. He performed party-leadership functions, such as speaking at get-out-the-vote rallies, but he also expressed his displeasure with the party's agenda on cultural issues such as abortion and LGBTQ-related topics.[15]

Perhaps the best indication of talk radio's growing political impact was that, during the 1992 election, Limbaugh and his ilk created new opportunities for Republican messaging and even, to some extent, steered its content. Because talk radio's audience leaned right—albeit, not as far right as it does today—the airwaves became a forum in which politicians could safely talk to the base without worrying that other voters would listen in. (The highest-powered politicians were exceptions; any interview they gave would reach the public at large, no matter the context in which they spoke.) This encouraged politicians to throw red meat and address topics about which their base cared more than the electorate writ large. Candidates and officials could also use this new forum to fire up their base with information that might be dubiously sourced and would provoke skepticism from a mainstream reporter.

Before talk radio entered the political scene, the mainstream media had served as an uncompromising gatekeeper, determining whether stories were newsworthy and sufficiently verified and only then sharing them with the public. Talk radio broke down the gate, enabling conservatives to share any message they wanted.[16] As Limbaugh explained, "I am here to find the things that you may spot yourself, but certainly the mainstream media would not."[17]

Limbaugh's interview with Bush presents a stark case of a host opening up new possibilities for GOP messaging. During the interview Limbaugh blew the lid off the controversial issue of Clinton's evasion of service in

Vietnam. Bush himself had scrupulously avoided the matter throughout the campaign. But Limbaugh offered a venue where the president could change that, addressing an issue important to his base and doing so before an audience that he knew would be receptive to it. On Limbaugh's show Bush could comfortably jab Clinton for a "total failure to come clean with the American people about his draft record." After some observers were angered by the apparent attack on Clinton, Limbaugh even played public-relations man for Bush, framing their exchange in the president's favor. Limbaugh argued that Bush wasn't attacking anyone but instead was simply responding to a question.[18]

This was party leadership for a new age. Limbaugh wasn't strategizing the president's messaging, but he was shaping it all the same. Under the leadership of talk radio, media gatekeeping took on an entirely different look, and there was little need to soften one's tone or compromise on one's convictions. In fact every incentive existed to do the exact opposite. This was especially so in talk radio's early days, when the medium wasn't taken seriously enough to attract attention from liberals concerned about what hosts and listeners were saying—except perhaps when the president was on the air.

After the election Limbaugh exhibited a degree of buyer's remorse over his support for Bush, foreshadowing the future of the relationship between talk radio and establishment Republicans. With Bush defeated, Limbaugh issued a prediction: "There's going to be a huge battle for the soul of the Republican Party. And I would make this contention. I would say to you that the moderate patrician wing of the Republican Party just demonstrated why we don't want to let them run the party anymore. The conservatives are going to have to move in and take over."[19] This declaration provided a clear signal of the direction in which talk radio hosts would guide the party. The next patrician Bush would have to wear cowboy boots.

6

Bill Clinton, Talk Radio Innovator

THE PERIOD BETWEEN 1992 and 1994 was a transitional one for talk radio. The medium was emerging as a potent political force on the right, but Bill Clinton was still its most committed user. Many of the key players from Clinton's campaign, such as Strauss and Eller, joined the White House communications staff and continued investing in radio from within the administration. Clinton's eager embrace was a reminder that talk radio was nowhere near the conservative monolith that would throw its weight around during the 2000s and 2010s.

The administration understood that talk radio was not only a valuable tool for winning elections but also that it would help determine the fate of Clinton's presidency. Clinton's rocky first days in office provided a stinging reminder of this: talk radio was instrumental in scuttling his nomination of Zoë Baird as attorney general. Baird had illegally employed two undocumented aliens, a nanny and a driver. Though Baird earned $507,000 a year, she paid them less than minimum wage and did not pay taxes on their wages.

Initially most of official Washington—Republican, Democrat, and journalist alike—minimized the scandal. Orrin Hatch, the highly conservative ranking Republican on the Senate Judiciary Committee, called Baird's infraction a "hypertechnical violation." But talk radio listeners fumed. Hiring an illegal-immigrant domestic worker under the table was just the sort of hypocritical behavior they expected from the overpaid Washington elite, while law-abiding citizens scrambled to secure childcare on meager salaries.

Angry callers flooded the airwaves. From there the fury spread to the White House and senators' offices, which were bombarded with complaints.

Talk radio spotlighted the situation, driving down public opinion and forcing officials and the mainstream media to reappraise the nomination. This reappraisal, in turn, generated even more negative sentiment, eventually dooming Baird's chances and inducing her to withdraw.[1] Clinton also backtracked on his second attorney general choice, Judge Kimba Wood, when the press learned that she too had hired an illegal immigrant as a nanny, in 1986. Unlike Baird, Wood had complied with all tax and registration requirements. But talk radio, especially Limbaugh, had rendered the potential nomination toxic. If Clinton nominated Wood, hosts would bludgeon the young administration, which couldn't afford to lose again.[2]

The Clinton team's talk radio strategy was to harness the medium rather than be its victim. Talk radio's influence could harm the White House, but, if exploited effectively, the medium could also provide opportunities to advance the president's agenda. The White House communications team had two primary goals for talk radio. First, they wanted to expand talk radio's ideological palette. They bolstered friendly or less hostile hosts and tried to convey to the press and the public that talk radio consisted of more than Limbaugh and his ilk.[3] In a 1994 interview with a talk radio trade publication, presidential adviser George Stephanopoulos affirmed the administration's belief in talk radio but also made a plea for balance and diversity of opinions on the airwaves.[4] Second, the White House hoped to use talk radio to circumvent the White House press corps and speak directly to the public.

Clinton's staff constructed the first dedicated White House talk radio outreach operation. As the first ever director of radio, Strauss aggressively pitched guests and discussion topics selected and designed to match individual hosts' interests. For example, he encouraged the administration's drug czar, Lee Brown, to appear with Oliver North. North disagreed with the administration on most issues, but he shared Brown's views on drug policy.[5] Strauss didn't mind booking guests with conservative hosts, as long as he thought they were fair and willing to let administration officials have their say. More combative hosts, who promised to interrogate guests, might get political adviser James Carville or other brawlers on the Clinton team.[6] The White House also targeted local morning shows, which reached a broad audience but had largely been ignored by previous administrations.[7]

Strauss made sure the president himself took advantage of the medium's intimacy to showcase his likability. Clinton's radio appearances ranged from Imus's show to an interview with ESPN Radio, on which the president talked about his beloved Arkansas Razorbacks' trip to the NCAA men's basketball Final Four. During these appearances he might touch on broad political themes, but the objective was to leave the audience wanting to have a beer with him. Talking on the radio broadened the audience for Clinton's charm, exposing Americans who opposed him or were disconnected from politics.[8] During a 1994 chat with Imus, Clinton fielded questions about policy and Whitewater, but he also bantered with the host about his cholesterol level and joked about whether the White House was "America's most beautiful public housing or the crown jewel of the penal system."[9] Listeners who paid attention to these humanizing interviews might give Clinton the benefit of the doubt in the future.[10]

In an effort to win over hosts, Clinton spoke to them directly as a collective. In 1994, after igniting a firestorm of criticism with comments perceived as attacking talk radio, Clinton sat down with *Talkers Magazine* Publisher Michael Harrison for an interview. Clinton stressed that call-in shows were a "very positive thing for democracy."[11] Expanding on the president's views, Stephanapoulos told the 1996 National Association of Radio Talk Show Hosts luncheon that, for as long as he had known the president, Clinton had been telling him that radio was the surest way to reach voters and get ideas into the marketplace.[12]

The White House skillfully employed talk radio to produce news and advance its agenda. In September 1993, in conjunction with the unveiling of Clinton's health care plan, the communications team staged a multiday talk radio bonanza at the White House. The president, first lady, vice president, and aides briefed 200 hosts on the plan's details. Two days later, in an unruly sight that Eller likened to the bar scene from *Star Wars*, sixty hosts broadcast live from the White House lawn, with high-profile administration officials jetting from table to table for interviews.[13]

Clinton's team understood that they needed a charm offensive in order to overcome hosts' skepticism about their top policy priority. Hosts were clearly formidable: not only had they played an important role in harpooning Baird's nomination, but they also had stoked public opposition to the president's plan to allow LGBTQ Americans to serve openly in the military, resulting in the scaled-back don't-ask-don't-tell policy. The health care plan was likely to face similar headwinds. But even if the White House couldn't win outright support from many hosts, it might at least soften their opposition or get its slant onto the airwaves. Phil Tower of WOOD in Grand Rapids gave the administration credit for its effort. Compared to its predecessors, the Clinton White House was more aware that "image is everything and we're the conduit to the rest of the country," Tower said.[14]

Clinton's communications team invited its most potent on-air critics to the briefing, including Limbaugh. The same Limbaugh who opened his Clinton-era shows by counting the days America had been hostage to "the Raw Deal"—a spoof of *Nightline's* coverage of the Iranian hostage crisis.[15] The host, however, would have no part of the White House's public-relations program. Instead he sent a camera crew to cover the event. At one point White House staff asked the crew to stop filming, then confiscated the camera after the request was ignored. Republican congressmen made outraged inquiries. Their letters offered a reminder of how powerful Limbaugh had already become.[16]

While this wasn't the sort of attention the White House dreamed of receiving, the administration welcomed the widespread media coverage the talk radio commotion generated. The presence of radio hosts broadcasting from the White House was itself newsworthy, and the mainstream media, ranging from the Associated Press to NBC, reported on it, drawing further attention to the rollout of the health care plan.[17] This sort of echo coverage offered an added benefit to the aggressive courtship of talk radio.[18]

By June 1996 President Clinton had appeared on more than a hundred radio shows, while Hillary Clinton had appeared on more than two hundred.[19] Mark Gearan, who spent two years as White House communications director during the Clinton presidency, said he couldn't think of a single big legislative effort in which talk radio was not "a staple of the basic architecture of how we'd communicate it."[20] Talk radio was similarly integral to Democratic political efforts, and Clinton himself did a radio barrage in advance of the 1994 midterm elections. Producers were shocked to learn that Clinton wanted to be on their shows. Strauss recalled an episode when he reached a station for a last-minute interview and was nearly turned down because the producers thought he was pulling their leg. To convince them it wasn't a hoax, and impart the proper "wow" factor, Strauss had the producers call the White House switchboard and ask for him in the president's residence. During these midterm appearances, the president lamented negative ads, stumped for Democratic candidates, touted his crime bill, lacerated Republicans' Contract with America, and criticized their unwillingness to work with him on health care and other issues.[21]

Targeting talk radio made sense. Any political observer could see that it was affecting politics and public policy alike.

7

Stopping Legislation in Its Tracks

DURING PRESIDENT CLINTON'S first term, the deep bond between hosts and listeners began to have a profound impact on public policy. Talk radio came of age as a tool of the legislative process—above all, one of obstruction.

Just as they pitched advertisers' products, hosts pitched conservative ideas. They defined and framed issues in terms that motivated listeners to act. Members of Congress accustomed to deciding arcane matters of policy among themselves were suddenly pressed by conservative constituents at key moments in the legislative process. Usually what those constituents said was "no thanks." Listeners' engagement prompted squeamish Republicans to refuse compromise and to withhold and block votes. Occasionally talk radio had similar influence on Democrats. But by 1995—with the medium's conservatism hardening, and the virtual extinction of conservative Democrats in the federal legislative branches after the 1994 elections—this influence waned.

Talk radio's outsize effect in scuttling initiatives had its roots in historical circumstances and structural conditions. Realistically, in Clinton's first term, talk radio was never likely to be a driving force behind the enactment of legislation. After all, Democrats enjoyed universal control of government. Whatever impact talk radio had was going to be on defense, preventing progressive legislation and preserving the status quo to the extent that it served hosts' and listeners' interests.

Structurally, talk radio was most potent in the hands of the opposition, regardless of party. That is because talk radio was particularly effective at stirring great passion in a relatively small number of voters. This positioned the medium to take advantage of minoritarian features of U.S. law and legislative practice, which make it easier to kill proposed laws than to enact them. In particular talk radio was ascending as the Senate was increasingly erecting a sixty-vote hurdle to passage of legislation.[1] With this cloture threshold in place, a relatively small number of senators could torpedo legislation.

Members of Congress feared losing, so they were acutely sensitive to signals from their constituents on pending bills.[2] Leadership, in particular, also saw hazards beyond their own electoral imperilment. They worried that pushing hard for one bill could generate collateral damage and ignite intraparty wars. Or an issue push might deplete valuable political capital, thereby endangering other legislation of greater import. Since going all in on one bill could easily kill three others, it was comparatively easy to convince legislators to give up in one or another instance.

Talk radio was well-placed to capitalize on this bias against action. Hosts concentrated listeners' attention in ways that increased vulnerable legislators' perception of risk. Shows could trigger scores of calls, faxes, letters, and eventually emails on a topic.[3] Deluged lawmakers may have understood that talk radio had generated all the messages, but that didn't necessarily blunt their impact. Why hazard voter blowback? When there was no corresponding pressure from supporters, the benefit of voting in favor seemed small.

Hosts also took advantage of their daily contact with listeners to deepen listeners' commitment to causes and drive activism earlier in the legislative process, when bills were most vulnerable. Americans and the mainstream broadcast media tended to follow politics like a casual fan follows a football game: in the last two minutes, and only when a big win is on the line. Typically it was just the climactic stages of the legislative process that got airtime. This left an opening for talk radio to get out ahead of mainstream press coverage of policy proposals. While hosts and listeners were scrutinizing and criticizing legislation, most Americans, including many who might view the legislation more positively, did not know it existed.[4] At this stage, when a bill's future hinged on gaining momentum—adding crucial cosponsors and committee supporters and demonstrating that it wouldn't entail great risk—even a small, unrepresentative slice of the electorate could have a large impact.

In some cases the mainstream media never gave widespread coverage to issues highlighted on talk radio, allowing hosts to influence public opinion without any informational counterweight. For example, on his Election Day 1992 show, Limbaugh reminded listeners of a hideous "hidden House bill" about which he had previously sounded the alarm, but which other outlets never treated as significant. A House committee had stealthily and without debate bottled up HR 4848, which lowered the threshold at which assets became subject to the estate tax.[5] Limbaugh bemoaned the bill's redistributive intent and warned listeners that they could easily find their assets in excess of the new $200,000 threshold. For the moment, the specter of HR 4848 was a distant one, but with a Democrat in the White House, its prospects would improve substantially. It was another reason why Clinton had to be defeated.

Early, concentrated action gave talk radio another advantage: it could pierce the veil of secrecy that legislators on both sides of the aisle had long relied on to hide the costs and authors of bills.[6] Such secrecy prevented accountability but also enabled complex compromise legislation with significant costs. Hosts specialized in airing the specifics of bills during delicate stages of negotiation, when attention could impede or destroy prospects for passage. Hosts often exposed legislation drafted in secret and "outed" legislative gimmicks or other attempts to hide a bill's costs, fiscal and otherwise. Unhappy legislators or staffers found that they could kill bills by sharing information with powerful talk radio hosts, who then rallied allies on and off Capitol Hill and transformed the politics surrounding the issue.[7]

In essence, talk radio was working around the pattern Frank Baumgartner and Bryan Jones have detected in the mainstream media's influence on agenda setting. Baumgartner and Jones show that, because the establishment media consult a small group of sources, they tend to highlight the same issues and to view similarly the implications of a given debate at a given moment.[8] Talk radio—and later its progeny, such as cable news and conservative digital outlets—looked to other sources and issues, or dove deep into issues the mainstream press covered lightly. Even when hosts focused on the same stories as the mainstream press, they often zeroed in on different aspects of the debate, directing attention in whatever way benefited their position.[9] Frequently, even when hosts could not stop a bill, they could force changes to a distasteful provision or two.[10] That's what happened, for instance, to 1994 legislation aimed at limiting gifts members of Congress could receive.

The Gift Ban

Hosts' first legislative win had come in 1989, when they helped to stymie a congressional pay raise.[11] But the medium's true legislative might was displayed only in the fall of 1994, on the eve of the midterm elections. If members of Congress were previously unaware of talk radio's political capacities, the failure of the Lobbying Disclosure Act of 1994 was a dramatic wake-up call. Talk radio stirred a hornet's nest of opposition—small but fierce—forcing legislators to spend political capital on a bill that at one time seemed guaranteed to pass without controversy.

The Lobbying Disclosure Act—or the "gift ban," as it was popularly known—was hard to vote against. The bill banned lobbyists from paying for any gift, meal, entertainment, or travel junket for lawmakers, and it required lobbyists to register and disclose financial information. Privately, the bill aroused the ire of the "congressional golf caucus"—members who liked to frequent the links. But that was precisely why supporting the bill was almost a political must: to avoid looking like one wanted to preserve perks. Some members were insulted by the implication that they could be bought for a sandwich or event ticket, but they too fell in behind the law.[12] A better reason to oppose the bill might have been electoral strategy: as the legislative calendar crept toward the 1994 midterm elections—the bill eventually stalled a month before Election Day—Republicans had incentive to deny the Democratic majority achievements to tout on the campaign trail.[13] Finally, there were legitimate policy disagreements over how best to regulate lobbyists.[14] Yet, in spite of all that, the legislation had been breezing through Congress. In 1993 the Senate approved a version of the bill 95-2.[15] The House followed in 1994 by a 315-110 vote, sending the bill to a conference committee to work out lingering differences.[16] Coming out of conference committee, the bill's supporters "thought we had a clear path to enactment."[17]

They may have until House Minority Whip Newt Gingrich and colleagues Tom DeLay and Ernest Istook undertook a last-minute charge to crush the legislation. They enlisted the aid of conservative groups ranging from the Christian Coalition to the National Rifle Association, who feared that the law would hamper their lobbying activities.[18] Gingrich and his allies also had a new partner in the fight: conservative media, especially talk radio. The mainstream media weren't paying much attention to the bill, which was complex and seemingly too technical to bother with.[19] But talk radio was ready to fill the vacuum.

DeLay sent a fax opposing the bill to 500 conservative radio hosts. Gingrich faxed his talking points to Limbaugh. Istook alerted conservative activist Paul Weyrich, who lambasted the bill on his television show and on Michael Reagan's nationally syndicated radio program. The Christian Coalition helped to spread the word to conservative broadcasters, religious and otherwise. Reverends James Dobson and Pat Robertson implored their audiences to urge senators against the bill.[20]

The conference report eventually made it out of the House, but only after considerable struggle. Sensing the tightness of the fight, Texas Democrat John Bryant, the bill's lead House sponsor, accused Republicans of falsely claiming to oppose the bill on the grounds that it violated the free-speech rights of grassroots organizations. Bryant told Republican Deputy Whip Bob Walker, "There is no grassroots gag. If you want to keep playing free golf, admit it."[21] The House approved the conference report by a 306-112 margin, but in many ways Gingrich and his allies got what they wanted: they shook the bill's aura of inevitable passage and ruffled Democrats' feathers. So fierce was the debate that Republicans accused Bryant of impermissibly attacking Ohio Representative Michael Oxley. In response Bryant almost had his words taken down, a harsh penalty that precludes a House member from speaking for the remainder of the day.[22] And in several procedural votes, the bill's sponsors won by far closer margins of 216-205 and 215-202, with the vast majority of Republicans opposed.[23]

Limbaugh's assault on the bill began that same day the conference report passed the House, eight days before the Senate would bring the bill up for cloture. After receiving Gingrich's talking points, the host pilloried the "anti-American" and "unconstitutional" bill, telling his television viewers:

> Ladies and gentlemen, the United States Congress today, late on Thursday afternoon, actually, passed a bill that one congressman has called "Hillary's revenge." This is the Lobby [sic] Disclosure Act of 1994 and what this bill will do if taken to its full length, or full breadth of possibility, is consider any citizen, member of a grassroots organization or anybody who just happens to call

Washington—if you spend more than 10 percent of your time trying to influence the outcome of legislation in Washington, you could be considered a lobbyist and the federal government could require you—will require you—to report your existence, the names of yourself and anybody else in your organization, how much time you're spending trying to influence legislation. And if you fail to report this information to them and they find out about it, you could be subject to $200,000 fines for not reporting it.[24]

Limbaugh also criticized a carefully crafted provision designed to protect religious groups and leaders as being ambiguous, which astounded a House staffer involved in its drafting.[25]

Limbaugh's analysis spawned outlandish allegations about the bill. A Senate staffer remembered one rumor "about how churches were going to have to list their members and how much they donated, and disclose all of their fundraising activities." The rumors spread rapidly, inspiring intense resistance.[26]

Paul Brubaker, the staffer working on the bill for its Senate Republican cosponsor, William Cohen of Maine, remembered the Senate switchboards lighting up after Limbaugh began talking about the issue. Brubaker also recalled the discord Limbaugh sowed in official GOP ranks. Brubaker started hearing from other staffers who believed that, thanks to the vocal opposition, supporting the bill had become too risky for their bosses. After Republican senators devoted one of their weekly lunches to the topic, a senator approached Brubaker outside the meeting and remarked, "So you're the asshole responsible for this."[27]

The bill's primary Senate sponsor, Michigan Democrat Carl Levin, made a bold move to stem the tide of misinformation: he went on Limbaugh's show. In doing so he became the only significant Democratic elected official to appear on the nationally syndicated radio program during its entire thirty-year run.[28] Levin felt like he had nothing to lose by stating his case, so he took to the air to argue that the bill was nowhere near as dangerous as opponents alleged. But he never had a chance to rebut Limbaugh's next guest. After Levin signed off, Limbaugh welcomed Istook, who charged that Levin had lied about the bill.[29]

Amid the continuing fervor, and with the midterm election just a month away, Levin and Cohen even offered to delete offending provisions from the bill. But the opposition smelled blood. Senators blocked the attempt, citing other qualms they had with the legislation, and the bill died in early October, a victim of a bipartisan filibuster.[30]

There is little doubt that the conservative-media campaign played a major role in killing the Lobbying Disclosure Act of 1994. West Virginia Democrat Robert Byrd certainly believed as much, explaining in a press statement that a deliberate campaign of misinformation had prompted what he considered unwarranted, but genuine, fears among his constituents. Byrd was facing reelection, and the sincere concerns of his constituents, however misguided, compelled him to vote against cloture.[31] A House staffer who worked on the bill and spoke anonymously for an interview firmly believed the lobbying reform would have become law in 1994 had it not been for Limbaugh's influence. In a demonstration of that influence, the Republican-led 104th Congress passed a version of the Lobbying Disclosure Act without opposition after sponsors altered the provisions that had prompted the greatest controversy on talk radio.[32]

As the work of Gingrich, Istook, and DeLay illustrated, even in these early days, hosts didn't just organically weigh in on legislation. Republicans courted them, and in increasingly organized and institutionalized ways. Beginning in 1993 the Republican National Committee's Scott Hogenson faxed daily segment ideas to producers, hosts, and bookers. He offered hosts everything necessary to produce a segment, including suggested guests and sources. Although, legally, the RNC could not expressly advocate for or against a candidate or legislation, it could use talk radio to that end, providing hosts the means to advocate the RNC's position on their own.[33] Meanwhile GOPAC, Gingrich's political action committee, included talk radio hosts in conference calls designed to foster a message of the week.[34] These sorts of efforts would dramatically expand over the years to come, with hosts receiving talking points, booking recommendations, and story ideas from countless Republican organs, in addition to individual legislators such as Istook.

This outreach signaled an important change in conservative media's relationship with politics and politicians. If talk radio began as a commercial enterprise unaffiliated with any party, by the time of the Clinton era, it was becoming the Republican Party surrogate that many assume it has always been—but, crucially, only when this suited hosts' purposes. They fiercely maintained their independence and resisted taking direction from the GOP, even as they often proved helpful in legislative fights.

Elevating and Transforming Small Issues

Talk radio's influence on policy stemmed from hosts' ability to transform even complicated, highly technical matters into something understandable and ominous. On talk radio the fortunes of the most arcane legislation turned into a referendum on bedrock principles. While hosts used their ample airtime to delve into legislative minutiae, other media outlets ignored the issue or only talked about it in order to address the controversy talk radio had stirred.

Pat Schroeder, a Democrat who represented Colorado in the House from 1973 until 1997, recalled a 1990s patent-legislation proposal that spurred massive public debate. Ordinarily the bill would have been the narrow province of the few legislators who could converse on intellectual-property issues. Yet somehow patent legislation made for compelling radio. The reason was that the bill sought to comply with an international treaty. Talk hosts therefore incorporated the legislation into their broader argument against anything related to global governance or the sacrifice of American sovereignty. By distorting the issue or changing the focus, talk radio caused hysteria and made passing legislation arduous.[35]

Another dense policy debate that talk radio contorted to the point of listener outrage—the sort of debate that the mainstream press invariably left to Washington insiders only—concerned "pioneer preferences." The FCC awarded these preferences, which included free licenses, to developers of breakthrough communications technologies in an effort to spur development of cellular telephone systems, reward innovators, and avoid the caprice of lotteries. While the FCC was in the process of awarding the preferences to three companies, Congress enacted a statute requiring the commission to auction licenses to the highest bidder. In 1994 powerful House Energy and Commerce Committee Chair John Dingell of Michigan proposed bipartisan legislation to mandate that the three pioneer licensees pay roughly 90 percent of the market rate for their licenses. The FCC then demanded on its own that the companies pay up. The result was a lawsuit from the companies, which argued that the FCC had no right to charge them.[36]

Dingell worried that if the companies won the suit, they'd get their licenses for free, so he continued to press his bipartisan legislation to ensure that the companies paid, regardless of the outcome of the lawsuit.[37] But this result still would have amounted to a discount for the three existing pioneer preference licensees, frustrating their competitors, who benefited from no such largesse. One of them, Pacific Telesis, pounced after the *Washington Post* published an editorial in favor of a bill expanding the General Agreement on Tariffs and Trade, the unrelated bill to which Dingell had appended the legislation enshrining the 90 percent rate. Pacific Telesis bought ads in the *Post* and the *Washington Times* flaying the *Post* for the editorial's failure to disclose that the paper had a financial interest in passage of the legislation, as the Post Company owned 70 percent of one of the licensees, American Personal Communications.

On talk radio this complex maze was simplified and recast as an explosive story. Hosts and listeners erupted, claiming that the *Post* was deceptively trying to win a government handout. This argument fit nicely with the usual talk radio trope about a liberal media in bed with Democrats.[38] While the details of pioneer preferences might have put the public to sleep, listeners could easily comprehend cronyism and media bias.

After the debate caught fire, Dingell staffer David Leach had to explain to Gingrich that, far from providing a gift to the *Post*, the bill compelled its parent company to pay for a license that it might otherwise get for free.[39] Energy and Commerce Committee staff prepared a fact sheet for the benefit of the rest of the House. And a House subcommittee held an emergency hearing at which members from both parties castigated a Pacific Telesis executive.[40]

In the end talk radio didn't get exactly what it wanted. The uproar forced Congress to delay action on the bill until after the 1994 elections, but the bill eventually passed in the lame duck session. Still, critics managed to extract a concession that implicitly recognized their complaint that the *Post* was taking the country for a ride. The bill passed only after an agreement between President Clinton and Senator Dole in which the administration committed to working with Congress to make pioneer licensees retroactively pay more for their licenses if policymakers concluded that the government had not received "a fair return."[41] Talk radio, by essentially flipping the purpose of the bill on its head, spurred enough outrage both to delay the bill's passage and force the parties into a side agreement.[42]

Talk radio's influence was no mystery, at least to some members of Congress and their staffers. As Virginia Republican Representative Tom Davis explained, talk radio turned complex policies "into hot-button issues that aroused public passions and polarized the parties on ideological lines." This put Republicans who supported legislation on its merits in an impossible position politically, compelling them to vote against a bill they agreed with or pay a political price because radio hosts and their fans were upset about ideological principles that were barely at stake, if at all.[43] Republican aide Brett Shogren understood the situation clearly, noting that issues about which members did not have strong views were particularly susceptible to this simplification effect. When members faced key votes on policies that really did implicate their core philosophies, they followed their instincts. But in other cases, talk radio could manipulate listeners into activism that made minor bills into high-stakes purity tests.[44]

The lobbying-reform, pioneer-preferences, and patent-legislation cases were signs of what was to come. Even as talk radio was growing closer to the Republican leadership, working with Gingrich and his allies to advance their agenda, hosts were staking their own claims to conservative principles. They placed themselves at odds with many Republicans by rejecting even relatively unimportant compromises as betrayals of conservative values. The smallest vote, they warned implicitly, would be assessed on talk radio's terms, which increasingly took the form of bad-faith argument and misinformation.

8

The Political Earthquake

IN 1994 TALK RADIO took two major steps along its decade-long path toward becoming the doctrinaire medium that dominates the airwaves today. At the time the format was spreading like wildfire. The number of talk stations grew from roughly 300 in 1989 to between 800 and 1,031 in 1994, depending on how one was counting, and increasing at a rate of about 20 stations per month.[1] But its consolidation as an all-conservative medium was nowhere near complete, and its relationship with Republican politics was very much in flux.

The first of the two steps came in San Francisco, where Mickey Luckoff seized a rare opportunity. Luckoff was president and general manager of KGO-AM, the city's top-rated full-service talk station, airing a variety of perspectives, news, and nonpolitical programs. He worried that another company might purchase KSFO, a run-down local station for sale, and build it into a rival to KGO. So he convinced his bosses at Capital Cities/ABC to purchase KSFO. But the acquisition left Luckoff with a station that needed a format. He tried a few different ideas, but none stuck. Then he started thinking about KVI, the all-conservative Seattle talk station whose success had caught the eye of many in the business.

Luckoff wanted to know whether the KVI model would be viable in ultra-liberal San Francisco, so he checked in with Jack Swanson, his former program director who was then working in Seattle. Swanson, himself a card-carrying liberal, suspected that all-conservative talk would make it in San Francisco, precisely because of the Bay Area's politics. San Franciscans celebrated tolerance, but that tolerance had limits: they accepted all

types of people, except for conservatives, whom they scorned and ostra-
cized. This made San Francisco an ideal market for talk radio: a big city
with an underserved conservative minority, seeking validation and likeminded community. Swanson returned to San Francisco to program
KGO and KSFO.

KSFO ramped up quickly and soon was soaring as an all-conservative
talk station. Station managers throughout the influential Capital Cities/ABC
network took note and began tinkering with conservative shows, which
took the place of liberal or apolitical ones. Ratings went up.[2] KVI and
KSFO proved that conservative talk could thrive in America's most liberal cities, suggesting that it could work just about anywhere.[3] This may be
surprising on its face, but it reflects the baked-in economics of the radio
industry at the time. A major market station such as KSFO needed to
draw just 3 to 5 percent of the local listening audience to turn a profit.
Conservative talk could do that routinely in even the most liberal places.[4]

KSFO's success also marked a turning point because it demonstrated the
viability of all-conservative stations before the format had become a tried-
and-true business model. In 1994 there were still good reasons to be skittish
about the financial prospects of entirely conservative talk formats. For one
thing, while the audience leaned right, it was more ideologically diverse
than we have come to expect. A survey that year from the Benchmark
Company found that 35 percent of listeners identified as conservative,
29 percent as moderate, 24 percent as liberal, and 11 percent as "other."[5]
Catering only to conservative listeners therefore risked alienating large
numbers of potential listeners. KVI, KSFO, and their most immediate followers showed that the reward of all-conservative talk was worth the risk,
throughout the country.

A second 1994 development also pushed talk radio rightward, and it happened to be the political story of the year: the midterm elections, in which
Republicans did the unthinkable by capturing the House of Representatives for the first time in four decades. Entering the election cycle, the notion that Republicans could retake the House generated derisive laughter.
Even National Republican Congressional Committee Chair Bill Paxon,
who spearheaded the GOP effort to win back the House, admitted in February that gaining a majority would be "a four-year process—1996 is our
opportunity."[6]

But Republicans had a new secret weapon in talk radio.[7] Bob Michel had
announced his retirement in 1993, leaving House Republican leadership

to the likes of Gingrich, Armey, and Tom DeLay.[8] All three were talk radio fans who grasped the medium's potential. The Gingrich-aligned GOPAC distributed training tapes urging candidates to embrace talk radio, while Armey and Gingrich himself integrated regular talk radio usage into the Republican battle plan for the elections and beyond.[9]

The medium boosted Republicans from the campaign's nascent stages through Election Day. Before the races were under way, talk radio encouraged Republicans to take the plunge. Paxon argued that conservative radio gave Republicans hope, a sense that victory was possible and opportunities awaited nominees.[10] After campaigns launched, local conservative hosts fulfilled many traditional party-leadership roles on candidates' behalf. For instance, at a luncheon for candidate Steve Chabot featuring two Republican senators, "The tone . . . was set by the master of ceremonies, noted Democrat-basher and WLWRadio talk show host Bill Cunningham." The *Cincinnati Post* reported Cunningham warmed up the crowd with praise for Chabot—a "truly great American"—and a warning that his opponent, Representative David Mann, was "a threat to the American Way."[11]

Talk radio also provided Republicans an outlet, which in many cases offset the media-access advantage Democrats held by virtue of incumbency and their status as members of the majority party. Just mentioning a race on local radio could generate excitement for the Republican candidate. When Bob Grant discussed Michael Forbes's campaign to unseat New York Congressman George Hochbrueckner, the phone lines in Forbes's campaign office lit up. Forbes eventually won his race. Seattle host Kirby Wilbur contributed to Republican challenger Randy Tate, canvassed for him, emceed a fundraiser, and frequently hosted Tate on his show. Wilbur dispatched angry listeners to disrupt campaign events held by Tate's opponent, Representative Mike Kreidler.[12] Tate also won.

Republican George Nethercutt, who upset House Speaker Tom Foley in the election cycle's marquee matchup, gave talk radio credit for helping him do what many thought impossible. After all, though the Eastern Washington district they vied for leaned right, Foley seemed secure thanks to the mystique and power that accompanied the speakership. Only two challengers had ever defeated a sitting speaker, and none since 1862. Foley also had a huge financial edge, outspending Nethercutt $2.1 million to the challenger's $1.07 million.[13] And most traditional media outlets in the district were deferential to the speaker because of his position.

Nethercutt had to take coverage by any means available. He chatted regularly with Richard Clear, a supportive local host. The Republican upstart felt radio galvanized his backers, and there was evidence to prove it.[14] All day long the phones in his campaign office rang off the hook with callers who had heard about him on the radio.[15] Local talk radio was all in; none of the major hosts in the district backed Foley. Indeed, hosts were positively hostile. During an interview one host asked the speaker about rumors that he was gay. Another dubbed him the "sphincter of the house."[16]

Mark Souder's experience was similar to Nethercutt's. The Indiana challenger didn't face the speaker, but he was trying to unseat a popular incumbent Democrat. Representative Jill Long had a large cash advantage and had won her previous two elections easily. But talk radio helped keep Souder in the race. He kicked off his campaign on Paul Phillips's local morning program, and Phillips promoted his candidacy through Election Day. Daily appearances on radio and cable TV allowed Souder to stealthily build momentum. Souder's campaign both benefited from conservative hosts' favor and actively reached out to targeted radio audiences by devoting a large budget to ads on talk, Christian, and country-music stations. In these spots the candidate responded personally to charges, winning over voters.[17] Long might have smothered Souder early on with her financial might, but her campaign team wasn't paying attention to the conservative talk radio audience. She didn't detect the rising challenger until it was too late, when he was too well defined and capitalized to squelch. Souder went on to serve fifteen years in the House.

Saxby Chambliss, another member of the freshman class elected in 1994, summarized the dynamic that fall: "We all used [talk radio] on the Republican side to a great extent." Chambliss noted that hosts and candidates enjoyed a win-win relationship. Candidates such as him got opportunities to raise money and win support, and talkers burnished their status with listeners by hosting the candidates.[18] At the time many shows were just getting off the ground; hosts needed the credibility infusion.

Limbaugh used his stardom to press the Republican cause on a larger stage. A documentary released the year after the elections labeled him "a national precinct captain for the conservative movement and the Republican Party."[19] He labored to keep his listeners and television viewers energized and to discredit any press narrative that might damage Republicans' chances. He also focused on stories that made high-profile Democrats look bad. If voters came to see powerful incumbents as arrogant, entitled, hypocritical, or disingenuous, then even they were ripe for the picking.

In one case of big-game hunting, Limbaugh trained his sights on Tennessee Democratic Senator Jim Sasser, who was in line to replace retiring Senate Majority Leader George Mitchell after the election. Sasser shrewdly purchased ad time on Limbaugh's radio program to trumpet his support for school prayer and school choice, but Limbaugh killed any potential benefit. On his television show, he questioned the authenticity of the ads, accusing Sasser of pandering to voters with promises he had no intention of keeping. Beyond the circumstances of the campaign, Limbaugh contended, a Democrat would never associate himself with conservative positions on such issues. Four days before the election, Limbaugh accused Sasser of being a liberal masquerading as a conservative during the campaign.[20]

Limbaugh did not limit himself to the largest trophies, such as Sasser and Speaker Foley. The host kept tabs on various close races on which he might have an impact. In one television program, he played three ads in which Democratic senators touted stands they had taken against President Clinton's agenda and suggested that the candidates must have been back on their heels. Limbaugh also fact-checked one of the ads and argued that the Democrats were lying.[21] Clinton's supposed toxicity was a major theme of Limbaugh's coverage and a vehicle for attacking lesser figures. Democrats are doing "everything they can to convince you that they never heard of Bill Clinton, they've never supported Bill Clinton, that they've never seen him, they've never been around him," Limbaugh observed.[22]

When he wasn't going after Democrats, Limbaugh did his best to elevate Republican candidates and deflect potentially damaging charges against them. For example, when Ross Perot backed Texas Governor Ann Richards in her reelection fight against George W. Bush, Limbaugh wrote off the endorsement as "nothing but sour grapes at the Bush family."[23] Limbaugh also celebrated Florida gubernatorial nominee Jeb Bush. Whereas Limbaugh and many of his listeners thought the forty-first president was unacceptably moderate, the younger Bush was deemed a "legitimate conservative."[24]

To hear Limbaugh tell it, the GOP exuded fairness and common sense. He lauded the agenda contained in House Republicans' Contract with America and argued that, with Republicans in the majority, "the people [would] debate these issues for the first time, because the Democrats . . .

won't even let these issues come to the floor of the House for a debate, much less a vote."[25] Meanwhile proposed Republican tax cuts represented a simple and reasonable calculation in the public interest. "You will make better decisions with your money, spending it as you see fit, which will benefit the economy, than giving it to somebody like Tom Foley and letting him decide how to spend it," Limbaugh said. "And that's what the decision we all face is."[26]

While hosts cheered hardest for conservatives and relished their successes, the election also provides a clear window into the complicated détente between talk radio and moderate Republicans in the early to mid-1990s. Listening to talk radio now, only one creature is more reviled than Democratic luminaries such as Barack Obama, Nancy Pelosi, and Hillary Clinton: the Republican in name only, or RINO. Conservative hosts and listeners target these Judases for extinction; they are disloyal, unable to pass an ever-more-rigorous purity test. But this unremitting hostility is a relatively new development. Between 1988 and the mid-2000s, conservative talkers accepted the presence, and sometimes even recognized the utility, of moderates in the Republican Party.

True, it was a grudging acceptance. Limbaugh touted his preferred 1994 candidates on the basis of their conservative credentials. And hosts never hesitated to bitterly decry moderates who complained about talk radio's influence. Back in 1990, when President Bush bowed to the necessities of divided government and reached a budget deal with Congressional Democrats that included tax increases, some hosts had grumbled and others howled.[27] They certainly weren't willing to accept a violation of Bush's famous 1988 pledge, "Read my lips no new taxes."[28] That same year when a fan at a promotional appearance asked Limbaugh which three Republicans he wished were Democrats, and vice versa, Limbaugh named three moderate Republicans he would cast off and no Democrats he'd take in exchange.[29] He seemed to prefer a purely conservative Republican caucus to a large Republican caucus.

Yet hosts, Limbaugh included, were capable of tolerance, at least when moderates were the most conservative candidates electable from a given district or state. It was not party loyalty that motivated such concessions; it was strategy. Hosts understood that accepting some deviation from their policy goals could indirectly advance those goals by boosting the only party that could, in theory, pursue a conservative agenda. The first step toward a conservative government was a Congress controlled by Republicans, even if some were themselves insufficiently conservative.

Limbaugh epitomized this posture in 1994. For instance, when Republican New York City Mayor Rudolph Giuliani endorsed liberal Democratic Governor Mario Cuomo for reelection—something almost unimaginable today—Limbaugh, equally unimaginably, responded by gently chiding Giuliani. He tried reason. "Mayor, you don't defeat liberals by joining them," he said. "You defeat them with taxes, and you defeat them with lower taxes. You defeat them with economic policy. You defeat them with policies that enrich personal freedom which they stand against. You do not defeat them by joining."[30] Similarly, Limbaugh advised the moderate businessman Mitt Romney, who was running against Senator Kennedy, "You think you can make these massive monumental momentous changes with 'can't we all get along.' . . . You've got a week to turn this around, and I don't mean to hit you too hard, but you come out as a partisan, identify yourself as things—for things you stand for."

This was light prodding, featuring none of the harshness with which Limbaugh later castigated moderates. There also was no demand for ideological purity. Limbaugh counseled his television viewers not to be angry at Romney, or to oppose him. Electing a moderate over Kennedy would be a huge shift to the right. Even if Romney was not "the ultimate guy we want," electing him would constitute change "in the right direction—at least Romney's in the right direction."[31]

Limbaugh also rejected the ideological purity of single-issue voting, on the grounds that it was a tactical miscalculation. Single-issue voters needed to understand that you did not win in one election. It might take five elections to accomplish a policy goal—but only if voters took the first step, which sometimes meant voting for an imperfect Republican. As a cautionary tale, Limbaugh recalled an example from his Sacramento days: the 1986 California Senate election, when pro-life conservatives had refused to support pro-choice Republican Ed Zschau against Democrat Alan Cranston. Limbaugh lamented that these voters shot themselves in the foot, because only a Republican-controlled Senate, which would have confirmed President Reagan's judicial nominees, provided any chance of doing away with *Roe v. Wade*. Replacing Cranston with Zschau might also have helped keep the liberal Barbara Boxer out of the Senate. When Cranston retired in 1992, Boxer didn't have to beat a Republican incumbent. Limbaugh also advised a caller to back Nethercutt even though she disagreed with the candidate's support for fetal-tissue research. Limbaugh warned the caller that sitting out the race would keep Democrats in power and leave her shut out of the game.[32]

In many ways 1994 represented the pinnacle of talk radio hosts serving a fairly traditional party-leadership role. As Republicans bore no responsibility to govern, talk radio focused on elevating them to power and obliterating President Clinton's agenda. That meant coaxing moderate Republicans, not excising them; advocating and aiding Republican candidates of all ideological stripes; and assailing President Clinton and Democrats. Crucially, talkers had minimal expectations for Congressional Republicans, which fostered synergy between their goals and those of elected Republicans. As Republicans had little power, hosts didn't expect them to enact a conservative agenda or derail Clinton's entire program. All that hosts demanded was opposition to Clinton, a low bar easily cleared. In 1993 and 1994, the pressure was off, with hosts and party loyalists striving together to oppose Clinton and get Republicans elected. Equally important, good business happened to be good politics: eviscerating Clinton stirred up listeners while furthering the Republican cause.

But the synergy between hosts and elected Republicans would not survive the transition to power and the heightened expectations it fostered. As related by Congressman Bob Walker, a member of the Republican leadership at the time, many hosts disapproved of the compromises and the nuance necessary to govern after 1994. This dissatisfaction would complicate the relationship between talk radio and Republicans for the next quarter century, although that relationship remained, on balance, beneficial to both sides well into the 2000s.[33]

9

Everything Changes

THE DAY AFTER the 1994 elections, Speaker-elect Gingrich called Limbaugh to thank him. "You helped us overcome the elite media bias," he told America's number-one talker. "Just by hammering home the truth about issues, you helped arm I think literally millions of people across the country with the facts that let them argue in October and November so successfully."[1] Accolades for Limbaugh and his peers poured in from Republicans. The House freshmen made Limbaugh an honorary member of their class and invited him to speak at their orientation in December. When he showed up, new representatives flocked to meet him, pose for pictures, and ask for autographs. Former Representative Vin Weber, Gingrich's old Conservative Opportunity Society partner, introduced the host to what he called "the Limbaugh Congress." "I think everybody in this room probably has the idea you're the beginning of forty years or more of conservative or Republican domination," Limbaugh told the exultant group.[2]

Whether talk radio actually swung the election to Republicans is difficult to determine, but most elected Republicans and their staffers fervently believed it did. This conviction is what truly mattered to the future of Republican politics. After their surprising win, Republican leaders were suddenly eager participants in the talk radio universe. "It all . . . went back to '94," said Kyle Downey, who ran the House Republican Conference's outreach to talk radio in the late 1990s. Talk radio was "such a factor in taking back the majority."[3]

The belief that talk radio won the election also had an impact on the radio business. As the new House majority credited Limbaugh with their ascension, radio executives became that much more likely to associate Limbaugh's popularity with his conservatism, not his entertainment value.[4] This was not an obvious call at the time. Talk radio's special appeal to conservatives was evident, but the medium remained fairly diverse ideologically. A 1995 *Philadelphia Inquirer* story labeled 60 to 70 percent of the nation's talk radio hosts as right of center—not conservative. At that time, unlike today, hosts were not unyielding in their views, which were wide ranging.[5] A Times Mirror survey that year found that only 36 percent of talk show hosts described themselves as conservative or very conservative.[6] The audience also remained mixed; a 1995 *Talk Daily* survey found that only 38 percent of listeners identified as Republican.[7] Even the audience for specifically conservative radio was more varied than might be assumed. A 1996 Annenberg study found that only 47.8 percent of listeners to non-Limbaugh conservative radio identified as conservative, while 34.1 percent were moderate, with 18.1 percent liberal.[8] Reflecting this diversity, many stations maintained an eclectic slate of programs. Their lineups leaned right, but they did not feature doctrinaire conservatives discussing national politics all day.[9]

Republican politicians' all-in embrace of talk radio therefore furthered the ongoing process of talk radio's transformation but did not complete it. Even at this stage, to call talk radio a conservative medium would have been premature. Its political persona was emerging, but it had not crystallized. Yet the new wave of Republican leaders, looking to their own experiences, were convinced that to ignore talk radio would have been foolish. The ensuing marriage, however, was a complicated one from the start. The most outspoken hosts especially admired conservative Republicans who defiantly stuck to their guns, and vice versa, often leaving party moderates and pragmatists to endure an onslaught of invective from the very media personalities their leadership courted.

The leadership itself found its room for maneuver constrained, thanks to talk radio's influence over the Republican caucus. In his speech at the freshmen orientation, Limbaugh warned new legislators that the Beltway would try to change their behavior, rewarding go-along-to-get-along bipartisanship. "This is not the time to get moderate," he told them. "This is not the time to start trying to be liked. This is not the time to start gaining the approval of the people you just defeated." The warning came with an implicit threat. As Limbaugh explained to the freshmen before him, a reporter had asked him whether Gingrich would moderate his posture now that he was speaker. Limbaugh replied, "Better not."[10] Even in the honeymoon phase, right-wing media were turning to ideological warfare and opening a new chapter of the ideological purification of the GOP.

The new alliance developed quickly, with Republicans inviting hosts to broadcast live from the Capitol during the first week of January 1995, when the official changeover of power occurred.[11] Such broadcasts happened repeatedly while Republicans controlled the House. Hosts flocked to Washington and set up in the Capitol or House office buildings, where they heard from a parade of the chamber's Republicans. Each talk radio day centered on a major issue leadership wanted to spotlight.

The mastermind of this operation was Chad Kolton. The fresh-faced twenty-year-old was taking night classes to finish his degree at American University while helming the House Republican Conference's talk radio operation. Kolton booked House Republicans as radio guests, refusing no request from stations big or small. Initially he confronted some reticence from Republican members because of his age, the novelty of the radio effort, and press secretaries' inherent risk aversion. But Republican communicators soon warmed to Kolton's vision and his plans. In some respects, practices once confined to the fringes now became standard operating procedures for the House Republican leadership. Kolton produced daily tip sheets for talk hosts and answered any questions they and their producers might have. This contact cemented relationships and gave radio people a chance to provide feedback, often funneled from their listeners, which helped Republicans avoid any surprises percolating on the airwaves.[12]

The new leadership understood that talk radio could be valuable both for campaigning and in passing its agenda. With respect to the former, Kolton's outreach operation built support for freshman members in marginal districts preparing to face strong Democratic challengers in 1996.[13] With respect to the latter, the operation used talking points and broadcast days to drum up public support for GOP policies. For example, the third gathering of hosts in 1995 came as the House was considering welfare-reform legislation.[14] Dick Armey, now the majority leader, had learned early in his career that large and controversial legislation advanced only when it had support within Congress and without.[15] The few nationally syndicated conservative shows during the period—hosted by the likes of Limbaugh and presidential son Michael Reagan—were an especially useful tool for sending a message to constituents whose opinions could drive perceptions in Congress.[16]

Gingrich fully embraced talk radio. On many occasions he called Limbaugh unsolicited to chat about pressing issues. Gingrich's leadership team recognized that Limbaugh carried more influence with their base than maybe anyone else and sought to cultivate him. The two men also developed a personal relationship and reportedly vacationed together during one holiday weekend.[17]

Talk radio was a perfect match for Gingrich, who was eager to circumvent newspapers, many of which were hostile. Whereas the speaker might fight for a line or two in the *Washington Post* each day, he had no trouble getting on regional radio shows; hosts were thrilled to have a moment of his time.[18] And he was a good guest. Gingrich's bold, sometimes-incendiary style, and his willingness to traffic in rumor and innuendo, fit the medium. He even sounded like Limbaugh. Once he charged on NBC's *Meet the Press* that "up to a quarter of the White House staff" had used drugs in the four or five years before joining the administration, causing an infuriated Chief of Staff Leon Panetta to threaten that the White House would refuse to conduct business with Gingrich if he didn't "stop behaving like an out-of-control radio-talk-show host."[19] During the December 1994 orientation speech, Limbaugh had done a bit lampooning the White House employees' drug screen as a "multiple-choice test."[20]

As Republicans tuned in to talk radio, the medium shaped their activities. Consider one episode from 1994. Limbaugh fielded a call from a paratrooper who asserted that, because of budget cuts, the Army had equipped some of his comrades en route to Haiti with only fifteen rounds of ammunition. Senator Hank Brown of Colorado was listening. He inquired with the Pentagon about the veracity of the allegation and the rationale behind the policy. Brown and fellow Republican Senator Don Nickles of Oklahoma also wrote to President Clinton about the issue. Afterward Brown appeared on Limbaugh's television show to discuss his efforts to rectify the problem.[21]

In another case, in 1997, Gingrich was driving south on Interstate 95 to visit his daughter, when he heard Limbaugh read on air a memo from conservative publisher Steve Forbes about an IRS attempt to extend the Medicare payroll levy to business partnerships. Gingrich pulled over to call congressional staffers, whom he instructed to scuttle the proposal, which had been issued months earlier. Then, for the second time that week and the third time in sixteen days, Gingrich hopped on the phone with Limbaugh. The speaker assured the host and his listeners that he would take care of the problem. All three calls were aimed at mollifying Limbaugh and his audience in response to criticism of House Republicans by some conservative commentators.[22]

These are just two representative instances; one could find many more. For Brown, Gingrich, and many other elected Republicans, Limbaugh provided useful information, a platform from which to communicate with their base, and opportunities to demonstrate their responsiveness to the base's concerns. There also was no better podium from which to silence conservative critics.

Limbaugh, in turn, reaped many rewards. He gained standing as a news-breaker, and he appeared well-connected and politically powerful. These qualities endeared listeners to him and made his program a daily must-listen. As Gingrich told Limbaugh in his first call of the sixteen-day stretch, "I know more Americans listen to you and talk about what they hear than any other place by a huge margin, Rush, and that's why I wanted to call and report directly so you can say that you and I discussed this."[23] Gingrich was referring to charges that he was abandoning a push for tax cuts. Such moments also enhanced Limbaugh's importance in political circles: he really was well-connected and politically powerful and there-fore not easily ignored. From a Republican communications standpoint, Limbaugh was, as Downey put it, "the Super Bowl, the Holy Grail. . . . He was the Beatles. He was in his own little category."[24]

But while Limbaugh was often receptive to elected Republicans' atten-tion, he also was careful to maintain distance lest he risk his perceived independence. He grasped that the necessities of governing might lead officials to adopt stances that he and his listeners would loathe, and with which he did not wish to be associated. Thus, when hosts descended on the Capitol in January 1995 for the official Republican takeover of the House, Limbaugh headed off for a planned vacation. "I do not tie myself to politicians," he explained.[25]

Limbaugh held firmly to that posture in years to come. While he had the power and influence of a party chief, he was not completely devoted to the cause in the manner that an elected or appointed leader could be expected to be. What mattered most was the quality of his show and his relationship with his audience. Other hosts had similar priorities.

In 1999 Gingrich was succeeded as speaker by Dennis Hastert of Illinois. Unlike the front man Gingrich, the new speaker preferred working in the back room to achieve legislative victories. He left talk radio primarily to other members of the leadership, including Majority Whip Tom DeLay of Texas and Conference Chairman J. C. Watts of Oklahoma. But this did not mean talk radio faded from the House GOP's priority list. Even Hastert took advantage of radio from time to time, often to boost other members as he stumped with them in their districts. Hosts who wouldn't cover the local congressman's fish fry would happily interview Hastert, and he obliged.[26]

Beyond the leadership, members remained eager to talk with local hosts in their districts and states in an effort to target messages to their constituents. Souder, who had called on talk radio heavily in his election contest with Jill Long, even cohosted his own program during his initial years in Congress.[27] Other Republican members, such as John Linder of Georgia, jumped at the chance to substitute for vacationing hosts. Linder, who "enjoyed the hell" out of talk radio, described his stint filling in for Boortz as "the fastest three hours I ever spent in my life." Jack Kingston, Linder's Georgia colleague, used relationships with local talk radio to improve his position at home. He would go on radio to blunt attacks from the national press and get in front of the hubbub about controversial legislation. And when he appeared with hosts who were at odds with him on an issue, he could count on their rapport to prevent matters from getting out of hand. As Kingston relates, a host whose program he frequented would continue to see him as "part of the solution"—as well as someone accessible and accountable—even while disagreeing.[28]

Kingston and Linder were amazed by the publicity advantage talk radio could generate. Constituents would tell Kingston about times they had heard him on the air, even if they didn't recall what he said. During a contentious primary fight in 2002, Linder found that Boortz was one of his most important boosters. Linder's opponent had made what Linder considered the "stupid mistake" of picking a fight with the powerful Atlanta-based host. Every day people approached Linder to share Boortz's commentary "whether it was about me or something else," Linder said. It felt like Boortz's reach extended farther than all the commercials Linder ran, no matter how much money his campaign spent.[29]

Senate Republicans' approach to talk radio was less organized and centralized than that of their House colleagues. In particular, senators' conference-wide booking operation was not as developed and aggressive. Utah Republican Senator Bob Bennett, a talk radio regular, observed that the Senate was the last place where people caught on to the benefit of talk radio.[30]

It makes sense that the Senate lagged the House in embracing talk radio. For one thing, most senators did not need talk radio in order to gain media opportunities. As one in a club of a hundred, each senator is better known than the average House member. Parliamentary rules also empower individual senators to a greater degree than their House colleagues, which translates into higher profiles and greater influence on the legislative process. For these reasons, even a junior senator could expect the mainstream media to pay attention. Furthermore, in the mid-1990s, many senators were older than their House colleagues and had been in government for a long time, elevating their perception of talk radio's risks: Why would veterans such as Jesse Helms and Strom Thurmond turn to the new kid on the block after decades in office? The rewards of talk radio also seemed fewer for politicians who shut down their campaigns and stuck to Washington for six-year terms.

Senate Republicans' less ambitious radio operation focused on providing technical expertise rather than courting hosts, booking members for interviews, and sharing talking points. The conference had a radio studio, which senators used to talk to stations in their states, distribute radio actualities, and host their own shows. In most cases, this was enough to support senators' communication strategies.[31]

But some Senate Republicans did go farther. Arizona Senator Jon Kyl, first elected in 1994, maintained a good relationship with many local hosts and chatted regularly on KFYI in Phoenix. Talk radio provided Kyl an outlet to "talk about my issues . . . with an audience that was generally supportive, but always, I thought, needed background and information and education about how the issues were really playing out in Washington, D.C., something they probably couldn't figure out from the other media." Appearing on these programs also gave Kyl "some element of endorsement."[32]

Other senators used talk radio "to be a presence in the area when you can't be everywhere at once," as staffer Chris Paulitz, who worked for multiple senators during his time on Capitol Hill, explained. Talk radio was potentially a huge asset for senators from large states with numerous media markets. Crisscrossing the average House district was easy; covering the biggest states, especially in the three to four days per week senators were home, was not. As Paulitz explained, before local radio appearances, a senator's communications and policy staffers might huddle to craft a message answering three key questions, "What have we done for [our constituents] lately, what are we promising to do for them, and what issues are we tackling nationally as a Senate that they care about?" Aides would then turn over to their bosses lists of points relevant to the local community, which senators would try to work into their on-air conversations.[33]

While senior senators generally shied away from talk radio, Mississippian Trent Lott, who took over as majority leader in 1996, included a major talk radio component in his communications program. Lott gladly accepted interview requests from Hannity and other hosts.[34] Dating back to his earliest days in office, Lott had grasped the opportunity that radio offered. When a political adviser counseled not to do radio, Lott replied that he had to do the morning drive to reach a crucial constituency: workers on their way to Mississippi's shipyards. After he won his Senate seat in 1988, he regularly appeared on the Mississippi-based Radio News Network and on an Alabama station that reached Mississippi voters. Nationally, Lott found talk radio useful for creating interest in welfare reform and balancing the budget and for providing leverage as he negotiated with President Clinton.[35]

Even as the GOP leadership embraced talk radio, a note of discord was emerging—one that would grow louder in later years. It was already evident that leadership couldn't control the medium's political interventions. Hosts followed their instincts, which meant that talk radio remained a weapon for rank-and-file members bold enough to grab hold of it. As Armey noted, talk radio gave entrepreneurial members a chance to generate public support for their pet causes, regardless of what leaders wanted. From there, these members could build coalitions within the House, forcing the hands of influential colleagues.[36] In one 1995 case, freshman Republican Congressman Van Hilleary of Tennessee used talk radio to circumvent leadership and press an amendment to a term-limits bill. Leadership either opposed Hilleary's amendment or ignored it. But Hilleary spent weeks appearing on talk radio programs, galvanizing listeners who pressured his peers to support his amendment and term limits more broadly.[37] While Hilleary's amendment and the wider term-limits effort failed, his push vividly illustrated how talk radio provided even the most junior members with a communications stream that did not depend on leadership input.[38]

Challenging leadership generated exactly the sort of engaging, controversial, and combative content that made hosts salivate. Contentious discussion left listeners glued to their radios, so hosts were not above offensive rhetoric and conspiracy mongering. Talkers were, as they frequently reminded the world, entertainers rather than journalists, and they showed it by reporting dubiously sourced "scandals" that bordered on the preposterous. Famously, in 1994, Limbaugh and others told listeners that Deputy White House Counsel Vince Foster, who committed suicide, had been murdered in an apartment owned by First Lady Hillary Clinton.[39] Limbaugh later went so far as to assert that "the only difference between Watergate and Whitewater is that Whitewater has a dead body."[40] Resulting rumors to the effect that the Clintons were responsible for Foster's death persisted straight through the 2016 presidential campaign.

Such explosive, entertaining radio, however, sometimes made for bad politics. Republicans felt trapped between their base, which practically frothed at the mouth to nail President Clinton, and centrist voters who considered talk radio's scandal-mongering absurd, petty, and vituperative. But once hosts had generated intense interest in these topics, elected Republicans often had to address them, sometimes by holding official hearings. This could have a corrosive effect on Republicans' agenda by occupying finite committee and floor time, distracting from issue pushes, and turning off middle-of-the-road Americans. Moreover, the rumors and allegations circulating on talk radio hardened base voters' opposition to Clinton, making it that much more difficult for Republicans to reach the compromises necessary to govern alongside a Democratic White House. In turn the heated rhetoric—and elected Republicans' variously grudging and enthusiastic acceptance of it—drove President Clinton toward his base, undermining his taste for compromise as well. For instance, as Steve Gillon details in his 2008 book *The Pact*, a secret deal between Clinton and Gingrich to reform entitlement programs fell apart when discussion of impeachment—pushed strenuously by talk radio—began. Clinton and Gingrich each needed base support in the impeachment fight, and their entitlement proposal promised to anger both bases.[41]

As much as the disreputable gossip, rumors, and flat-out conspiracy theories on talk radio bothered moderate Republicans, moderates themselves bothered talk radio. Détente still governed the relationship between the two in this era, but that relationship was nonetheless uneasy and prone to conflict. For, with Republicans in control—especially in the House, where the minority party has few options for stopping legislation—the primary obstacle to conservative outcomes was the moderate bloc within the party: it would decide how far a generally conservative Congress could go.

More doctrinaire hosts wanted no part of the bipartisan legislative bargaining that moderates favored and attacked any moderate who dared cross them or impede their agenda.[42] One example came in 1995, when Senate Appropriations Committee Chairman Mark Hatfield of Oregon refused to provide the final vote necessary to pass a balanced budget amendment. In response Limbaugh raged, "Do the Democrats have something on Mark Hatfield? Does Hatfield owe the Democrats something rather than the Republicans? . . . Just pull his chairmanship away from him. This is a war. . . . Obviously Hatfield isn't on the team."[43]

Other moderate Republicans, such as Representatives Connie Morella of Maryland and Amo Houghton of New York, also confronted this sort of vitriol and its repercussions. They took fire from talk radio listeners for their positions on the 1994 assault-weapons ban, the 1995 government shutdown, and later the second Iraq War. When Morella received letters and postcards from infuriated constituents, she and her staff followed up with the authors and discovered that many got their information from Limbaugh.[44]

Yet, in the mid-1990s, there was a long way to go before hosts achieved their current levels of disdain for Morella's ilk. Pragmatic toleration was still possible, as Massachusetts Congressman Peter Blute discovered. Blute enjoyed some slack from hosts in New England, who, the congressman believed, generally understood that he was the best they were going to get in Massachusetts.[45] Blute himself would later become a conservative talker.

Moderates also did not always feel overwhelming pressure to engage talk radio. Unlike more conservative colleagues, they did not listen regularly and many rarely knew what talk radio said about them.[46] New York Congressman Jack Quinn, for one, did not listen to talk radio at all. So disengaged was he from the medium that he did not realize Limbaugh was a critical supporter of his 1993 effort to make public the anonymous signers of discharge petitions, which could be used to dislodge bills from recalcitrant committees.[47] Many moderates such as Quinn also shrugged off talk radio criticism if and when they became aware of it.[48] Senator Hatfield's chief of staff, Steve Nousen, recalled that Hatfield did not care what Limbaugh or any other member of the media thought about his vote on the balanced budget amendment.[49] With time, however, this posture would present increasing danger.

Unique among moderate Republicans, Senator Arlen Specter of Pennsylvania zealously cultivated conservative talk radio, perhaps because his constituency leaned farther to the right than most in the Northeast.[50] Specter was always prepared to discuss pertinent local issues with conservative hosts throughout the state. He distinguished himself by always being ready to hop on conservative radio, local or national, to refute accusations against himself. He believed that failure to do so was tantamount to accepting mischaracterizations of himself and his record. Specter and his staff also used the medium to appeal to conservative talk listeners, not just to go on defense. The senator would appear on air when he agreed with conservative positions on key issues, such as judicial appointments. This outreach might have shielded Specter, at least partly, from hosts' venom, though he did occasionally scrap with them, including Ingraham after her show launched in 2001.[51]

The truce reflected in Specter's and Blute's experiences helped enable the mutual gains of the GOP–talk radio relationship in the 1990s. What tension existed was not enough to outweigh the benefits. But there were ominous clouds on the horizon: even aggressive outreach like Specter's wasn't always enough to protect a Republican perceived as a heretic in conservative media.

For instance on one 1996 TV show, Limbaugh upbraided a number of Republicans, including New York Senator Alfonse D'Amato, New Jersey Governor Christine Todd Whitman, and California Governor Pete Wilson, for challenging conservative proposals or agreeing with Democrats. Then Limbaugh zeroed in on Long Island Congressman Peter King. King had criticized the House Republican leadership for displaying a "Southern anti-union attitude that appeals to the mentality of hillbillies at revival meetings." On his radio show that day, Limbaugh denounced the congressman as a Northeastern elitist. Ripping a page from Specter's playbook, King fired back, faxing Limbaugh a response defending himself in pro-conservative terms. King said he was upset that Republican leadership was attacking a potential conservative Republican voting bloc—the blue-collar Reagan Democrats of organized labor, who happened to be a key constituency of his. Limbaugh was having none of it. On TV he brushed aside King's re-joinder, arguing that the attack on blue-collar conservatives came from "the union bosses . . . because those are the people who are out there spending $35 million of union dues and telling lies about conservatives, making up all sorts of things about cuts in Medicare and cuts in education that don't exist." He closed the segment by lamenting that "Republicans continue to beat themselves up when they ought to be focusing all their energies on Bill Clinton and the liberals who are running Washington right now."[52]

The truce between talk radio and moderate Republicans, or even Re-publicans who might dissent from the party line on a position or two, was clearly tense. It would fray in coming years, thanks to both political and financial forces. Eventually the rise of talk radio helped pull the party's center of gravity to the right, threatening moderates' political survival.

10

The Democrats Wake Up

CONGRESSIONAL REPUBLICANS weren't alone in hopping aboard the talk radio train in 1995. Talk radio appealed to the marginalized, who truly needed the medium, and after the 1994 election that meant House Democrats. They had been forty years in the majority, their leaders conspicuous on television and page A1. But in the minority, like House Republicans before them, they were starved for media oxygen. The national storyline was President Clinton's titanic clash with Speaker Gingrich and the Republican leadership, which eventually produced multiple government shutdowns in the fall and winter of 1995–1996. Congressional Democrats were bystanders, except when they too were feuding with President Clinton. If they ever hoped to regain power, they were going to need new ways to reach the public and sway its attention.

The project of resurrecting House Democrats fell to Dick Gephardt of Missouri and his team. The mild-mannered, sandy-haired St. Louis native had been majority leader under Speaker Tom Foley, but Foley was one of many high-ranking casualties in the 1994 tsunami, leaving his former deputy in charge of the caucus.

Gephardt and his staff concluded that, to recapture the majority, they needed more exposure from media they once considered marginal. That included talk radio. Democratic members who had never done talk radio outside of their districts agreed and embraced the medium. Talk radio was an undertaking, but, as Texas Representative John Bryant explained, "I think we realize we have to take time out to do this." After all, he said, "We let the right wing have a free run in the last elections and it cost us dearly."[1]

Gephardt had been on talk shows before, but they had not been a central outlet for him or his caucus. In the wake of the election, though, Democrats ramped up their efforts. Even before the new term kicked off, Gephardt arranged a briefing for colleagues on the importance of engaging with interactive media. Democrats also got tips on handling their radio appearances.[2] And Gephardt's team filled a glaring hole at the staff level by hiring the minority leader's, and House Democrats', first ever aide devoted to talk radio outreach.[3] Their man was Fred Clarke, who had been a producer for nationally syndicated host Gene Burns. Clarke originally had no intention of taking the job. He only agreed to interview with Gephardt's staff because he wanted to get Democratic guests on Burns's show.[4]

Clarke arrived for his interview acutely aware that Democrats' problems with talk radio included more than ideological disagreement with hosts. When it came to securing the political advantages talk radio had to offer, Democrats simply weren't trying as hard as their Republican rivals. Clarke showed Gephardt and his staff—Communications Director Laura Nichols, Press Secretary Dan Sallick, and Chief of Staff Tom O'Donnell—the reams of information Republicans sent him every day. He told them how the RNC made his job easier by faxing a daily one-page document listing hot issues and the guests who were prepared to discuss them. Typically the Democratic National Committee sent Clarke information only when he asked for it. Not only did Democrats often fail to reach out, but when they did make overtures, they gave him materials he couldn't use—long policy memos whose language, methods, and themes didn't fit the talk format. Democrats, Clarke concluded, needed to engineer a talk-friendly message by making their priorities clear to hosts and their members available for comment.[5]

Achieving this meant changing the culture among House Democrats who weren't comfortable with talk radio. And, for Clarke, it meant making his former colleagues' lives easier by giving them access on a silver platter. He arranged a radio-actuality line to provide stations with soundbites from House Democrats. He also wired a room in the Capitol to serve as a talk radio cafe, complete with coffee and cookies. During key votes, hosts were invited to broadcast interviews with Democrats from the cafe.

Clarke booked Gephardt and the rest of his caucus on conservative programs, as long as the host was willing to treat them respectfully. Clarke also prepared background materials for House press secretaries to help them navigate the booking process. Eventually he got permission from Nichols to build a portable radio studio so that hosts could broadcast from the Capitol without having to bring equipment or an engineer. Even Republicans had no such facilities in the Capitol. Sometimes conservative hosts would use the Democrats' equipment to talk with House Republicans, but Clarke would also supply Democratic guests for them to spar with, injecting some balance into even the most right-leaning programs.[6]

The outreach paid off, with more and more Democrats going on air. Many who had never appeared on talk radio before, or who had done so infrequently, proved to be adept, repeat guests. Gephardt, who before 1995 had done approximately two radio interviews per month outside his district, did six to twelve per week in 1995 and 1996. His appearances set the tone, encouraging other members to follow suit.[7]

Another source of encouragement was even more important: constituents. Clarke won friends in the caucus in no small part because members couldn't ignore talk radio's grip on voters. Members would go home and hear constituents parroting Limbaugh's lines.[8] House Minority Whip David Bonior recalled one such instance. As the Democratic point person responsible for attacking Gingrich over ethical lapses, he had come on Limbaugh's radar and earned himself an unflattering nickname. Playfully conveying how unthreatening Bonior was, Limbaugh took to calling him the "Pit Yorkie." Once, parched after a summer labor rally in Decatur, Illinois, Bonior went to a local bar where he heard one blue-collar patron turn to another and say, "That's the Pit Yorkie." On several other occasions, people stopped him to ask, "Aren't you the Pit Yorkie?"[9]

While Clarke was getting House Democrats air time, the members themselves were trying to make their messaging more appealing, building on an effort that Gephardt had launched after his failed 1988 presidential campaign.[10] Representative Rosa DeLauro, who cochaired the new messaging operation, encouraged her colleagues to make one-minute floor speeches, reach out more aggressively to the media, and hold attention-grabbing special events.[11] Talk radio fit into this strategy. When, in 1995, Democrats wanted to protest proposed cuts to the National School Lunch Program, they held a media event including celebrity endorsements, daily floor speeches, "Save the Children" ties and scarves, and a talk radio blitz. They organized another blitz that year to contest Republicans' proposed cuts to Medicare and other budget items.[12]

But even when Congressional Democratic outreach to talk radio was at its peak, tensions lurked beneath the surface. Sallick recalled that while

Clarke always advocated more engagement with talk radio, many communications staffers were less enthusiastic. To them, the challenge was not to equalize the message on talk radio but to work around it—to counterprogram in a way that got House Democrats' message out on the airwaves.[13] Talk radio had yet to complete its evolution into a doctrinaire, far-right medium preaching to the converted, but Democratic staffers understood as well as anyone that the listenership leaned conservative. There were more effective ways to reach the voters they most wanted to connect with.

Despite the efforts of Clarke, his successors, and a core group of members, Democrats struggled to overcome Republicans' talk radio advantage. Julianne Corbett Waldron, who took over from Clarke as radio coordinator, felt her caucus was no less available to talk radio than Republicans were. Yet hosts seemed to think Republicans were more accessible.[14] Talkers didn't call Republicans for taped radio actualities; they got live guests. Host Tom Leykis explained that Democrats were just too reticent, too picky. "When you call the average Democrat, they say, 'Who's going to be on the show? What's the subject? Are you going to be taking calls? Hmmmmm, I don't know.' And then their aides tell you, 'I can get him on a tarmac on a cellular phone for a couple of minutes before he takes off. But no calls, and he wants to talk about this transportation bill that's coming up.'"[15]

The sense of frustration was mutual. Democrats, including Gephardt, felt that they rarely received a fair hearing on talk radio. The effort of trying to have a rational conversation didn't seem worth it, and over time they became harder to coax into appearances.[16] Corbett Waldron and her successor Kimberlin Love found many in their caucus hesitant to appear with conservative hosts.[17] DeLauro observed that going on talk radio required a "junkyard dog" mentality her colleagues often lacked: they didn't run for Congress to engage in on-air donnybrooks. She also noted that the failure to recapture the House in 1996 and 1998 disheartened many members and prompted doubts about the new messaging strategy. The intense media push seemed to be going nowhere.[18]

In interviews, members attuned to the value of communications suggested that their colleagues failed to understand the connection between power and public messaging.[19] Representative Pat Schroeder retired in 1997 in part because she believed that her colleagues' refusal to focus on messaging ensured the party would be unable to regain and maintain congressional majorities.[20] And while messaging failures are not the sole culprit, her prophecy has proven correct, as Democrats controlled the House for just four of the twenty-four years between 1994 and 2018.

On the other side of the Capitol, the relationship between Senate Democrats and talk radio unfolded similarly. When Tom Daschle of South Dakota—a prairie populist and, by Senate standards, a boyish forty-seven-year-old—became Democratic leader in 1995, he and his staff realized that they were a beat or two behind Republicans in using radio. They also understood that it would no longer suffice for senators to communicate with their constituents through recordings. Radio was now a two-way medium, not just a source for top-of-the-hour newscasts. Daschle and his staff built a radio studio and initiated other upgrades to enhance senators' ability to converse with their constituents in real time.[21]

But technology wasn't the only problem. Daschle sensed that his colleagues wanted proof they could succeed on talk radio before fully engaging with the medium. As staffer Laura Quinn recalled, most senators viewed talk radio as "hot and hostile." Roger Lotz, a radio producer newly hired by the Senate Democratic Technology and Communications Committee, initially had great difficulty convincing senators, or their protective press secretaries, that they should appear on conservative talk programs.[22]

Quinn and Lotz would have to persuade senators that most hosts would be polite and respectful to interviewees, even if they disagreed. By 1997 their encouragement had begun to pay dividends. While buy-in from senators varied widely, some got used to the medium and readily grappled with hosts from across the ideological spectrum. Stalwarts such as North Dakota Senator Byron Dorgan appeared routinely on conservative programs seeking alternative voices.[23] Others were willing to do radio and prepared thoroughly but were more reactive than proactive in seeking on-air opportunities.[24]

It may come as a surprise that Joe Lieberman was one of the Senate Democrats' true champions of talk radio. The senator from Connecticut exposed a dry, buttoned-down speaking style during the 2000 and 2004 presidential campaigns, but he was good on radio. He appeared weekly and even spoke at a national radio convention. He had been joining talk shows at least since his successful 1982 run for state attorney general. Lieberman enjoyed chatting with hosts, and they liked having a guest who got the rhythms of the medium. He had a quick sense of humor and, according to his former communications director, Jim Kennedy, could "mix it up" and avoid being "too stiff" or resorting to talking points. Lieberman appreciated talk radio as a tool for communicating with constituents.[25] Radio fit Lieberman's personality better than did television, which precluded viewer feedback and cut everything down to brief soundbites. While Lieberman could do "short, soundbite environments" or the partisan back and forth of cable television, Kennedy didn't think his boss was "a *Crossfire* kind of person." On talk radio, by contrast, the senator could speak expansively about issues to a large audience in a conversational format, which was more "conducive to his style of presentation." As Lieberman himself put it in a discussion of talk radio, "It gives you a chance to show the range of your personality."[26]

Lieberman accepted the challenge of talk radio without equivocation and endeared himself to hosts across the ideological spectrum. For instance, he turned out to be a favorite of equal-opportunity critic Don Imus, although he didn't start out that way. A month into Lieberman's Senate career, an Imus producer attempted to book him, but one of the senator's staffers, Kathie Scarrah, turned down the request. She didn't know who Imus was, and she was put off by the producer's demanding inquiry. However, as she was on the phone declining the interview, Lieberman's chief of staff, who was familiar with Imus, came over and tried to get her to stop talking. According to Scarrah, he said to her, with a panicked look, "Oh my god, he's recording everything you said." The chief was petrified because Scarrah had "basically dissed" Imus's producer, and it would get back to his boss.

Sure enough, the next day Imus launched into an on-air "rampage about Kathie-something-unpronounceable who works for Lieberman who thinks he's too good to be on my show." Calls flooded into Lieberman's office. When word of Imus's sharp criticism reached the senator, he bristled and insisted on appearing on the show. It turned out to be just the right move. Not only did Lieberman join Imus on the air, but the two developed a rapport and the senator became a frequent guest. Later Lieberman unofficially hosted Imus when he broadcast from Washington. Lieberman's team showed Imus and his sidekicks around the Capitol and took him to lunch in the senators' dining room. Thereafter Lieberman would continue to welcome Imus whenever he visited D.C.[27]

Lieberman also chatted with many conservative hosts, including Hannity. During Glenn Beck's shock jock days in New Haven, Lieberman made campaign stops bearing lox and bagels. Such appearances reflected and reinforced the friendly reception Lieberman received from conservative radio, his comfort with the medium, and his respect for his conservative and independent supporters. It also spoke to Lieberman's standing as a different kind of Democrat. While he compiled a liberal voting record, he was far from doctrinaire and agreed with conservatives on a few issues, especially on foreign policy and cultural topics.[28]

Not every senator would join Lieberman or Dorgan on rough-and-tumble conservative programs, but Quinn understood that it was better to appear than not. She tried to teach members and their staffs that hosts would treat guests well but also would abuse Democrats who declined bookings. Democrats who stayed away would get far worse than colleagues who took their lumps in person and fought back. She refused to blacklist conservative hosts, because abstaining from a show left its airwaves without the Democratic message. If members wouldn't appear, she would find surrogates. Quinn did a lot of this kind of outreach, pitching topics and guests to hosts, most of whom were receptive if she offered a smart and credible interviewee on a hot topic.[29]

At the very moment when Congressional Democrats were most enthusiastic about talk radio—albeit, with many reservations—President Clinton's outreach effort was foundering. In the second half of Clinton's first term, the scope and vision of his radio strategy narrowed, and tensions with hosts continued to mount.

The mechanisms by which the White House communicated with talk radio remained largely the same, and Richard Strauss and his successors as radio director, Rica Rodman and Megan Moloney, used the medium strategically. They were still able to secure the president's time when they needed it. For instance Clinton did roundtables with agricultural and urban radio.[30]

But the emphasis on the medium faded. This decline was epitomized by a debate among Clinton's staff over whether he should do a proposed talk radio town hall with middle-of-the-road host Larry King. The town hall had been proposed by radio impresario Norm Pattiz, the chairman of the board of syndication giant Westwood One, who in 1995 met with DNC Chair Don Fowler and subsequently President Clinton himself to discuss how Democrats might achieve more ideological balance on the medium. Though the White House initially agreed to the event, dissension emerged among staff, delaying the town hall and leading a frustrated Pattiz to fire off a memo warning of the consequences of canceling.[31] Press Secretary Mike McCurry, who joined the White House in 1995, was one of the main sources of Pattiz's irritation. On an internal memo, McCurry commented that he had "tried several times to put [the town hall] off to 1996." He made his disinterest abundantly clear. "We have other priorities now and there is no reason press wise to do this in the middle of POTUS vacation or in 1995 for that matter," he wrote, underlining "no reason" twice. "If we have to do this for political or $$ reasons, I'll understand. But we have higher press priorities at moment."[32]

McCurry's attitude was fairly typical among staffers who joined Clinton's team in the second half of the first term and beyond. The big question was how best the White House could drive the news cycle, and they didn't see talk radio as a significant part of the answer. Clinton's earliest aides had seen firsthand how the 1992 campaign had capitalized on talk radio. But new aides without this campaign experience tended to view talk radio as intractably hostile and far down the media hierarchy. Even successful talk radio messaging wasn't going to dominate water-cooler chatter. Aides' views only hardened with time, as the scandals surrounding President Clinton mushroomed and the White House's needs and talk radio's interests further diverged.[33]

President Clinton himself grew frustrated with the increasingly conservative direction of talk radio and with hosts' efforts to hamstring his initiatives. In a June 1994 radio interview, he accused talk radio and conservative Christian commentators of using misinformation and demeaning personal attacks to create a culture of cynicism that made governing more difficult. Much of talk radio, he bemoaned, was "a constant unremitting drumbeat of negativism." The president lamented that, when he got off the air, Limbaugh would have three hours on the same station to say whatever he wanted without submitting to rebuttal or any sort of "truth detector." These remarks delighted Limbaugh; he was getting under the president's skin.[34]

After the 1995 Oklahoma City bombing, Clinton accused media personalities of essentially inciting violence through their hateful rhetoric.[35] He didn't mention talk radio specifically, and his aides insisted that his criticism was aimed at the media broadly. But there can be little doubt of his true target, as journalists reporting on the issue—and hosts themselves—understood. The coverage at the time singled out talk radio as the object of the president's ire. At the very least, the "loud and angry voices" Clinton decried could be heard on the AM dial. The medium still was well suited to Clinton's talents and political style, and the president respected talk radio's special capacity to reach voters and drive conversation. But by the time of his reelection, that conversation was running decidedly against him.

Conservative media was only getting started. In Clinton's second term a new antagonist would emerge in the form of Fox News. The content, style, and verve of talk radio were coming to cable, inaugurating another chapter in the right-wing press's decades-long transformation of the Republican Party.

11

Talk Radio Takes Over Television—
and Tries to Impeach a President

In OCTOBER 1996 the programming model that was fueling the rise of talk radio arrived on Americans' television screens. Fox News gave talk fans the chance to watch the visual equivalent of their favorite radio programs. Over time Fox joined talk radio as a key building block in the foundation of the conservative echo chamber.

Fox came of age during a moment of superheated partisanship. Clinton's second term was even more polarizing than his first, as the various scandals and investigations surrounding him came to a head in the form of impeachment. Each of Clinton's woes was a source of glee on talk radio—hosts and listeners pushed hard for impeachment and carried some reluctant Republicans with them. As Clinton weathered the onslaught, the White House fought back against talk radio's hardening conservatism, criticizing hosts and distancing itself from the medium. But while the decision to withdraw was understandable, it also invited an unintended consequence: absent the administration's input, talk radio became that much more saturated by conservative voices.

Fox News turned the partisan flame up even higher. The brainchild of media mogul Rupert Murdoch and veteran Republican political consultant and television executive Roger Ailes, Fox did not explicitly brand itself as a conservative outlet. But Ailes and Murdoch targeted the same audience that, alienated by mainstream news coverage, was flocking to talk radio. As political consultant Ed Rollins explained, Ailes "knew there were a couple of million conservatives who were a potential audience, and he built Fox to reach them."[1] Brit Hume, who left ABC to become a Fox anchor and the network's D.C. managing editor, told a reporter, "We believe we are eligible to pick up the audience of the disaffected—those who are looking for news but whose sensibilities are continually assaulted when they watch other news outlets."[2]

Fox's leaders knew the best way to reach their intended audience: Limbaugh. The network paid for him personally to read advertisements touting Fox's fairness. Unlike other news networks, Limbaugh told his listeners, Fox would provide more than "just the liberal slant or the reporter's own bias." It would be "television news for the independent thinker." Fox viewers were "thrilled to finally have a fair and balanced alternative to the other news networks." After hearing Limbaugh hammer away at media bias for almost ten years, listeners could at last exhale. "Remember," he advised, "Fox News is fair news."[3]

Whether Ailes and Murdoch consciously based the network's content on talk radio is hard to say, but there is no doubt that they knew the medium well. Ailes was the perfect bridge from talk radio to TV, having produced Limbaugh's television show from 1992 to 1996. He and the host were friends. Advisers also explicitly recommended to Murdoch that Fox News be "news talk-radio with video."[4]

Regardless of intent, talk radio was the blueprint for Fox's product, with AM-dial style and content translated for the less-intimate medium of television. In many time slots, Fox mirrored talk radio by rejecting dry, dispassionate, fact-based reporting in favor of entertaining commentary that left no doubt of the host's sympathies, which his or her audience was expected to share. Although discussion covered many apolitical topics, the conversation was steered by a conservative cultural worldview.

Talk radio and Fox had the same chip on their shoulders when it came to the mainstream media. Both covered issues important to conservatives that other media outlets ignored. And both maligned, challenged, and discredited the "liberal establishment," including journalists. Fox thereby placed itself alongside talk radio as a standard-bearer in the right-wing crusade against perceptions of media bias, a campaign that dated back at least to the 1940s.[5]

From day one Fox elevated conservative opinion and delivered hard news in a manner designed to respect and promote the values of conservative viewers. Fox's first debate show, *Hannity and Colmes*, featured the conservative fighter matched up with mild-mannered New York talker Alan Colmes, ensuring that the "good guys" would always pummel the opposition. This was part and parcel of the talk radio style, as well: liberals might be included on panels—after all, argument made for good broadcasts—but conservative debaters benefited from built-in advantages.

While Fox's bent was frequently obvious, it also used subtler techniques to correct the cultural bias that conservatives saw as endemic in mainstream reporting. John Moody, Fox's vice president of news, pointed to the network's coverage of executions. Its stories began "with a declarative sentence of what the person was convicted of." By contrast, other outlets would use lines like "thousands wailing outside, and then, a sudden hush." It was the mainstream media that was guilty of "editorializing" in Moody's eyes, and in those of Fox's target audience.[6] Before Fox launched, Moody held seminars for new hires in which he passed around packets of *New York Times* articles marked up to highlight liberal bias.[7]

Although Fox's reporting was intended to feel unbiased—at least to conservatives—its opinion programming fully adopted talk radio–style "infotainment," a fusion of news and entertainment. In contrast to news, this sort of material did not need, or even attempt, to be factually accurate. Nor did it necessarily focus on the most politically significant stories. What mattered was selecting stories that lent themselves to entertaining presentation while fitting into a conservative narrative or spotlighting issues important to conservatives. When talk hosts got called out for sharing something factually wrong or dramatically overstating the importance of a story, they quickly reminded listeners that they were entertainers or talk show hosts, not journalists. A case in point: recently Hannity batted down criticism of his kid-gloves interviews with President Trump by explaining that he is "not a journalist."[8] The open embrace of infotainment on the opinion side of Fox has produced tension with the network's reporters. At times they have professed themselves uncomfortable with opinion hosts' inaccuracies and conspiracy theories and worried about the resulting damage to the network's reputation.[9]

Infotainment on Fox reinforced changes to journalistic practices that were under way thanks to talk radio. Talk radio had already begun reshaping the media's gatekeeping role by exposing the sorts of red-meat stories for which listeners hungered—and that inspired their activism. When talk hosts stirred up a hornet's nest around an issue, news organizations felt compelled to cover the story, even if journalists wouldn't otherwise have considered it newsworthy. The alternative was to be ignored—left out of the water-cooler chatter. Talk radio buzz might itself be a story. It also got people in Washington talking, which meant journalists had even more reason to cover the underlying story. As Fox grew in popularity, it amplified this effect, earning the network influence over coverage priorities across the media landscape.

A month after Fox launched, Americans reelected Clinton. The White House's waning enthusiasm for talk radio had carried over to the reelection campaign, which paid the medium far less attention than its 1992 predecessor had. In an interview, campaign Press Secretary Joe Lockhart admitted he did not remember spending much time strategizing for talk radio. The campaign did view talk radio as an important venue for reaching the election's key group of persuadable voters: lower- to middle-class, white, married people. So Lockhart did radio interviews and sparred on conservative shows. But he felt the campaign gained little from these appearances. At most, he was hoping to connect with 10 percent of the talk radio audience, and then purely on defense. When Clinton was on offense, he turned to other forums.[10]

This attitude persisted into the second term, and the White House continued downgrading its radio effort. Whereas early in the first term Richard Strauss and his team brought hosts to the White House for the unveiling of the president's signature domestic policy proposal, in the second term, radio outreach focused on smaller matters, such as procuring local interviews with teacher-of-the-year-award winners. New initiatives included a radio-actuality line to provide audio to smaller and medium-sized stations for news reports—not aggressive booking with big-time hosts. Megan Moloney, who oversaw the talk radio apparatus, confirmed that radio took a backseat, especially to television.[11] By 1998, when Lockhart replaced McCurry as the administration's press secretary, talk radio was pretty much a dead letter in the White House. Lockhart and his colleagues believed there was no chance of a fair hearing on talk radio; hyperbolic criticism of Clinton clearly offered the best formula for building and maintaining an audience. The White House wanted to talk about the robust economy, but on talk radio, it was all brushfires and conspiracy theories du jour.[12]

The administration's withdrawal from talk radio may have left Clinton and his team breathing easier. Officials wouldn't have to take part in explosive interviews or field so many awkward questions about the president's sex life. And to some extent the DNC picked up the slack, deploying surrogates widely on the airwaves to beat back calls for impeachment.[13]

But even with the DNC mustering the full force of its talk radio operation, the administration's retreat ensured that talk radio's message became still more one-sided. Listeners received even less of a counterweight to talk radio's anti-Clinton perspective. This was another foundation stone for the right-wing echo chamber.

Impeachment

The drama surrounding President Clinton's impeachment was high entertainment on talk radio and the emerging Fox News network. Impeachment was, of course, a major source of strain between the White House and conservative media. But not all Republicans were happy about talk radio's obsession with Clinton's scandals, either. Throughout the impeachment process, talk radio demonstrated its independence, further undermining the view that the medium was a Republican puppet.

Conservative hosts energetically fanned the flames of impeachment. They also hammered any Republican, moderate or conservative, who was opposed or on the fence. Representative Amo Houghton, an entrenched New York moderate, faced threats from local and national talk radio. Souder, a conservative who nonetheless worried that impeachment would set a bad precedent, experienced similar pressure. Fort Wayne host Dave Macy proclaimed Souder "a traitor to the rule of law" and attacked him to such a degree that Macy eventually lost advertisers and his time slot.[14]

Limbaugh implored listeners to call Connecticut Representative Chris Shays, one of four Republicans who ended up voting against all four articles of impeachment. The host also publicized a town hall Shays was holding on the issue. Twelve-hundred people jammed the event space, and another 6,000 could not get in. Would-be attendees sat in a half-mile of traffic on the New England Thruway. Talk radio's battering did Shays lasting damage. As a Republican in a marginal district, Shays needed every supporter he could find. But he believed that some Republicans irrevocably turned against him after the pounding he took on the airwaves. He suggested that Connie Morella, another Republican who opposed impeachment, eventually lost her Maryland seat for similar reasons.[15]

During the impeachment process, talk radio pushed Republicans to do something that was very popular with the conservative base, at the expense of everyone else. Americans as a whole didn't feel the same enthusiasm. A Gallup poll from mid-December 1998, the month the House impeached Clinton, found that just 36 percent of Americans wanted their representative to vote in favor of impeachment. An ABC News/*Washington Post* poll came to a virtually identical conclusion: only 38 percent of respondents wanted to see Clinton impeached and removed from office. Other polls showed majorities considered House Republicans excessively partisan and out of touch with the public's views on impeachment.[16] But if the country at large opposed impeachment, grassroots pressure applied by talk radio helped force the House to its decision.

Republicans paid politically for embracing the right's cause. Even before the House voted to impeach Clinton in December, Republicans suffered a midterm election setback, rare for the party that doesn't control the White House, especially in a president's second term. Democrats gained four seats in the House, while the partisan breakdown of the Senate remained unchanged.[17]

To hear them say it, some hosts didn't mind if their outrage took down an elected Republican or Republican candidate who had unacceptable positions on big issues. For instance, Milwaukee host Mark Belling had no qualms about endorsing liberal Democrat Tammy Baldwin over Republican Josephine Musser, because he objected to Musser's position on "partial-birth" abortions. "With Republicans like these, who needs the Democrats?" Belling asked. "Tammy Baldwin is an honest left-wing crackpot. Jo Musser is a duplicitous left-wing crackpot. I'll go with the honest one."[18]

At this stage, though, Belling was something of an outlier. Many hosts were still capable of pragmatically tolerating moderates, and all-out campaigns to defeat them were years away. Limbaugh had vowed after 1992 to promote hard-right opposition to the "patrician moderate" wing of the Republican Party, yet he couldn't bring himself to back Pat Buchanan again in 1996.[19] Hosts generally understood that Republican victories still gave conservatives their best chance to legislate and control Congress, and even moderate Republicans agreed with hosts on far more issues than did Democrats. For example, most moderates, including some who didn't believe Clinton should be removed from office, voted for at least some of the articles of impeachment.[20] If Democrats had controlled the House, impeachment would not have been an option. Further, moderate Republicans might, out of party loyalty or in response to pressure from leadership, at least vote the "right" way on procedural measures.[21]

Overall the second half of the 1990s was an adjustment period as politicians on both sides of the aisle got used to conservative media as a political player. Talk radio aided Republicans as they sought to enact an ambitious agenda, but Democrats did not cede the field, at least at first. For a time they built outreach structures similar to those Republicans implemented. And even during this period of deepening partisanship, radio talkers were anything but Republican mouthpieces. They never hesitated to bash Republicans who failed to meet their expectations, and they pushed Republicans into can't-win fights such as the government shutdown in the winter of 1995–1996.

The impeachment battle also was unwinnable, but amid talk radio's ongoing rightward drift, hosts and listeners were implacable. We cannot lose sight of the principal reason for that drift: money. By 1998 there were new commercial imperatives to keep in mind. As we will see in the next chapter, a piece of 1996 legislation changed the structure of the radio business in ways that unintentionally invited more uniform and more strident conservatism.

12

Money Propels Talk Radio
to the Right

ONE OF THE CLINTON era's most important contributions to talk radio's deepening conservatism had nothing to do with the medium's hatred of the president, or, indeed, with partisan politics. A piece of bipartisan legislation inadvertently served to solidify talk radio into the medium we now know, delivering nearly all-conservative programming, all the time, in virtually every market.

The 1996 Telecommunications Act paved the way for today's vertically and horizontally integrated radio industry, in which large, publicly traded corporations own hundreds of stations and syndication companies.[1] The legislation—a no-brainer, winning 507 of Congress's 535 votes—eliminated the national cap on station ownership, which had prevented any one company from owning more than forty stations. The law also raised ownership limits in individual markets.[2] The regulatory changes accelerated an ongoing process of consolidation, which had been spurred by earlier relaxations of limits in 1984, 1992, and 1994.[3] Within five years of the 1996 law's passage, the three largest radio conglomerates—iHeartMedia (formerly Clear Channel), Infinity Broadcasting, and Cumulus Media—owned close to 1,700 stations.[4] By 2002 twenty-one companies owned more than forty stations, and the ten largest companies controlled 67 percent of the industry's revenues.[5]

These large media conglomerates had no political interest in pushing conservative messaging on their airwaves. But when they assumed control of struggling stations, they made an understandable business decision: they reprogrammed stations to broadcast the profitable, "in" format of the moment. In the second half of the 1990s, that format was conservative talk.[6] The success of Limbaugh and all-conservative stations such as KVI and KSFO signaled to corporate chieftains that conservative talk promised the best rate of return. Additionally, as syndicators provided more conservative programming to meet demand, the combination of the barter method and vertical integration made predominantly conservative formats more economical. Syndication allowed stations to air shows without paying for talent and production. Instead of paying cash upfront for programming, stations handed syndicators a fixed number of commercial slots per hour to sell in exchange for the right to air a show.[7] And vertical integration ensured even more conservative talk reached listeners because owners could save money by airing shows produced by their own syndication arms.

If syndication spread conservative talk more widely, it also encouraged hosts to spend more of their airtime on conservative politics. Many hosts, including Hannity and Liddy, spent more hours on politics after their programs entered syndication. In syndication, they faced pressure from executives to adhere to the theme and format stations were selling to listeners, usually conservative talk. And hosts had to appeal to listeners across the country, which meant discarding apolitical or less partisan topics that worked with local audiences but wouldn't translate nationally.

Hosts also found that they had to skew farther right if they wanted to maintain and grow their new, national audiences. Los Angeles star John Kobylt recalled that, when he and partner Ken Chiampou took their show national in the late 1990s, they couldn't possibly satisfy the audiences many of their stations attracted. The other hosts on these stations spewed such venom toward President Clinton that listeners perceived the populist, less doctrinaire Kobylt and Chiampou as insufficiently far right.[8]

Large corporate owners also pushed conservative media because, from their perspective, it was usually safe. Conservative hosts sometimes got themselves in trouble, but not with their own audience. Crucially, many of the people most offended by conservative radio's content weren't listeners in the first place, and during this period, before stations streamed on the Internet, only the most egregious talk radio howlers reached the ears of nonfans. In any case, the antics on conservative talk radio were almost never scandalous, rude, and shocking like the stuff on "hot talk" and "guy talk" formats. For instance, no one on syndicated conservative radio ever pulled a stunt like guy talk hosts Greg "Opie" Hughes and Anthony Cumia did in 2002. The popular, nationally syndicated duo was fired by Viacom, their station's parent company, for orchestrating and broadcasting a bit in which a couple purportedly had sex in St. Patrick's Cathedral while one of the hosts' sidekicks provided blow-by-blow commentary.[9]

Edgy talk like this, often produced locally, posed risks that predictable political shows didn't. That sounded good to corporate owners with lots of debt on the line. It also sounded good to big companies such as Disney and Viacom, whose many nonradio interests might be sullied by controversy. Conservative hosts were unlikely to expose ownership to fines, put a station's license at risk, or threaten spillover consequences.[10]

Radio-centric companies and individual owners were comparatively tolerant of controversy and offense, even though a single serious case could upend their business, especially in markets with smaller advertising bases. In bigger cities, radio-focused owners had the flexibility to stand by such content. They didn't have to worry about other businesses, and they knew that entertaining radio would keep attracting listeners in a competitive marketplace, even if some people were offended.[11] When the controversial and often lewd Tom Leykis broadcast in Miami in the 1980s, station management made clear that he didn't have to worry about losing advertisers. There were more queued up. He just had to be sure he didn't lose the station its license.[12]

The 1995 firing of top-rated WABC host Bob Grant is a study in the finer sensibilities of big corporate owners. Disney had just taken over the station after buying Capital Cities/ABC, when Grant was let go in response to one of the more veiled racist comments of his long career. After news broke that Commerce Secretary Ron Brown, who was black, had been in a plane crash, Grant made a very crude joke. Because Grant counted himself "a pessimist," he said, it might just turn out that Brown was the crash's only survivor. Other owners had tolerated Grant's insensitive, provocative verbal grenades for decades. To name but two, he referred to blacks as "savages" and described David Dinkins, New York's black mayor, as a "washroom attendant." But, facing threats of protests and boycotts, Disney wasn't about to put itself on the line for him. Less than two weeks later, Grant returned to the airwaves on WABC's main competitor WOR, operated by the family-owned, radio-centric Buckley Broadcasting Corporation.[13]

As the years went by, conservative radio would become riskier. Increasing competition during the 2000s drove hosts toward more outrageous and incendiary commentary in an effort to distinguish themselves. At the same time, Internet streaming and watchdog groups such as Media Matters brought hosts' words to broader, less-agreeable audiences, who were ready to apply pressure to advertisers. But during the consolidation of the late 1990s, conservative hosts were a comparatively safe bet. What mattered to the bottom line was programming suitable to economies of scale, and conservative hosts provided it: radio that appealed to audiences throughout the country and that was sufficiently inoffensive—and isolated in a right-leaning echo chamber—that it wouldn't raise many hackles from advertisers or other business partners.

Once again conservative media was spreading and becoming more strident not because broadcasters wanted to change the political landscape but because talk radio made better business sense than the alternatives.

13

Talk Radio in the 2000s: Big Changes for the Medium and for Politics

CONSERVATIVE MEDIA EXPANDED DRAMATICALLY in the new millennium. Talk stations became almost universally conservative, replacing what variety remained in their schedules with wall-to-wall right-wing opinion. In 2002 Fox News overtook CNN as the top-rated news network on cable.[1] In the second half of the decade and the early 2010s, conservative digital outlets blossomed. Eventually rivals to Fox sprang up on cable as well.

Competition produced a kind of arms race. Hosts feared being outflanked, so they became more extreme, both ideologically and rhetorically. Lobbing ever more, and bigger, verbal grenades, talk radio stoked and reflected the right's rising disgust with Republicans, especially moderates and pragmatists.

The medium's relationship with the party changed in turn. On the whole, talk radio was supportive of the GOP when it held unified control of government from January to May 2001 and from 2003 to 2007. But in 2003 hosts groused about the new prescription drug benefit that President George W. Bush and a Republican Congress added to Medicare. And in Bush's second term, hosts helped derail a signature policy initiative and a Supreme Court nomination. They were not willing to be good partisan soldiers when the stakes were so high and Bush wasn't meeting their expectations.

The alliance solidified again during President Barack Obama's first two years in office, when Democrats also controlled Congress. It was a repeat of the political dynamics that had bound talk radio and elected Republicans together in the first half of Bill Clinton's first term. But the cooperation evaporated almost as soon as Republicans regained the House in 2010. Once again hosts proved uncompromising, excoriating Republican leaders for purportedly surrendering to Obama's demands. Ignoring the basic realities of divided government, talk radio fueled a sense among conservative voters that elected Republicans were sniveling cowards who could have delivered on their promises had they just fought harder.

Hosts' tactics made governing more difficult, with mixed results for talk radio but decidedly negative results for Republicans. By rejecting any form of accommodation with Democrats who controlled the White House and Senate, talk radio helped to ensure the passage of more liberal legislation. In cases where legislation had to pass—for example, bills to raise the debt ceiling or keep the government running—hosts' unwillingness to countenance compromise left Republican leaders with little choice but to allow votes on more liberal bills that would secure Democratic support. Many rank-and-file Republicans didn't dare upset hosts, so Republican leaders had to find votes elsewhere.

Yet, for conservative hosts, these were small, largely irrelevant setbacks. In the first decade and a half of the twenty-first century, talk radio was enormously successful in reshaping the GOP. The party lurched to the right along with hosts and listeners, adopting extreme rhetoric and losing its appetite for compromise. Its standard-bearer went from Bush, preacher of compassionate conservatism, to Donald Trump, whose words sounded more suitable to the AM dial than the White House. During these years the Republican Party became talk radio's party.

The Next Conservative Star

The talk radio that we know today—and that had such an impact on politics in the new millennium—crystallized in 2001. That year Sean Hannity emerged as the next syndicated conservative star. Hannity hadn't generated particularly high ratings on WABC in New York. But executives at ABC Radio, including John McConnell, the senior vice president in charge of programming, understood from experience that Hannity was the kind of host who could flourish nationally. His Fox News show, *Hannity and Colmes,* and his work as Limbaugh's vacation substitute ensured name recognition. And Hannity possessed all the qualities of the best hosts. He was likable, the sort of regular guy to whom his audience could relate. McConnell recalled a charming story Hannity told on the air about the shocking price of a Louis Vuitton handbag he wanted to buy for his wife. The host had just started making some real money and wasn't used to high society; he was still one of the people, just like his listeners. Hannity liked to laugh, and while he made fun of others—a necessity in the irreverent, anti-PC world of talk radio—he also made fun of himself, something not everyone in the business would do.[2]

Hannity entered the national radio business with the wind at his back. Consolidation provided him distribution unprecedented for a host making his national debut. ABC, which was syndicating Hannity's show, arranged for it to air on stations it owned in seven of the top ten national markets. Hannity also benefited from happenstance: his national debut occurred on September 10, 2001.[3] The terrorist attacks the following day sent shock waves through the United States and increased demand for all sorts of media, including talk radio. Much as the Gulf War prompted people to tune into Limbaugh, 9/11 introduced listeners to Hannity, and large numbers liked what they heard. Finally, Hannity had the advantage of riding Limbaugh's coattails. Limbaugh was the biggest ratings tentpole in the industry; he boosted listenership for everyone else on the stations that aired him, and Hannity would be going on right after his show. The six-hour block of conservative political programming kept the audience engaged and drove Limbaugh's listeners toward the new guy.

Limbaugh and Hannity back-to-back was format changing. Between the two of them, they could define a station's audience. Executives who previously resisted the idea of an all-conservative format now had even more reason to take the plunge. Adding other conservative political talkers to complement Limbaugh and Hannity would help to maintain a consistent audience throughout the day—the one looking for just their brand of politics.[4]

An executive looking to build an all-conservative lineup around Hannity and Limbaugh had a buffet of talent to choose from. Much had changed since the 1990s, when Limbaugh was the lone syndicated conservative superstar. Indeed, the only other syndicated hosts of his stature were Howard Stern and Dr. Laura Schlesinger. Stern was the opposite of a conservative firebrand, and Schlesinger, though herself highly conservative, talked mainly about lifestyle topics rather than politics. But between 1997 and 2002 syndicators started giving station executives many more conservative options. Ingraham, Boortz, Michael Medved, Glenn Beck, Mike Gallagher, Michael Savage, Dennis Prager, and Bill O'Reilly all entered syndication or launched syndicated shows during this period.[5] Others would soon follow. As these shows took off, listeners could feast on a full day of popular national programming.

It is in this respect that the repeal of the Fairness Doctrine a decade and a half earlier played its biggest role in the development of talk radio. Uniformly conservative talk stations were only possible because the doctrine's requirement for balance was eliminated. The doctrine mandated that radio stations operate "on the basis of overall fairness," by "making their facilities available for the expression of contrasting views of all responsible elements in the community on the various issues which may arise."[6] That meant that a station couldn't be all-conservative. It could have conservative shows, but they needed to be balanced by liberal ones. Hosts often misinterpret the Fairness Doctrine as a now-defunct obstacle to their work and rage whenever discussion of its revival pops into the news. But while the doctrine never entailed that shows such as Limbaugh's couldn't be aired, one can't ignore the fact that, had the mandate remained in place, all-conservative stations would have violated FCC rules and potentially subjected stations to penalties.[7] Business incentives were the primary force underlying the all-conservative revolution, but their impact would have been more limited if "overall fairness" had been retained. Instead, by 2007, 91 percent of weekday talk radio was conservative.[8]

Format Purity

Constructing an all-conservative lineup around six hours of Limbaugh and Hannity made sense to the many radio executives who saw format purity as their recipe for success.[9] The theory was that listeners wanted reliable, consistent programming: rock music stations eschewed country music, and vice versa; sports stations didn't play Mozart. As former CBS Radio executive Scott Herman put it, "You don't go to Dominos for a hamburger."[10]

There were other paths to success, no doubt. San Francisco's KGO, which aired diverse Bay Area voices on a range of topics throughout the day, topped the local ratings for a whopping thirty-one years straight until losing its crown in late 2009. But generating that sort of content wasn't simple. It required creativity, substantial investment in talent and advertising, and ties to the community. Turning ideological diversity into a strength often required expensive branding campaigns. And some of these local talk stations were news hubs, making them especially costly to run.[11]

By contrast, by the 2000s a pure, niche format such as conservative talk was easy to buy, brand, and sell: it reduced costs and was constructed from "off-the-shelf" components offered by syndicators. It also maximized profits, as intense listener loyalty ensured high advertising rates.[12] Perhaps Phil Boyce had in mind these benefits—especially intense listener loyalty—when he replaced John Mainelli at WABC in 1995. Boyce believed that, in order to survive, stations couldn't "just be benign. You can't do a little bit conservative. And a little bit liberal. You can't be mushy in the middle." He built an all-conservative lineup, and the results speak for themselves. By surrounding Limbaugh with likeminded hosts Hannity and Mark Levin, Boyce extended the station's time spent listening (TSL), an audience measure that accounts for the time, on average, listeners spend tuned to a given station. When Boyce left WABC in 2009, it had the highest TSL of any news/talk station in the country. Thanks to its huge TSL advantage, WABC led the local ratings even though local all-news station 1010 WINS had a million more listeners. Listeners tuned in to WABC for around seven hours per week, on average.[13]

Format consistency was also attractive to programmers because, by their own admission, they weren't very creative. In interviews many described themselves and their peers as lemmings, followers, and the like. They tended to copy whatever format was thriving elsewhere.[14] This is also what senior executives wanted: when programmers suggested a format, the first question from their bosses was often, "Where is it working?"[15] Each station that prospered with conservative talk inspired more programmers and executives to try the formula. It seemed less risky than doing something new and unproven.

Audience expectations formed as a result of this dynamic, and reinforced it. As stations invested in ideological consistency, listeners came to anticipate it. Previously stations could expect some crossover audience between ideologically disparate shows. For instance, in the 1980s and early 1990s, KFI in Los Angeles thrived as the same listeners tuned into both Limbaugh and the left-leaning, if not doctrinaire, Leykis. By the 2000s, however, most conservative listeners wanted nothing to do with liberal hosts, and liberal listeners had, in large part, given up on the entire AM dial. Building a new blended-talk format came to seem very dicey. When any attempt failed, executives saw another sign that ideological consistency was the key to success.

Of course, consistency doesn't preclude doctrinaire liberalism. Yet liberal radio never took off. To some extent, this reflected a first-mover advantage enjoyed by all-conservative programming, and the listener expectations it created. Conservative talk radio locked down stations with the most powerful signals, ensuring that hosts could be heard clearly and crisply for hundreds of miles. As conservative talk experienced success, and consolidation swept the industry, these stations were able to secure large budgets from parent companies that prioritized the sales and promotional efforts of their biggest, most profitable broadcasters. Limbaugh himself embodied something of a head start: as the first star in political talk radio, he got the ball rolling for conservatives involved in the medium. Liberals never developed such a bright star around whom to develop a format.

But even if doctrinaire conservative stations came first, accruing these advantages, why didn't a robust liberal talk industry emerge organically to contest them? In a country closely divided on political lines, the opportunity was there, even if the best transmitters were already taken. After all, Limbaugh had ignited a revolution starting out on small stations in the late 1980s. Yet, while some liberal hosts carved out successful niches for themselves, their audiences paled in comparison to those enjoyed by the biggest names in conservative talk.

There are many reasons why liberal hosts never took off to the same extent as their conservative peers. A full discussion of liberal talk's struggles goes beyond the scope of this book, but it is worth at least introducing a few of the factors underlying liberal radio's checkered history because this failure to compete had a massive political impact.[16]

It turned out that liberal hosts' style and goals often were not conducive to good radio. Left-leaning political talkers didn't focus on entertainment. Instead, they placed their agenda front and center. Many liberal hosts, such as former New York Governor Mario Cuomo, came from the political world; they lived and breathed policy and coalition building. The resulting content often was dry and boring, sometimes verging on a lecture. Even left-leaning hosts plucked from the entertainment world, such as Janeane Garofalo and Al Franken, joined talk radio with political goals foremost in mind, ahead of putting on the most engaging possible show every day. Undoubtedly Limbaugh and his ilk cared about politics and policy, but, as we have seen, conservative political hosts knew how to amuse audiences, and they recognized that politics had to come second behind keeping listeners glued to their radios.

Radio companies also had less incentive to persevere with liberal radio. Executives understood that liberal listeners didn't have conservatives' thirst for loud, in-your-face political radio. That's because liberal listeners found voices they appreciated beyond AM political talk. They could go without their own Limbaugh because they already had National Public Radio, African American/urban and Latino talk radio, and culturally liberal shock jocks such as Stern and the hosts of FM "morning zoo" and guy talk shows.[17] Morning drive stars such as Preston Elliot and Steve Morrison in Philadelphia, and Tom Griswold and Bob Kevoian nationally, presented largely apolitical discussion and fun, but their topics and humor appealed to liberal listeners. From a commercial standpoint, counting these hosts and formats as liberal talk had real merit. They satisfied the needs of many liberal listeners, and their success fragmented the potential audience for opinion-driven liberal talk to rival Limbaugh and company.[18]

But while it is reasonable, in business terms, to call these products liberal radio, they did almost nothing to right the imbalance in on-air political advocacy. Liberal consumers may have enjoyed NPR and Howard Stern, but the vast majority of media outlets appealing to liberals—including the mainstream press—either eschewed partisan politics or aimed to provide a neutral perspective on the news of the day, even if they failed miserably by conservatives' standards.

No matter how many times conservative hosts accused mainstream journalists of being Democratic cheerleaders, they had a fundamentally different goal than advocacy broadcasters. That meant that conservative-advocacy radio played a very different role in the political process than did the mainstream media, shaped though it undoubtedly was by liberal sensibilities. While both conservative and mainstream media have contributed to Americans' embrace of distinct news bubbles, their effects on electoral and policy battles are night and day. With no liberal counterweight to conservative talk and Fox News, explicit media advocacy would be found only on one side of the debate. And this advocacy influenced outcomes, according to policymakers on both sides of the aisle. Before the mid-2000s, when MSNBC shifted to the left and liberals took to the burgeoning blogosphere, the left had nothing like Limbaugh or Hannity on a national scale. And even after MSNBC and digital outlets became major liberal media voices, they still didn't reach enough people to match the political impact of conservative talk.

14

The Parties Go Their Own Ways

THE NEW MILLENNIUM BROUGHT a political reality that hadn't prevailed since talk radio's infancy: there was a Republican president. For some of the George W. Bush years, there was even unified Republican control of government. And now talk radio was a political powerhouse.

Talk radio's relationship with Republicans remained close, steadfast, and mutually beneficial during the Bush years. Talk radio continued to favor Republicans electorally and labor on their behalf. For their part, elected Republicans worked as hard as ever to maintain their relationships with hosts, who used their rhetorical skill to deflect from Republicans' scandals, play up their more conservative policy ideas, and keep listeners focused on the flaws of the Democrats and the mainstream media.

But on-air criticism of Republicans was growing harsher and more constant. As the end of Bush's presidency neared, hosts became more combative toward moderate Republicans. In power, Republicans earned hosts' and listeners' ire by trying to chart a wider course. The majority and the presidency gave Republicans a huge opportunity: they could enact legislation, not just stymie it. But passing big, consequential bills for the most part required bipartisanship, which was anathema to talk radio. The base voted for Republicans who promised adherence to conservative principles. Yet once they got to Washington, they were looking to compromise on issues from prescription drug coverage to immigration.

*   *   *

Republicans took a double-barreled approach to talk radio outreach during the hotly contested 2000 presidential campaign. On one side was the Republican National Committee, which served as hatchet man, unleashing a torrent of criticism about Democratic nominee Al Gore. Radio Director Chris Paulitz expanded a talk radio–oriented daily tip sheet, "Light Up the Phones," and RNC staff wrote and distributed scripts to hosts. The scripts were designed for talk radio, dripping with incendiary charges one tends not to find in traditional press releases. Some hosts read the scripts on air; others adapted them to their own purposes and style. This followed a pre-campaign effort from Paulitz's RNC colleague Mark Pfeifle. A former talk radio host, Pfeifle compiled a CD of Gore's snafus and misstatements and distributed it to radio shows. He dubbed the material *The Best of Al Gore: Hits of the 80's, 90's and Today!* The RNC also had a hotline hosts could use to book a guest in as few as five minutes.[1]

The other prong of the GOP outreach to talk radio was Governor George W. Bush's presidential campaign itself. By doing the dirty work, the RNC freed up the campaign to focus its talk radio operation on selling Bush. The initial strategy was to book Bush as a guest. He could introduce himself without the strictures of four-minute television interviews. With more time at his disposal, Bush could showcase his personality while making his pitch. Susan Phalen, the campaign's radio director, aimed to get the candidate on morning and afternoon drive shows in markets where he would be appearing. Phalen tightly controlled the terms of Bush's radio appearances. They occurred either on conservative outlets or with ground rules designed to prevent ambushes. Producers knew that an unwanted surprise would harm the show's standing with the campaign even if it might produce great ratings.[2]

Bush curried favor with talk radio early in the campaign by giving a speech at the annual talk radio convention and circulating for interviews. Over time the operation expanded beyond the candidate himself to include surrogates, who were trotted out to praise Bush's character, qualifications, and passion for the job.

After Bush captured one of biggest cliffhangers in presidential election history, he brought to the White House the radio strategy that had propelled him to victory. The administration ran a robust booking and outreach operation designed to advance the president's policy agenda. While the president—who didn't particularly enjoy doing media appearances, especially radio interviews—was an infrequent guest, Vice President Dick Cheney appeared regularly on talk radio.[3] When Bush's policies left hosts disgruntled, the White House often dispatched the vice president to calm the talk radio waters. Cheney was popular with conservatives, and his counselor Mary Matalin understood the importance of radio. She had spent time during the 1990s as a host and had witnessed Limbaugh's power during the 1992 presidential campaign.[4]

The Bush team sought to make life as convenient as possible for talkers, matching guests to hosts and employing facts and information tailored to each host's state. Every morning communications staff would meet to determine a message of the day. Then the radio director—first Taylor Gross, then Trey Bohn, and finally Nick Piatek—would work the phones, personally appealing to hosts with that message in mind. During his time as radio director, Bohn tried to fulfill every guest request he received. The White House also distributed fact sheets and reached out aggressively to define and clarify issues for hosts. To make sure everything went smoothly, media staffers followed the campaign model of establishing ground rules, especially for a host looking to book Bush or Cheney.

It was a dexterous radio operation, nimble enough to move between partisan combat and policy battles. If national security dominated the day's news, Bohn would request twenty minutes with then-National Security Adviser Condoleezza Rice before going to hosts with the day's talking points. If an attack by Nevada Senator Harry Reid, then the Democratic whip, warranted a reply, Bohn would book a guest with Heidi Harris or Alan Stock, key radio hosts in Reid's home state.

The Web made it easier for White House staff to monitor the fruits of their efforts and offered an early warning system to catch trouble percolating in real time. As stations began streaming their shows online, Bohn started tracking key shows he would otherwise have been unable to hear and reported their contents to his superiors. But know-how, tenacity, and enthusiasm were at least as important as new technology. Piatek developed the capacity to listen to two or three shows simultaneously.[5]

But while the White House's attentiveness helped ensure good relations, talk radio wasn't always able to reciprocate by solving the administration's problems. The first political jolt of Bush's term became a cautionary tale about talk radio's limits: its conservatism narrowed its impact. Hosts were so predictable, and their listeners so strident, that many of the opponents they sought to influence simply paid them no attention, figuring there was no point in engaging an unmovable obstacle. Vermont Senator Jim Jeffords, who delivered the jolt, personified this tendency.

In 2001 Jeffords occupied a critical position as one of the undecided senators on President Bush's signature tax cuts. The White House radio operation tried to prod the senator by placing surrogates on Vermont radio shows, where they would turn up the pressure on Jeffords from hosts and callers.[6] But the senator continued to hold out, insisting on increased special education funding and a smaller tax cut as conditions for his vote.

Jeffords either ignored, or was unaware of, the discourse on talk radio. He had long since accepted that conservative talkers and their fans would not support him; one conservative host had even challenged him in a primary. Jeffords didn't need talk radio, because he didn't care about his national image, and in liberal Vermont he won elections despite being a Republican, not by running to the right. According to his former chief of staff, Susan Russ, talk radio also played no role in his decision to switch parties in May 2001, because the medium was totally off his radar.[7] That move flipped control of the Senate to Democrats, depriving Bush of unified control of government after a mere four months.[8]

Jeffords's switch made the 2002 midterm elections that much more important. If Democrats retained the Senate, large parts of President Bush's agenda would not be enacted without major concessions. The RNC saw talk radio as a crucial asset in the midterms and targeted key stations in battleground districts and states.[9] Six days before the election, the White House welcomed fifty talkers for a thirteen-and-a-half-hour talk radio day.[10]

For the most part Republicans in 2002 could count on their talk radio outreach to yield good things come election time. Talk radio didn't have to be an outsized contributor; by simply doing their thing, hosts provided an almost-daily boost. For instance, in Georgia, talk radio didn't do anything unusual for Saxby Chambliss in his effort to defeat popular Democratic Senator Max Cleland. But the medium did provide Chambliss regular benefits en route to his critical win. Georgia's seat was one of four that flipped in the chamber that year.

Regular talk radio appearances allowed Chambliss to "be" in multiple towns at once and provided access to a large, captive audience as people languished in traffic. Michelle Grasso, the Chambliss campaign's communications director, explained that people tended to tune in to one station and stay there, especially during drive time. One of their favorite shows was hosted by Martha Zoller, whose program gave Chambliss an outlet for speaking to his base.[11]

The race was an uphill battle for Chambliss. Though he was well liked in the pivotal swing area of Middle Georgia, where his congressional district was located, he couldn't win with that region alone. He needed the Atlanta suburbs. But while they usually supported Republicans, initial polling showed him trailing Cleland significantly in this crucial location. The trouble was that these suburbanites simply didn't know him.

Enter talk radio. The medium fueled Chambliss's come-from-behind victory by providing a forum for introducing himself to a key cadre of conservative voters.[12] Chambliss also used talk radio to dent Cleland. In interviews and hard-hitting fifteen-second ads, the challenger criticized his opponent's record, about which Georgians knew little.[13] As the national significance of the race grew, Chambliss chatted regularly with syndicated talkers, especially Hannity and Hugh Hewitt. These appearances unleashed a flood of online contributions to his campaign.[14] On Election Day he appeared on Boortz's Atlanta-based program to urge voters to the polls. No one could claim that talk radio handed the victory to Chambliss or that it was decisive. But the medium aided him at every step along the way.

The midterm elections restored Republicans to unified control. Before they got started governing, they hoped to spend the sleepy post-election month planning initiatives for the upcoming session. But they were derailed when a major firestorm erupted during, of all events, a birthday party. Talk radio would jump to Republicans' rescue.

The trouble started when Trent Lott, the incoming Senate majority leader, saluted his South Carolina colleague Strom Thurmond on his hundredth birthday. Lott joked that the country would have had fewer problems if more states had supported Thurmond's 1948 presidential campaign. The press, with little else to focus on during the lame-duck period, pounced: Thurmond's explicitly segregationist 1948 campaign was not something a party or one of its leaders should have been celebrating.

Radio talkers sprang into action in an effort to mitigate the damage to the Republican Party. Hosts knew they could not defend the substance of Lott's remarks, so instead they hammered home what they saw as the unfairness of the media scrutiny. Limbaugh highlighted Republican contributions to civil rights legislation and reminded listeners that prominent Democrats had opposed it. He attacked Democrats and the media for hypocritically failing to condemn equally intemperate remarks from

Democrats over the years. He focused on West Virginia Senator Robert Byrd, a Democratic Party leader and, during the 1940s, a member of the Ku Klux Klan. In the same vein, Hannity pointed out that liberals didn't go after Clinton for awarding the Presidential Medal of Freedom to Senator J. William Fulbright, "a known segregationist." Both hosts eventually acted to protect the party's image by suggesting that Lott step aside as majority leader.[15]

Citing double standards and hypocrisy was not only easier than defending Lott, it also was a tried-and-true strategy. Listeners were familiar with hosts' criticism of the get-out-of-jail-free card Democrats and the media gave Byrd. C-SPAN 2 aficionados may have recognized Byrd for his natty dress and fiery orations: he spent the 2000s with a pocket copy of the Constitution in the breast pocket of his three-piece suits, delivering Senate-floor speeches studded with history lessons dating to antiquity.[16] But in the world of talk radio, Byrd had never outrun his KKK membership of six decades prior. Hannity regularly referred to him as Robert "KKK" Byrd. Limbaugh opted for the nickname "Sheets."

For talk radio, Lott's case became a touchstone. Long after the episode had disappeared from the news, hosts brought it up to excoriate press bias. In 2005 Hannity declared that if any Republican or conservative had a Klan past, or if any Republican had uttered the "N-word" in an interview, as Byrd had several years earlier, he or she would not be leading the Republican Party. "Even though Dan Rather is gone, this institutionalized media bias still exists," Hannity told listeners. (Rather had resigned from CBS after it was discovered that his story questioning Bush's National Guard service was based on forged documents. CBS and Rather both claimed he had been planning to leave and was not being punished, but the story likely played a role in his departure.[17]) Hannity then played a clip of Byrd declaring that his KKK affiliation was in the past and that he had apologized for it. "Did Trent Lott get a pass?" Hannity wondered. "Trent Lott apologized five separate times for telling a joke about Strom Thurmond. Telling a joke about a guy. . . . And the same people who were calling for his head give this guy, the former Klansman, a pass. This drives me nuts."[18]

A full decade after that, following a horrific 2015 mass shooting in a Charleston church that sparked debate over the propriety of displaying the Confederate flag, conservative host Mark Levin dusted off the tactic Limbaugh and Hannity had used so effectively. Levin quoted Clinton's praise of Fulbright and read from the infamous Southern Manifesto resisting desegregation, which Fulbright signed in 1956. Levin also described Byrd, who at this point had been dead five years, as "the Klansman who ran the Democrat Party for twenty years in the United States Senate." (In fact Byrd had been Senate Democratic leader for twelve years.) Levin's analysis demonstrated the enduring power of the double-standard narrative in the minds of hosts and listeners. Rather than address politically thorny issues of racism and gun control, the narrative kept listeners focused on the supposed hypocrisy of Democrats and journalists.

This consistency in hosts' rhetorical leadership reflects both the cohesiveness and the insularity of what Kathleen Hall Jamieson and Joseph Cappella call the conservative media establishment. They argued in 2008 that Limbaugh, Fox News, and the *Wall Street Journal* editorial page formed the heart of that establishment; today, the conservative media establishment is broader. This was no sinister cabal. Conservative media personalities did not meet in a war room to plot political strategy. Rather, they consumed each other's work. Talk radio hosts read conservative digital sites and publications during commercial breaks and as they prepared for their shows. Fox News hosts listened to conservative talk radio during their commutes. Many top conservative talkers, including Limbaugh, Hannity, Boortz, and Levin, were friends who communicated regularly, sometimes even sending each other digital messages as they broadcast.[19]

In the echo chamber of the conservative media establishment, various outlets reinforced and amplified the same message, while insulating that message from rebuttal by Democrats or the mainstream media.[20] In particular, this message sidestepped Democratic attempts to stratify voters along economic lines and instead defined the political battle as one between conservatives and a godless, patronizing, liberal cultural elite who threatened socially conservative values and common-sense ideas. In this way conservative media personalities gave their listeners a common enemy. That common enemy, in turn, was crucial to establishing and sustaining a group identity.[21]

As Jamieson and Cappella discuss, conservative talk show hosts also harnessed emotion to bond their audiences together and distance them from the enemy.[22] Thus, more than a decade after Limbaugh, Liddy, and their fellow early hosts had taken to the airwaves with testosterone-fueled bravado, hosts were still up to the same tricks. In late 2002 Limbaugh dubbed Massachusetts Senator and presidential hopeful John Kerry, "Lurch Kerry-Heinz" and "Mr. Big Ketchup," suggesting that he was stiff, robotic, and dominated by his wife, ketchup heiress Teresa Heinz. One goal of such emasculation was to humorously convey the Republican message that Democrats were weak on crime and national security.[23] When it came to Democratic women, talkers flipped the script, often portraying strong liberal women as shrill. On one 2005 show, Hannity introduced comments from then-Senator Hillary Clinton with Helen Reddy singing "I am woman, hear me roar," overdubbed by Clinton screaming.[24]

Conservative hosts wielded three critical rhetorical weapons to encourage listeners' support for Republican candidates and causes: priming, framing, and inoculation.[25] Priming involves elevating the importance of one decision criterion over others. For example, a host seeking to undermine a candidate might highlight her unpopular position on abortion rather than her popular position on health care. Or a host might talk about the part of a bill he was most upset by, instead of its most well-liked provisions.

Media frames, following Jamieson and Cappella's definition, are organizing structures that tell audiences "what the issue is through the use of selection, emphasis, exclusion, and elaboration." They "affect the likelihood that particular options will be selected" by the audience. Talkers framed issues by challenging facts that supported Democratic claims and policy proposals, while sharing information that bolstered conservative assertions. Essentially they argued that the pro-conservative points were the only ones that should matter to voters' decision-making. Limbaugh, for one, routinely presented and then rebutted charges that could damage conservatives.[26]

As they demonstrated in the Lott case, hosts' truest rhetorical arrow continued to be inoculation, which took the form of consternation over a miserably biased mainstream media. By fostering distrust of journalists, hosts could protect listeners against the doubts that might arise from reporting.

This was, of course, a long-standing trope. Conservative media activists dating back to the 1940s had routinely slammed journalists for liberal bias. Conservative politicians, most notably Vice President Spiro Agnew in the late 1960s and early 1970s, often joined the pile-on.[27] Modern talk radio hosts leveled this charge in their usual fun manner, branding mainstream and avowedly liberal media outlets and personalities with snarky, derisive nicknames in an effort to discredit them. Limbaugh called MSNBC, "PMSNBC"; again, the opponents of conservatism took the form of a shrill, angry woman. Not to be outdone, Levin painted the network as the delusional "MSLSD." He nicknamed the *Washington Post* the "Washington

Compost." Limbaugh reminded his listeners that the mainstream media were boring and inaccurate: *U.S. News and World Report* was "U.S. Snooze," *Meet the Press* was "Meet the Depressed," and ABC News's Sam Donaldson was "Sam the sham."[28]

The distrust sown by talk radio diminished listeners' willingness even to consult mainstream media sources.[29] Hosts' decades-long assault on the fourth estate laid the groundwork for the rapid rise, on the right, of the concept of fake news. Long before the term was coined, and then co-opted by Donald Trump, talk radio was equating mainstream media and fake news in the minds of conservatives across America.

The media-bias frame proved especially important during campaign season. With Democrats and Republicans hurling nonstop claims and counterclaims, voters needed neutral arbiters to ferret out the truth. Talk radio hosts portrayed themselves as just such arbiters, while dismissing the mainstream media as hopelessly unfair. Between September 5 and November 1, 1994, Limbaugh discussed some form of media bias on seven episodes of his television show. Given that he had six times as much airtime on radio as television, he likely discussed the theme significantly more with listeners. The same thing happened in the run-up to the 1996 presidential election. Jamieson and Cappella found that between September 3 and November 11 that year, Limbaugh attacked the mainstream media fifty-two times and reframed its reporting fifty-eight times.[30]

All these rhetorical weapons—priming, framing, and inoculation—served to rally talk radio listeners behind Republicans and helped the party win the ideas war. Using data from the National Annenberg Election Survey in 2004, Jamieson and Cappella found evidence suggesting "that audiences for Fox and Limbaugh are more likely to accept Republican claims and reject Democratic ones than the audiences of other media sources."[31] In short, in the Bush years, talk radio was working for the GOP.

Democrats Sour on Talk Radio

As Republicans worked with talk radio and reaped the benefits of the medium's political might, Democrats turned away. Over time most, but not all, Democratic members of Congress gave up on talk radio. Democrats instead focused on media outlets that were more likely to reach their core audience—outlets that also offered a better chance to spread their message as they designed it, not a version of that message distorted by hostile questioning from a conservative host.

Exasperated Democrats did for a brief moment attempt to support a liberal counterweight to conservative talk. During the second half of George W. Bush's first term, several private companies tried to do liberal radio in a big way. They wanted urgently to improve liberals' media infrastructure, which had fallen far behind the competition: liberals lacked dedicated advocacy outlets and lagged conservatives in other areas such as think tanks and media monitoring. Liberals' sense of marginalization—Democrats were completely out of power in Washington—lent further urgency to these efforts and fostered on the left the sorts of conditions that, on the right, had proven ripe for exploitation by radio entrepreneurs.

Liberals also felt poorly served by the mainstream media. As they saw it, on the media's watch, an election had been stolen and the country had committed to an unnecessary war in Iraq. Liberals were looking for media that explicitly aired their frustrations. Randi Rhodes, one of the more successful liberal hosts, summarized this sentiment during her May 4, 2004, program, when she accused the media of being "bought off" and "paid for" and a "wholly owned subsidiary of the White House." She lamented, "I don't see anyone in the media who sounds like me."[32] This fury provided a fertile climate for liberal-advocacy media, much as the needs of dejected and alienated conservatives provided opportunity for Limbaugh in the late 1980s.

Senate Democratic Leader Tom Daschle and Senator Byron Dorgan became boosters of private liberal radio efforts. They had spent years trying to get their side heard on talk radio. They were successful disseminating a Democratic message using the infrastructure they had created, but results in the commercial market were more mixed. So they were supportive when upstarts came offering a new strategy, and they worked to build the cachet of local liberal hosts in hopes of getting them into national syndication. Senate Democrats even fundraised on behalf of one of the new liberal radio organizations.[33]

But few other leading Democrats joined Daschle and Dorgan, and results were, again, middling at best. Democratic donors and political leaders never truly prioritized these efforts, in part because they hated what they heard on the radio. When Daschle encouraged leading Democratic funders to invest in liberal talk, they declined, lamenting the vacuous and poisonous nature of the medium.[34] Liberal radio entrepreneurs similarly ran into a wall when they tried to recruit financial support.[35] This was a major blow because investment was crucial to overcoming the structural obstacles liberal radio confronted. Thanks to conservative radio's years-long head start, liberal radio was left with low-wattage stations and budgets too small to pay for serious promotion. Of course, those disadvantages hadn't stopped Limbaugh in his early days, and, despite the skepticism among Democratic elites, several liberal hosts, including Rhodes, Ed Schultz, and Stephanie Miller, did find a degree of national success.

But the boldest liberal radio gambit of the early 2000s was a catastrophic failure, furthering the left's view that talk radio was permanently infertile ground. In 2004 the hugely ambitious Air America radio network debuted amid much fanfare and celebrity involvement. But the network quickly ran aground for reasons wholly unrelated to its ideology. They included poor and ever-changing management, grossly insufficient resources for a hugely expensive undertaking, a constantly changing programming vision, and inexperienced hosts. Hosts also were paired in teams without first developing any chemistry or really working out the kinks in their shows.[36]

While ideology wasn't the reason for this flop, liberals responded to Air America's travails not with a new radio strategy but by shifting resources and energy to other media. In particular, liberals reached into the growing digital world. Politicians and other Democratic leaders found that appearing at a blogger conference such as Netroots Nation (formerly YearlyKos) or joining a conference call with bloggers produced a far better response than a liberal talk radio call.[37] As time passed, Democratic staffers and strategists concluded that cable television and social media also offered larger audiences than liberal talk radio.[38]

The Internet and cable outlets need not have served as substitutes for talk radio. Indeed, for most Democratic strategists and staffers in the early to mid-2000s, outreach to talk radio and the Internet weren't mutually exclusive. Even after Howard Dean's 2004 presidential campaign sparked Democratic investment in online infrastructure and communications, talk radio outreach continued at a fairly high level for a few years in both houses of Congress.[39] Right before the 2006 midterm elections, for example, House Democrats hosted a radio day during which they did more than eighty interviews on various outlets.[40]

Nonetheless, the option to go online did lessen the perceived need to invest in talk radio. Talk radio had had two primary selling points for Democrats in the 1990s: the opportunity, first, to target messages to local audiences and, second, to circumvent the mainstream media and speak directly and interactively with Americans. Over time, however, digital communications performed both of those functions, especially the latter.

In fact, the Internet was an even better outreach tool than talk radio, at least for the left. It finished what talk radio started: a progression toward pure, unfiltered messaging from politicians to their constituents, enabled by new media. The Internet was taking off just as talk radio's utility in achieving this goal was seriously declining thanks to national syndication. A national show wasn't a good conduit to local audiences, and in many places, nationally syndicated shows filled the majority of the programming day. Even if liberals were wrong to believe that talk radio was somehow inherently a conservative medium, they were right to see that, in the era of syndication, the Internet offered greater potential for voter targeting and interaction.

Democrats had sensed this potential in the 1990s. After President Clinton's final State of the Union address, he fielded questions from the public online. The president also did a live Internet town hall and became the first president to do Christmas shopping online.[41] In 1996 the president's communications director, Don Baer, conducted an Internet chat from the White House in conjunction with the launch of MSNBC.[42] The beauty of it was that there was no talk radio host to steer this contact between Democrats and citizens.

Not only were many spots on the Internet unguarded by gatekeepers of any sort, digital messaging also evolved to be much more precise than talk radio. Online services could target voters exactly and generate concrete response-rate numbers. If a radio show reached small parts of five House districts, it was less useful than an online system that could target users district by district. This was possible by the second half of the 2000s. And YouTube, Facebook, and other online tools enabled staffers to track the impact of their media campaigns with real, if imperfect, data, and eventually learn many details about the audience reached. By contrast, when a member of Congress ventured onto talk radio, his or her staff got a rough estimate of the audience, and how many calls or letters the appearance generated.[43]

But while the attraction of the Internet played a role in Democrats' declining relationship with talk radio, it's also easy to overstate that role.[44] It is not the case that Democrats, tired of being punching bags and sensing that they would never cut into the Republican advantage on the radio dial, quickly recognized and grasped the emerging Internet's potential. It took significant time for Democrats to understand that the Internet could be their talk radio. Many elected Democrats were dragged kicking and screaming to the online world.[45] Karina Newton, who directed new media for House Minority Leader and Speaker Nancy Pelosi between 2006 and 2012, recalled having to educate members about the Internet's potential exactly as Fred Clarke, Roger Lotz, and Laura Quinn had to educate members in the mid-1990s about the workings and benefits of talk radio.

It took most politicians, staffers, and political operatives a long time even to experiment with the Internet, and still more time to integrate the Web into communications operations. Political operations are risk-averse and rarely dive into new media as early as they could. For instance, even after Howard Dean generated significant grassroots support online during the 2004 Democratic presidential primary, the Kerry campaign, during the general election, viewed the Web primarily as a fundraising tool, not a means for engaging people or getting out the vote.[46] On the left the early enthusiasm for online politics came from grassroots groups and bloggers more so than politicians. Much like conservative talk radio, the liberal blogosphere developed organically without a push from the political establishment.[47]

While retreating from talk radio, and embracing the Internet, was rational for Democrats, avoiding the airwaves had some negative consequences. For one thing, it meant giving up chances to share their message and sway the opposition. After all, there was no rule saying Democrats couldn't go on talk shows. Quite the opposite: hosts appreciated Democrats who would enter the lion's den. As host Marc Davis told *National Journal*, when he had Democratic strategist James Carville as a guest in the 1990s, they had "beaten each other to a pulp. And . . . loved it." Most conservative hosts treated Democratic guests civilly and sometimes even protected them from unruly callers. Former New Mexico Governor Bill Richardson remembers hosts, including Oliver North, rebuking callers who treated him rudely. Even if conversations got heated, there were opportunities for Democrats to benefit from engaging the medium.

That was Richardson's experience. The governor, whose distinguished career also included stints as a congressman, secretary of energy, and ambassador to the United Nations, understood the power of talk radio because it was popular in the rural areas of his home state of New Mexico. Whereas Democratic consultants thought that putting their clients on talk radio only stirred up critics, Richardson felt increased dialogue engendered respect from some opponents. This respect, in turn, might earn Democrats the benefit of the doubt on a vote.[48] Nebraska Senator Ben Nelson, another rural-state Democrat, frequently went on conservative talk programs and left disarmed hosts acknowledging that, while they disagreed with everything he said, he was also a nice guy.[49]

For Democrats representing rural or right-leaning constituencies, such outreach was essential to survival. But even some Democrats in safely liberal districts chose to keep working with talk radio in hopes of advancing the fortunes of the party writ large. Representative Rosa DeLauro, whose Connecticut district includes New Haven, placed critical importance on Democrats appearing on talk radio. Using facts, not just rhetoric, Democrats could challenge accusations that hosts leveled against them. Party figures could provide an alternative perspective that listeners would never otherwise hear.[50]

Senator Joe Lieberman, a longtime talk radio guest, was received warmly on the medium during his 2004 presidential campaign. On almost every show Lieberman appeared, the host introduced him by mentioning that, while he or she disagreed with the senator on many issues, Lieberman was a Democrat who was willing to listen to common-sense ideas and cross party lines.[51] This welcome came in spite of Lieberman's decidedly nonconservative credentials: in 2003 and 2004, the American Conservative Union gave him scores of zero; his lifetime score was seventeen. His lifetime DW-NOMINATE score—a measure of ideology from −1 to 1, with −1 being most liberal and 1 most conservative—was −0.205. This made him only the ninth most conservative Democratic senator out of 49 (including Jeffords, who at this point was an independent who caucused with the Democrats).[52]

Two years later, when Lieberman confronted a strong primary challenge from anti-war activist Ned Lamont, even Hannity opined that the senator was a good man and lamented that his praise would probably hurt Lieberman. Brimming with hubris, Hannity mused that one of the most potent weapons against Lieberman was their mutual admiration and the senator's appearances on Hannity's show.[53] The host explained that he liked Lieberman because "he represents a level of civility and decency. He's the last of the John F. Kennedy Democrats. Scoop Jackson. Guys who understand the need for homeland security and national security." Hannity made clear that he disagreed with Lieberman on 90 percent of the issues, but he also respected the senator as a man of honor and integrity.[54] Lamont went on to win the primary race, but Lieberman became an independent and overcame Lamont in the general election.

New York Democratic Congressman Gary Ackerman received similar plaudits from Hannity during a 2002 encounter. Ackerman shared similarities with Lieberman; both agreed with Hannity on issues related to Israel, Iraq, and national security. Ackerman had a more liberal voting record than Lieberman, with a career American Conservative Union score of 4 and a DW-NOMINATE score of −0.429, making him the 78th most liberal out of 215 House Democrats and aligned independents.[55] Yet Hannity lavished him with praise as they were wrapping up an on-air debate. "We have had shootouts on taxes, on Democratic policy," Hannity said. "But when it comes to Israel, but when it comes to police officers, when it comes to the war in Iraq, Gary, I've gotta tell you, you've been Hannitized. No honestly, you are a man of intellectual honesty and integrity and I appreciate the fact." Hannity laid it on thick, warning playfully, "You know if I endorse you anymore, you're going to get defeated by a Democrat in your district who is going to say, 'Even Hannity likes him.'" Before letting Ackerman go, Hannity reiterated that he was both a Democrat and a great guy.[56]

By contrast, hosts denigrated Democrats who refused invitations to appear. During an aside about support for police, Hannity contrasted his praise of Ackerman with criticism of then-Senator Hillary Clinton because, "There are a lot of liberal Dems, a lot of Congressmen, that refuse to come on this show. Hillary Clinton will never come on this show because she really isn't a person that has the courage of her convictions . . . she'll do media interviews only with people that like her and only if they agree to a certain set of questions ahead of time." Hannity's comments reflected a reality Pat Schroeder observed: hosts did not respect Democrats who refused to come on their shows and defend their beliefs.[57]

Yet even talented Democratic communicators, including Schroeder herself, often hesitated to appear on talk radio for reasons beyond a desire to avoid confrontation. Schroeder saw talk radio as a significant contributor to declining civility in politics, and she preferred only to appear in studio with hosts. On the phone they felt empowered to be rude, like people who shout from their cars terrible things they'd never say on the sidewalk. But she also rejected invitations from prominent conservative hosts Liddy and Michael Reagan because Reagan had falsely accused her of not knowing the words to the Pledge of Allegiance and because Liddy's success bothered her, given his checkered past. She had similar qualms about North and forced him to court her before she would chat with him on the air. He responded by sending her flowers and chocolates.[58]

Dorgan was another Democrat who understood the political importance of talk radio but also had his hesitations. Earlier in his career, he routinely joined conservative programs, including Scott Hennan's popular show in his home state of North Dakota. But over time Dorgan cut back his appearances because he found so much of the content on talk radio thoughtless and devoid of facts.[59]

While these principled stands might have been morally admirable, strategically they were shortsighted because fewer Democrats appearing on talk radio meant more listeners receiving an exclusively conservative message. And when Democrats failed to respond to charges levied against them on talk radio, the charges stuck and grew more outlandish. As DeLauro and others pointed out, Democrats' rejection of talk radio left a segment of the population unaware of what Democrats stood for and believing the worst accusations against them.[60] This may have played a role in their continuing decline in the South, in the Plains states, and in parts of the Mountain West. Notably Daschle lost his South Dakota seat in 2004, and the party lost open seats in Florida, Louisiana, South Carolina, North Carolina, and Georgia. By 2019 Democrats held only one Senate seat south of Virginia and none in the Dakotas or Nebraska, where they had held five of six before Daschle's loss. Withdrawing from talk radio meant, to an extent, withdrawing from competition—in the marketplace of ideas and in elections.

15

Disgruntled but Still Loyal— Unless You're a Moderate

Republicans had barely reassumed unified control of government when Bush's reelection campaign launched its talk radio operation. It was August 2003, more than a year before Election Day, giving the campaign far more time than its predecessors to ramp up radio outreach.

Initially Brian Walton, the campaign's radio and TV director, focused on local radio and some national conservative programs. Walton's team built relationships with key hosts, who tended to pose gentle questions. He could book surrogates, who addressed thorny, locally important issues, such as lifting steel tariffs, on the campaign's terms. While much of the media focused on the Democratic primary, talk radio gave the campaign an outlet to share messages and motivate its supporters.[1] Phil Valentine, a conservative host in Nashville, summarized the mutual benefits of the Bush reelection campaign's outreach: "They wanted to get their voice out, and I got to interview Karl Rove and Andy Card."[2]

That outreach was extensive. Kevin Madden, one of the campaign's five regional spokesmen, joked that he and his colleagues were like morning DJs because they'd be on the air from 6:00 to 7:00 a.m. doing hits with various stations. State press secretaries working under Madden spent much of their time aggressively pitching material and guests to local shows. The campaign especially relied on talk radio to get its message out in markets that had hostile print and television reporters. Madden singled out West Virginia, a state that Bush had to work to win. West Virginia had long leaned Democratic in presidential elections, and Bush had barely taken its electoral votes in 2000.[3]

But even as the Bush campaign was wielding talk radio effectively to boost the president's reelection prospects, the winds of change were blowing for another set of Republicans.

Growing Hostility

There is no single reason why the détente between talkers and moderate Republicans collapsed. Rather, one can point to a combination of business and political factors that coalesced to produce a newly strident talk radio. Some hosts may have had buyer's remorse, leading them to rethink their willingness to support or tolerate moderate Republicans. Hosts also were horrified over the free-spending George W. Bush administration. And many expressed a sense that, after incremental gains throughout the 1990s and early 2000s had delivered unified Republican government, the time had come to take the final step toward uncompromising conservatism. In 1994 Limbaugh had argued that achieving political goals was a multistep process often involving several election cycles. Ten years later conservatives were ready to realize those goals. Indeed, they were disgusted by the failure, so far, of unified Republican governance to achieve the policy outcomes they desired.

Furthermore, during the second half of the 2000s, hosts might have become more conservative, less pragmatic, and less willing to countenance compromise. They would have been joining their audience on this journey.[4] With each passing year, hosts also increasingly had to contend with the explosion in conservative media, which drove them toward more rigidly right-wing positions. To differentiate themselves and compete for audience share, they embraced ever-more-extreme ideology and rhetoric. And after Democrats regained control of Congress in 2006—the first time they had controlled both houses since talk radio gained national prominence in the mid-1990s—conservative talkers likely felt liberated to challenge Republican apostates because they no longer had to worry about risking the party's majority.

Regardless of their reasoning, hosts steadily adopted a more combative posture toward moderates as the 2000s progressed. Hosts pride themselves on being consistent, even stubborn, exponents of their beliefs. But if their beliefs did not change, their behavior certainly did.

By the mid-2000s national hosts wanted moderate Republicans on their programs essentially for the same reasons they wanted Democrats: to produce confrontational, audience-gripping radio. Democrats, and now moderates, weren't invited on air so they could have a fair chance to persuade listeners. Hosts wanted punching bags and verbal combatants. Virginia Representative Tom Davis, a moderate and former Republican leader, learned as much from his appearances on Ingraham's program. He went on a few times, only to discover that Ingraham wanted to make an example of him.[5] Connecticut Republican Chris Shays had his own such experience when he joined Hannity. After Shays got off the air, Hannity misrepresented the campaign finance reform legislation he was championing in the House. Shays jumped back on the phone and asked Hannity to let him clarify. Hannity acquiesced, but he never again had Shays as a guest.[6]

Hosts' handling of Arlen Specter's 2004 campaign vividly demonstrated talk radio's changing mentality toward moderates. The Pennsylvania senator's DW-NOMINATE score of 0.068 was the second most moderate of any Republican senator.[7] Specter fit his state, with its long tradition of electing moderate Republicans such as Hugh Scott, Richard Schweiker, William Scranton, John Heinz, and Tom Ridge. After narrowly capturing his seat in 1980, Specter dispatched Democratic challengers comfortably in 1986 and 1998. (His 1992 campaign was nastier and far more closely contested, after he enraged the left by interrogating Anita Hill during the Clarence Thomas hearings.) Specter also beat back primary challenges from the right during all his reelection campaigns.[8]

By 2004 Specter was a popular four-term senator. With credentials like that, mortality should have been the only threat to his seat. Instead Specter confronted the most serious primary challenger he would ever face from the right.[9] The conservative Club for Growth backed his opponent, Congressman Pat Toomey, while Specter maintained the support of the Republican establishment, including President Bush. Party brass fretted that Toomey wouldn't win the general election in a state that had gone Democratic in three straight presidential elections. Such worries appear well-founded: while Specter won reelection by 590,954 votes, President Bush lost Pennsylvania by 144,248 votes, a clear indication that moderation was critical to victory in the state.[10]

Limbaugh's handling of the race reflected the old style on conservative talk radio. He wasn't wild about Specter, but he wasn't trying to push the senator out, either. Limbaugh discussed the race occasionally, and, as the election approached, he pointed out to listeners that a big upset was possible.[11] Owing perhaps to his pragmatic impulses, Limbaugh didn't rabidly attack Specter. In addition the senator had always been available to Limbaugh, which might have earned him the host's respect.[12]

On one occasion Limbaugh informed listeners that Specter stood to benefit from George Soros's $50,000 donation to the Republican Mainstream Partnership, even as the liberal billionaire was pouring millions into the effort to topple President Bush. Yet, rather than endorse Toomey or hammer Specter, Limbaugh gave the senator the opportunity to defend himself on air. Specter told listeners he had no idea that Soros had made the contribution and denied having anything to do with it. Limbaugh even permitted Specter to claim he had "no connection with the Mainstream Partnership," when in fact, as *National Review* pointed out, Specter was a member of the organization.[13] Limbaugh speculated that the donation could be a setup to tarnish Specter; "There's been no indication Soros is supportive of you prior to this, so it sort of stunk," he said. In fact, as Specter then admitted, Soros had contributed to him in 1996. But the senator downplayed that donation. Finally, when Limbaugh grilled Specter on issues, the host stuck to the senator's comfort zone. Specter was able to trumpet positions that placed him well within the conservative camp, rather than account for his deviations from orthodoxy.[14] After the interview Limbaugh refused a request for equal time from the Toomey campaign.[15]

While Limbaugh protected Specter, albeit without endorsing him, other national hosts such as Lars Larson thought Specter was too moderate and wanted him out. As the race tightened, critical hosts amped up their coverage and their support for Toomey. Radio play drove funds to the Toomey campaign and the Club for Growth.[16] Most of Pennsylvania's significant local hosts backed Toomey, though cautiously, to avoid antagonizing the senator in case he won reelection.[17] One exception was Philadelphia star Michael Smerconish, who championed Specter to such a degree that he earned the first thank-you of the senator's eventual victory speech.[18] Specter turned back Toomey 51 to 49 percent.

Talk radio's widespread opposition to Specter's reelection was especially striking considering that he was a longtime friend of the medium. Specter had cultivated talk radio hosts over the years and plowed advertising dollars into stations. That didn't mean every host liked him, but even critical voices tended to treat him fairly. Yet all that mutual goodwill earned Specter little aid come 2004 primary season. It was a sign of things to come. By 2009 Specter switched parties after concluding that he couldn't win another Republican nomination.[19]

Another illustration of talk radio's competing ideological and pragmatic impulses came a year after Specter's heart-attack win over Toomey. In November 2005 Limbaugh read on air the names of Congressional Republicans who voted against drilling for oil in the Arctic National Wildlife Refuge (ANWR). Again he noted that these apostates were winning praise for their position from the Soros-funded Republican Mainstream Partnership. He likened the offending representatives to Mafia sellouts.

> It is just unacceptable when a tiny, tiny, tiny fraction of Republicans in Congress also rear up in opposition and join the liberal Democrats to derail an agenda. . . . Your family is your family, and when you go to battle with other families, folks, you want your family on your side, not joining the family across the street firing back at you—and that's what's happening here, and it's because liberals hate conservatives and liberals fear conservatives. I don't care if they're Republican liberals or Democrat liberals, they're still liberals. They're not "moderates." Don't hit me with that. There's no such thing as a moderate. A moderate is just a liberal disguise, and they are doing everything they can to derail the conservative agenda.

But while Limbaugh's tongue-lashing couldn't have been politically comfortable for many of these Republicans, the host didn't call for their defeat.[20] He wanted listeners to know who the ANWR traitors were, the better to pressure them on future votes. Weighing pragmatic and partisan considerations when evaluating Republicans was not yet heretical, but the day was coming.

Anger toward moderates reflected broader frustration with the results of unified Republican government. Conservatives fumed about President Bush's spending and immigration policies and many had opposed the addition of a prescription drug benefit to Medicare. The right also staged a full-scale revolt, aided and abetted by talk radio, when Bush nominated his White House counsel, Harriet Miers, to the Supreme Court in 2005.[21] Ingraham, for one, was proud that she helped torpedo Miers's nomination.[22]

By the fall of 2006, the fissures in the GOP–talk radio alliance were obvious, and hosts had a choice to make. Would they come out in force for Republicans in the midterms, or would they instead hang back as voter frustration turned into electoral rebellion? Congressional Republicans knew they needed all the help they could get: the president's party traditionally fares poorly in his second midterm election, and the tumultuous Iraq War and bungled response to Hurricane Katrina were not helping.[23] Add to those a wave of scandals afflicting Congressional Republicans, and 2006 was looking bleak. Any hope of holding Congress rested on strong base turnout.

Against these headwinds, the administration doubled down on talk radio. In mid-September Bush invited Hannity, Ingraham, Boortz, Medved, and fellow big-time national host Mike Gallagher to the White House for a private, off-the-record meeting. They wouldn't be able to quote the president on their shows, but they would be able to convey to listeners his tone, demeanor, and general sentiments and their overall impressions.

Over the course of ninety minutes, Bush presented his case to the hosts. They liked what they heard. Gallagher was amazed at the president's warmth, humor, and passion. Boortz left the meeting certain of Bush's sincerity. Boortz described a devout president who truly believed that anyone who shared his faith in God would have a burning desire to be free—an ideal that motivated his decision-making in Iraq. Boortz also came away understanding that Bush was "absolutely convinced" the United States would prevail in Iraq and in the war on terror. Both hosts shared these observations with their listeners. Medved, too, gave his audience a taste of Bush's thinking on policy and the upcoming elections.

The meeting offered the hosts an opportunity to see Bush at his best: in private. Bush was cautious in the presence of cameras and satellites that beamed his every word around the world. Behind closed doors, however, he was engaging and candid, which impressed and reassured the hosts.[24] Bush also used the opportunity to query hosts about how listeners were feeling on key issues.[25]

A month later, with Election Day just a few weeks away, the Bush team again turned to talk radio to tamp down conservative anger and keep the base engaged. Forty-two hosts descended on the White House, where they sat in a tent broadcasting interviews with a steady stream of high-profile guests. As the biggest star present, Hannity scored interviews with Vice President Cheney, Secretary of State Condoleezza Rice, and Defense Secretary Donald Rumsfeld.[26]

The meeting, the talk radio day, and other outreach undoubtedly helped Republicans' cause with talk radio. Many hosts were as disgruntled with

Bush's policies as their listeners were, but in 2006 talk radio again embraced the more traditional side of its party-leadership role, boosting GOP candidates and setting aside criticisms until after the election. Hosts might have let Republicans hang, or even stoked right-wing fury. Instead they used their position to calm, or postpone, the outpouring of conservative displeasure. It was a task to which talk radio was ideally suited.

During the campaign Hannity seemed to be everywhere for Republicans. He headlined events for, among others, Arizona Representative J. D. Hayworth; Wisconsin, Ohio, and Michigan gubernatorial candidates Mark Green, Ken Blackwell, and Dick Devos; Pennsylvania Senator Rick Santorum; and Maryland Senate candidate Michael Steele. The host promoted Steele's candidacy, and many others', on the air. Hannity also accompanied Florida Senate candidate Katherine Harris on a bus tour and held fundraisers for Santorum and Virginia Senator George Allen.[27] Hannity's aid extended to lower-profile Republicans as well. He invited little-known challenger Diana Irey on his show to solicit donations for her campaign against veteran Pennsylvania Representative John Murtha. Hannity exhorted listeners to contribute and volunteer through her website.[28] This sort of appearance could generate a financial windfall for an under-the-radar Republican: a ten-second mention on a popular show was all it took to reach the national network of donors who paid close attention to conservative talk radio.

By this point the Internet had strengthened the role of talk radio hosts in Republican fundraising by lowering the barrier of entry for donors. In contrast to the cumbersome and relatively time-consuming process of contributing by mail, the Web allowed for "impulse" donations. When a conversation between a host and a candidate moved a listener to donate, online tools gave him a chance to do so before changing his mind.[29]

In addition to helping fill the GOP's coffers, hosts dipped adroitly into their rhetorical toolbox to frame the election on Republicans' behalf. Hosts minimized the party's foibles, downplayed and countered Democrats' strongest arguments, and primed audiences to focus on Republicans' best traits.[30] To demoralized Republicans who complained that there was no difference between the parties, Medved pointed out that Republicans had lowered taxes every year since President Bush entered office, whereas Democrats increased taxes many times during the Clinton presidency and wanted to raise them again. Medved acknowledged that Republicans had not gone far enough to reduce the size and capacity of government, but he counseled that having Democrats in power would undermine any chance of achieving that goal. As Medved put it, one party was capable of making progress, and the other was not. There would be a time to prod Republicans, to shame them into actually living up to conservative principles. But that time wasn't during the critical campaign. Like Limbaugh before him, Medved made a case for electing imperfect Republicans, even while recognizing his listeners' frustration.[31]

Hosts also did their best to make Democrats look ominous, to scare wavering listeners back into the fold. Hannity warned that Michigan Representative John Conyers, who would chair the House Judiciary Committee if Democrats gained control of the House, was laying the groundwork to impeach President Bush. Hannity observed that even a bare majority in the House would enable Democrats to impeach Bush. "Don't think these hate-Bush people wouldn't do it," he cautioned. "It's all at stake."[32] A few days later he warned again, "Don't think it can't happen. It can happen."[33]

Perhaps the best summation of talk radio's posture that fall came from Nashville host Steve Gill. "The Republicans certainly deserve to get spanked," he told the *Washington Post*'s Howard Kurtz during the talk radio day at the White House. "The problem is, if you turn the Senate over to Hillary [Clinton] and Ted Kennedy, and Nancy Pelosi in the House, it's America that gets spanked."[34]

Grudging though their support was, hosts came out in top form. And Republicans were grateful for the help. With scandals swirling, the 2006 midterm was a moment of crisis for the GOP—just the sort of situation in which Republicans most needed to take advantage of talk radio. In the 1990s, whenever Newt Gingrich had faced a barrage of criticism, he'd pop onto Rush Limbaugh's show for a chat.[35] In 2006 Republicans had many more options to choose from, and they were keen to talk. With so much on the line and new problems arising seemingly every minute, Republicans had to hustle. Hosts had no trouble scoring exclusive interviews with the principal figures of the biggest stories.[36]

It was conservative radio that came to the rescue during one of the most significant scandals Republicans faced that fall. Allegations of improper relationships with teenage House pages had surfaced against Florida Representative Mark Foley, and the press and even conservative critics were asking questions about Speaker Hastert's response. Hastert claimed he learned about Foley's behavior from news stories, but evidence showed that he knew months before the story broke yet took no action. A decade later

Hastert's behavior looked far more sinister, after the world discovered that he had molested teenagers during his days as a high school wrestling coach.[37] But in 2006 Hastert could still seek refuge in conservative radio. Amid condemnation and calls for his resignation, Hastert talked with at least nine national hosts. When Limbaugh suggested to him that the uproar over the scandal reflected an attempt by Democrats and the liberal media to suppress conservative turnout in the elections, Hastert was only too ready to agree.[38]

Ron Bonjean, Hastert's communications director at the time, acknowledged that talk radio was a lifeline in choppy waters. Talking exclusively to friendly hosts ensured an embattled Republican leader would avoid journalists' questions while getting his message out. Reporters still needed quotes from Hastert, so they were forced to repeat what he said on radio shows.[39]

As Election Day drew closer, talk radio got a chance to do what it did best: boost Republicans by blowing up an unimportant story that cast a Democrat in a bad light. Republicans often employed talk radio to share these sometimes-unverified, sometimes-salacious stories with their base and wedge them into mainstream media coverage. At other times, talk radio could originate such stories on its own and force the political class and the press to address them.

That was the case when, on the eve of the midterms, Senator Kerry attempted to tell a scripted joke during an appearance at a college. Kerry, who was not known for his humor, flubbed the punchline. "Education, if you make the most of it, you study hard, you do your homework and you make an effort to be smart, you can do well," the senator said, by way of setup. "And if you don't, you get stuck in Iraq."[40] It was supposed to be a zinger directed at President Bush, but Kerry omitted a crucial word from the prepared text: "you get *us* stuck in Iraq." What came out of his mouth sounded like a slap in the face of America's soldiers.

Initially the gaffe received little attention, but that changed when Los Angeles host John Ziegler happened to catch a local news report that mentioned the remark in passing. Ziegler played the clip ten times during his three-hour show. Bloggers picked it up from Ziegler's website, prompting conservative news aggregator Matt Drudge to promote the clip prominently on his site, the Drudge Report. Drudge's site was the online equivalent of a billboard that the entire media drove past, and from there the story went viral. The next morning Senator John McCain, a decorated veteran and friend of Kerry's, demanded that Kerry apologize. The story led the day's news cycle.[41] Democrats had to disavow Kerry's statement, and some candidates canceled scheduled events with him.[42]

Talk radio dug in, refusing to let the story fade from view. A few days later, Milwaukee star Charlie Sykes posted on his website a picture of American servicemen holding up an intentionally misspelled sign reading, "HALP US JON CARRY—WE R STUCK HEAR N IRAK."[43] The image generated so much online traffic that it crashed Sykes's Web server.[44] Again, the mainstream media jumped on the story. Finally, Limbaugh asked Bush about Kerry's quip, and journalists dutifully reported Bush's response.[45]

The verbal equivalent of a typo earned Kerry three separate humiliations in the mainstream media and distracted from Democrats' message on the eve of Election Day, all thanks to talk radio's tenacity and creativity. Kerry wasn't even on the ballot that year; the national media might never have paid attention if talk radio hadn't pushed the story. But hosts saw an opportunity to discredit a well-known Democratic messenger and, in so doing, paint all the Democratic candidates with the same brush. Advancing familiar conservative radio themes, the story suggested that Democrats in general were weak on defense and unfriendly toward the military. They were haughty elitists who looked down their noses at average Americans. It was great radio and good politics.

In the campaign's final week, hosts closed by urging listeners to go to the polls. On the day before the election, Hannity hosted several vulnerable Republicans, informing his audience that there were five races within one to three points. "There is hope," he said. "That means there is opportunity. That means you have an unbelievable responsibility as you head into the voting booth tomorrow. If you were thinking about being lazy, tomorrow's not the day to do this. If you don't want to see Nancy Pelosi third in line for the presidency. . . . Your destiny, your power comes tomorrow." A few minutes later, he exhorted, "There are more people in the collective talk radio audience, that if everybody voted, and was resolute in their defying of the news media and defying these liberal polls, you could have a significant impact on all of these races. A lot of these polls are unreliable; I don't know how these elections will turn out and frankly, neither do they."[46] Limbaugh, too, questioned the polls. He argued that they were simply a new way for the "drive-by media" to report faux news and help Democrats.

Although he rarely hosted guests, Limbaugh welcomed both Republican Senate leader-in-waiting Mitch McConnell and White House Press Secretary Tony Snow on the eve of Election Day. Limbaugh and McConnell worked in tandem, prodding listeners to vote. Later in the show, a caller reported receiving a robocall from Limbaugh encouraging her to vote Republican and warning of the consequences should Democrats prevail.[47]

Thus, even as Republican behavior left hosts dissatisfied, they protected the party's interests. They devised frames to motivate their listeners to support Republicans, while deferring attempts to correct the party's wayward trajectory until after they had vanquished the threat from Democrats.

But one class of Republicans didn't receive the benefit of the doubt from talk radio in 2006: moderates. The campaign marked another escalation along the road from détente to outright warfare. The main front in the battle against moderates in 2006 was the Rhode Island Senate primary, which pitted incumbent moderate Republican Lincoln Chafee against Stephen Laffey, the conservative mayor of a Providence suburb. Talk radio's treatment of Chafee was a clear signal that hosts' priorities were tipping away from pragmatism and toward purity.

Chafee, with his DW-NOMINATE score of 0.003, hugged the center. He was arguably the only Republican capable of winning a Senate race in liberal Rhode Island, where Democrats had won the last five presidential elections by 21, 29, 33, 18, and 11.5 points, respectively.[48] Chafee also hailed from local royalty: his father John had served as governor in the 1960s and occupied what would become his son's Senate seat from 1976 until he died in office in 1999. The younger Chafee succeeded him and was elected in his own right in 2000.

The Republican establishment, including the National Republican Senatorial Committee, rallied aggressively behind Chafee. The establishment feared that Laffey would lose the general election, potentially costing Republicans their precarious Senate majority. Yet radio hosts vehemently opposed Chafee's reelection, regardless of the consequences. In July 2006, infuriated by Chafee's apparent advocacy of a cease-fire between Israel and Lebanon, Limbaugh railed against the senator. "He needs to be defeated. It's about time we get rid of these—whatever you want to characterize Linc Chafee as being—out of the Senate."[49] A couple weeks later Limbaugh summed up his attitude toward Chafee and moderates generally: "May as well have a Democrat."[50]

Even Hugh Hewitt, perhaps the firmest party stalwart among conservative hosts, publicly opposed Chafee's reelection. It was the first time in fifteen years on the air that Hewitt came out against a Republican. Hewitt supported other moderates, including Specter in 2004. But Chafee crossed a line by voting against the party on several litmus-test issues, including the invasion of Iraq and the confirmation of Supreme Court Justice Samuel Alito. Chafee didn't even vote for President Bush's reelection. As far as Hewitt was concerned, Chafee simply wasn't a Republican.[51] After Chafee won the primary, Hewitt labeled the victory "an unfortunate development" and reaffirmed his belief that Chafee's defeat would be in the best interest of the party. Extending his principled stand, Hewitt even refused to donate to the National Republican Senatorial Committee because it supported Chafee.[52]

Ultimately talk radio, for all its bluster, did not have much impact on the outcome of the race. Chafee won the primary but lost the general election, a contest in which talk radio was inconsequential. But the medium showed some muscle anyway, helping to generate out-of-state contributions for Laffey. Only 16 percent of individual contributions to Laffey's campaign came from within Rhode Island.[53]

An exchange between Hannity and caller Ken on August 4 laid bare the tension between hosts' pragmatic impulses and their disgust with RINOs such as Chafee. Ken railed about a few RINOs and charged that if Republicans lost in November it would be their own fault. He warned RINOs they would pay a price if they didn't start meeting the expectations of the voters who elected them. Hannity agreed and expanded Ken's list of RINOs to include maverick Senators McCain, Chuck Hagel of Nebraska, and Lindsey Graham of South Carolina. All three had compiled far more conservative voting records than Specter or Chafee, but they hailed from conservative states and had bucked Republicans—and conservative hosts—on a few high-profile issues such as immigration.

Their inclusion in Hannity's rogues gallery indicated not only that moderation was becoming less acceptable to hosts, but also that hosts were expanding the definition of impermissible moderation. To New York Representative Sherwood Boehlert, the notion that his former classmate McCain was a fellow moderate was just silly. "McCain is no more moderate than I am a Communist," Boehlert quipped. "He's not moderate; he's very conservative."[54] The pool of ideological moderates had diminished to such a degree—Boehlert himself was retiring—that any dissent, even from otherwise conservative politicians, shone in stark relief.[55] Republicans, Hannity argued, had weakened their standing with their base by allowing closeted liberals such as McCain, Hagel, and Graham to "maneuver more left-wing positions" onto their agenda.

Importantly both Hannity and caller Ken resolved that they still had no better option than these RINOs. As the host put it, the sins of moderates were nothing compared to the risk of "Nancy Pelosi being speaker and third in line to the presidency."[56] This conclusion reflected a dilemma experienced throughout talk radio. As far as hosts and listeners were concerned, it was high time elected Republicans started acting on the conservative principles they espoused in campaigns. Yet talk radio was still following Limbaugh's earlier recommendation that incremental change was the way forward.

Despite talk radio's best efforts, the 2006 elections went poorly for Republicans—moderates and conservatives alike. Democrats regained control of both houses of Congress. But if anyone thought that talk radio's impact was diminishing, such notions would soon be erased by the medium's vigorous intervention in the immigration debate. It would prove to be the biggest policy fight of Bush's final two years in office, and its outcome would be decided in large part by talk radio.

16

The Titans of Talk 1 - Bipartisanship 0

WHEN IT COMES to public policy, talk radio has left its most indelible mark on immigration reform, or the lack thereof. The issue fit talk radio perfectly. Complicated policy specifics could be distilled into the simple black-and-white themes talk radio had long since made its own. Hosts could rail against soft-on-crime, weak-on-national-security liberals who rewarded lawbreaking. And hosts could trumpet "American culture," the well-being of American workers, and the preservation of the Republican Party. Repeated attempts at immigration reform also gave hosts multiple chances to take aim at compromise measures supported by both party establishments. Elite bipartisanship was inherently suspect in talk radio's world, an easy bogeyman given the framing of Washington insiders and dealmakers as enemies of hosts' and listeners' shared values.

Momentum for a comprehensive legislative solution to the vexing, multifaceted problem of illegal immigration started building on Capitol Hill in 2001. President Bush seemed open to a path toward legal status for undocumented immigrants, and the Senate odd couple of arch-conservative Kansan Sam Brownback and liberal-lion Ted Kennedy was working on a legislative fix. Brownback saw supporting immigration reform as a profoundly conservative endeavor because, in his view, reform would spur economic growth and fulfill biblical injunctions to care for orphans, strangers, and foreigners.[1]

But 9/11 changed the electorate's mood.[2] Before the attacks nativists had been struggling to find a message that connected with voters. As longtime immigration reform activist Marshall Fitz put it, after 9/11 nativists' "fear of the other" translated into national security terms. Anti-reform groups ran ads featuring the hijackers and the towers, driving home visceral warnings about invading immigrants and the dangers they posed. Conservative media joined the fear-mongering, helping to move public opinion against the sorts of legislative proposals Washington was considering. Fitz and other reform advocates devoted all their time to combating misinformation disseminated by conservative media, including Fox News, then-CNN host Lou Dobbs, and local and national talk radio.[3] This new political climate killed the nascent bipartisan immigration effort in the Senate.

After President Bush won reelection in 2004, he selected Social Security reform over immigration reform as his top domestic priority. Nonetheless the Senate again tried to inch immigration reform forward. But talk radio passionately decried what hosts viewed as amnesty. During the summer of 2005, the Minutemen, a group whose members advocated for border security and went on border patrols, became a staple on talk radio and cable television.[4]

Hosts left the studio to emcee events and encouraged listeners to rally against illegal immigration. Hosts also freely blasted President Bush on the issue. Roger Hedgecock took his advocacy a step further by organizing the now-annual Hold Their Feet to the Fire lobbying trip in partnership with the Federation for American Immigration Reform (FAIR), a restrictionist group. Hosts from across the country descended on Washington with several hundred "listener lobbyists" trained by FAIR. The hosts broadcast live from a makeshift radio row, and the citizen lobbyists met with legislators and their staff.[5] As early as 2005, these trips appeared to pay dividends. Host Lars Larson told *Talkers Magazine* that when that year's trip arrived in Washington, the visitors learned to their dismay that the Real ID Act was dead. The legislation, which established federal standards for state-issued drivers' licenses and other ID cards and prohibited federal agencies from accepting state IDs that did not meet these standards, was a priority for immigration hard-liners. By the second day of lobbying and broadcasting, the bill was headed into law with support from President Bush and even some Democrats.[6]

In December 2005 the Republican-controlled House, partly inspired by talk radio's activism, passed a punitive, enforcement-only bill that criminalized violations of immigration law, such as being in the country illegally. The bill also funded enhanced border security. None of its provisions offered benefits for guest workers or a pathway to legalization for those already in the United States.[7] The bill sparked a massive backlash. Opponents, some organized by Latino radio, marched in the street.

The spring of 2006 featured a duel between liberal reformers and immigration hawks, supported by Latino and conservative media, respectively. Each camp jockeyed to influence the ongoing legislative debate in the Senate.[8]

The rhetoric on conservative radio was stern. Liddy warned his audience that the Senate was trying to shove an amnesty bill down their throats and urged listeners to call their senators. He accused President Bush of disingenuously supporting renewable green cards for guest workers that would allow them to stay in the country forever. The host also went after Bush for supposedly encouraging illegal immigrants to have "anchor babies"—children whose birthright citizenship would eventually lead to regularized status for everyone in their family. An outside group bought commercial time on one of Liddy's Tennessee affiliates to urge Bill Frist, the Tennessee senator and Republican majority leader, to support effective immigration enforcement legislation. The ad ominously warned Frist not to back down.[9]

Limbaugh spent more than two months criticizing the Senate bill and Republican motivations.

> Reform, my rear end! . . . Even if we stipulate that a guest worker program helps to deal with people who are here illegally, how does that help stem the flow of future illegals? It does just the opposite. It's going to increase it. . . .
>
> The illegal influx continues, and the politics of this has to make you laugh. It cracks me up. It probably makes you laugh, too. They argue that we need to attract this vote. You know the best vote, the highest Hispanic vote total George W. Bush ever got, was about 44 percent when he ran for governor of Texas. So if we continue to get a smaller percentage of the vote by a growing community in this country, will we win elections? We ought to be talking about taking our principles to all people regardless of race or religion and win the day with those arguments, not by pandering and embracing illegal behavior.
>
> You've got some elites in Washington who are just hell-bent on this election angle, and they're worried that too much focus on keeping the illegal immigrants out of the country will make the Republican Party a minority party for the long term—and

they call people like me "nativists." Yeah nativists, xenophobes, racists, what have you. I mean, it's quite interesting. But what good is being a Republican or a conservative if you're going to throw it all out in order to attract certain votes from people who have grown up and been weaned on an entitlement mentality and expect that?[10]

Limbaugh argued that a cabal of moderate Republican dealmakers, conspiring with leadership, was using secrecy and subterfuge to get the bill passed, a clear suggestion that they were trying to pull a fast one on conservative members and voters.

I am told that basically five Republican senators were holed up last night trying to put together some sort of face-saving compromise. Those senators are McCain, Hagel, Specter, Mel Martinez, and Frist, and the other Republican senators had no idea what they were doing. The initial bill that came out of this committee was 500 pages long, and they're trying to push it through today without anybody having had a chance to read it. That's why you're seeing stories that Republicans are prepared to filibuster their own bill. Yes. Republicans are preparing to filibuster this thing if it comes up for a vote, because they don't know what's in it and they weren't included in the hole-in-the-wall gang that was working on this last night to put this together.

"I don't know that I have ever seen anything like this," he concluded. "Security is *secondary*. The rule of law is *secondary*. All these clowns are doing is blatantly buying votes by making more citizens."[11]

In spite of talk radio's opposition and some initial procedural defeats, in May 2006 the Senate passed, sixty-two to thirty-six, a bipartisan immigration reform bill sponsored by Kennedy and McCain.[12] But the bill was vastly different from the House's immigration bill, and the House refused to impanel a conference committee to hash out the incompatibilities. Instead House leaders intended to use the issue to rally the conservative base during the 2006 midterms.[13]

The campaign was a crushing loss for Republicans, as Democrats gained control of the House and Senate. That seemingly made 2007 the moment for immigration reform: both the Democratic majority in Congress and the Republican president supported it. A bipartisan group in the Senate, along with the Bush administration, spent months fashioning a new bill.

According to Joel Kaplan, the deputy White House chief of staff, the specter of talk radio hovered in the background. Republicans tried to address the right's objections to the 2006 bill, understanding that, if they didn't, their effort faced a potentially fatal response on the AM dial.[14] In deference to the Republican base, McCain assumed a lesser role in negotiations—a sign of problems that lay ahead for his 2008 presidential campaign.[15] In his place was Arizona colleague Jon Kyl, who thought the 2006 bill was "a very bad piece of legislation" that "went way too far in terms of amnesty." Kyl believed that, with Democrats controlling Congress, someone like him needed to get involved to shape a bill that was as "benign as possible" and that could otherwise achieve Republican objectives. Graham joined the process, with Kennedy continuing to take the lead for Democrats.[16]

The negotiations generated real optimism from President Bush and congressional leaders. Larson recalled an event where the president confidently told onlookers he would see them at the signing ceremony.[17] But the bill failed on the Senate floor in large part because conservative radio hosts, their guests, and pressure groups advertising on talk programs galvanized a huge grassroots outcry against the bill. Opponents blasted the bill for providing amnesty to illegal immigrants without adequately securing the border.[18] Speaking for most talk hosts, Limbaugh declared that the bill would "fundamentally, and perhaps permanently, alter American society for the worse." He dubbed the legislation the Comprehensive Destruction of the Republican Party Act of 2007. "It is an utter disaster," he said, "and it must be defeated. There's no middle ground here."[19]

According to one Senate Republican staffer who watched the process unfold, talk radio was able to exploit a tactical blunder on the part of the negotiating group. After agreeing on the framework of the bill, the senators held a press conference to explain its provisions in general terms. But there was not yet any legislative language indicating how the federal code would change. Talk radio filled in the details with its own interpretation of what the bill would do.[20] True, hosts and listeners probably would have pilloried the bill as amnesty regardless. But, as another staffer conceded, the drafting process was a nightmare, producing a sloppy product that left the effort vulnerable to attacks.[21]

The onslaught began in March, two months before the Senate even debated the bill. Kyl, Lott, Chambliss, and other Republicans found their offices inundated with negative feedback. Lott received death threats. Lott and Chambliss liked to answer the phones themselves, so they knew conservatives were apoplectic. When Chambliss informed swearing, raging callers that they were talking to the senator, and started to tell them about the bill, he could hear them "gasping for air"—they were prepared to eviscerate a staffer, but they never expected to talk to the senator himself. Utah Republican Senator Bob Bennett paid staffers a bonus for handling the volume of vituperative phone calls he received as the Senate debated the bill.[22]

In May, with the Senate debate now under way, Hedgecock brought Hold Their Feet to the Fire 2007 to Washington. The week-long extravaganza included more than forty hosts, who reached 75 percent of the national radio market, imploring listeners to call senators. On the last day, there were enough callers to shut down the Capitol Hill switchboard. Three hundred and fifty citizen lobbyists descended on Capitol Hill. They also used nascent social media to swamp senators with messages.[23] According to a Pew study, between mid-May and mid-June talk radio hosts devoted 23 percent of their airtime to denouncing the immigration bill.[24]

Crucially, in the middle of the debate, Congress jetted off on its annual Memorial Day recess. Before the recess the bill's supporters believed that sixty senators were prepared to vote for it, which would have been enough to shatter a filibuster. The recess, however, gave grassroots conservatives and conservative media an opportunity to demonstrate to senators just how unpopular the bill was with their constituents. (Some liberal groups, such as organized labor, had other reasons to oppose the bill; they also used the recess to air their displeasure to senators visiting home.)[25] When the Senate resumed debate after the recess, the bill's prospects had dimmed. Supporters found themselves unable to secure a sixtieth vote.

Chambliss and fellow Georgia Senator Johnny Isakson cosponsored the bill, but, after withering attacks from talk radio and outcry from constituents, they joined the opposition. Chambliss admitted that he and Isakson could have done more to communicate with constituents about the bill. The information vacuum gave opponents—who would have rejected any immigration reform, and some of whom profited from their opposition— an opportunity to fill in gaps. They did just that, taking over the airwaves with what Chambliss called the "magic word": amnesty. During the Senate debate, Chambliss and Isakson flew to Atlanta for the Georgia Republican

Convention. Such was the buzz surrounding the bill that, on the drive to the convention site, Chambliss's wife called him to ask what in the world he had done to infuriate people. In his convention speech, Chambliss addressed the issue directly, prompting five convention attendees in the back of the room to boo him. The heckling made national headlines. One of the hecklers called Chambliss the next week to apologize.[26]

Senators had little success quelling the discontent on talk radio. Chambliss consulted with the Atlanta-based Boortz, but, as the senator's spokeswoman put it, Boortz "popped us pretty good."[27] When Kyl tried to engage old friends on talk radio, many no longer wanted to talk to him; the hosts on Phoenix station KFYI, where Kyl appeared regularly, were at least courteous enough to allow him on for a "constructive conversation," even as they disagreed. Kyl also conversed with Hugh Hewitt. The host was convalescing from a back injury when the Senate negotiators unveiled the bill; without much else to do, he read page after page of the text. Hewitt concluded that it provided "blanket amnesty" and proposed changes to Kyl. The senator turned around and introduced several of them as amendments.[28] But that didn't mollify opponents in conservative media. Michael Savage bluntly warned senators, "We will deport you from office."[29]

Conservative talkers also skewered guests from the Bush administration. Ed Gillespie, a veteran Republican Party hand and Bush counselor, had to survive some tough interviews. Deputy Press Secretary Tony Fratto equated his dealings with hosts to "whack-a-mole" because there were "a lot more of them than there were of us." At times, Fratto said, it seemed like hosts just wanted to attack guests trying to sell or explain the plan, not engage them. "You could be explaining it all you want, and they'd just call it amnesty."[30]

At the height of the debate, Lott's frustration boiled over. Talk radio was "running America," he complained. "We have to deal with that problem."[31] Hosts and listeners pounced. Limbaugh used Lott's comments to reframe the debate over the "amnesty bill" as "a battle between Washington and the people." Supposed conservatives were selling out the base, "and they know it. So you got a Republican talking about talk radio the way liberals talk about talk radio, which tells you—it tells me—what the real objective of most elected officials in Washington is anyway. It's to perpetuate themselves and their jobs and to spend money."[32] Ratcheting up the pressure, Limbaugh read on air the names of each Republican senator who voted to cut off debate.[33]

Heading into the climactic floor vote, leaders had commitments from fifty-nine senators to vote to cut off debate. But once it became clear that the last vote wasn't forthcoming, leaders released senators from their pledges.[34] Only forty-six senators voted to cut off debate, and the bill foundered.[35] It was a sign of how many senators, even some supporters of the bill, didn't want to be publicly associated with it.

Hold Their Feet to the Fire took credit on behalf of talk radio. Its website declared, "Hold Their Feet to the Fire successfully defeated the McCain-Kennedy-Bush amnesty bill in 2007, which was hatched in secret and sprung on the American public at the last minute with no time for review, even by lawmakers. The bill died when talk radio roared, and activists fanned out across the Capitol and citizens flooded their lawmaker's switchboard."[36] This assessment was self-serving and overstated. Nonetheless, talk radio's uncompromising position does seem to have grown more popular in the Senate. The numbers tell the story: in 2006 twenty-three of fifty-five Senate Republicans voted for immigration reform. In 2007 the bill moved significantly to the right but got less Republican support—only twelve of forty-nine Republicans voted yes on cloture.[37] It is reasonable to suspect that some of the same Republicans who backed the 2006 bill would have been even happier with the 2007 version. Yet, ten of them flipped and voted against the 2007 bill. While some likely had pledged to vote for cloture had their votes been potentially decisive, the picture was striking all the same. It was clear to many observers that conservative media deserved credit for the outcome—or blame, depending on one's position. Conservative media accepted nothing less than total opposition, and members of Congress had good reason to toe the line.

Congressman David Dreier learned as much. Back in 2004 star Los Angeles hosts John Kobylt and Ken Chiampou had taken the California Republican to task for his immigration stance. On one show they selected five Republican House members with "bad" voting records on illegal immigration for a *Survivor*-style tournament in which the hosts and their listeners would pick one to "vote off the island." Dreier, who supported a relatively free flow of goods and people across borders, got the nod. Kobylt and Chiampou invited the five lawmakers to appear on their show, but Dreier declined rather than be forced to back off his positions or else be skewered for them.[38] While immigration was a critical political issue for Kobylt and Chiampou, their beef with Dreier was also about something more fundamental: they claimed that he told constituents one thing, and voted another way. In Kobylt's words Dreier was a hypocrite, "as blatantly two-faced as a politician could be." The hosts urged Dreier's defeat in that year's midterms and invited his Democratic opponent, Cynthia Matthews, to join them at a live broadcast outside of one of Dreier's offices.[39] Many of Matthews's volunteers were Republicans.

Dreier eventually won the race, but not without a tougher fight than he had anticipated. Forced back on his heels, he spent the last two weeks of the campaign promising a new focus on immigration. He even ran ads and had robocalls featuring Governor Arnold Schwarzenegger, who, with characteristic cheesiness and bravado, proclaimed Dreier "tough as nails" on illegal immigrants. The congressman had the worst showing of his career, then twenty-five years strong.[40] He outspent Matthews dramatically and beat her back 53.6 percent to 42.8 percent in a year when President Bush won reelection and Republicans gained seats in both houses of Congress. The contrast to 2006 places the power of talk radio in sharp relief: that year Kobylt and Chiampou left Dreier alone, and he won a rematch with Matthews 57 percent to 37.9 percent during a Democratic wave election.[41]

In many ways the revolt against the 2007 immigration bill foreshadowed the right's response to the Obama presidency, especially his signature health care legislation and another attempt at a bipartisan immigration bill.[42] Like the members of Hold Their Feet to the Fire and its fellow travelers, Tea Party activists would style their movement as a populist, conservative uprising dead set against any elite-driven plans they perceived as threatening their vision of America. It didn't matter who supported these plans—Democrats, Republican elites, business interests, or all the above. Talk radio was at the center of this fray, exhorting these movements, stoking their fury, and helping to channel their passion into legislative advocacy campaigns. The outcome—derailing a major bill—was novel in 2007, but it would become familiar over the next decade, as both partisan and bipartisan legislation fell to uprisings on the right. Talk radio's role in knocking down an initiative cherished by President Bush, the most powerful Republican in Washington, offered the best evidence yet of the medium's independence from the party apparatus.[43] Talk radio was a power player in its own right, pushing its own agenda and demanding that elected officials fall in line or suffer the consequences.

17

Never a Republican Puppet

TALK RADIO'S CONTRIBUTION to the immigration debacle wasn't a re-sult of failed or insufficient Republican outreach. During the Bush years, the White House and Congressional Republicans worked hard to keep talk radio in the fold. After Bush's first pre-midterm meeting with hosts came several more. The White House selected hosts for each meeting carefully, prioritizing popular, influential, widely distributed talkers who, in combi-nation, would cover the entire country and who cared especially about the specific issues the president wished to discuss.[1] For instance, in 2007 Bush met with ten hosts for a little more than an hour to talk about foreign policy and the budget and to clear the air after talk radio had spent the spring and early summer trashing the immigration bill. Afterward Hannity got his own hour with the president.[2]

Like Hannity, Limbaugh wasn't at the group meeting. But, in his nine-teenth year on national radio, Limbaugh remained the king of talk. Bush staffers marveled at how he still drove the conversation on talk radio.[3] If the host wasn't on the guest list for the group meeting, it was only because he was too politically important to be just one among ten. Two days after the meeting, a caller asked Limbaugh why he had not joined his peers at the White House. He revealed that he had gotten something much better than even Hannity: a private audience with the president for an evening of drinks, cigars, dinner, and conversation in the White House residence.[4] A year later White House staffers would cap a week of congratulations for Limbaugh's twentieth anniversary on national radio by arranging a surprise on-air phone call from President Bush, his father, and his brother Jeb.[5]

A producer interrupted Limbaugh midsentence with a note that the president was on the phone. It was one of the few occasions in Limbaugh's lengthy career when he was flustered on the air.

Congressional Republicans also kept up their outreach to talk radio, albeit with new leaders at the helm trying to recapture the majority. In 2007 the profane, chain-smoking John Boehner, who wore his emotions on his sleeve, replaced Hastert as Republican leader while the party transitioned into the minority for the first time in thirteen years. Talk radio was a central element of Boehner's communications strategy. He continued Hastert's practice of appearing on talk radio when traveling to members' districts. Boehner also did regional or national talk radio once a week and encountered a generally friendly reception. Mindful of his constituency, he made sure to chat regularly with Cincinnati star Bill Cunningham, too.[6]

On the other side of the Capitol, Kentuckian Mitch McConnell, a master tactician and political animal, took leadership of the Senate Republicans as they too transitioned into the minority. McConnell's staff quickly diagnosed that Senate Republicans were not competing for news cycles. Their communications operation had languished and needed a refresh. To that end, they launched a communications center, with staffers designated to cultivate individual media.

The center's talk radio experts treated their medium with the same seriousness that communicators devoted to television. They developed ears for the sort of content a particular host most wanted and monitored the airwaves for opportunities. The radio staff encouraged senators to stay in touch with hosts, just as senators spoke to reporters around the Capitol daily. Stories of liberal hypocrisy were like catnip to hosts and producers, so the radio team generated downloadable audio to suit this preference. All the information shared with hosts was verified, helping to cement a strong relationship between radio producers and the communications-center staff. The radio specialists understood that making producers look good with their hosts—and providing audio, which made producers' jobs easier—improved the odds of getting clips played.[7]

One of these specialists spent virtually all day listening to shows. Each morning she would peruse the news and send hosts individually tailored updates. She aimed to make her update the first item in hosts' inboxes. She understood that if she could get one big national show to tackle a topic, other hosts would pick it up as well. Some stories fit into the category of "oh wow, this is talk radio bait, this is awesome." Other stories were better geared toward one or two particular hosts. For instance, Limbaugh was unusually interested in climate change. Part of the job was also defense. When a host said something McConnell didn't want to hear, the staffer would pass along a background document explaining the senator's point of view. At times her zealousness irritated talkers; Mark Levin complained about getting "that McConnell girl" to stop calling.

McConnell himself routinely chatted with hosts on and off the air. On the air he adhered to rigid message discipline but without sounding scripted or shutting down a topic of conversation. McConnell was an artful exploiter of the radio limelight. He was engaging and willing to talk about virtually any subject, but on his own terms. Hosts persistently wondered what his favorite bourbon was, but he would never tell. More seriously, talkers couldn't pry newsworthy soundbites from McConnell because he would always wait for the right moment to speak his mind or make any announcements on behalf of Senate Republicans. The only big reveals were the ones he intended.[8]

All of this is to say, in the final years of Bush's presidency, Republicans did just about all they could to skillfully and passionately pursue the advantages talk radio had to offer. They could hardly have been more invested. Indeed, the private meetings with talk radio hosts continued right up until the last week of Bush's presidency in January 2009, when he met with a group of ten hosts. Around the same time, Bush also had one-on-ones with Hannity and Limbaugh. It was Limbaugh's birthday—another opportunity to fete the number-one name in conservative radio. Bush's staff presented Limbaugh with a cake decorated with a chocolate microphone. The outgoing president even joined in singing "Happy Birthday." It was a sign of how far Limbaugh had come. "I just wish my parents were alive so that I could be able to show them the pictures here and to tell them about this," he told listeners.[9]

But this final White House charge, like the immigration effort, was for naught. Hosts could not be wooed so easily. For all their pro-Republican efforts, hosts weren't Republican puppets, and they let Bush know it. As he left office, he urged the hosts to give President-elect Barack Obama a chance.[10] The request was destined to fall on deaf ears. The retiring president could focus on what he thought would be good for the country, which meant giving Obama the best shot at a successful presidency. Hosts had other goals. Their listeners felt great angst about Obama, the policies he campaigned on, and the onset of unified Democratic government. Whether they shared this angst or not, hosts gave voice to the sentiment, lest they find themselves squeezed out of the ever-more-crowded conservative media landscape. Two days after Bush's plea, Limbaugh incited a firestorm when he said of Obama, "I hope he fails."[11]

This was emblematic of the sometimes divergent priorities of hosts and elected Republicans. During the Bush years, no host woke up in the morning pondering how to aid the GOP that day. Instead hosts consistently prioritized good radio and the special bond with their audiences above party loyalty. As before, when Republicans controlled the levers of power, talkers were particularly allergic to the compromise required by governing. They demanded rigid adherence to their principles and policy preferences; advancing policy in a conservative direction, even amid divided government, was not enough. Only total victory sufficed. As former Congressman Bob Walker observed, the stock and trade of radio hosts was entertaining listeners with a "very sharp," unambiguous message. There was nothing "very entertaining about nuance."[12]

It is no wonder that Ed Gillespie, the former Republican staffer and RNC chairman, thought the term "coordination" ill fit his outreach to conservative talkers. While their perspective left them more open to the information he proffered than were the *New York Times* or NBC News, hosts did not simply mouth talking points.[13] Some hosts, such as Oliver North, loathed talking points because they wanted to form their own opinions.[14] And those hosts who accepted plenty of material from Republicans shared it with listeners only a fraction of the time. Conservative host Scott Hennen estimated that he accepted a tenth of the pitches from Republican operatives. Occasionally Hennen booked a guest he did not particularly want in order to help out the Bush White House or Congressional Republicans. But he wasn't, he explained, being a team player—he was trying to protect his access to guests he did want.[15]

Republican communications professionals weren't blind to such motivations. They understood that there was a transactional element to their relationship with talk radio. Several observed that hosts provided support only when they saw an opportunity for mutual benefit. These Republican communicators pointed out that, though they worked constantly to cultivate relationships with talk radio, only occasionally could they expect to flip a switch and deploy hosts for party purposes.[16] Veteran Republican hand John Feehery even saw the relationship between hosts and Republican leaders largely as "quietly antagonistic" because, on issues such as immigration, the interests of the party and of talk radio diverged so severely that hosts were never going to be an asset.[17]

Even hosts who agreed with a Republican position were mindful of their need to entertain. Theirs was a forum for lively interviews and discussions, not recitations of ponderous speeches and platform language. Hennen, for one, strove to ask a guest something he or she had not been asked fifty times already that day. He and Larson said they wanted their interviews to generate news.[18] Ingraham rejected all but the biggest-name politicians unless she thought the proposed guest had something unique or interesting to say that she couldn't say herself.[19] Hosts got fed up with the likes of future RNC Chairman Reince Priebus because he stuck rigorously to talking points and often repeated himself in multiple interviews. This rankled hosts and tempted them into asking Priebus "gotcha" questions in an effort to draw out something interesting or newsworthy.[20]

Hosts mostly refrained from discussing Republican agenda items ad nauseam for fear of boring their audiences.[21] Inescapable issues such as immigration reform could earn an exception, but even the 2007 immigration push proved the point: although the bill was the top item on the airwaves, it still accounted for less than a quarter of talk radio's content during the critical month of debate.

Similarly, talkers sometimes declined guests who had recently joined them, lest their programs get stale.[22] As a result many politicians left their pet legislation largely unmentioned during talk radio appearances and instead used the time to convince audiences of their likability and dedication to doing the right things for the country.[23] Or a guest might settle for a quid pro quo: he or she got to mention a pet bill or cause but only in exchange for discussing a topic of the host's choosing.[24]

In all these ways, hosts sought to maintain their image as independent outsiders, which was essential to their bottom line. Asserting independence meant that Washington would remain a target no matter who was in power. Hosts were acutely sensitive to accusations of carrying water for Republicans. When Dan Bartlett, who served as communications director and counselor to President Bush, told a reporter that conservative media personalities such as Hewitt "regurgitate exactly and put up on their blogs what you said to them," Hewitt howled.[25] Similarly, Milwaukee star Charlie Sykes angrily swatted aside charges that he and a colleague based their shows on Republican talking points and that they selectively disagreed with Republicans in order to fake their independence without actually posing a risk to the party. Sykes labeled the charges a liberal conspiracy.[26]

Ironically hosts' independence enhanced their power within the party coalition. Independence earned hosts credibility, which they spent mobilizing listeners behind causes. Over time, hosts' influence over party affairs grew in part because they stepped up criticism of Republicans who failed to meet their standards. This practice reinforced their independence and their role as guardians of conservative values.

But they performed a delicate dance between, on the one hand, appearing—and being—connected and, on the other, not looking like puppets. Maintaining relationships meant hosts couldn't go too far in demonstrating their independence. Hosts risked access to guests if they ambushed and trashed a Republican on air. Being disrespectful, or violating prearranged interview terms, might result in blacklisting. That threatened what hosts valued most: the quality of their programs. But while hosts might avoid ambushing a guest, talk radio still thrived on disagreement. Conflict gripped the audience. Ingraham, for one, built the second hour of her show each day around a confrontation with a guest.Ingraham's approach to these encounters was so combative that she sometimes struggled to find oppositional guests. Congressional Democrats were generally smart enough not to appear, so Ingraham and her staff often resorted to guests who were less familiar with her show. These guests didn't know that they were running into a buzz saw.[27]

Ingraham's case illustrated why eviscerating guests of any ideological stripe or sparring with a guest who wasn't prepared for it could be a bad idea: it made getting guests hard. Hosts had to husband their relationships with Republicans, just as Republicans and their handlers husbanded their relationships with talk radio. Audiences rarely knew how often their favorite hosts talked off the air with Republican officials and their staffers.

Hosts who were good at the dance only saw their power within the Republican Party mount, and everyone—listeners, elected officials, the mainstream media—could tell. On any number of occasions in the late 2000s, hosts' outrage compelled swift corrective action from Republican politicians.[28] For instance, a week after Bush left office, Republican Congressman Phil Gingrey was forced to apologize to Limbaugh. The host had criticized Republican leadership, to which Gingrey responded, "It's easy if you're Sean Hannity or Rush Limbaugh . . . to stand back and throw bricks. You don't have to try to do what's best for your people and your party. You know you're just on these talk shows and you're living well and plus you stir up a bit of controversy and gin the base and that sort of thing." The next day, with the phones in his office ringing off the hook, Gingrey rushed to reverse course, calling into Limbaugh's show, joining Boortz on air, and chatting with Hannity. Gingrey admitted to "putting my foot in my mouth," expressed regret, and described hosts as "conservative giants."[29]

Little more than a month later, RNC Chairman Michael Steele made the mistake of asserting that Limbaugh was an entertainer and decrying his program as "incendiary" and "ugly." After Limbaugh roasted Steele, the chairman too apologized and lamented that his thoughts had come out wrong.[30] It was a revealing moment: hosts gladly adopt the label of "entertainer" when they need to distance themselves from their own false statements and other failures to uphold journalistic practices, yet they bristle when others use the same label to dismiss them. But no Republican, Steele included, was interested in pointing out talk radio's hypocrisy on this front. Hosts were too powerful to antagonize.

Local hosts often held similar sway over state officials and their representatives in Congress. In 2006 a reporter dubbed Milwaukee talk titan Charlie Sykes "arguably [Wisconsin's] most influential conservative voice." Sykes considered the label "ridiculous" and "unhealthy," but Dale Schultz, a moderate Republican who had been the state senate leader, did not disagree. He lamented that WTMJ, Sykes's southeastern Wisconsin station, had "every legislator in that area shaking in their boots." After Wisconsin Senate Republican leader Scott Fitzgerald promised Sykes and his listeners that Republicans would not allow any new taxes, Schultz noted, "It's humiliating when legislators have to be hauled in there to swear allegiance."[31]

Another example of talk radio's might came courtesy of a 2007 fight between two Republicans with megawatt star power: Limbaugh and Schwarzenegger. It marked a reversal for the two men, and another sign of talk radio's rising pique with moderates. In 2003 Limbaugh had given Schwarzenegger the benefit of the doubt during a California gubernatorial recall election. The host acknowledged that the candidate was not a conservative but also reminded listeners that there were reasons to vote for him. As with Romney in 1994, Limbaugh hoped to persuade the candidate to adopt more conservative stances rather than see him lose.

By 2007, however, Schwarzenegger had been governor for three and a half years, and he and Limbaugh were engaged in a war of words over policy. It had been a civil clash, until Schwarzenegger went on national TV and dismissed Limbaugh as irrelevant—perhaps the most stinging insult one could lob at a talk radio host.[32] The moderate Schwarzenegger had little to lose: he was term limited and didn't have national political aspirations, not least because his Austrian birth precluded a run for the presidency. Yet Schwarzenegger knew he had gone too far. After insulting Limbaugh, he called the host to make nice and turn their discussion back to policy. "We'll smoke a stogie together, and we'll be talking about this from here to eternity," the governor said. "The key thing is that people should know that you and I, we don't have a fight. We don't argue over those things. We just have different opinions, and, you know, and I am enjoying that because I think the Republican Party has a big tent."[33] The attempt to placate Limbaugh vividly illustrated the host's influence, even among politicians who seemingly needed nothing from him.

In Bush's final years—with hosts savaging Republicans who failed to meet their lofty standards and Republicans prostrating themselves in fear of political repercussions—it became impossible to deny that elected officials had helped to create something of a monster. Their cultivation of talk radio had helped hosts accumulate such influence within the Republican Party that listeners had come to trust talkers more than the officials who relied on them to smooth their path to election and policy victory. After a couple decades of validating hosts' inflamed, unyielding rhetoric and tossing red meat to their base, elected Republicans found their freedom of action circumscribed.

The end of the Bush presidency did nothing to improve the rocky relationship between talk radio and elected Republicans. Republicans needed a new standard bearer, and they went with a RINO, as far as talk radio was concerned. John McCain was widely considered a war hero and a blunt speaker, qualities talk show hosts and listeners might be expected to admire. His forthrightness was so much a part of his personality and his brand that he had spent his 2000 presidential campaign riding a bus dubbed the Straight Talk Express. Yet talk radio opposed McCain's run for the nomination. Kathleen Hall Jamieson and Joseph Cappella, and separately David Barker, have all found evidence that Limbaugh damaged McCain's candidacy in the 2000 Republican primary.[34]

During his 2008 campaign, McCain continued advocating for policies, such as comprehensive immigration reform and a troop surge in Iraq, that talkers and listeners considered anathema. One McCain media staffer described the first six months of 2007, as the primary was just kicking off, as the "most violent" in his life. He was engaged primarily in survival messaging: trying to defend McCain, or deflect attention from him, because much of talk radio disagreed with many of his stances.[35] For example, Iowa's WHO—known as a "flamethrower" station thanks to its massive 50,000-watt signal, which ensured wide geographic reach—pounded McCain over immigration and moved the issue to the forefront of the campaign conversation, to the candidate's detriment.[36] Local hosts were typically less hostile to McCain, offering better prospects than their national counterparts, but not in WHO's case. Regardless, McCain never wavered in the face of aggressive hosts and appeared regularly on talk shows where he faced opposition.

Not that conservative media damaged only McCain. During the primary blogs and talk radio actually landed a punch for McCain by propelling into the mainstream media a story about rival Mitt Romney's mistreatment of his dog Seamus. The key for McCain's team was to feed the beast before it ate them: hosts didn't have to agree with the senator, but if the campaign could deliver them something negative about Romney, McCain didn't get singed that day.

During the general election, McCain labored to keep talkers on his side by focusing the conversation on issue positions he shared with conservatives. Previous Republican nominees had it easier. They could go on talk radio to rally their base. Talk radio listeners, however, were not McCain's natural base: they needed to be convinced. McCain engendered skepticism and risked alienating listeners if a conversation turned toward his departures from orthodoxy.

Overall, though, talk radio bolstered McCain during the general election and motivated Republicans to turn out to vote. The addition to the ticket of Sarah Palin, Alaska governor and emerging conservative rock star, helped to win over talk radio. Whatever hosts' and listeners' suspicions of McCain, the alternative—Barack Obama—was clearly worse.[37] Andy Polesovsky, who oversaw the RNC radio operation in 2008, took full advantage of the McCain campaign's uneasy alliance with conservative media. In particular he made good use of new technologies. He produced YouTube clips to share with hosts and always tried to add audio snippets to the research he shared with radio producers. He'd pull video clips from campaign rallies, sometimes catching Obama off-message, and include those in his morning roundup for hosts and producers. Polesovsky also worked closely with Liz Mair, who conducted blog outreach for the RNC at the time.[38]

What Polesovsky, Mair, and others in their line of work understood was that, in a digital environment, radio, TV, and online sources were converging. But while new technology had enabled this convergence, the result was marked profoundly by the imprint of its forebears. The conservative media empire that bloomed in the digital age took its style, sensibility, and priorities—profits, not party loyalty—from talk radio.

18

The Conservative Media Empire

THE PROLIFERATION OF IDEOLOGICAL news sources in the twenty-first century—primarily cable news and digital outlets—reduced talk radio's direct political influence, simply because it ended talk radio's monopoly on unfiltered access to the Republican base. But these new outlets also increased talk radio's impact indirectly, by reinforcing and amplifying its message. The empire that talk radio spawned ensured a far more potent conservative media presence in the late 2000s than during any previous moment in the modern history of the medium.[1]

Talk radio and cable news could not help but work in concert, because many of the same personalities populated both arenas. Hannity served as a primetime Fox host from the network's inception in 1996. O'Reilly, Fox's biggest star until he was undone by a sexual harassment scandal in 2017, had a radio show from 2002 to 2009. Glenn Beck, another popular radio talker, hosted a Fox program from 2009 to 2011. Later Fox would add Ingraham to its primetime lineup. Many other local and national radio talkers, including Larson and Gallagher, appeared regularly on Fox, either as guests or guest hosts.[2]

Similar connections abounded between talk radio and the digital world. Salem Communications, which owned a network of conservative talk radio stations, purchased conservative opinion sites Town Hall in 2006, Hot Air in 2010, and RedState in 2014. As the Internet grew, many conservatives started writing columns for Town Hall, Newsmax, and other sites, which allowed them to cross-promote. In one very early example, Gallagher demonstrated the potential of cross-promotion on his November 10, 2000, program. He mentioned several times that he wrote for Newsmax, a publication at the epicenter of the election-recount controversy in Palm Beach, Florida. He then interviewed Newsmax's founder, Christopher Ruddy.[3] In some cases hosts were compensated for writing columns, but, contrary to a belief swirling on the left, radio personalities didn't make big bucks writing online. The major benefit to them was an opportunity to attract listeners to their programs.[4]

Blogs also became a proving ground for talk radio, with columnists moving from the screen to the airwaves. In 2011 Erick Erickson, then editor of RedState and a CNN commentator (he'd later become a Fox News contributor), began hosting an Atlanta talk program. His style was shaped by advice from Limbaugh: "Your job is to entertain people and be their friend in their car."[5] Ben Shapiro, a syndicated columnist who wrote for Breitbart before launching the multimedia site the Daily Wire, worked a talk radio stint in Los Angeles. Later, in 2018, his podcast entered national radio syndication. By the mid-2010s, many conservative media personalities had multiple avenues for reaching their fans. And much of the information they shared originated with conservative print and digital publications, some of which had financial relationships with radio programs.[6]

Like Fox News, digital conservative media adopted talk radio's content model—sites such as Breitbart, the Daily Caller, and Newsmax were very much online print versions of the AM dial, albeit with video capacity that challenged hosts to adopt more of a multimedia approach.[7] Breitbart launched in 2005 as a content-aggregation site and quickly gained a following thanks to the Drudge Report, which linked back to it. Breitbart then burst into wider consciousness in 2009 after posting a deceptively edited undercover sting video purportedly demonstrating illegal activity at ACORN, the community organizing nonprofit. (No illegal activity was proven, but ACORN took a major financial and public-relations hit.) A year later the site had another moment in the mainstream spotlight when it posted video of a Department of Agriculture official named Shirley Sherrod apparently declaring that she once gave short shrift to a white farmer. The clip was taken out of context, but it succeeded in stoking widespread outrage and condemnations. Eventually the misleading edits were revealed, forcing even O'Reilly, who shared the video, to apologize. Still, the story left a mark and raised Breitbart's profile.

Both videos were intended to highlight exactly the sorts of liberal hypocrisy and scandal that were red meat to talk radio listeners conditioned to believe the worst about the left.[8] And both used deceptive tactics to push false conspiracy theories about individuals and institutions conservatives viewed as enemies. It was a sign of how completely Andrew Breitbart, the site's founder, embraced talk radio's strategy and its values. Indeed, Breitbart credited Limbaugh as an ideological inspiration who opened his eyes to the media's liberal bias and alliance with the Democratic Party. Breitbart, a onetime liberal, claimed he had originally tuned into Limbaugh expecting to hear the personification of everything he hated, and only because his girlfriend's father had challenged him to. But "one hour turned into three. One listening session into a week's worth," Breitbart explained. "The next thing I knew, I was starting to doubt my preprogrammed self."[9]

In addition to embracing talk radio's views, Breitbart grasped the genius of its style. His site offered the very same soap opera heard across the AM dial, with heroes and villains that readers recognized and experienced viscerally. Like the titans of talk, Breitbart focused on stories the mainstream media ignored and delighted in skewering liberal political correctness and timid establishment Republicans.[10]

Other sites, such as RedState, were more user-oriented but equally important to digital conservative media's embrace of the talk radio model. Along with microblogging and social media services such as Twitter and Facebook, user-oriented sites enabled everyday readers to post their own content. This got people talking with each other, and sometimes a story that started with users worked its way up the food chain to a media figure who could push it onto the radar of the mainstream press.[11] Talk listeners did the same kind of thing, bringing stories to the attention of hosts who promoted them into the wider consciousness. What mattered most was the story, not its origins. As long as the story had the heat of a talk radio bit—the independent, tell-it-like-it-is streak; the scathing mockery of liberal sacred cows; the uncompromising defense of conservative first principles—it could catch fire. Fox News unintentionally demonstrated as much in 2016 and 2017, when it maintained ratings while changing over all but one show in its primetime lineup. A strong personality was critical—milquetoast hosts flopped—but audiences flocked to talk radio–style content more than specific personalities.

So rabid were audiences for this sort of content that digital on-demand video subscription services such as CRTV and Glenn Beck's The Blaze cropped up to serve them in the 2010s. The two merged in 2018 just as Fox News entered this space as well. While the delivery device was different, the programming was not: it remained true to the familiar talk radio model, and included radio stars such as Beck and Levin. Even Blaze shows that strayed from politics had a right-wing worldview. The Blaze sports show featured veteran conservative talker Steve Deace and former Major Leaguer Curt Schilling, an all-star pitcher and Breitbart host known for his incendiary political commentary.[12]

As new conservative outlets flourished, older ones, such as Fox and long-standing radio programs, became the mainstream of conservative media, generating suspicion just as the political establishment did. Breitbart and its ilk explicitly positioned themselves as the places to turn instead of establishment conservative media. They were harsher, still farther to the right, and more populist.[13] Once again the effect of increased competition was playing out, forcing media incumbents to greater ideological extremes in order to retain their bona fides. The result was an even more strident conservative media that openly scorned pragmatism, demanded purity, and eviscerated Republican politicians who brooked compromise.

For their part, politicians and their aides generally did not dwell on the distinctions between establishment and upstart conservative media, or radio versus digital. They viewed cable news, talk radio, digital outlets, and social media as complements and tried to foster and wield all of them. What mattered was attitude, not medium or stature: so long as an outlet wasn't looking to claim a scalp, Republicans could see it as a part of a fruitful, well-balanced communications strategy.

Although there were now many more media organizations to court, technology made it relatively easy to reach them. Thanks to high-quality cell phones, senators could do radio appearances from home, from a car, or even while walking from their offices to the Senate floor. The Senate GOP conference set up servers and video-recording software so that staffers could clip a relevant soundbite from an appearance on Fox News and email it to important home-state bloggers and radio hosts.[14] One interview could easily reach multiple media sources.[15] To engage new digital outlets, staffers adapted many of the communications strategies they had pioneered with talk radio. For instance they came up with bloggers' rows, a direct analogue to the radio rows they had begun staging in the 1990s.

Eliding the differences between talk radio, cable news, and conservative websites may have upset the new impresarios of right-wing media, who sought instead to emphasize distinctions from crustier, stale competitors.

But doing so was understandable from the standpoint of members and their aides. Whatever their divergences, these media formed one network. They were intricately intertwined and provided a largely consistent message. They were all talk radio writ large, driving politics to the right and toward the sensationalism and conspiracy theories on which hosts had thrived for more than two decades.

19

I Hope He Fails

THE ELECTION OF BARACK OBAMA was a revolutionary moment in American politics. Above all the nation had its first black president. And the nation had its first digital president. The Obama campaign carried forward the 1992 Clinton campaign's passion for new media. Whereas the Clinton campaign had great success innovating with talk radio, in 2008 the Obama team harnessed digital technology and microtargeting and rode them from insurgency to the presidency.

After entering the White House, Obama and his team continued their dramatic reconfiguration of Democratic communications strategy.[1] The administration took advantage of detailed information on the reach and footprint of various media outlets to better target audiences. For instance, the White House largely scrapped radio rows because the targeting data made clear that regional-television rows were a better approach. According to Dag Vega, who was special assistant to the president and director of broadcast media, regional television offered "maximum impact for a national initiative." Thus it was television anchors, not talk hosts, who flocked to the North Lawn, invited for a day of broadcasting and interviews with heavyweights, the president included. Furthermore, messaging was targeted not just geographically and demographically but also ideologically: all progressive media outreach ran through a dedicated staffer. Finally, the communications staff established the first White House social media operation, which grew dramatically during the president's eight years in office.

The Obama team thought broadly about venues from which to disseminate their message. The president appeared on "Between Two Ferns," a digital celebrity-interview show hosted by comedian Zach Galifianakis. Obama chatted with popular podcaster and comedian Marc Maron and set the political world aflame when he used the N-word while discussing race relations on the show. He even did a Reddit AMA ("ask me anything"), the modern equivalent of Bill Clinton's foray into the post–State of the Union digital Q&A.[2] In an effort to reach a young and male audience, Obama, a massive basketball fan, picked a yearly bracket for the NCAA tournament and appeared on ESPN and other sports programming, chatting courtside with broadcasters.

This, too, was redolent of Clinton, who had joined ESPN radio to dish on college basketball. While microtargeting offered a newfound precision, much of the Obama team's media outreach involved an intensification of earlier efforts. The White House took ideas from predecessors' playbooks and applied them in what was now a much larger media environment with many more opportunities to reach voters.

The smorgasbord of available media inspired new messaging approaches. Gone were the days of radio directors pushing the White House message to everything from morning talk shows to conservative outlets to NPR. Instead radio got divvied up: regional shows were handled by staff focused on regional press; staffers tasked with booking television interviews also booked national radio, with their priority being the former; staff in the constituency press office addressed black and Spanish-language radio outlets; and the staffer focused on progressive media covered liberal radio.

The result was a diverse radio strategy. The Obama White House held talk radio days for select issue blitzes, the president did occasional radio interviews, and the White House dispatched surrogates to radio in a targeted fashion. For instance Agriculture Secretary Tom Vilsack, a former governor of Iowa, did turns on Iowa farm radio. But most of the focus was on neutral, nonideological radio and on programs aimed at black or Latino audiences. While radio targeted to minority listeners was not necessarily all political, all the time, it reached the Democratic base in much the same way that conservative talk radio reached the Republican base. NPR was also on the White House's interview radar, in part because the network offered an opportunity for a ripple effect: other elite media paid attention to NPR, so its interviews could echo throughout the press.

But in a variety of ways, the radio effort was also significantly downgraded. Jen Psaki, one of Obama's communications directors, explained that Obama's team employed radio in a "selective and specific" manner.

This was not the daily use of the George W. Bush administration, or even the early Clinton administration. The Obama team even turned the president's weekly radio address into an online video series.

When it came to conservative media, the White House engaged with Fox News but not talk radio. Sometimes staffers went on Fox for interviews or to correct the record. In general Obama's team believed that engaging Fox was worth its time because, as a channel that drew large audiences for hard-news programming, it catered to some persuadable viewers. National conservative talk radio was another story. As far as the White House was concerned, talk radio promised only fruitless, combative argument, and none of the listeners were open to persuasion from a Democrat. Devoting resources to talk radio, or serving up guests, didn't make sense to a disciplined operation such as Obama's. His communications team knew that there was a more effective medium for just about any message the White House wanted to send.[3]

Obama's presidency marked the culmination of a decade of partisan divergence with respect to communication strategies. Today this may seem like a trivial observation: of course Democrats and Republicans talk to different audiences through different media. It's also not without ample precedent in American history; partisan newspapers dominated the nineteenth century. But that doesn't make the development any less shocking or less of a departure from recent times. The beginning of the talk radio era, in the early 1990s, looked very different. By the time Obama was in office, talk radio, a major player in American political dialogue, barely existed from the White House's perspective. In Congress and state governments, however, Republicans were still devoted to talk radio, despite the ups and downs of their relationship with the medium.

In many ways, the relationship between talk radio and Democrats had been doomed from the start. While it was hot and heavy for a short while, many rank-and-file Democrats were never going to embrace talk radio, because they perceived the medium to be implacably hostile. Party leadership understood talk radio's importance and directed outreach, but, with a few exceptions such as Bill Clinton, they lacked any real affinity for the medium. Some Democrats conceptualized the necessity and the potential benefits: they wanted good relations with hosts, they wanted to make hosts' lives easier through radio-friendly outreach, and they wanted to flood the airwaves with prominent Democrats sharing the party's message. But too many didn't see matters that way. Certainly Democrats' enthusiasm was never, on the whole, close to that of Republicans. And even at the peak of their engagement with talk radio, the savviest Democratic communicators used talk radio more defensively than did their Republican counterparts. Their best hope was to ensure that radio listeners heard both sides of the story, as opposed to hearing an entirely anti-Democratic message.

Maybe the situation would have been different if conservatives hadn't gotten to the airwaves first. Conservatives' early advantage set in motion a culture in which elected Democrats didn't listen to talk radio as much—at least, those Democrats who lacked a major host or station in their districts or states rarely listened. Elected officials, their aides, and party operatives therefore often held skewed perceptions about talk radio. They underestimated its reach and importance and exaggerated its hostility. Longtime Michigan Representative David Bonior argued that many of his peers saw radio as the "red-headed stepchild in the media world."[4] They mistakenly believed that hosts were likely to turn an interview into a screaming match where they would not get a word in edgewise. In reality a few hosts did behave this way, but most at least let Democrats say their piece.[5]

A geographic element contributed to the awkward fit between Democrats and talk radio. Many Democrats came from urban districts and states dominated by cities, whereas the brand of talk radio shaped by Limbaugh tended to be a more significant part of the media diet in rural places.[6] Those who did listen in urban areas tended to be trapped in cars commuting and looking for companionship—not a likely condition for members of Congress. Senator Daschle—who lost his seat in a close 2004 election, as rural America moved away from Democrats—noted that in his native South Dakota, people passed long hours on highways listening to talk radio. Senator Ben Nelson prioritized radio because, as one of his aides noted, in his home state of Nebraska, a significant number of people weren't reached by the Internet or even by cable.[7] But from the perspective of most leaders and the party as a whole, talk radio was at most one among many tools for communicating, and not an essential one given that their base was concentrated in urban areas and mostly didn't tune into the conservative breed of spoken-word radio. Bill Richardson, for one, lamented the missed opportunity: he believed that many aspects of the Democratic agenda would have appealed to rural and moderate voters who got their news and entertainment from talk radio.[8]

Hardened "red-and-blue" thinking also contributed to this difference in the parties' media priorities. Before the second half of the 2000s, when voter targeting became more sophisticated, Democratic campaigns might have ignored conservative-leaning programs outside of top-priority areas. As targeting improved, however, Democrats realized that they had potential voters in these places, and these voters might tune into talk shows because the hosts cared about issues they cared about, too. That offered an opportunity for a candidate or a surrogate who agreed with the host on the issues in question, or who at least was inclined to address them.[9] But for many years Democrats left the field uncontested.

Even with improved targeting, talk radio occupied a far more significant place in Republican communications strategy, in part because talk radio needed to serve a larger function for Republicans than it did for Democrats. Both sides saw the medium as important for disseminating and amplifying a message. But for Republicans talk radio was a two-way street. They used it to take the pulse of their base—to hear the concerns of their most crucial and engaged supporters. Liberal talk radio never had enough listeners to serve that function for Democrats. That meant, as well, that there just weren't that many voters to reach in many situations. Resources being limited, Democrats accordingly devoted more attention to media that offered access to larger groups of persuadable or supportive voters.

Sensible though this decision was, Democrats missed an opportunity to balance the message talk radio listeners received. Though conservatives constituted much of talk radio's audience, the medium offered access to many persuadable voters, and there likely would have been more had Democrats been a consistent presence over the years. Democrats might even have benefited from reaching conservative listeners who voted reliably Republican. Instead, by vacating the talk radio airwaves, Democrats allowed the medium to harden into an echo chamber, which, along with Fox News and conservative digital outlets, fueled polarization. From there the level of vitriol and hysteria in conservative media only escalated until, by the time of Obama administration, right-wing outlets routinely targeted even midlevel Democratic staffers.[10]

Had Democrats stayed in the game, they might have blunted some of these developments. Access to the talk radio audience at least would have allowed Democrats to muddy the waters factually for conservative listeners, who typically parroted talk radio–derived diatribes about Democrats and their policy positions. And by challenging more visceral claims, Democrats could have reduced the personal animosity that many talk radio listeners felt toward them. Democrats such as Lieberman, who routinely ventured onto conservative talk radio, shattered stereotypes and defanged hosts. Instead of wrath, they confronted respectful disagreement. Had others gone on the air and earned hosts' esteem, listeners may have felt less hostile to them and therefore been less active in opposition. As Jamieson and Cappella demonstrated, Limbaugh listeners who felt more intensely about the 1996 presidential candidates were more likely to participate in political activities near the time of the election, which wasn't good for Democrats.[11] While some hosts, such as Ingraham, only wanted Democratic guests to serve as piñatas, Hewitt and others would have asked tough questions but then allowed their guests to answer, engage in debate, and try to turn down the volume on voter outrage.

By giving the opposition a lot of uncontested time to sell their agenda, Democrats probably made it progressively harder to correct the problem of imbalance. Their absence from talk radio not only meant that listeners weren't getting Democrats' message, it also meant that hosts had free rein to caricature their positions and villainize them personally. This would have increased the chances that the audience accepted Republican claims, even if Democrats had at last come on the air to defend themselves.[12] By the Obama era, it was arguably too late to correct this mistake, given the intense mixture of scorn, disgust, and fear that talk radio listeners felt toward Democrats. The resulting disparity in messaging likely contributed to Democrats' steadily decreasing competitiveness in small towns and rural parts of America, including in the Midwest, which culminated in Donald Trump's stunning ascension.

None of this is to say that Democratic outreach would have transformed talk radio into a friendly medium. While many conservative hosts would have welcomed information from Democrats and happily talked with Democratic guests, they still fundamentally disagreed with Democrats on most major issues. And they aired that disagreement through harsh criticism. That's what the bottom line demanded: flamboyant disdain, delivered with panache. Nonetheless the rejection of the medium, which reached near totality during the Obama years, helped to ensure the seemingly unbridgeable disconnect that emerged between the Democratic Party and large swaths of the country.

20

The Relationship Sours

FOR TALK RADIO the Obama presidency would mark an important mile-stone: the moment when the medium became more hindrance to Republicans than help. That moment, however, would come in 2011, after Republicans regained control of the House. Before that, talk radio coalesced around Republican efforts to impede Obama's agenda.

Republicans were on the outs during the first half of Obama's first term: Democrats controlled both houses of Congress and, for seven months in 2009 and early 2010, had enough votes in the Senate to overcome a Republican filibuster. While this was the sort of powerless position from which Republicans previously could have expected talk radio's full-throated support, signs of the medium's growing consternation were visible. When it came to special elections and primaries, talk radio repeatedly went its own way, though doing so meant harming Republicans' chances of winning back Congress. And even before Republicans returned to power, talk radio firmly and finally gave up GOP moderates.

In the early Obama years, Republican talk radio outreach continued at its usual energetic pace. Indeed, some staffers worked harder than ever. During the intense 2009 debate over the Affordable Care Act, Senate Republicans' talk radio point person spent twenty hours a day clipping audio from floor speeches and passing it along to hosts virtually in real time. She also arranged hundreds of interviews and directed several radio rows. In one case she put together a radio row on a mere week's notice. When it was over, the exhausted staffer's boss asked if she could set up another later that week.[1]

Even with Republicans struggling for legislative relevance, talk radio continued to cast its spell over Congress, albeit in ways less visible than before. This subtle influence arguably was on display during the 2009–2010 effort to pass the financial regulatory reform bill that came to be known as Dodd-Frank. As Robert G. Kaiser describes, every time Senate Banking Committee Chairman Chris Dodd and Republican Ranking Member Richard Shelby seemed close to a bipartisan agreement, Shelby hardened his position. At times Shelby also seemed hamstrung by his caucus, preventing him from negotiating freely.[2] Discussing negotiations between Dodd and Tennessee Senator Bob Corker, Kaiser writes, "Once, a senator was a potentate in his own right, in most matters a free agent who could build his own alliances and pursue his own goals with colleagues in either party. But in the modern era every senator was subject to party discipline, and they all knew it."[3] Rule changes played a role in this shift. But we might also see conservative media—and talk radio in particular—as a silent force behind the impasse between Shelby and Dodd.[4]

As Kaiser notes, Shelby dreamed of chairing the Senate Appropriations Committee, which made him leery of crossing McConnell and fellow Republicans. If Shelby did upset his caucus, his Republican colleagues on the Appropriations Committee would hesitate to vote for him as chair. So Shelby had to safeguard against allegations of disloyalty from leadership and rank-and-file colleagues alike. Supporting Dodd's bill, which appeared to have few Republican votes behind it, was a huge political risk, especially for a former Democrat such as Shelby.[5] Talk radio would undoubtedly have tarred him as a RINO and campaigned against any future ascent to the chairmanship. This was precisely the sort of small, inside-baseball matter that talk radio could influence. Few Americans cared, and the decision would be made only by Republicans, most of whom had far more to worry about in primary elections than general elections. Talk radio could make the committee assignment seem like a matter of core principles, compelling Republicans to choose between voting with hosts or facing severe backlash.

Talk radio also affected delicate legislative processes through the threat of transparency. Twenty-five years before Dodd-Frank, senior members would have negotiated quietly in private, but talk radio made the back room a perilous place to be. Over and over, hosts provided a sympathetic outlet for disgruntled conservative leakers: by going to talk radio, they could scuttle deals no one even knew about. That meant Shelby—and Republicans broadly—courted disaster with every secret concession. It might escape notice, but it also might not, so the watchword was caution. Dick Armey considered this elevated transparency talk radio's principal source of impact on the legislative process and public policy. The medium made legislators more accountable, which, in turn, made it harder to pass legislation through regular order. In Armey's words, politicians did not respond to increased accountability with "very much courage." Instead they often resorted to passing vague legislation in moments of crisis and allowing the executive branch to fill in the details.[6]

To legislate in the talk radio era demanded nerve and daring that ambitious, risk-averse Republicans such as Shelby were loath to demonstrate. Shelby spent 2009 and 2010 fighting tooth and nail for Democratic concessions to Dodd-Frank, and, even after he won several, voted against the final bill. In 2018 he got his Appropriations Committee chairmanship. This was a far cry from how legislating worked when Shelby joined Congress in 1978.

If hosts were traditional political actors, unified Democratic control would have prompted talk radio to revive the pragmatic posture it adopted in the early Clinton years. Hosts would have accepted the few moderate Republicans who survived the wave elections of 2006 and 2008. And they would have boosted any Republican on the ballot in hopes of restoring GOP congressional majorities.

But the political and media landscapes had changed dramatically over the previous fifteen years, and the Limbaugh who would chide conservative single-issue voters or back the then-moderate Mitt Romney for Senate was no more. In general, that kind of conservative media was hard to find. Talk radio would help Republicans only insofar as they resisted President Obama and pursued a purely conservative agenda; otherwise Congressional Republicans, no less than Democrats, were the enemy. Republican support for insufficiently conservative moves, such as the Troubled Asset Relief Program (TARP), inflamed the conservative grassroots, including many hosts, who used their microphones to voice the base's fury.[7]

Under such circumstances, pragmatism held no attraction for talk radio. Any ideological slippage on a host's part would give ground to farther-right media, potentially alienating listeners and harming the bottom line.[8] And, politically, hosts were free to move to the right and keep up with online upstarts. They no longer faced the burden of supporting a governing party and its necessary compromises. They felt no reason to look the other way, or to focus on Republicans' conservative achievements, as they once had. In 2006 Hannity and caller Ken agreed that the dangers of Democratic control demanded that conservatives remain loyal to the Republican Party, no matter its failings. But now there was little to lose. Talk radio seized the moment by pushing for a purer GOP shaped in its image.[9]

Talk radio's gloves-off posture matched listeners' rising anger during Obama's presidency. Many of those angry listeners joined a new movement that would have considerable impact in Washington: the Tea Party. Hosts were good at reading and projecting the feelings of their Tea Party–heavy audience, but while it might be tempting to see the Tea Party as the cause of talkers' increasing aggressiveness, that interpretation misses the mark. Hosts certainly did channel listener sentiment, but they also drove it. Many hosts began souring on moderates and compromise years before the Tea Party movement coalesced. The shifts on talk radio were a harbinger of the movement, not a response to it. In fact, many hosts helped to shape the priorities of the Tea Party. As Theda Skocpol and Vanessa Williamson explain,

> The Tea Party cannot be understood without recognizing the mobilization provided by conservative media hosts who openly espouse and encourage the cause. From Fox News to right-wing radio jocks and bloggers, media impresarios have done a lot to create a sense of shared identity that lets otherwise scattered Tea Partiers get together and feel part of something big and powerful. Media hosts also put out a steady diet of information and misinformation—including highly emotional claims—that keep Tea Party people in a constant state of anger and fear about the direction of the country and the doings of government officials.[10]

It was in the Tea Party era that talk radio fully matured as a RINO hunter. A case in point is Limbaugh's handling of a carbon cap-and-trade system enacted by the Democratic House in June 2009. Conservatives viewed the policy as a tax. On the day it passed, Minority Leader John Boehner lacerated the bill on the House floor and then blasted it again in multiple talk radio appearances.[11] But talk radio was no blindly loyal ally to Boehner's party. Such an ally would have kept the spotlight solely on the Democrats driving the legislation. Limbaugh, however, was outraged by the eight moderate, mostly Northeastern, House Republicans who voted for the bill. He accused them of selling out for campaign contributions from Wall Street types who stood to benefit from carbon-credit trading. "These eight Republicans made this happen," he fumed.

But the matter did not end there, with a standard-fare Limbaugh tongue-lashing of GOP Judases. "This whole bill . . . is so un-American," he declared, "everybody who voted for it from Pelosi on down needs to be jacked out of there in the next election."[12]

Here was something different. Here was America's preeminent conservative voice calling for the defeat of elected Republicans. Not just any Republicans, but ones who would surely be replaced by Democrats. To pick one example from the eight, Congressman Mike Castle hailed from Delaware, where a moderate was the only kind of Republican who could win. Delaware elected its lone U.S. representative statewide, and the Democratic presidential nominee had won the state by an average of fifteen points in the elections of 1996–2008. A hard-right candidate could never match Castle's popularity across the state, though the representative and former governor was vulnerable against a more conservative primary opponent.[13] That a conservative nominee would have little chance in November was hardly a concern to Limbaugh, however. It made no difference if all eight moderate Republicans were replaced by Democrats, so grievous was their crime against conservative principles.

Because 2009 was an election off-year, RINO-hunting opportunities were mostly limited to five House special elections and local races, some of which became arenas of intense focus. One was the race for a vacant New York congressional district, which pitted liberal Republican State Assemblywoman Dede Scozzafava against Democrat Bill Owens and Conservative Party candidate Doug Hoffman. President Obama had captured 52 percent of the vote in the district, suggesting that a strong conservative such as Hoffman would have a hard time winning the seat.

The Republican Party backed Scozzafava. Gingrich, now on the sidelines, and Boehner endorsed her, and the National Republican Congressional Committee spent over $900,000 bolstering her candidacy. Limbaugh, Hannity, Levin, and Bèck all endorsed Hoffman.[14] "See, I'm a conservative," Hannity said, explaining his opposition to Scozzafava. "I'm not a Republican. I am a Reagan conservative." He drew a parallel between the special election and Reagan's primary challenge against Gerald Ford in

1976. In both cases, the party had strayed from conservative principles, and only a revolt could right the situation.[15]

Limbaugh was enraged that the party would back Scozzafava over Hoffman. "We actually have two liberal Obama Democrats, one calling herself a Republican," he argued, "and you've got the Reagan conservative Hoffman in there."

> I ruined two hours of my day when I saw that the Republican Party was running ads against Hoffman. They have a death wish. The Republican Party has a death wish. Gallup: 40 percent of Americans now say they are conservative, 20 percent say they're liberal, 36 percent say they're moderates. And of those three groups, which one is being ignored—not just ignored—which one is being attacked by the Republican Party? The conservatives! . . . The Republican Party, as constituted, is as dangerous to this country as the Democrat Party is.[16]

When Scozzafava withdrew from the race and endorsed Owens, the Democrat, Limbaugh responded with glee. Another moderate had been exposed as an unprincipled liberal. "Dede Scozzafava has just delivered a teachable moment for those who lack a keen sense of the obvious," he told listeners. "RINOs cannot be trusted. . . . They aren't principled. You vote 'em into office and you're going to get cap and tax, you're going to get some version of Obamacare, you're going to get tax increases, you're going to get TARP bailouts, you're gonna get amnesty."[17] Owens defeated Hoffman in the election, but again, this mattered less than imposing talk radio–style conservatism on the GOP.

Although talk radio scorned moderate Republicans in the Tea Party era, there were moments when their goals happened to overlap. Another special election, with the highest of stakes, found hosts boosting a moderate Republican: Scott Brown, who was running against Massachusetts Attorney General Martha Coakley in a January 2010 election for the Senate seat previously occupied by the late Ted Kennedy. Talkers had a large impact on the race, thanks in part to more robust Web tools and social media, which made talk radio an even greater financial powerhouse for Republicans seeking campaign contributions.

Conservative hosts had several reasons to pull for Brown. If Brown won Democrats would be deprived of the sixty Senate votes they needed to pass a final version of the Affordable Care Act—or any other legislation—without concessions to secure at least one Republican vote. At the time, both houses had passed versions of the health care legislation, but they still needed to reconcile the two bills. The race also carried deep symbolic significance because the seat had been in the Kennedy family for all but twenty-six months dating back to John F. Kennedy's election in 1952. And while hosts might have opposed Brown's moderation on many cultural issues, he was at least a solid fiscal conservative.[18]

As the race progressed and tightened, it catapulted into hosts' field of view. Brown would go on shows, mention his website, and watch the traffic and donation numbers spike.[19] Accordingly, his advisers increased his bookings on conservative media. Talk radio, in particular, drove donations. Staffers would discover clusters of donations from unexpected zip codes at odd times of day—say from Boise at 10 o'clock at night. It turned out that the race had been discussed on talk programs airing on tape delay in the relevant markets.[20] A mention by a national talker could produce up to $20,000 in donations. In the week between Christmas and New Year's, mentions by Ingraham and Herman Cain, filling in for Hannity, brought in hundreds of donations apiece.[21]

Brown's campaign came up with a "money bomb"—a multifaceted effort that included a media blitz designed to generate a burst of donations on January 11, eight days before the election. They hyped the money bomb on social media and other sites. They also built a site that took pledges and, on the designated day, reminded donors to pay up. Also on the appointed day, Brown appeared with Ingraham in the morning and Hannity in the afternoon. The results dramatically exceeded the campaign's expectations. They raised $1.3 million on the 11th alone, and that turned out to be the campaign's weakest online fundraising day that week.[22] Donors were encouraged to fill out a form telling the campaign how they heard about the money bomb, and four of the most popular sources they listed were Fox, Hannity, radio, and Ingraham.[23]

Remarkably, Brown came out on top in one of the most liberal states in the country. His victory dealt a major blow to Democrats and buoyed Republicans heading into the 2010 midterms. But while talk radio was no doubt cheered by the outcome, hosts and listeners weren't looking for more Scott Browns. His case was a fluke, albeit one that demonstrated the enduring and expanding power of talk radio.

In the 2010 Delaware Senate race, that power swung sharply against a similar moderate, seriously undermining the Republican Party in the process. The race was another rare GOP chance in a blue state. Castle, the state's congressman, was the perfect Republican for the seat Democrat Joe Biden had vacated when he became vice president. Castle's moderation—his DW-NOMINATE score of 0.229 made him the ninth most liberal House Republican in the 111th Congress, and his lifetime American Conservative Union score was a middle-of-the-road 51.69—positioned him as the GOP's best bet in a state that typically rejected strident conservatives.[24] Castle had been winning elections in Delaware since the mid-1960s, and most analysts considered him the heavy favorite against Democrat Chris Coons in the general election.

But the primary split conservatives. While the establishment backed Castle, the Tea Party and talk radio hosts wanted Christine O'Donnell. A conservative activist with a checkered history, O'Donnell had lost the 2008 Senate race to Biden by almost thirty points.[25] That result was a glaring warning sign about her chances against Coons, but Hannity, at least, didn't care. "Christine O'Donnell, the establishment is just trying to assassinate her character, smear her," he told his TV audience. "And here's a guy, Mike Castle voted for Obamacare, voted for TARP, voted for cap and tax; the establishment wants him."[26] In fact Castle hadn't voted for the health care law, but the damage was done. On election night, as it appeared O'Donnell would win, Hannity justified his support for the surefire general-election loser and argued that voters had made the right choice:

> I don't think we can make progress in the country with RINO Republicans. I don't think you are going to stop Obama's radical agenda without people that are really committed to cutting taxes, to stopping spending, really strong principles. How could this guy be one of several Republicans to vote for a killing bill like cap and tax and expect conservatives in a primary to vote for him? You know what? I'm sorry, he brought this on himself.[27]

The race prompted Limbaugh to announce a Limbaugh rule, to replace what had been known as the Buckley rule. In an earlier time, conservative luminary William F. Buckley urged primary voters to pick the most conservative candidate who could win a general election. The Limbaugh rule counseled differently: "In an election year when voters are fed up with liberalism and socialism, when voters are clearly frightened of where the hell the country is headed, vote for the most conservative Republican in the primary, period." Clearly Castle was not that. He would "be just another liberal but he's going to have an 'R' next to his name," Limbaugh said. "Now somebody tell me how that helps the conservative movement? I can understand the Republican Party being for Castle. . . . But I don't understand people who profess to be conservatives supporting this guy." Limbaugh acknowledged the risk of running O'Donnell in November, but, he explained, "The bigger risk to me is that RINOs, Republicans-in-name-only like Mike Castle, tarnish the conservative brand. They confuse and turn off the electorate who end up thinking, 'Well, they're all alike.'"[28]

It was an exact 180-degree turn from Limbaugh's position sixteen years earlier, when the king of talk helped Republicans retake the House by arguing that GOP moderates provided advantages over Democrats. Now he contended that moderates diluted the conservative brand and had no business winning primaries, let alone seats. Michael Medved was a lone voice in the wilderness on conservative talk radio, lamenting that so many of his colleagues demonized Castle, who had been "a very good governor and a fine member of Congress, and emphatically not the enemy." Medved regretted talk radio's "shameful" posture and denounced hosts backing the "moron side" in the election. But he was drowned out by the chorus of purity seekers.[29]

Talk radio threw its full weight behind O'Donnell in the general election. The day after the primary, when Limbaugh encouraged his listeners to donate to O'Donnell's campaign, the response crashed the candidate's website. The call for support produced over $1 million in contributions in twenty-four hours.[30] It didn't matter. Coons crushed O'Donnell in November, 56.6 percent to 40 percent.

The position of conservative hosts in 2010 reflected years of evolution. Whether or not their views had changed, the political landscape had shifted in ways that left them emboldened to express those views even at the expense of the Republican Party. In 2004, when Toomey challenged Specter, only one elected incumbent Republican senator had lost a primary election in the previous twenty-four years. In that case New Hampshire's Bob Smith—the second most conservative senator in his final Congress, according to DW-NOMINATE—likely lost over fears that he could not win the general election, not because he was thought of as insufficiently conservative.[31] Dating back to World War II, only eight elected Republican senators had lost primaries.[32] Yet in 2010 alone conservatives got O'Donnell over Castle and before that denied renomination to Bob Bennett of Utah and Lisa Murkowski of Alaska, Republican senators deemed excessively moderate or pragmatic. (Murkowski went on to win reelection as a write-in candidate.) The most conservative forces in the country were ascendant within the party, making once-unthinkable results reality. The substantial advancement in Web technology, which allowed talk radio to become a more muscular fundraising force, also significantly enhanced the odds of defeating an establishment-supported moderate.

These changes—in technology, in conservative activism, in attitudes about conservative purity—meant that hosts could be confident of their prospects for unseating moderates. In the Clinton days, hosts primarily used their influence to help advance the party's goals. Under Bush, hosts clashed with leadership more frequently and used that influence to hold members accountable, but seldom by directly threatening their seats. By the time Obama was in office, hosts could wield their influence to evict from the party the ideologically indefensible. For talk radio in 1994, party leadership meant putting as many Republicans in Congress as possible. In 2010 it meant driving moderates to the brink of extinction, damn the consequences.

21

Hunting RINOs

TALK RADIO'S SWAY was always greatest when information about a policy debate or an election was scarce. That meant the impact of talk radio typically was inversely related to the size of the electorate and the importance of the office.[1] In presidential general elections, with massive national electorates and billion-dollar campaigns behind the candidates' messages, talk radio played a relatively small role. At most it was one source among many, doing its best in a crowded field to sustain listeners' enthusiasm and frame the races.[2] By the 2010s voters were bombarded with information about the presidential candidates from every direction: the campaigns, which planted ads everywhere from bus kiosks to video games; numberless media sources, including many that usually didn't concern themselves with politics; and social media. In these circumstances, no one source could muscle out all the others in the contest for influence.

But at the opposite end of the electoral spectrum, in sleepy Republican congressional primaries, talk radio could have an outsized impact. That's a big part of why talk hosts were able to end the political careers of moderate and pragmatic Republicans: they were exposed in precisely the sorts of elections in which talkers possessed the most clout. House primaries, in particular, featured small electorates heavily weighted toward the types of politically engaged conservatives who spent hours glued to their favorite talk programs.[3] Chris Mottola, a Republican media consultant, said it was not unusual to find that 60-plus percent of Republican primary voters who responded to campaign surveys were regular talk radio listeners.[4] In four surveys of the 2004 Pennsylvania Republican primary electorate that gave the moderate Specter such a hard time, 26 to 35 percent of respondents said they frequently or sometimes listened to Limbaugh.[5] These data probably understate the primary electorate's talk radio habits, since many Pennsylvanians would have been unable to tune into Limbaugh, who aired in the state from noon to 3 p.m. Counting those who listened during their commutes likely would have shown even greater talk radio penetration among Pennsylvania primary voters.

Findings such as these show why talk radio developed into a go-to venue for reaching Republican primary voters.[6] The late Utah Senator Bob Bennett understood that talk radio enabled him to contact a significant slice of the primary electorate for free, which is why he never refused an opportunity to appear on air.[7] Nonetheless he was one of the Republicans whose pragmatism got the better of him. In 2010 he wasn't even on the primary ballot, after he came in third at the state party convention behind Tea Party–backed challengers Mike Lee and Tim Bridgewater.

As much as a national star could motivate primary voters, prominent local hosts such as Cunningham in Cincinnati, Sykes in Milwaukee, and Nashville's Phil Valentine likely were even more influential in nominating contests.[8] These conservative pillars of the community could focus on a race for weeks, repeatedly dissecting it from every angle. By contrast a national host could mention a given primary only now and then. Those mentions might spike an underdog's fundraising or volunteer recruitment, but they did not drive sustained interest in the way that concentrated local attention could.

It made sense that, as one ventured farther down the ballot, the potential impact of talk radio would grow simply because candidates were less well known and had less money to spend on messaging. Listeners' opinions accordingly were more malleable. Additionally, in primaries, voters could not rely on party identification to make their voting decisions for them; voters had to do research if they wanted to differentiate one Republican from another. Talk radio provided the information voters were looking for, and the medium's intimacy made it a particularly potent delivery mechanism. When people knew little about the candidates, they naturally relied on what they learned from friends or family, and many listeners considered their favorite hosts to be friends.[9]

Talk radio's special impact on primaries also reflected the dynamics of electoral competition in right-leaning districts saturated with listeners. It wasn't that talk radio couldn't be a force in general elections. But in these districts, general elections tended to be uncompetitive, meaning there wasn't much for talk radio to influence in the run-up to November. This had not always been the case. In 1994, when talk radio was coming into its own, a hundred Democrats held districts that had voted for President Bush in 1992, fostering conditions for high-impact talk radio right up to Election Day.[10] But by the 2010s, general elections like these were few and far between, making primaries the only game in town.

Data limitations make it difficult to quantify the impact conservative hosts have had on Republican primaries. Given the tiny electorates involved in many primaries, it often is not cost effective to generate polls with sample sizes large enough to produce statistically significant information on voters' media habits. As a result few pollsters bother querying primary voters on the matter. What little evidence we have about the impact of talk radio on primaries is limited to presidential primaries, which are not at all analogous to congressional primaries, because typically far more is known about presidential than congressional candidates.[11]

But those who have watched talk radio throw its weight around in primaries—including politicians who have been on the receiving end of hosts' criticism—have few doubts about the medium's power. Sympathetic Limbaugh biographer Zev Chafets argued that conservative hosts destroyed Scozzafava's candidacy.[12] And Castle believed talk radio contributed to his defeat. He pointed out that he did especially poorly in Sussex County, home to one of his most vehement and outspoken talk radio opponents. Castle lost his primary by 3,542 votes; in Sussex County he lost by 5,429.[13]

Castle's pollster, Jan van Lohuizen, also believed that talk radio deserved credit for the congressman's primary loss. In one of his polls, van Lohuizen asked respondents where they got their information. Those respondents who listed talk radio programs as their principal source of information supported O'Donnell by a 56.2 to 43.8 percent margin. The only other group that favored O'Donnell were respondents who listed online sources. Respondents who got their information from television, radio news, or newspapers overwhelmingly favored Castle. The sample size for this question was too small to provide a statistically meaningful result, but the finding was at least consistent with what pollsters discovered in other surveys: talk radio listeners tended to be more sympathetic to ultra-conservative candidates than were Republicans who got their news from other media.[14]

Years of political experience left other moderate officeholders feeling much like Castle. While the Republican Party writ large saw talk radio as an ally, Sherwood Boehlert, the New Yorker who retired from Congress in 2007, confessed that moderates did not share this view. Rather, they understood that they couldn't ignore talk radio, because doing so was perilous. Unlike establishment media, talk radio eagerly gave even obscure primary challengers a platform. Over the years Boehlert had five primary challengers as an incumbent; talk radio came out against him every time, energizing and encouraging his opponents' supporters to work harder against him. He won "by the skin of my teeth." According to the late Representative Steve LaTourette, talk radio "gave aid and comfort" to aggressive conservative groups such as the Club for Growth and Heritage Action, which "don't think that we should have moderate Republicans." These organizations specialized in funding and otherwise supporting primary challenges against insufficiently conservative Republicans.[15]

Whatever the empirical evidence concerning talk radio's effect on primary outcomes, Republican officeholders perceived the medium as holding sway over voters, and this is what truly mattered when it came to empowering hosts as agenda makers. As long as Republicans thought angry hosts could be their electoral downfall, they would be skittish about policies talkers decried and more likely to adopt the positions they espoused. For, as R. Douglas Arnold explained, "Reelection is [a congressman's] dominant goal. This means simply that legislators will do nothing to advance their other goals if such activities threaten their principal goal."[16] If establishment Republicans felt threatened, it was also because talk radio erased two of their traditional advantages: high name recognition and the massive fundraising lead that came with incumbency or official GOP support. Hosts got the word out about otherwise-unknown candidates and turbocharged fundraising for insurgent hard-liners such as O'Donnell.[17]

It is hard to overestimate how important the incumbency funding advantage can be, and therefore how significant talk radio can be in equalizing challengers' chances. Andrew Hall's research indicates an incumbency funding advantage of roughly twenty-two percentage points; if a challenger is able to secure 50 percent of the funding flowing to their race, in the next election, as an incumbent, the candidate can expect to secure 72 percent of the funding in the race. Hall's research also indicates that when the incumbency funding advantage is removed, incumbents can expect their electoral advantage, measured as a share of votes, to drop by as much as half. Hall also suggests that boosting challenger spending, which talk radio does, is the main factor in reducing this electoral advantage.[18]

Talk radio also helped upstarts by giving them chances to spread their message even if they lacked the money incumbents could count on. Without much money, candidates have few opportunities to define themselves. A well-capitalized incumbent can easily frame an opponent's candidacy and his or her own through paid advertising. But when unknown candidates lacked money for their own ads, hosts spoke for them and gave them chances to speak for themselves.

As conservative media drove Republicans to the right, the party's candidates increasingly struggled to win moderate districts and states. The candidates who best competed in those places often could not survive primaries against more conservative opponents, which meant that the GOP ended up running extremists in swing-state general elections. Sharron Angle is a case in point. A Tea Party–backed Senate candidate, Angle beat a mainstream Republican for the 2010 Nevada Senate nomination as conservative media cheered. She received huge fundraising bumps every time she chatted with a conservative media star.[19] But in a year that was very good for Republicans nationally, Angle lost the general election to Senate Majority Leader Harry Reid by a relatively small margin, suggesting that a less rigid conservative had a decent chance of unseating him.

Not only did this primary dynamic hurt Republicans electorally, but it also had a serious impact on governance. Fear of primaries reduced the appetite for compromise among Republicans from conservative districts who might otherwise have voted against hard-right principles in the name of governing. Critics derisively dubbed these legislators the "hope-yes-vote-no" caucus—they privately rooted for bills to pass while refusing to vote for them. What's more, it used to be that pragmatic members in "safe" congressional districts routinely swallowed tough votes—politically unpalatable, but necessary from a policy standpoint—because they knew they would survive reelection. This way, peers in swing districts could vote as their more challenging electoral prospects demanded, which typically resulted in a more moderate voting record. The rise of conservative media and purist grassroots groups made it far more difficult for Republicans to vote strategically in this way—they had to support the conservative position, no matter what. Instead of covering for moderates, once-safe members now voted uncompromisingly—with one eye on potential primary challenges—and left moderates to walk the plank. One result was that achieving basic governmental tasks such as passing appropriations bills became far more challenging for Republicans, because doing so often required making concessions to win Democratic support.[20]

If talk radio's stridency over policy didn't make life hard enough for moderate Republicans, the medium's disdain for President Obama did. Red meat and outlandish rumors were of course nothing new for talk radio, and they had created problems for Republicans during the Clinton years. But in many ways Clinton had it easy compared to Obama. Talk radio did everything it could to oust Clinton, but as a white man with two U.S.-born parents, he was shielded from some of the worst that Obama would face. The first black president, with the middle name Hussein and a complicated background that included a Kenyan father, Obama aroused deep suspicion among many conservatives. Toxic, racist rumors abounded on talk radio, Fox News, and conservative digital outlets, which charged that Obama was foreign-born—and therefore ineligible for the presidency—and Muslim. This was not some one-time spasm: conservative media continued to push the "birther" lie throughout Obama's presidency, to considerable effect. In 2008 16 percent of Republicans thought Obama was a Muslim; in 2012 that number was 30 percent, and 34 percent among self-identified conservative Republicans. Indeed, a full seven years into Obama's presidency, 43 percent of Republicans believed he was Muslim. The rhetoric on talk radio also ratcheted up with respect to policy. Hosts decried Obama's programs as socialist and government takeovers. This despite the fact that many of Obama's policies, such as his signature health care legislation, were more centrist than those proposed by twentieth-century Democratic presidents.[21]

This inflamed talk radio discussion trapped Republicans, as South Carolina Representative Bob Inglis learned. The congressman was no liberal RINO. True, he had voted for TARP, supported comprehensive immigration reform, and opposed the troop surge in Iraq. He also acknowledged that climate change was real and caused by humans, and he demanded corrective action. Still, during six terms in the House he compiled a DW-NOMINATE score of 0.518, which placed him in the most conservative third of the Republican caucus during his final Congress. But Inglis discovered during the Clinton years that reviling a president from the other party damaged not only the country but also his soul. Given that, he tried to avoid the venom toward Obama coursing through the right, while remaining true to his conservative principles. Thus, when an attendee at a 2010 campaign breakfast fumed that the unpatriotic Obama refused to place his hand over his heart during the Pledge of Allegiance or the national anthem, Inglis allowed his conscience to outweigh political strategy. He understood that commiserating with his enraged supporter was the right move from an electoral perspective, but instead the congressman pointed out that, in fact, he had seen Obama place his hand over his heart during recitations of the anthem and the pledge. A Republican operative counseled Inglis not to make such "concessions."[22]

Inglis found that it was futile to try to overcome talk radio's mudslinging. On another occasion he met at a South Carolina church with four couples who had donated to his previous campaigns but had given no money to his 2010 reelection effort. He spent an hour and a half trying to persuade them that their worst fears about Obama were not true. In spite of his efforts, one of the donors eventually asked, "Inglis, what don't you get? Obama is a socialist, communist, Muslim." These couples repeated what the local morning and afternoon-drive talk radio shows had been peddling, and nothing Inglis could do or say would dissuade them.[23]

Inglis went on to suffer the second worst primary defeat for an incumbent member of Congress in modern history, netting a mere 29 percent of the vote in a primary runoff.[24] His unwillingness to embrace talk radio's vitriol toward Obama had angered hosts and left voters crying for the head of a latter-day Benedict Arnold. Inglis's voting record and policy preferences couldn't insulate him from the talk radio buzz saw: either he would adopt conservative media's contempt for—and lies about—Obama, or he would suffer the consequences.[25]

That even Inglis could find himself in talk radio's crosshairs demonstrates how successful talk radio and its allies were in weeding out moderates. By the time hosts turned on Inglis, RINOs were an endangered species, and talk radio had to go elsewhere for hunting. Even a strong conservative such as Inglis could be next in line. He espoused a few policy heresies, but most of all he rejected the conservative media's warfare mentality, and he foundered as a result.

22

Trying (and Failing) to Govern

DESPITE TALK RADIO'S intolerance for Republicans who didn't hew to their demands to demonize President Obama and oppose him 100 percent of the time, Republicans recaptured control of the House in the 2010 midterm elections. Once again the GOP had some responsibility to govern, leading to elevated tensions with talk radio. But while this was nothing new—the same dynamic played out in the Clinton and George W. Bush years—the context had changed in ways that made life much harder for Republicans in Congress.

By 2010 the base had moved farther to the right. As their expectations for right-wing wins rose, they became that much less willing to accept excuses from Republicans who broke big campaign promises. Establishment officials and elected and unelected conservatives were therefore on a collision course, because Republicans could not likely achieve the goals they campaigned on while Obama was in the White House, and certainly not while Democrats also controlled the Senate. Their number-one agenda item, repealing the Affordable Care Act, was doomed from the start. This was a moment for internecine warfare on the right, driven by conservative media.

The tense conditions emerging from the midterm provided further evidence of the predicament Republicans had created for themselves by cultivating talk radio and its progeny. Elected officials had given talk radio credibility. They had also adopted hosts' overheated rhetoric and often-hysterical claims, as well as their penchant for blunt, unambiguous commitments, all in an effort to excite the base. And much of the time, it worked, helping Republicans win office or at least compete. But arguably it worked too well. When Republicans took power, those commitments were inevitably revealed to be outlandish—the sort of stuff that made for a great radio soap opera but couldn't possibly find its way into law under the circumstances. Then Republicans were left appearing feckless and disingenuous in the eyes of hosts and listeners.

By 2010 the acrimony between elected Republicans and talk radio was taking a serious toll on their relationship. Boehner, now Speaker of the House, decided to be much more selective about his media appearances. As Speaker he didn't have as much time available for talk radio, but he freely admitted that there was another reason he was less interested in appearing with conservative hosts: "I used to talk to them all the time. And suddenly they're beating the living shit out of me," he told Politico. By 2015, the last year of his speakership, Boehner had dramatically reduced his appearances on national talk radio. He did continue conversing with hosts off the air, once telling Hannity, "Listen, you're nuts." Hannity bashed Boehner less for a few months before reverting to form.[1]

But neither this souring mood nor even the digital revolution changed the core of the House Republican communications strategy. Local talk radio remained the bread and butter. The conference continued to hold radio rows, often luring members to participate by including hosts from their districts. What talk radio's increasingly antagonistic posture did mean, however, was that, while the Republican conference continued to communicate with and rely on hosts, engagement was more often an uphill fight.[2]

This hostility was palpable at every level of the House Republican caucus, not just in the relationship between hosts and leadership. According to a House staffer, during the 2010s a majority of House Republicans grew reticent to appear on national talk radio for fear that a combative, unpleasant exchange would cause more harm than good. (Most local hosts remained friendly with their members, because maintaining good relationships guaranteed regular appearances, which benefited both hosts and members.) And, as members and staffers got younger with turnover, their affinity for talk radio diminished alongside rising interest in more controlled media environments such as Facebook Live and Google Hangouts. A friendly host could ask softball questions, but taking no questions at all, as with a YouTube video, was still preferable because it left nothing to chance.[3]

A similar situation prevailed on the other side of the Capitol. Senate Republican aides scrambled to deflect talk radio's negative attention away from their bosses. Even senators who cultivated relationships with hosts couldn't totally avoid the wrath of talk radio, but they absorbed somewhat less of it thanks to this outreach. Staffers got a chance to plead their case with hosts and producers before hosts pulled out their verbal sledgehammers.[4]

With or without outreach, by 2012 no Republican was safe from talk radio's influence at the ballot box. Even Senator Richard Lugar, who had been winning elections in reliably red Indiana for decades, was on the chopping block. Lugar did have certain liabilities—he ran for reelection unopposed in 2006, so his political machine was rusty. He was also a longtime creature of Washington: his residency in Indiana was open to challenge, and his focus on policymaking meant that he was less engaged politically back home. Yet Lugar also was a legend, the sort of entrenched politician who seems unbeatable. The former Indianapolis mayor—Richard Nixon's favorite mayor—had upended an incumbent senator in 1976 and comfortably held his seat for thirty-six years.[5] And he had earned respect on both sides of the aisle as a foreign-policy expert.

In 2012 Indiana State Treasurer Richard Mourdock decided to take his chance, in spite of the odds. He pounced on Lugar's perceived weaknesses and moderation. Outside groups such as the Club for Growth spent heavily against Lugar. The residency issue also took a massive toll. In the face of this onslaught, Lugar's atrophied political operation and damaged political instincts simply couldn't keep up.[6]

Talk radio hosts and other conservative media personalities did their part, magnifying Lugar's alleged RINO status. During his long Senate career, Lugar accumulated a record that hugged the borderline between moderate and conservative (DW-NOMINATE score of 0.304). In his first Congress, he was only the twentieth most liberal Senate Republican out of thirty-eight and more conservative than his party's top leaders. But by 2012, thanks to the attrition of moderates, Lugar was the seventh most liberal Republican out of forty-eight in the Senate.[7] President Obama's affinity for Lugar—he frequently cited working with the Indianan during his 2008 campaign— provoked conservative media's suspicion and disgust.[8] It is no wonder that in an interview with Mourdock on the day before the election, Ingraham noted that she had been criticizing Lugar for her entire on-air career, then eleven years.[9]

Talk radio boosted Mourdock in several ways. He appeared regularly on national talk radio as well as podcasts and Internet radio shows that reached small but engaged and ideological audiences. He even did local shows based outside Indiana, because they promised access to potential donors. Prominent Indiana hosts, especially Greg Garrison on WIBC in Indianapolis and Pat Miller on WOWO in Fort Wayne, provided platforms from which Mourdock could discuss Indiana issues and share his views with primary voters, helping to overcome Lugar's advantage in name recognition.[10]

Nationally, Levin plugged Mourdock early and often, beginning with an August 2011 interview during which he endorsed the candidate. In March 2012 Mourdock chatted again with Levin, who encouraged listeners to donate to the challenger's campaign. Levin implied that Lugar was outspending Mourdock, and the host mentioned Mourdock's website five times during the interview. The appeals produced a spurt of contributions, netting Mourdock's campaign a five-figure dollar amount. The two men spoke on air a third time on the eve of the primary.[11]

Four days before the vote, Limbaugh mentioned that Mourdock was up ten points but was being outspent ten to one, an unspoken exhortation to donate. And on primary day, Limbaugh trashed a Lugar ad. The king of talk called the ad "unconscionable" and said Lugar was not the "kind of Republican" who opposed big spending or wanted to downsize government. Limbaugh even observed that the media, so loathed by his audience, wanted Lugar to win.[12]

Bloggers also championed Mourdock and ripped Lugar. RedState editor Erick Erickson, maybe the most influential conservative blogger at the time, was ahead of just about everyone, singling out Lugar in 2010. Erickson was incredulous over Lugar's support for the DREAM Act, which sought to provide certain undocumented youth a ten-year path to legal residency. Erickson continued hammering Lugar as the primary approached. In February 2012 Erickson linked to a post from Club for Growth President Chris Chocola discussing a National Review op-ed explaining the club's endorsement of Mourdock. In an April post, Erickson chided Lugar's campaign and called for his social media director to be fired. On the eve of the May 8 primary, Erickson headlined a post, "Tomorrow, Retire Dick Lugar."[13]

The following day Mourdock prevailed. That he lost the general election mattered little to conservative media personalities. They smelled blood and saw an opportunity to purify the party, even if it meant losing seats and narrowing the GOP's ideological appeal. Although talk radio and its media allies couldn't elevate Mourdock to the Senate, their crusade facilitated the ever-increasing conservatism of the Republican Party and enhanced polarization in Washington by eliminating from the Senate one of the few remaining Republicans willing to countenance bipartisanship and seek policy solutions. From hosts' perspective, unseating Lugar was a win.[14]

The rush to take out Lugar also reflected the geographic narrowing of the GOP brought about by this insatiable quest for purity. With moderates unable to survive and thrive, the GOP couldn't compete on either coast. When Limbaugh went national in 1988, Republicans held eighteen Senate seats from New England; the mid-Atlantic (counting Virginia); the upper-Midwest states of Minnesota, Illinois, and Michigan; and the West Coast— an increase from fifteen in Lugar's first Congress. But in the Congress sworn in as Lugar departed, that number had dwindled to four.

Talk radio's hard-line posture also influenced the 2012 presidential campaign. Republicans nominated Mitt Romney, another candidate who failed the purity test. Ironically, Romney had become the conservative candidate of choice during the 2008 primary, as conservative media sought to stop the even-more-suspect McCain. But by 2012 talk radio had moved right. It had even less patience for candidates unwilling to engage in political warfare. The Republican field also included challengers far more conservative than Romney.[15] He therefore confronted hostility and skepticism from talk radio during the Republican primaries. In October 2011 Limbaugh declared, "Romney is not a conservative. He's not, folks. You can argue with me all day long on that, but he isn't."[16] In interviews, hosts peppered the candidate with tough questions.

Some talkers never warmed to Romney, even after he captured the Republican nomination. This despite the campaign's avid outreach. During the general election campaign, Romney employed two radio bookers, who labored to build relationships with hosts, channel fitting materials their way, and supply shows with interview questions that would serve Romney's message while appealing to the audience and hosts' particular interests. The campaign also shared notes with hosts, explaining what the candidate and his team had planned for a given day or week, as well as the themes they aimed to convey. The staff was at pains to remind hosts about the issue positions they shared with Romney.

Still, the nominee faced attacks from some conservative media personalities right up until Election Day.[17] Some hosts didn't find Romney militant enough or sufficiently willing to fight back. In August Ingraham asserted that Romney was losing even though "conservatism wins. When you are debating the other side on substance, when you are attacking with substance, when you are laying out a vision with passion, that marries conservative ideals to the problems of the day, you will win." But Romney and his team had brought a "down pillow to a gun fight." A month later she ripped Romney's campaign and the consultants running it, noting, "If you can't beat Barack Obama with this record, then shut down the party. Shut it down. Start new, with new people."[18] Other hosts doubted the courage of Romney's conservative convictions. When, less than a month before the election, the candidate tried to moderate his stances to court swing voters, Iowa host Steve Deace groused, "I'm running out of fingers and toes to count the number of positions he has taken on abortion."[19]

After Romney lost the election, conservative media returned to the project of hampering bipartisanship, which for practical purposes meant impeding governance, since Republicans retained control of the House, while Democrats held the Senate and the White House. One might have expected to find Republicans in a conciliatory mood in late 2012. After all, President Obama had just won reelection, and Democrats gained seats in both houses of Congress. Circumstances also presented a perfect opportunity for the parties to come together over a point of agreement: rescuing the country from the so-called fiscal cliff—a looming, artificially constructed economic disaster resulting from the expiration of Bush's signature tax cuts and from mandatory spending cuts. Members of Congress on both sides objected to the budget slashing—Republicans to reduced defense outlays and Democrats to reduced support for domestic programs. The perverse theory was that opposing partisans, eager to avoid a recession, would have to cut a deal. In an earlier era, such an agreement would have been a no-brainer.

Boehner sought to negotiate. His initial offer would have raised $800 billion in new tax revenues by capping tax deductions for the wealthy, in exchange for $800 billion in cuts to entitlement programs.[20] Democrats rejected this plan as a skewed compromise. They pointed out that the president had just triumphed electorally while calling for higher taxes for the wealthy—not for entitlement cuts. In remarks weeks earlier that had both extended an olive branch and drawn a line in the sand, Obama observed, "This was a central question during the election," one that "was debated over and over again. On Tuesday night, the majority of Americans agreed with my approach."[21]

Had Democrats squandered their leverage and accepted Boehner's deal, it would, by any reasonable calculation, have been a huge win for Republicans. But Limbaugh's standards were higher. He called the press conference announcing Boehner's proposal "a seminar on how to surrender." Limbaugh's view was that Boehner's plan implicitly accepted Obama's premise that the rich weren't paying their fair share in taxes, an apostasy against the church of conservatism. Boehner and his colleagues had "no interest" in defending conservative values, Limbaugh said, because "many of them really aren't conservatives." There was no greater insult on talk radio.

The host made plain that he didn't care about preventing the damage that would follow a drop from the edge of the fiscal cliff, if protective measures could only be achieved by abandoning conservative principles. Limbaugh conceded that maybe Republicans couldn't win this fight against Obama—and, of course, the media—but this was irrelevant. "The point is what you stand for when this is all said and done," Limbaugh explained. "You have something to fall back on and go back to, in order to move forward. We've just given away something that used to be part of our brand." Furthermore, there was "no common ground here. There is no bipartisanship to be had. Isn't gonna happen. There is no compromise. None! There is only concession. That's all that can happen, and that's what will happen." Limbaugh had no strategy for inducing the White House or the Senate Democratic majority to capitulate and no ideas about how to escape the economic risks of a stalemate. All that mattered was conservative purity.[22]

A few weeks later, after negotiations with the White House broke down, Boehner crafted a plan B, which would give Democrats the tax-rate hike they demanded but only on those making more than $1 million per year.[23] Boehner hoped to shield as many Americans as possible from tax hikes while winning Republicans leverage to negotiate spending cuts. Grover Norquist—the godfather of the anti-tax movement, who had secured pledges from hundreds of Republicans never to increase taxes—blessed the proposal. But other hard-liners opposed the deal. The Club for Growth, the Heritage Foundation, and the Tea Party–aligned advocacy group FreedomWorks all blasted Boehner's plan B.[24] They operated from the same playbook as Limbaugh: Republicans should oppose tax hikes, period.[25]

Despite a furious whip effort that included personal pleas from the entire leadership team, plan B couldn't get enough votes to pass the House. Many in Boehner's caucus felt that supporting even a modest, narrowly targeted tax increase promised political hazard, including a primary challenge. These no-votes didn't necessarily disagree with the policy, but they wanted to be sure they were not perceived as heretics. As one member announced in a meeting of the House Republican conference, he could vote for the proposal, but not until *after* the cliff deadline, because then it wouldn't be a tax increase but rather a tax cut for everyone making under $1 million. This was a face-saving move, having nothing to do with governance, fiscal discipline, or even conservative anti-tax principles. The policy result would have been identical whether Republicans voted for plan B before or after the deadline.

But if this congressman's notion was too clever by half, it did express a truth about the GOP's relationship with the hard-right entertainers and activists it had cultivated on the AM dial, on cable, and online: by the end of 2012, Republicans feared what they had created and could only hope to govern by spinning their votes to avoid backlash. They had tailored rhetoric and promises to fit the new political culture on the right and now were so hemmed in that they couldn't fulfill their most basic duties.

During a dramatic emergency conference meeting days before Christmas, Boehner conceded the humiliating defeat of plan B. In a moment of what looked to be honest reflection on his impotence, he recited Reinhold Niebuhr's Serenity Prayer. The death of such a proposal from the Speaker, at the hands of his party, would have been unimaginable a generation earlier. The failure of plan B made it clear that Republicans couldn't pass anything in the House without Democratic votes. The whole country now knew that even with a deadline staring them in the face, Republicans were no longer capable of basic governance—at least not under divided government—whether or not observers recognized the role conservative media played in reaching that historic point.[26]

The result of conservatives' intransigence was, by any objective measure, a less conservative policy than plan B. Because Republicans couldn't pass their own plan through the House, they had no leverage with which to bargain. This put Democrats in the driver's seat. Boehner pledged to allow a vote on a plan that passed the Senate, ensuring that the eventual deal would be more enticing to liberals than even plan B. And so Vice President Biden and Senate Minority Leader McConnell reached an agreement that raised taxes on individuals making more than $400,000 and couples earning more than $450,000 per year—a more expansive tax hike than Boehner proposed—while delaying the spending cuts by two months.[27] In the House the agreement passed with 85 Republican and 172 Democratic votes.[28]

As plan B crashed and burned, Limbaugh never wavered. A few weeks before the final agreement was reached, he preemptively absolved himself and fellow conservatives of responsibility for any outcome that did not meet their demands, including a more liberal bill that might result from the right-wing pressure on Boehner. Any blame for such a bill lay with the Speaker alone, for he had strayed from principle. Limbaugh reminded listeners that he "didn't take a position on plan B." He went on, "If you have been listening carefully and closely, you know that I believe this whole thing went up in smoke weeks ago when Boehner agreed to raise taxes on the rich. That's what Obama's been after. He got it. You can't put that genie back in the bottle."[29]

This pattern would repeat itself often in the 2010s.[30] Time and again conservative media, thirsting for a fight, urged elected Republicans to adopt hard-line tactics and harebrained schemes that could never be implemented. That such maneuvers had virtually no chance of working, and that they came with the potential for major self-inflicted damage, was of little concern to hosts. Their bottom line was maintaining an audience and making money, not passing legislation.[31] They had only to protect their right flanks from upstarts who might better reflect the seething anger they had spent years stoking. And to the extent that hosts genuinely cared about conservative principles and policies, they could afford to be patient: demanding purity might hurt in the short term, but the price was worth paying if eventually it helped to produce a party that delivered on its promises. For the moment, elected Republicans could deal with the fallout on their own.

The best example of talk radio hanging Republicans out to dry in the Obama years emerged from the issue about which conservatives had become most passionate: immigration. After 2007 the battle to reform immigration laws was publicly dormant for more than five years. When Democrats assumed complete control of the government in 2009, they rushed to legislate on bigger and more immediate priorities such as health care reform (a Democratic dream for more than a generation), financial reform aimed at addressing the drivers of the 2008 meltdown, and a stimulus bill designed to jumpstart the flagging economy. When Republicans recaptured the House in 2010, they too steered clear of immigration reform. The issue was simply too hot to handle, given the right wing's strong concerns. There was no chance of getting Obama's signature on an immigration reform bill without inflaming the grassroots.[32]

The 2012 presidential election, however, catapulted immigration reform back into the spotlight. President Obama had captured 71 percent of the

Latino vote, prompting fears among establishment Republicans that a large and growing segment of the electorate would soon be out of reach. An autopsy commissioned by the Republican National Committee concluded, "We must embrace and champion comprehensive immigration reform. If we do not, our Party's appeal will continue to shrink to its core constituencies only. We also believe that comprehensive immigration reform is consistent with Republican economic policies that promote job growth and opportunity for all."

In essence, if Republicans wanted to restore one of their own to the White House, they needed to demonstrate to Latinos that the party cared about their communities and was worthy of their votes. Passing immigration reform also would take off the table an issue that kept Latino voters from considering Republican policy positions that might otherwise be attractive. The thinking among Republicans was that many Latinos were "pro-business" or social conservatives who would prefer to vote for GOP candidates, if only the party first got over the immigration hump.[33]

This conclusion in favor of immigration reform transcended the usual ideological fissures within the Republican coalition. South Carolina Representative Mick Mulvaney—first elected in the Tea Party wave and described by fellow House Republican Mario Díaz-Balart as the kind of legislator who "makes the Tea Party look like left wingers"—supported the effort.[34] To Mulvaney, the existing system provided de facto amnesty. He also understood the electoral calculus. At a Republican breakfast gathering in his district, Mulvaney warned that the party could not continue to write off blacks, Latinos, libertarians, and LGBTQ people, because that left just 38 percent of the country open to the GOP's message—nowhere near enough to win elections.[35] Even conservative broadcasters temporarily subscribed to this line of thinking. Two days after the election, Hannity explained to his radio listeners that he had "evolved" on the issue and supported legislation that would provide a pathway to citizenship for illegal immigrants.[36]

Once again, the Senate took the legislative lead, this time with Senators Charles Schumer of New York, Dick Durbin of Illinois, Michael Bennet of Colorado, and Bob Menendez of New Jersey in charge. They partnered with Republican immigration reform stalwarts McCain and Lindsey Graham and two of their new colleagues, Jeff Flake of Arizona, who had long sponsored bipartisan comprehensive immigration reform measures in the House, and Marco Rubio of Florida.

Rubio was brought on to mollify conservatives. Veterans of the earlier Senate immigration push knew they needed someone from the right flank of the Republican caucus to forestall the kind of outrage that had doomed their earlier efforts. Initially, they courted Utah Senator Mike Lee. But Lee was unwilling to commit to what a staffer described as a "basic tenet of joining the gang": willingness to countenance a bill that would include legalization as a "general concept." In conversations with his colleagues, sometimes at the Senate gym, Rubio had shown himself more open to the possibility of legalization. He was also a young, charismatic, media-savvy Tea Party darling and budding political powerhouse. He had built such a commanding lead in the 2010 Senate primary that his opponent, Florida's incumbent Republican governor, left the party to run as an independent. Rubio also felt he was a good fit for the negotiating role. As a resident of Miami, with its huge population of immigrants, he was interested in and knowledgeable about the issue. And he thought it made more sense to craft a bill than to sit on the sidelines, waiting to vote on something he might not like.[37]

This "gang of eight" understood the pivotal role conservative media would play in determining whether their effort succeeded. After all, talk radio had been a major force in bringing down the 2007 bill. Quietly, the Senate negotiators reached out to conservative stars to make the case for passing immigration reform. The stealth outreach had begun even before the 2012 election. On March 9, 2011, Schumer and Graham pleaded their case to Limbaugh and Fox News honchos Rupert Murdoch and Roger Ailes in a private room at the Palm steakhouse in New York. The senators shared their vision for immigration reform and explained why the label of amnesty was so lethal to any legislative push. At a second meeting, in January 2013, Ailes and Murdoch urged Rubio and Schumer to consult again with Limbaugh.[38]

Rubio communicated frequently, on and off the air, with many of the leading talk radio hosts, including Limbaugh and Hannity. Two weeks after the January 2013 meeting with Ailes and Murdoch, and one day after the gang of eight unveiled principles that would guide their eventual draft legislation, Rubio chatted with Limbaugh on the air. The host was skeptical. He pressed Rubio on the president's willingness to agree to enforcement provisions and other measures important to conservatives. Limbaugh was also concerned about whether the bill was needed and what might be its political consequences. But he was respectful and praised Rubio.[39] That

same afternoon, the host alluded to what he gleaned from his private conversations with senators. "They've said to me, 'People support this. If you
call it "amnesty," it's dead.' They were trying to convince me how it's not
amnesty. They were doing everything they could to tell me, 'We're not
talking amnesty.'"[40]

Initially some of this outreach paid dividends. Fox's most popular hosts,
including Hannity and O'Reilly, were less antagonistic than in previous
years. Ailes and Murdoch skewed coverage in a favorable direction, inspiring Graham at one point to exclaim, "God bless Fox."[41] Rubio had also
tried to keep conservative media on board by insisting on an open drafting
process. Some of talk radio's most effective attacks on the 2006 and 2007
bills focused on the relative secrecy with which they were prepared.
This time opponents would be free to air grievances and get votes on
amendments.[42]

But while it was important to court Limbaugh and Fox, the gang of eight
wasn't prepared for the changes the Web had wrought upon the media
landscape since 2007. Back then, conservative digital outlets were just getting their bearings. By 2013 they were flourishing, and they were not
onboard. Especially important was Breitbart, which had become strongly
nationalist after Steve Bannon took over the reins following Andrew Breitbart's sudden death in March 2012. Under Bannon, a future adviser to the
Trump campaign and White House, the publication launched a major
expansion already in the works. The site took on its new editor's pugilistic,
anti-establishment vision. Bannon loathed immigration and globalization
and pushed Breitbart's writers to attack Republicans who disagreed. He
plowed the organization's resources into the immigration issue, opening a
bureau in Texas and cultivating sources among Immigration and Customs
Enforcement agents.[43]

If Limbaugh's coverage of immigration reform was skeptical, Breitbart's
was fire-breathing and hysterical. When the Senate passed its bill in June,
the main Breitbart story carried the headline "Senate Passes Amnesty by
Vote of 68-32." For good measure, a companion piece listed every GOP
senator "who voted for amnesty over border security and interior immigration law enforcement."[44] Breitbart carried major segments of the conservative media over to its position. During the summer of 2013, conservative
personalities gradually bowed to pressure from Breitbart, other competitors,
and the audience they influenced. Eventually Hannity—he of the "evolved"
position—unevolved and teed off against the Senate bill.[45]

Arguably, conservative critics need not have bothered. The Senate bill was dead on arrival in the Republican-controlled House. Roughly three-quarters of House Republicans opposed the bill, which included a pathway to legalization for undocumented immigrants without first and separately passing some border enforcement mechanism. Most House Republicans favored almost exactly the opposite: only after acceptable enforcement measures became law would they consider a pathway to legalization.

Indeed, many House conservatives saw little to gain in tackling the issue at all, whether that meant taking up the Senate legislation or drafting something else. Eighty-four percent of House Republicans hailed from districts that were less than 20 percent Latino.[46] They didn't see why they should care about reaching Latino voters. And their constituents, who consumed large doses of conservative media, were convinced that illegal immigration and open borders were a scourge. Most of these members agreed, at least in part. They thought comprehensive reform rewarded lawbreaking, was unfair to people pursuing the legal immigration process, and left in place out-of-control border conditions that enabled illegal immigrants to flood the country. And even if a Republican was personally open to comprehensive reform, voting that way meant handing a powerful weapon to a potential primary opponent, not to mention local talk radio and bloggers.[47]

The only option for passing the Senate bill through the House was no real option at all. Like the fiscal-cliff compromise, the immigration bill would need support from Democrats, plus a clutch of Republicans.[48] So House leadership refused Democrats' demand to bring the Senate bill to the floor. Boehner knew that either Republicans would kill the bill or it would barely make it over the line, after which the rank and file would have his head for allowing a vote on a bill that the majority of his caucus didn't support.[49] For Boehner and his team, the Senate bill was at best a waste of time that would raise the hackles of conservative members and activists and at worst political suicide.

That meant the House would need its own solution. Even the most optimistic and involved House staffers conceded that passing legislation was a monumental challenge. The traditional avenue was blocked because the House Judiciary Committee, which had jurisdiction over most immigration matters, was stocked with conservative hard-liners who had little interest in pursuing the sort of bill Obama might sign. The committee was only willing to pursue small, discrete bills on slivers of the issue. Time was also short; the debate would have to be settled before the 2014 election season got in gear, at which point action would become politically impossible for many crucial members.

Against the odds, some House members maintained hope for comprehensive reform. The House had its own negotiating group, feverishly and furtively plugging away.[50] The talks, which Boehner encouraged, dated back to the failure of the Senate bill in 2007. At various points the talks involved up to twenty different members. In 2013 the core Democratic negotiators were John Yarmuth of Kentucky; Luis Gutiérrez of Illinois, the House's most tireless advocate for immigration reform; and Zoe Lofgren and Xavier Becerra of California, the latter, pivotally, a member of the Democratic leadership. The Republican side included several immigration hawks. One was Tea Partier Raúl Labrador of Idaho, who, as an immigration lawyer, had deep knowledge of the system. He joined Sam Johnson, a staunchly conservative war hero whose website read, "If you break the law, you should be deported." Rounding out the team were the equally conservative Texan "Judge" John Carter and the more moderate Díaz-Balart of Florida.[51] The talks were so secretive that multiple members of the group refused to confirm they were even happening.[52]

The House group of eight came agonizingly close to a deal. Matters came to a head in the spring of 2013, as Carter, Labrador, and Johnson were coming under enormous pressure from the right. On May 15 Carter, tired of the tedious negotiations, threatened to pull out unless the group immediately struck a deal on the thorny issue of how to handle health care for undocumented immigrants. Working on an iPad, Lofgren and several staffers hashed out compromise language. After breaking into partisan huddles for the first time, seven of the eight members of the group accepted the Democratic-drafted language. But Becerra insisted that he needed to check with House Minority Leader Nancy Pelosi. An annoyed Carter snapped at Becerra, "I don't have to check it with John [Boehner], why do you have to check with Nancy?" The press reported that a deal had been struck in principle, but the next day Becerra insisted on changes.

What followed was an angry meeting of the eight negotiators, with no staffers present. Gutierrez reportedly accused Becerra of sabotage, and the group couldn't come to an agreement on the health care provisions. Labrador quit. He felt burned after making significant concessions, though Democrats suspected he was cynically trying to kill a bill about which he was ambivalent.[53] Three months later Carter and Johnson threw in the towel, citing Republicans' biggest worry: that President Obama wouldn't enforce the tough security and enforcement provisions of whatever bill they passed.[54] Politically, they couldn't afford such an outcome—not with conservatives so riled up about Obama. The danger Republican base voters perceived in his agenda was only augmented by rhetoric on talk radio and other conservative media, which gave the grassroots a deeply distorted impression of the president as an un-American, non-Christian "other." Too many voters had too little tolerance for Republicans such as Carter and Johnson, who wanted to accomplish bipartisan legislation.[55]

The departure of Johnson and Carter from the gang of eight marked the collapse of any truly bipartisan effort at immigration reform in the House. Further legislative efforts were driven by Republicans, with Gutiérrez the only Democrat still engaged—behind the scenes.[56] The House also missed its crucial window to handle immigration before campaign season kicked off. The timing made it far more difficult for conservatives to support such legislation.

In December Boehner made a last-ditch attempt. He hired Becky Tallent—a former top McCain aide who had been intimately involved in the 2006 and 2007 Senate immigration negotiations—to revive the House negotiations. "Boehner Hires Adviser Who Helped McCain Push Amnesty," Breitbart proclaimed. The accompanying story warned that bringing Tallent aboard meant Boehner might want to include a pathway to citizenship in an immigration bill, which would, according to the Congressional Budget Office, "lower the wages of working class Americans." The story depicted Ana Navarro, a pundit and strategist who praised the hire, as "the establishment Republican best known for criticizing conservatives while pushing amnesty."[57]

With Breitbart and more firebrand talkers such as Levin and Ingraham pushing a nationalist agenda, Hannity, Limbaugh, and other stalwarts who were willing to engage negotiators had to follow suit.[58] As Boehner memorably put it after his retirement, "Who was that right-wing guy, Levin? He went really crazy right and got a big audience, and he dragged Hannity to the dark side. He dragged Rush to the dark side."[59] No longer could Republican policymakers woo a few key figures in hopes of neutralizing conservative media or influencing its message. Nor could they count on once-friendly hosts to treat them and their initiatives fairly.

By January 2014, when Boehner revealed his principles for immigration reform, any semblance of neutrality that had once existed on talk radio had vanished. Instead of respectfully interviewing Boehner and gently disagreeing, Limbaugh hammered the Speaker, railing for two days in a manner reminiscent of his rants against the 2006 and 2007 Senate efforts.

> See, my take is, we ought not be granting citizenship to people that don't love the country. . . . We shouldn't be granting citizenship to people who come here and want to undermine it. But we do, in the interest of the fairness and multiculturalism and being nonjudgmental and all this. But the real reason we do is because the people granting citizenship to people like this share that opinion: This is no place special. And that's what's so damn frustrating and inconceivable about the Republican Party wanting to open the country up to this kind of immigration. It just doesn't make any sense! It's the end of the Republican Party. It's the end of the country as we know it.[60]

On March 13 House Republicans got a reminder about the risk of supporting immigration reform. That morning Renee Ellmers, a largely unknown second-term congresswoman from North Carolina, ventured unsuspectingly onto Ingraham's program. The result was an excruciatingly awkward, heated exchange that likely had the staffer who booked it pondering if it was too early in the day to start drinking.

Ingraham and Ellmers started out discussing the Affordable Care Act, but the host quickly steered the discussion to illegal immigration. Ingraham repeatedly accused Ellmers of parroting liberal lines, including one purportedly authored by the Latino advocacy group La Raza. Ingraham charged that unions and countless liberals, including President Obama, supported Ellmers's position. Ellmers replied, "We have to deal with those who are here who are living in the shadows, that's what we have to deal with," after which Ingraham cut her off and unloaded. "What you just said is infuriating to my listeners. I'm speaking for them right now. Your responsibility, I imagine, is to your constituents who are legal residents and American citizens. Whose lives are slipping away from them right now. Whose middle-class lives are being flattened."

When Ellmers invited Ingraham to talk with some of the farmers from her district struggling to find workers, Ingraham exploded again.

> If you're a farmer and can't make a living by following our laws right now, then you shouldn't be in business. If you're an American landscaping company and you can't pay a decent living

wage, and hire people, then move aside because I know a lot of landscapers who actually have gone out of business because illegal immigrants have taken good people's good-paying jobs from them. So yes, if you can't operate in a free-market economy and respect sovereignty, the rule of law, and American immigration law, you're right congresswoman, then I don't think you should be in business.[61]

The next day, Ingraham welcomed Ellmers's primary challenger onto her show. The host replayed a clip from the interview, remarking, "Yeah this crazy idea that it's probably worth preserving America, you know your focus as a congresswoman should be on the American people, the legal people in your district who depend on the ability to support their families in order to have dreams of their own. Yes, that is a wild, locked-in position that I have. Guilty as charged."[62]

The Ellmers interview made news and created waves.[63] Assuredly, Ellmers's Republican colleagues heard about it. It was further evidence that backing immigration reform, even if it might be good for businesses in one's district, could pose political peril. At the very least, reformers could be sure they'd be turned into piñatas on the airwaves.

But Díaz-Balart and Budget Committee Chairman Paul Ryan, who had been the Republican vice-presidential nominee in 2012, persisted with little fanfare. Díaz-Balart worked on crafting a narrow bill that would tackle the two toughest issues: border security and the fate of undocumented immigrants already in the country. To figure out how best to frame his bill politically, he had its language focus group–tested and commissioned polling of primary voters in Republican districts.[64] When Díaz-Balart and Ryan felt confident that they had enough support for their version of immigration reform, they scheduled a meeting to brief Boehner.

Thanks to the unforeseen events of June 10, 2014, we will never know what may have come of their bill. Just two days before the scheduled briefing with Boehner, one of the biggest upsets in U.S. political history drove the final nail in the immigration reform coffin. Dave Brat, a little-known economics professor, toppled House Majority Leader Eric Cantor of Virginia in a Republican primary. While many factors influenced the outcome— Cantor was accused of paying too little attention to his district, and Boehner later blamed his deputy for "the worst campaign ever run"—immigration appeared high on the list. Ingraham and Levin had latched onto the race and promoted Brat. Ingraham even attended a rally with the candidate. After Brat won, both hosts declared victory and took the credit. While autopsies of the race eventually showed that these boasts were dramatically overstated, Cantor's Republican colleagues saw no need to take chances. If there was any possibility that the grassroots anger bubbling over immigration reform had, in fact, accounted for Cantor's loss, then the issue wasn't worth touching. Díaz-Balart and Ryan's anticipated majority evaporated.[65]

The effort to enact comprehensive immigration reform spanned more than a decade. Two presidents, from opposing parties, and countless members of Congress struggled to shape the project, as did many outside groups. An alliance of conservative media, pressure groups, and grassroots activists undid all of their work. Whether Republicans were always right to fear the power of talk radio–style conservative media is in some ways beside the point, although it is unlikely that so many would err in evaluating the sources of their political vulnerability. The fact is that Republicans believed that if they supported immigration reform, indeed any bipartisan action, enraged media personalities could trigger a serious primary challenge.

As the country became more geographically polarized, conservative media's influence over legislation kept growing because the real battle for office increasingly happened in primary season. A safe Republican district was only safe for a Republican who toed the line. With talk radio and other conservative media on their side, upstarts could take out even entrenched, battle-tested Republicans. And where Republicans weren't safe, right-wing media didn't care. It was better to get rid of a RINO and empower Democrats than let an unprincipled conservative linger, tarnishing the Republican brand.[66] When every vote in Congress risked focused backlash from local talk radio and the insurgent-boosting invective of Breitbart or a national star, many Republicans felt they couldn't afford to act strategically or even follow their consciences, unless doing so happened to appease conservatives' relentless demands.

The result was paralysis.[67] In the 2010s, the Republican Party could no longer contribute to functional governance. Talk radio and the copycats it inspired on cable and online had obliterated the Republican Party that husbanded them and installed in its place a party of conservative purity incapable of accomplishing more than the bare minimum in divided government. In the years to come, even unified government would prove to be a challenge.

23

Turning the Power Structure Upside Down

SEETHING CONSERVATIVE ANGER over the GOP leadership's perceived heresies roiled the waters and made governance harder. But it was a boon for one group of Republicans: those on the far right ready to take up the mantle of Gingrich and the other bomb throwers who had recognized talk radio's potential decades earlier.

The new extremists—some elected to Congress in 2010 and after, others elected earlier but carried to prominence amid the Tea Party wave—understood and took advantage of their shared interests with conservative media personalities. They had been championed by right-wing hosts and columnists. Many, such as Texas Senator Ted Cruz, had received significant primary boosts from talk show hosts, television anchors, and bloggers.[1] The fresh faces of the right promoted themselves using social media, but they were still eager for the celebrity afforded by talk radio and cable news. And they also knew that defying or attacking leadership was a good way to earn conservative media's interest and applause. Strident politicians made great guests; their rhetoric fit talk radio and cable news, and their black-and-white issue positions captured the mood of hosts and audiences alike.

The rapid rise of hard-right figures such as Ohio Representative Jim Jordan and Texas Representative Louie Gohmert, who sometimes filled in for Hannity when the host went on vacation, exposed the disconnect between the new media power structure and the traditional congressional hierarchy. These men once would have been gadflies or curiosities—opinionated backbenchers with no real influence. Yet in the conservative media empire, they were rock stars, a status that empowered them to take on senior figures and in turn gain even more plaudits on the right. There was little leadership could do to respond. In the past junior members of the House would never have dreamed of publicly challenging the leadership, for fear of being banished to congressional Siberia. A representative from a landlocked district might have found himself assigned to the now-defunct Merchant Marine and Fisheries Committee. But by the 2010s retaliation was nearly impossible because it promised to enrage conservative media and create more headaches for leadership. Under this new dynamic, bold rejection of leadership was a ticket to prominence, not the gulag.

Members of Congress who specialized in incendiary rhetoric, pithy soundbites, and bellicose conservatism captured more attention than committee chairs and some members of the leadership, even as they exerted less influence internally on Capitol Hill and routinely damaged their party.[2] They had no chance of entering the leadership themselves—one staffer related that, during a leadership shakeup in late 2015, Gohmert could have secured perhaps four votes for the speaker's gavel, one more than he actually received when he challenged Boehner the previous January—but they served the purposes of talk radio.[3]

No audience wanted to hear a committee chair's boring talking points when it could listen to Ingraham and Cruz spitball about whether his Republican colleagues fought harder against President Obama's executive overreach or against Cruz's own conservative agenda. As far as Cruz was concerned, the contest was "not even close." This was 2015, long after Democrats had largely given up on the prospect of working fruitfully with Republicans. Yet Cruz lamented that his fellow Republicans "don't fight at all against Obama. Right now, Republican leadership spends all of their time fighting to defeat conservatives. They don't spend any time trying to honor the commitments that were made to the men and women who elected us. They don't spend their time trying to defeat Obama. In fact what they focus on is funding Obama's priorities." For a kicker, Cruz wondered, "What on earth is happening when Republican leadership operate as the most effective Democratic leaders Congress has ever had?"[4] That sort of line was talk radio gold, capturing the frustration of hosts and listeners in a memorable way.

To hear the likes of Cruz and Jordan, they were the ones fighting for hosts and listeners, while leadership was nowhere to be found. In a conversation with Ingraham, Jordan fretted that his colleagues in the House "didn't get done what we told the voters we were going to do on the president's executive amnesty issue." He went after leadership directly when he complained, "We pull a pro-life bill on the most pro-life day"—the day of the annual March for Life—"and now some people are talking about not repealing Obamacare."[5] It was of course leadership that had pulled the controversial abortion bill, which would have banned abortions after twenty weeks except to protect the life of the mother and in cases where pregnancy resulted from a rape that had been reported to authorities. Some Republicans objected to the reporting requirement.[6] The leadership, too, would decide whether repealing the Affordable Care Act was a priority worth pursuing, even if it wasn't achievable.

Along with conservative media, various factors including gerrymandering, geographic polarization, and fundraising by outside groups served to protect members who thumbed their noses at leadership. Whatever leadership and RNC brass thought of them, these politicians were well suited to the blood-red territory they represented, and they didn't need the party's money to run their campaigns. The leadership also lost an important carrot and disciplinary tool when Congress banned legislative earmarks in 2010. Earmarks, which allowed members to direct funds to projects within their districts through the appropriations process, had been an important means of achieving compromise and team spirit because leadership could dangle them in front of recalcitrant members or threaten to withhold them.[7]

Leaders tried to fight back against the tide. Boehner implored Ailes to stop putting on television members who had little credibility within the wider Republican conference, Gohmert chief among them. The speaker's pleading came to no avail. Mike Sommers, Boehner's chief of staff, was amazed that a member of Congress as insignificant as Gohmert got so much attention from conservative media. But Sommers also understood that Gohmert and his ilk gave hosts and listeners exactly what they wanted, even if these members were the rump of the Republican caucus. For, back in his high school days, Sommers himself had loved hearing Bob Dornan, "the Louie Gohmert of his day," fill in for Limbaugh. At the time Sommers thought Dornan was the "best thing since sliced bread." Decades later he could only shake his head as Dornan's successors got the same airtime.[8]

A clear example of the new, media-driven power relations came in June 2015, when an inside-baseball dispute exploded into a major story in conservative radio, TV, and online publications. The issue was esoteric: traditionally, House leadership, regardless of party, demands that its members at least support the caucus on procedural-rule votes, which dictate the terms under which bills come to the House floor. Without majority coop-eration on procedural votes, the House becomes virtually ungovernable, and the minority can hijack control.[9] Anyone in a position of power—a committee or subcommittee chair, the recipient of a desirable committee assignment—who bucks leadership on rules votes risks reprisals.

By the summer of 2015, conservatives had repeatedly flouted this impor-tant norm and others. More moderate Republicans and leadership allies were demanding consequences. The last straw came when thirty-four Re-publicans voted against a rule on a key trade bill. One of them was Mark Meadows of North Carolina, an arch-conservative who, earlier that year, had been among the twenty-five Republicans who opposed Boehner in the floor vote to determine the Speaker. As punishment for the rules vote, Over-sight Committee Chairman Jason Chaffetz yanked Meadows's chairman-ship of the panel's Subcommittee on Government Operations.[10]

The move was a long time coming, from leadership's perspective. Meadows had a genial personality; House Majority Leader Kevin Mc-Carthy nicknamed him "sunshine." But Meadows also had a habit of saying one thing to party leaders behind closed doors and then acting dif-ferently in public. One leadership staffer fumed that Meadows was a "lying fucking snake"; another labeled him "two-faced." In a post-retirement in-terview, Boehner called Meadows an "idiot."[11] Meadows was also a leader of the right-wing Freedom Caucus; while the group formed officially in 2015, its members, cheered by allies in conservative media, had been con-founding and challenging leadership since at least 2011.[12] Leadership took a stand against Meadows in the hope of regaining control more broadly.

As news of the rebuke spread, Meadows went on the attack, marshaling conservative media to prosecute his case against leadership. He chatted with more than fifteen hosts over the next few days, and the story caught fire online. Levin exploded over the news, unleashing an epic on-air tirade against Chaffetz and House leadership. He labeled Boehner a "fool" and a "moron" and McCarthy "the sleaziest of the bunch." Levin said he wouldn't even allow the majority leader "to sell me a used car." As the host saw it, Meadows was being punished because "he doesn't fall in line with Boehner, who falls in line with Obama. He's not the first one. He's not the first one. They've gone after a number of these conservatives and they in-tend to go after more." Levin concluded with a call to action against House leadership and the GOP itself:

We need a new Republican Party that's principled, that's conservative, that believes in America. Not this crap that goes on inside the Beltway. They fund Obamacare, they fund amnesty. They fund whatever Obama wants. . . . They want to destroy the conservative movement. . . . We need to go after these three guys: Boehner, McCarthy, and [Majority Whip Steve] Scalise. We need to find serious candidates, serious candidates who aren't going to screw up. And nationwide. All of us wherever we live, whomever we are, we need to contribute directly to those campaigns, and we need to target these three in particular.

Later in the program, Levin hosted Meadows, whom he labeled a "standup patriot and a conservative." Meadows endorsed Levin's call for leadership change and accused leadership of imposing "a culture of punishment here trying to keep conservatives silent. I for one am not going to be silent. The voice of the American people must be heard. . . . We've just got to stand up for freedom and the American way."[13]

In a conversation with Jordan, a staunch Meadows ally, Ingraham lashed out at House leaders, comparing them to the Mafia.[14] Fox host Neil Cavuto picked up the theme in an interview with Chaffetz, describing the maneuver against Meadows as "very Tony Soprano-ish."[15] Breitbart provided breathless coverage, with one headline reading, "'Courageous Conservative' Axed by GOP Leadership for 'Voting His Conscience.'" Breitbart's Sunday night talk radio show included an interview with Meadows, and the publication reported that conservative luminaries such as Palin, Cruz, and former Arkansas Governor Mike Huckabee were displaying solidarity with the scorned congressman.[16] Chaffetz's office was inundated with phone calls from angry conservatives.[17]

Jordan—whom the retired Boehner branded an "asshole" and a "legislative terrorist"—worked behind the scenes to organize an insurrection on the Oversight Committee.[18] Freedom Caucus members on the committee informed Chaffetz that they would refuse to replace Meadows, raising the possibility that his slot would remain vacant or that the committee might overrule Chaffetz. Though Boehner praised Chaffetz for stripping Meadows of his gavel, the chairman caved. Concerned more with protecting himself from an embarrassing defeat than sticking with the leadership that made him a committee chair, Chaffetz restored Meadows's position without securing even some sort of face-saving concession. Meadows then twisted the knife, defiantly vowing "to vote and conduct myself in accordance with my conscience, what my constituents want me to do, and what is best for the country."[19]

As a congressional staffer related, the lesson for Meadows was that the pressure he generated through conservative media made him "untouchable."[20] It was therefore no surprise when, a month later, Meadows doubled down by offering a motion to vacate the chair, which, if successful, would have removed Boehner from the speakership. The motion never went to a vote—and, if it had, it would have failed—but it was yet another sign of how the power dynamic had shifted in the House.[21]

That shift had everything to do with the influence of conservative media, not the usual news organizations of record. Though the Meadows case was a cause célèbre in conservative media and Beltway-centric publications such as *Roll Call*, it generated limited coverage, and no heat, in the national mainstream media. What moved Chaffetz wasn't fear of a *New York Times* editorial or tough questions on *Meet the Press*. It was conservative anger mobilized by Levin, Ingraham, Fox, and Breitbart that led the congressman to reverse course. The case also illustrates conservative media's continuing affinity for—and successful exploitation of—hypertechnical minutiae. Much as hosts had once made esoteric telecom rules the stuff of a passionate talk radio debate, twenty years later hosts and online outlets drew blood from the stones of procedural rules and subcommittee chairmanships.

By the fall of 2015 Boehner had had enough. On October 31 he retired from Congress, only to watch his successor join his chief GOP antagonists, the Freedom Caucus.[22] The right wing of the House had stymied every big deal Boehner tried to cut and made securing 218 votes for legislation a chore, even when that meant preventing Congress from doing the nuts and bolts of its job.[23] Yet hard-line conservatives were never satisfied; they still grumbled that the caucus wasn't fighting fiercely enough for conservative causes. Summing up right-wing opinion three days after the Speaker announced his retirement, Ken Cuccinelli, a conservative activist and former Virginia attorney general, told Ingraham that Boehner and McConnell were the "cochairmen of the surrender caucus."[24]

After significant arm-twisting, Ryan agreed to take over the Speaker job. He was viewed as the one figure who might be able to unite the badly fractured Republican caucus. Ingraham, for one, was skeptical. In a conversation with Alabama Congressman and Freedom Caucus member Mo Brooks, the two made clear that Ryan would inherit the same short leash that had so frustrated Boehner. Putting Ryan on notice, Brooks claimed that, according to his staff's research, the future Speaker had "the absolute worst record on border security of any Republican in the United States House of Representatives." While the congressman was reassured that Ryan had pledged not to put to vote an immigration bill that didn't have majority support from House Republicans, Ingraham worried that Ryan had "completely misled the American people" on trade, rendering any promises he made suspect. Brooks replied, "If he breaches his word, then I hope that the House will have the courage to do what is necessary to hold him accountable for the breach of his word." It was an ominous welcome to the Speaker's chair.[25]

Despite the heated rhetoric, Ryan was not about to join the Democrats in abandoning talk radio. He pledged to be a communicator, spreading Republican gospel far and wide, and talk radio was an integral part of his strategy. In his first three months as Speaker, Ryan did eleven national talk radio interviews, and his pace barely slackened for the rest of the year. On Mondays he routinely called in to radio programs in his home state of Wisconsin. Ryan chatted comfortably with national hosts ranging from his mentor Bill Bennett to the skeptical hard-liner Ingraham.

Ryan knew his relationship with hosts had to be less poisonous than Boehner's had become. But Ryan also recognized that hosts would never do for him what they had for, say, Gingrich. Republicans could no longer count on talk radio to be a steadfast ally, but it was worth cultivating hosts just to mitigate the damage they might do. By being accessible and establishing rapport, Ryan encouraged hosts at least to understand where he was coming from in moments of discord.

Ryan's communications team worked to make the most of his radio appearances, avidly repurposing interviews to gain additional coverage. His office advised reporters before he appeared on radio, so that they would listen in and write stories based on his comments. Staffers also recorded the interviews and distributed excerpts and transcripts. And hosts reciprocated by talking up what Ryan told them. When hosts ventured onto cable news, they would share tidbits from their conversations with Ryan, helping to spread his message.[26]

While Ryan's wooing of conservative media was largely successful, there was only so much his efforts could achieve. Hosts did not suddenly cease their outrage at the Republican leadership, their frustrations over immigration legislation, or their praise for congressional extremists such as Meadows. They remained intolerant of the pragmatic impulses even of highly conservative Republicans such as Ryan himself. They continued to stoke the Republican base's craving for unyielding candidates who saw politics as war and Democrats as evil. And they continued to demand a true champion—truer, certainly, than Ryan and his leadership colleagues, who had remained in place after Boehner retired.

In fact that champion had arrived months before Boehner picked up his ball and went home. The week after Meadows cast his fateful vote, Donald Trump rode the golden escalator into the lobby of the Manhattan tower bearing his name and announced his presidential run. The return of Hillary Clinton, one of the bigger villains of the talk radio era, set up the most unbelievable presidential race in recent history.

24

The President That Talk Radio Made

IN THE WAKE of the 2016 election, half of America walked around with giant, I-told-you-so grins plastered on their faces. The other half wore glazed, gobsmacked expressions as they tried to wrap their minds around the realization that the crass, uncurious reality-TV impresario Donald Trump was about to become president of the United States. Trump's election was a stunning plot twist that rattled and confounded the political establishment—Republicans and Democrats, journalists and scholars (this one included), just about every veteran Washington observer one could imagine. Yet Trump's election was also the logical conclusion to the story that began with Rush Limbaugh's ascent.

When the research for this book began in 2010, almost anyone would have laughed at the notion of Trump becoming president. His political involvement to that point had been slight, though he had flirted with a presidential run in the past. Ideologically, he was a dodgy fit for conservatives and the Republican Party. During the Obama years, Trump was in sync with the most vociferous conservatives on immigration, but he also had a long history of defying conservative orthodoxy and Republican priorities with respect to health care, gun control, and many areas of foreign policy. He was no lion of Christian conservatism, either, when it came to issues such as abortion. When he decided to run in 2015, he was practically a lone voice in his party on trade, pushing protectionism while other Republicans extolled the wisdom of free markets. Trump had his fans but was known primarily for firing people on his NBC show *The Apprentice*.

What is more, the 2016 Republican primary brimmed with experienced politicians who excited the Republican base; there was no need to look far afield for a candidate who would please conservative media personalities and their listeners, viewers, and readers. The large Republican field included Wisconsin Governor Scott Walker, whose career had been nurtured by powerful local hosts. There was Senator Ted Cruz, an ideal fit in terms of ideology and tactics. Fellow Senator Marco Rubio had been a Tea Party darling and was a long-standing presence on conservative media who had strong relationships with hosts. The front-runner at the outset, former Florida Governor Jeb Bush, held less appeal, but he was the son and brother of presidents who had welcomed Rush Limbaugh to the White House. He had joined the family call to talk radio's biggest name on his show's twentieth anniversary.

Yet if Trump, at least initially, appeared ideologically problematic, stylistically he was perfect for conservative media. Hosts had long decried political correctness and yearned for a blunt-speaking Republican who would eschew niceties and norms, take the gloves off, and pummel the hated Democrats and mainstream media. Hosts wanted a politician who sounded like them and voiced the grievances they had long stoked and aired, but which the establishment largely ignored. In this respect Trump was their man.

One quality that candidate Trump shared with the most successful conservative media personalities: he was always captivating, even to those who paid attention only to wince and seethe. To put on a good show, Trump ripped pages from the playbook that hosts employed every day.

Trump's style was evident from minute one of his campaign, an announcement speech that was nothing if not good theater. He boasted of his wealth, bragged about his golf courses, and ridiculed Secretary of State John Kerry for breaking his leg in a bicycle accident. It was a spectacle that had little in common with a traditional political speech. When Trump turned to policy, he excoriated China and Mexico as economic competitors "killing" America. He promised that Mexico would pay for him to build a "great, great wall on our southern border" to keep out the "rapists" and other criminals who were pouring across. He coined the tagline that would animate his campaign, proclaiming, "We need somebody that can take the brand of the United States and make it great again."[1]

The mainstream press latched onto the most outlandish and unusual elements of the address, framing them as disqualifying. But conservative media personalities understood what the rest of the press didn't: Trump's shocking language was not disqualifying; it was appealing. Limbaugh was riveted. True, he acknowledged the surreal, carnivalesque element of the speech. "Snerdley and I just spent the last half hour sitting here watching Donald Trump's announcement that he's going to run for president, and we were laughing ourselves silly," Limbaugh said, referring to his sidekick and producer James Golden, known to listeners as Bo Snerdley. "I mean, it was a howl session." But Limbaugh also saw the political genius wrapped in the crazy spectacle. "This is gonna resonate with a lot of people, I guarantee you, and the Drive-Bys are gonna pooh-pooh it. They're gonna relegate it to the carnival characteristics of the campaign and so forth, but it's gonna resonate, just like [1992 and 1996 presidential candidate Ross] Perot did. Do not misunderstand this." After his many years talking to the conservative grassroots, Limbaugh could be confident that "the more the media hates this and makes fun of it and laughs, the more support Trump's gonna get."[2]

Trump's speech took off immediately in the most influential right-wing spaces online. Breitbart wrote up the announcement under the headline, "Donald Trump Wants to Make America Great Again, Announces 2016 Campaign." Several paragraphs of the article were devoted to the candidate's pledge to crack down on illegal immigration.[3] Trump's online following was massive and admiring, thanks in no small part to Twitter—a new kind of platform impeccably suited to Trump's rhetorical style—and other social media.

The divergent responses to Trump's kick-off address made clear just how different the world looked in the conservative media echo chamber by 2015. Equating undocumented immigrants with rapists infuriated many on the outside, but, as Limbaugh knew, this was exactly the sort of thing talk radio listeners loved to hear and, indeed, heard often. To their ears, it was the sort of "straight talk" that had been purged from the public conversation by overzealous liberals worried about offending anyone. It was a masterpiece even by the standards of the most outrageous talkers, thanks in no small part to the succeeding disclaimer: "some, I assume, are good people." That addendum enabled Trump fans to write off as oversensitive anyone screaming about racism. It was pure AM-dial stuff: using mockery simultaneously to insult and disarm politically correct opponents, all while winking at the base.

To talk radio listeners, the comment wasn't even controversial. Limbaugh, for one, readily agreed with Trump that the Mexican government was knowingly sending rapists and other "debris" to the United States. A few months later, after Trump was pressed on the claim in the first Republican debate, Limbaugh remarked on how he'd covered the topic and credited Trump for inserting the issue into the debate. As far as Limbaugh was concerned, it was axiomatic that Trump was just sharing uncomfortable truths.[4]

Polling bore out the startling dichotomy in how the "rapists" claim was received. A 48 percent plurality of respondents in one poll said the comments made them less likely to vote for Trump. In a second poll, 53 percent of respondents said Trump's assertion was wrong. In a third, a 37 percent plurality of respondents found the remarks insulting, racist, and having no place in a presidential campaign. But the same polls also showed that the language worked well enough for Trump. In that last poll, another 36 percent thought Trump was raising an important issue but should have been more careful with his language, and 26 percent thought "Trump had the guts to say exactly what was on his mind about an important problem we need to deal with."[5] In the first poll, 44 percent of respondents—a minority, but a substantial one—thought Trump was basically right. In the second, 15 percent of respondents said they were more likely to vote for Trump because of the comments.[6] Undoubtedly Trump alienated many voters with his comments, but a sizable portion of the electorate bought what he was selling, just as millions appreciated the same language when they heard it on the radio.

How had Trump settled on a political style ideally suited to conservative media fans? And how did America's top talk radio host know that the candidate's proposals and rhetoric would resonate with his audience? Quite possibly because Trump had road-tested some of his key themes during years of talk radio appearances. He used these segments both to build a political brand and to promote his business endeavors. For instance he discussed immigration with Levin and others.[7] In one especially notable 2012 chat with Ingraham—which segued seamlessly from politics to *The Apprentice* and the Miss Universe Pageant, which Trump owned at the time—the future president mused:

> You know most of the people that talk like Jeb are mediators, they want to sort of come down the middle. I'm not sure that this country can afford a mediator at this point. I think you have to go all out. If we're going to be great again, and right now we're

not great, we're a debtor nation as you understand. I think if this
country is going to be great again, I'm not sure that we can have
a negotiator, a mediator, a person in the middle.[8]

Years before he urged voters to "Make America Great Again," Trump had
the tagline on his mind. He instinctively knew it would resonate with a
talk radio audience.

In fact the themes and key issue positions of Trump's campaign were familiar to Ingraham's listeners a full two months before his announcement
speech. In a chummy, playful April 2015 conversation in which Ingraham
laughingly suggested that Trump rename government agencies after
himself—for instance, the "Trump Border Patrol"—mentioned how often
she frequented his Florida club Mar-a-Lago, and counted herself among
those who didn't expect him to actually run for president, Trump laid out
what sort of candidate he would be. On trade, he explained:

> Trade is killing us. What trade is doing to this country is killing
> us. You know free trade, I believe in free trade. But one thing
> I've seen over the years, free trade is great if we have smart people
> negotiating for us. But if we have dummies negotiating for us,
> which is what we have, free trade is not so good. Because the free
> trade is good for them, but it is not good for us. And if you look
> at China, they've taken our jobs. You look at so many other coun-
> tries. We don't make good deals any more.

Trump boasted he would do a great job as president because "the China
thing would be over. It would be ended. Mexico and the borders and the
everything would be proper." And he unveiled his biggest promise. "Look,
I've built some of the greatest buildings in the world," he bragged. "Walls
are easy. I will tell you, you will have a wall like nobody's ever had. And
there won't be people coming across that border unless it's legal."

Trump employed his soon-to-be-famous tagline twice in the interview.
At one point he took a dig at Jeb Bush, telling Ingraham, "I want to think
about making America great again. And Jeb can't do that, but I can."[9]
Though he later appeared to be a fantastically undisciplined candidate
lacking core convictions, Trump had a vision and style in place well before he declared his intention to run.

The opening weeks of Trump's campaign set the tone for the entire
seventeen-month spectacle. Repeatedly he made incendiary statements of

the sort that would have ended the career, let alone the campaign, of any other politician. The media, the political class, and his rivals watched dumbfounded as the comments failed to dent his chances. His poll numbers might dip momentarily, only to rebound.

What Trump got away with may be unprecedented. For instance on July 19, 2015, he went nuclear on McCain, a former POW almost universally viewed as a war hero. "He's not a war hero," Trump insisted. "He was a war hero because he was captured. I like people who weren't captured." Trump's competitors immediately condemned him. Most Washington observers, already surprised at the month-old campaign's longevity, figured the circus was finally over.[10]

But Limbaugh had a hunch that Trump would survive without any long-term damage, and the host was right. After three decades behind the mic, Limbaugh knew better than anyone that conservatives were fed up with the very establishment figures who wrote Trump off for speaking his mind about McCain, an impure conservative respected by talk hosts and listeners for his military service but maligned for his politics. Limbaugh also presciently recognized that Trump was handling the outrage unleashed by his remark in an unusual way: he was pushing back. Typically when the establishment judged that a Republican had transgressed, "The perp apologizes, begs forgiveness, and is never to be seen or heard from again," Limbaugh explained. But Trump responded to criticism by renewing his attack on McCain and attempting to switch the discussion to veterans' affairs. Limbaugh observed that Americans were seeing something they hadn't seen in a while, "a target stand up and refuse to go away."

Without defending Trump's comments, Limbaugh articulated a rationale for continuing to support him. The host reminded listeners that it was not them but rather the wretched media—a Democratic Party appendage—that made "an arbitrary decision or judgment that some Republican has said something so intolerable, so politically incorrect, so reprehensible that civil discourse demands this person just go away. Maybe even die! But certainly get out of our sight and stop talking. That's always what happens, because the perps fall for the belief that the majority of the American people share that sentiment."[11] In Limbaugh's formulation, the media was hounding Trump, as they had other Republicans, but it was his listeners, the voters, who got to decide whether Trump should go away. He reminded Trump supporters in the audience precisely why they liked the man: he shot from the hip with little regard for what the media or the PC police thought. Limbaugh's framing essentially challenged listeners to come to Trump's defense or else allow the media to win.

To the media's amazement, Trump's comments about McCain didn't hurt him. With some voters, the remarks might even have helped. A late June Fox News poll of those who were "more likely" to vote in a Republican primary or caucus put Trump second at 11 percent. But a mid-July Washington Post/ABC News poll taken over the course of several days before and after the McCain comments showed Trump soaring to the lead with 23 percent. And four late July and early August polls, based on surveys taken only after the remarks, showed him still in first place, with levels of support ranging between 19 and 26 percent.[12]

This polling didn't surprise talk radio hosts in the least. Ingraham counseled the astonished establishment to go beyond rebuking Trump and instead think about why he was so popular. "How is it that the field is so susceptible to being, at least for the moment, Trumped?" she asked.[13] It was a rhetorical question. Hosts understood Trump's appeal because it was their appeal. The Republican base ate up his outrageous comments, just like it did hosts'. Over the years their incendiary rhetoric repeatedly got them singed by the mainstream media and watchdog groups, yet they thrived. Their audiences stuck with them through turbulent moments, even when advertisers did not. Hosts knew that their popularity was a function of saying what their listeners felt but were not comfortable expressing publicly. Why wouldn't listeners want the same from a politician?

After all, listeners had been demanding candidates who sounded like their favorite hosts for years. They had been telling hosts they were sick of ho-hum candidates who shrank from establishment criticism. Trump didn't shrink. Like hosts, he relished the establishment's disapproval. It was his selling point, the source of his power.

This endeared Trump to hosts and their audiences, but it didn't make him an automatic winner in talk radio land. Early in the campaign, many hosts were far bigger fans of Cruz than of Trump.[14] Like Trump, the senator appealed to fed-up Republicans by courting opprobrium. Like Trump, he was highly combative and absolutely unwilling to abide by the clubby norms of Washington. But unlike Trump he was thoroughly conservative in his views and to some extent in his manner; Cruz supporters didn't have to overcome niggling concerns about crudeness or previous liberalism.

When he said something provocative, it was typically an articulation or defense of a conservative principle, not a personal attack that left even some conservatives squeamish.

But one incident was different. About a week after the McCain remark, Cruz showed why Trump didn't have a monopoly on talk radio's heart. In what the Associated Press dubbed "a stunning, public attack on his own party leader," Cruz went after McConnell as a liar and no better than his Democratic predecessor, Harry Reid. It was a slur of epic proportions in Republican politics, and the perfect story for talk radio. There was no complexity or ambiguity to it; it was a simple and understandable case of hero versus villain, Cruz against the embodiment of the establishment and everything talk radio hosts and listeners hated about it.

Cruz had asked McConnell in a meeting of Republican senators if he had cut a deal to allow a vote on reauthorizing the Export-Import Bank in order to smooth passage of trade-promotion authority, which fast-tracked trade bills and made them easier to pass.[15] The business community favored both moves, but the right vehemently opposed the Export-Import Bank as an engine of crony capitalism. Pockets of the right also opposed trade-promotion authority, at least when Obama was in office. Cruz had agreed to vote for trade-promotion authority, which he supported, only after McConnell reassured him that no bargain on the bank had been struck.

On July 24 Cruz stood on the Senate floor and charged McConnell with perfidy. In doing so the Texan trampled on the Senate's norms and violated a rule prohibiting senators from disparaging one another. But Cruz was unapologetic, instead taking his crusade to a more hospitable forum. That very afternoon he began his talk radio blitz with—who else?—Limbaugh.[16] "It's what I refer to as a Washington cartel," Cruz said, describing McConnell and his ilk. "It's career politicians in both parties who get in bed with lobbyists and special interests." Cruz also worked several pitches for his campaign website into the conversation.[17]

Later that day he spoke with Levin, a major backer. The host routinely championed Cruz's initiatives, occasionally had the senator on, and frequently spoke with his Senate staff.[18] Before Cruz came on that day, Levin lionized him, equating him with the beloved fictional senator Jefferson Smith, from the 1939 movie *Mr. Smith Goes to Washington*. Cruz, like Jimmy Stewart's Smith, was "a man with absolute integrity surrounded by corrupt politicians," while McConnell was "intellectually and politically corrupt." Levin played more than six-and-a-half minutes of Cruz's floor speech, an eternity in talk radio time. The host described the speech as "iconic"; upon hearing it, he told listeners, "I called my buddy Rush, I called my buddy Hannity, I said listen to this."

To brush aside media critics who said Cruz's speech was a stunt designed to advance his campaign, Levin contended that the move wouldn't help Cruz politically. But once Cruz was on the air, he of course pitched his candidacy and platform. Levin also let the senator brag about how many people were donating via his website, which he mentioned four times. Levin equated Cruz to Ronald Reagan, a virtual deity among conservative Republicans. In all, more than a quarter of Levin's program for the day, excluding commercials and news breaks, was devoted to the story and interview.[19]

Cruz's gambit was another sign that 2016 would be a year of the outsider. He was willing to take the risk because he calculated that it would win more admiration from Republicans than it would lose. Base voters were tired of traditional politicians; they wanted the kind of Republican who took on the mainstream media and leaders in both parties. Cruz and Trump were both that kind of Republican. They had what it took to dominate the Republican pack, even if their qualifications on paper were less impressive than those of some competitors.

Unfortunately for Cruz, whatever momentum he might have gained from the move dissipated less than two weeks later when the Republican candidates gathered in Cleveland for their first primary debate. The debate confirmed that the race was still the Trump show. He got all the attention, whether it came in the form of praise or criticism. None of his rivals, including Cruz, could tear the spotlight away.

It's not that the debate moderators were trying to go easy on Trump. To the contrary, he confronted tough, probing questions from the Fox News crew of Megyn Kelly, Chris Wallace, and Bret Baier. Kelly asked Trump about his long history of disparaging women. When Trump tried to dismiss the question by claiming that he had only run down comedian and nemesis Rosie O'Donnell, Kelly swatted aside his denial, noting, "For the record, it was well beyond Rosie O'Donnell."[20] She also pushed Trump on some of his more liberal past policy positions. Trump spent the next twenty-four hours bashing the Fox moderators in media appearances and on Twitter. "I really enjoyed the debate tonight even though the @FoxNews trio, especially @megynkelly, was not very good or professional!" he tweeted.[21] He also retweeted fans angry at the Fox journalists. The media offensive culminated in an interview with CNN's Don Lemon that will live in the annals of political history. Trump first ridiculed Kelly as a "lightweight" who asked "all sorts of ridiculous questions." Then, he told viewers, "You could see there was blood coming out of her eyes, blood coming out of her wherever. In my opinion, she was off base."[22]

The political world melted down over the implication that Kelly's menstrual cycle somehow spurred her challenging questions, though Trump denied making any such connection. Even some conservatives were disgusted by his remarks. Erick Erickson uninvited Trump from a RedState gathering the next day in Atlanta. Trump's only female rival, former Hewlett-Packard CEO Carly Fiorina, tweeted, "Mr. Trump: There. Is. No. Excuse."[23]

But Erickson was the rare host who rebuked Trump. As they had after the McCain comments, most talkers went with the base, confident that listeners would—and should—shrug off what they'd heard. Ingraham justified voters' unyielding support for Trump, telling the *New York Times*, "People have to get their minds wrapped around the fact that the seething fury at the leadership of the Republican Party is real, and it's going to bubble over somehow with somebody, and right now it's with Trump."[24] As Limbaugh put it:

> There's a percentage of the population that is totally fed up with the political class, including the media. And they have wanted things said to people and about people for the people . . . for years and they haven't heard it. I mean, the media is not loved. The media in some cases is despised, and Trump is giving it right back to 'em in ways that many people in this country have dreamed of happening. And, as such, he comes off as refreshing.[25]

Limbaugh, with his finger always on the pulse of the base, read the situation perfectly. For many Republicans, disgusting remarks didn't make Trump a villain. The villains were newspeople who were trying to crush him and conservatives who sought to distance themselves. Chris, a Limbaugh caller, directly addressed Fox pundit and *Washington Post* columnist Charles Krauthammer, who had judged Trump's debate performance a "collapse."[26] Chris argued that Krauthammer and likeminded commentators didn't understand his and others' anger toward the Republican Party. They felt "almost betrayed. You know, we voted [Republicans] in and gave them the power, it's not being exercised, and that anger is so palpable, I almost don't view it as two parties anymore, like Republican versus Democrat. I view it like it's almost like two versions of one party, and the other side is the outsiders that aren't part of it."[27] This outlook would have seemed completely alien to most nonconservatives. To many of them, the differences between the parties could not have been starker in this moment, after Republicans had impeded Obama on everything from immigration reform to taxes. But Chris's comments likely had a lot of heads nodding along to their radios.

Even Levin, at the time no fan of Trump's, blasted Kelly and her Fox colleagues. During a Saturday morning call to Breitbart's talk radio program, which Bannon hosted, Levin took particular umbrage at the question about mistreating women.[28] It paid to get on the bandwagon. After Erickson rescinded Trump's invitation to speak at the RedState event, Trump supporters pelted him with vitriol. It was clear that the usual norms would not apply to Trump and that conservative leaders and pundits would face consequences for crossing him.

Trump dove into the controversy unleashed by his insult because he knew his fans loved him for it. They despised mainstream pundits, even conservative ones, and the politically correct norms that provoked outrage over his comments. He pushed back at his critics with the feistiness his supporters craved, refusing to give an inch. "Dopey @krauthammer should be fired," he tweeted. "The hatred that clown @krauthammer has for me is unbelievable—causes him to lie when many others say Trump easily won debate."[29]

The next day, as the Kelly comments continued to dominate the news, Trump dismissed the uproar as much ado about nothing, claiming that he was referring to blood coming from Kelly's nose. But he also tweeted, "Political correctness is killing our country. 'weakness.'" And, "So many 'politically correct' fools in our country. We have to all get back to work and stop wasting time and energy on nonsense!"[30] This was akin to the follow-up to the "rapists" comment, disclaiming the insult while laughing along with the base at the reactions of apoplectic PC liberals and spineless conservatives. It was music to the ears of Trump's supporters, exactly what they had yearned for a politician to say when under assault from the establishment.

Like the titans of talk radio, Trump grasped that a large segment of Republican voters cared more about a candidate's willingness to upset the establishment and its oppressive rules than about the substance of whatever was said. He also understood that a subset of Republicans *wanted* to hear someone trash liberals, moderates, and journalists. These voters did pay attention to the substance of Trump's repeated, crude assaults, and they liked it. After years of begging for a true fighter, these segments of the Republican coalition wouldn't abandon Trump when he stirred up controversy, even if they might have agreed that his remarks actually were offensive. The more aghast was the establishment—left, right, and media—the more confident were these voters in their champion.

Of course, not every Republican felt this way, and talk radio was divided like the rest of the conservative movement. Some hosts found Trump appalling—unqualified, vulgar, lacking in policy knowledge, and, most importantly, not a true conservative. They fumed about missteps on the trail, which confirmed their hunch that Trump was merely trying to mouth conservative tropes he didn't understand, let alone believe in. They cited his past heresies on issue after issue.

Perhaps for the first time, these hosts found themselves seriously out of step with their audience and the wider world of talk radio. Those who dared challenge Trump confronted blowback from listeners, colleagues, and, in some cases, bosses. But regardless of whether hosts liked Trump, they couldn't escape him. He sucked up all the oxygen on talk radio during the primary. Always mindful of the bottom line, even hosts who found Trump distasteful talked about him daily, as he made nearly constant news.

With Republicans badly fractured—and the staunchest conservatives split between Trump and Cruz—even the biggest stars in talk radio were bound to annoy one or another portion of their audience. In the wake of Trump's resounding win in the New Hampshire primary, Limbaugh made news with lavish praise for Cruz's conservative credentials, though the host stopped just short of an endorsement. "If conservatism is your bag, if conservatism is the dominating factor in how you vote, there is no other choice for you in this campaign than Ted Cruz," he said. "This is the closest in our lifetimes we have ever been to Ronald Reagan. In terms of doctrinaire, understandable, articulated, implementable conservatism, there's nobody closer." Limbaugh's remarks prompted a caller to question why he didn't break his longtime pledge not to endorse in primaries and throw his full weight behind Cruz. The ever-talkative and forthright host demurred.[31]

As tempers flared with each Trump primary win, no talk radio star had a rockier time than Hannity. In April 2016 he started generating ire from some conservatives for his fawning treatment of Trump. The instigating factor was an unusual one: a report from the liberal website Think Progress. The site found that Hannity had interviewed Trump a whopping forty-one times on his television program over nine months, in the process generating endless softball questions but no actual news. The gems included, "Do [the Chinese] buy Trump steaks, too?" and "Is there any state you don't have property in?"[32] Typically a liberal outlet ripping a conservative host would have warranted yawns or a swift counterpunch from the right. But RedState author "streiff" jumped on the report: regardless of its source, it exposed Hannity as an unprincipled mouthpiece for a candidate pretending to run as a conservative. "One thing this campaign season has showed us is who are actual conservatives and who are the cynical opportunists with no values beyond their own bottom line," the RedState author wrote. "One of the biggest offenders is Sean Hannity."[33]

Hannity responded furiously. RedState was "pathetic" for parroting Think Progress, "Hillary Clinton's surrogate, hit piece website." He challenged the veracity of the original report and the bias behind it and countered that he had chosen to remain neutral and provide his audience access to the candidates. He went no easier on Trump than on any other Republican, he claimed. His producers calculated that Trump ranked third in overall time on Hannity's radio airwaves, behind Cruz and Rubio; on television Trump was second in appearances to Cruz. Hannity freely admitted that his questions for Republicans would be a hundred times easier than those he would ask Hillary Clinton, but there was nothing unprincipled about that. He agreed with the Republicans more, and defeating Clinton was what truly mattered, not who won the primary.[34] But RedState's Leon Wolf fired back, "We know when someone is pro-Trump and only pretending to be neutral. . . . The reason Hannity is being criticized is that he is giving a ton of airtime to a not very good caricature of a conservative, and that he is doing absolutely nothing to expose a faker for what he is."[35]

Hannity's perceived pro-Trump stance affected his interaction with other candidates. After Cruz sidestepped a question implying that he was trying to poach delegates at a possible brokered Republican Convention, the two had a testy exchange. Cruz asserted that people cared about issues and beating Clinton, not process. Hannity countered that it was the question everyone was asking him, to which Cruz retorted, "The only people asking this question are the hardcore Donald Trump supporters." Hannity exploded. "Why do you do this?" he asked. "Every time I have you on the air, and I ask a legitimate question, you try to throw this in my face. I'm getting sick of it. I've had you on more than any other candidate on radio and TV. So if I ask you, senator, a legitimate question to explain to the audience, why don't you just answer it?" Cruz again avoided a straight answer, but Hannity kept pressing him until finally an exasperated Cruz exclaimed, "Let me be clear, I'm not mad at all. The Trump campaign wants to distract from the real issues. I want to focus on the issues, and so when you ask only about the nonsense, how 'bout we ask—you know what people ask me when I travel around? 'How do we bring jobs back? How do we turn our economy around?'" Hannity interjected, "Senator, I've asked you those questions a hundred times." Eventually they moved on to other subjects.[36]

Throughout the primaries and the general election campaign, conservatives searched for any hint of hosts' disloyalty to their preferred candidates. On Election Day, Limbaugh spoke to the pressures he and his peers confronted. "I've heard it from virtually every angle there is, every group of Republicans, conservatives, Never-Trumpers, quasi-conservatives, Tea Partiers, populists, nationalists, they've all had a beef with me at some point during the election."[37]

Listeners' zealousness reflected their understanding that talk radio wielded enormous influence, especially during the primaries. If a powerful host's message was at odds with a candidate's, that candidate might well lose. Never was this clearer than in Trump's biggest setback during the nomination fight: his April 5 loss in Wisconsin. Conservative talk radio boasted an avid following and outsized influence in that state, which went for Cruz.

The state's six most prominent hosts all opposed Trump. Somehow Trump's campaign either didn't know that these talkers opposed their candidate, or else concluded that putting him on hostile airwaves was good strategy. That led to several awkward and confrontational interviews, as hosts grilled and battered Trump. He even hung up on host Vicki McKenna after a fiery exchange about whether spouses and children of candidates should be off-limits. Trump had recently retweeted an unflattering image of Cruz's wife and threatened to "spill the beans" on her.[38]

Trump responded by lashing out at the hosts during his campaign rallies around the state. "In certain areas, the city areas, I'm not doing well," he complained at one rally. "I'm not doing well because nobody knows my message." He blamed talk radio hosts "giving misinformation." At another event he railed against Charlie Sykes, the most prominent conservative talker in Wisconsin. "This morning I was interviewed by a very good radio

guy—not the whack job that interviewed me—his name is Skyes? . . . Oh
he is the worst." Sykes's crime? During their interview he had broken the
news to the candidate that he was a never-Trumper.[39]

Trump's confrontation with talk radio in Wisconsin spawned a burst of
national media coverage.[40] But while the top Wisconsin hosts were unified against Trump, the mainstream press misread the situation. Talk radio
wasn't turning on Trump; Wisconsin was an anomaly. In key remaining
primary states, many hosts favored Trump. Kobylt and Chiampou, the wildly
popular afternoon duo on KFI in Los Angeles, were behind the candidate. Kobylt thought a Trump nomination was necessary to bust up the
system in Washington. While the duo sometimes called out Trump when
he made ridiculous statements, they mostly cheered his style and policy
positions. Their listeners were equally supportive, for familiar reasons. As
Kobylt explained, Trump endeared himself to listeners by rejecting political correctness and saying what listeners were thinking privately but felt
unable to say publicly. People were tired of being locked into two rigid
ideologies or having only two ways of looking at things; to Kobylt, a candidacy such as Trump's was long overdue.[41]

Even hosts in remaining primary states who weren't crazy about Trump
pledged to support him if he was the eventual nominee. Greg Garrison, a
longtime force at WIBC in Indianapolis, respected how Trump had "pulled
the pants down on some issues that nobody wanted to talk about" and "said
some things that needed saying." But he loathed Trump's juvenile and personal insults. Every time Garrison started to like Trump, the candidate
would jump back into the gutter. By contrast Garrison was an unabashed
Cruz fan and always had been. Garrison thought Cruz would be a good
steward of the Constitution, and the host wasn't shy about letting his audience know that the Texan was his guy. Even so, Garrison reserved his
caustic commentary for Hillary Clinton, and he pledged not to stay home
and refrain from speaking out in the fall if Trump secured the nomination. His hope was just that Trump "learns to control his mouth a little
bit" before a potential presidency.[42] Chris Stigall, the morning host at
WPHT in Philadelphia, blasted Trump's "verbal miscues and general lack
of preparation," which, he said, "embarrass people who are serious about
the direction of the country." But Stigall nonetheless vowed to support
Trump in the general election should he secure the nomination.[43]

While the titans of talk divided over Trump—some embracing him
wholeheartedly; others viewing him as a figure to be reckoned with, if not

the best choice in a crowded field; others rejecting him entirely—conservative media was changing in response to the candidate's growing popularity and influence. Trump had a penchant for citing and retweeting information from dubious sources, with no concern for its veracity, as long as the claims puffed him up or otherwise caught his fancy. In doing so he elevated a rogue's gallery of eccentric personalities. Suddenly the usual suspects on talk radio, cable news, and established digital outlets found themselves competing for attention alongside a newly prominent class of commentators.

One of the most significant was Alex Jones. A longtime radio host and conspiracy theorist who sold a vast array of products from his Infowars website, Jones struggled to crack the top tier of terrestrial talk radio because he was too outlandish and offensive even for an AM dial dominated by anti-PC firebreathers.[44] He drew the ridicule of comedians and media personalities ranging from John Oliver to Howard Stern to Glenn Beck, though his claims were no laughing matter. For instance he asserted that the 2012 massacre at Sandy Hook Elementary School and the 9/11 terrorist attacks were "false flags"—covert government operations carried out under phony identities. These appalling charges didn't prevent Jones from scoring an interview with Trump during the primary, something inconceivable with any previous Republican nominee.[45]

Another surprising figure who rode Trump's coattails to stardom was Mike Cernovich. A self-help author and advocate of hypermasculinity, he had flown beneath the radar until Trump, his family, and his staffers started retweeting and sharing his so-called reporting. Both Cernovich's inaccurate claims and his denigration of women placed him squarely in the talk radio tradition, dating back to Limbaugh's rants against "feminazis" a quarter-century earlier. Cernovich garnered hundreds of thousands of retweets and followers, who would employ hashtags he designed to get topics trending. More traditional conservative media, which had never been averse to a good conspiracy theory targeting Democrats, bought in to an extent. Cernovich promoted rumors that Clinton had Parkinson's disease and other serious ailments, earning him fans in the conservative broadcast world. Fox anchor Lou Dobbs followed him on Twitter.[46]

A gadfly and executive recruiter named Bill Mitchell, whose perfect mane of silver hair fooled some into believing that he was a prominent conservative broadcaster, epitomized the sort of personality who came of age in 2016. Mitchell's dogged support of Trump turned him into an Internet celebrity. He argued that lawn signs, crowd size, and enthusiasm at rallies were better metrics for gauging the state of the race than polling, and that on this basis Trump would win. Mitchell spent the fall as a whipping boy and source of derision and laughter for pollsters across the ideological spectrum, and on the left more generally. However, in the post-truth environment that was the 2016 campaign, he gained such a large social media presence that the MIT Media Lab listed his Twitter account as the twenty-sixth most influential of the election cycle.[47] On nine occasions, during the campaign and after, Trump retweeted Mitchell, quoted his tweets, or tweeted someone else quoting Mitchell.[48]

Following the long tradition of new conservative outlets outflanking incumbents, this emerging breed of online personalities told Trump fans what they wanted to hear when Fox and Limbaugh were insufficiently supportive. Other sources not so new, such as Breitbart and Jones's Infowars, blossomed with the Cernoviches and Mitchells of the world. During the primary Breitbart's readership and social media shares mushroomed as the site pummeled Fox News for not being pro-Trump enough, dramatically altering online discourse. According to an in-depth study by four media scholars from Harvard and MIT, Breitbart "became the center of a distinct right-wing media ecosystem," with Fox merely in its orbit.[49]

The 2016 election campaign was thus a remarkable moment in the evolution of conservative media. Less than thirty years earlier, there had been essentially no conservative broadcast media to speak of. Nationally there was Limbaugh—trying to do something that few expected to succeed—and hardly anyone else. What disparate strands of right-leaning media existed were operating on their own, with no broader network to amplify them. As the chase for profits led to the growth of conservative media, outlets formed an interconnected landscape that entrenched their style and ideological positions in the political and media worlds. By the time Trump ran for president, conservative media had flourished to such an extent that the newest conservative outlets were denigrating the fixtures that had developed over a quarter century.

But even as the range of conservative media personalities and outlets expanded, the titans of talk still commanded the attention of the Republican apparatus. When it became clear that Trump was pulling away from his GOP opponents, the Republican National Committee turned to talk radio to stifle a brewing mutiny that aimed to snatch the nomination from him at the Republican convention in July. Whatever RNC honchos thought of Trump, they knew that such a move would provoke a civil war within the party, with potentially catastrophic consequences. As part of the effort to head off the rebellion, the RNC courted the biggest talkers to try to heal its fractured party.

In April RNC Chairman Reince Priebus, along with several aides, ventured to Limbaugh's South Florida headquarters, known as "EIB Southern Command." (EIB, an acronym for Excellence in Broadcasting, is Limbaugh's tongue-in-cheek name for his fictional media network.) The meeting between Priebus and Limbaugh, scheduled for half an hour, lasted ninety minutes. RNC officials wanted to convey to Limbaugh what they were doing tactically and why they were doing it. They wanted to explain what they had invested money in and why and to make sure Limbaugh knew what data and field operations these investments had produced.[50] RNC personnel also tried to engage anti-Trump hosts such as Beck and Levin.[51] The outreach produced mixed success, but it demonstrated the party's recognition of talk radio's continuing importance. The RNC was convinced that a Republican candidate could not succeed without support from a majority of prominent radio talkers.

In August, after the convention lined up behind Trump, he formalized his embrace of the conservative media that championed him by naming Bannon chief executive of his campaign. Under Bannon Breitbart had been so rabidly pro-Trump that it sided with Trump's original campaign manager, Corey Lewandowski, over one of its own reporters, Michelle Fields, when she accused Lewandowski of assaulting her after a press conference. Some Breitbart staffers quit in response.[52]

Bannon appealed to Trump in part because he promised to allow the candidate to be himself at a time when his campaign chairman, Paul Manafort, and other staffers had been trying to rein in his worst verbal excesses and moderate his message for the general election.[53] Now the talk radio candidate had a talk radio host for his campaign CEO, encouraging him to keep launching verbal grenades and running an unapologetically far-right populist campaign in terms that sounded more appropriate to the AM dial than the corridors of power in Washington.

Trump took that rhetoric on the road, speaking at massive, raucous rallies. In many ways these carnival-like events brought the world of talk radio to life, with Trump as the host. Attendees echoed vulgar chants and paraded with paraphernalia—hats, signs, T-shirts, buttons, and so on—that they would never have displayed at work or in their communities. Like talk radio, Trump's rallies provided forums where supporters could air their true beliefs without fear of backlash from disapproving coworkers, bosses, family, or other nagging scolds. As Katy Tur, an NBC journalist who covered Trump's campaign from day one, described, "Inside a Trump rally, these people are unchained. They can yell and scream and say the thing they'd never say out loud on the outside. 'Obama is a Muslim!' 'Hillary Clinton is a cunt!' 'Immigrants need to get the hell out!' 'Fuck you media!' On the outside, this kind of behavior is disreputable. But inside a Trump rally, they can tell a woman she's ugly and needs more makeup."[54] For decades the anonymity of talk radio had provided listeners the thrill of hearing their closeted beliefs voiced by heroes on the air. Now Trump gave talk radio fans a live-action version of their favorite programs. Here was an environment in which political correctness was the only unsafe belief.

By early fall talk radio had largely coalesced around Trump. Hannity continued his enthusiastic cheerleading—so enthusiastic that he appeared in a promotional video for the campaign, earning a rare rebuke from Fox bosses struggling to maintain at least the appearance of independence.[55] Even Levin, who had been in the never-Trump camp, announced in September that he would vote for Trump, albeit reluctantly. "So I'm going to vote for Donald Trump. I'm going to wind up voting for Donald Trump on Election Day," he said.[56] "Voting for Donald Trump is not a full-bore endorsement of Donald Trump. It means I'm voting for him to stop her." Trump was not a conservative, as far as Levin was concerned. But with Hillary Clinton as his opponent, there was no other choice.[57]

Limbaugh conceded Trump's flaws while still jumping fully on the bandwagon. "Are you admitting Trump's not a conservative?" he asked himself during a mid-September show. "Damn right I am! Folks, when did I ever say that he was? Look, I don't know how to tell you this. Conservatism lost, in the primary, if that's how you want to look at it." Yet in the same segment, Limbaugh stumped passionately for Trump over Clinton by turning to the issue on which Trump most clearly reflected the feelings of talk radio: immigration. "Hillary Clinton has promised to expand the number of illegal immigrants and refugees pouring into this country," Limbaugh said, presenting his interpretation of her policies as though they were in fact her policies. "We are flooding the country with people who are not educated, who are not able to speak the language, and who are not capable of providing for themselves, and that's exactly what the Democrat Party wants." Limbaugh outlined the stakes. "This stuff has to stop—and, in this election, there is a candidate saying that he's going to stop it. We don't know if he really will, but we do know that Hillary won't."[58]

On Election Day Trump's running mate, Indiana Governor Mike Pence, joined Limbaugh for a friendly chat. While "El Rushbo" admitted that he could understand why people might have problems with Trump, he left little doubt that, conservative or not, Trump was the best choice for the country. Conservatives who couldn't see that, and either planned to vote for Clinton or for a third-party candidate, were making a major mistake. "I do not understand—and nobody's gonna ever be able to make me understand—how a Republican could vote for Hillary Clinton. I just am never going to understand that. Nobody can make me understand it, and nobody can make me accept it, particularly Republicans that have been around and paying attention for the last twenty-five or thirty years."[59] After decades of demonizing Clinton, hosts' apocalyptic depictions of a potential Clinton presidency sounded natural and reasonable even to talk radio listeners who were not totally behind Trump.[60]

Undoubtedly business motives also factored into hosts' eventual turn to Trump. Hosts were loath to damage the bond they had built with listeners because that relationship drove the bottom line. And many of their listeners had been vocal Trump backers from day one. In an interview Jeb Bush's communications director said a host had told the campaign, "Maybe you can talk some sense into my audience, but I sure can't."[61] Listener enthusiasm changed hosts' perspective, or at least compelled them to choose their words carefully as they expressed reservations or chose other candidates in the primary.[62]

A small group of hosts, most notably national stars Beck and Medved, remained steadfastly in the never-Trump camp, regardless of the pressure from their audiences and attacks from their peers. They paid a price. Medved fielded plenty of correspondence and calls from listeners promising never to tune in again. Some wished for his "speedy demise." His refusal to board the Trump train also strained his relationship with his syndicator, Salem Media. "I'm working with a syndicator that is enthusiastically pro-Trump and where all of the other syndicated hosts are pro-Trump," he pointed out. In one market Salem yanked Medved from a choice time slot. He was also excluded from the network's quadrennial election tour.[63] At the time Medved was protected by a long-term contract. But when the deal expired in late 2018, Salem dumped the host in favor of Trump cheerleader Sebastian Gorka.[64] The removal of Medved, who had been with Salem for twenty-one years, was part of a larger purge of anti-Trump voices from the company's properties.[65]

Another refusenik was Ben Shapiro, one of the new breed of precocious far-right personalities making waves in conservative media. In 2016 Shapiro left Breitbart over his opposition to Trump and the treatment of Michelle Fields. He lost speaking gigs and was pressed by colleagues to avoid badmouthing Trump on his radio show, which aired on Salem-owned KRLA, Los Angeles. One slapdash email from a Salem executive complained that Shapiro and cohost Elisha Krauss got "into negative minutiae of the Trump campaign and the GOP convention (e.g. criticizing Trump for having his kids speak at the convention.) Do we really need a side by side audio comparison of Trump's wife's speech with Michelle Obama's? How is that ultimately relevant to the big picture and advance the cause?"[66] Krauss, who ignored these complaints and "kept being me," thought criticizing Trump didn't hurt their ratings. Nevertheless both hosts lost their KRLA gigs shortly after the election.[67]

Sykes lost audience over his resistance to Trump in Wisconsin. The vitriol he confronted online included a picture of his face photoshopped into a gas chamber. Listeners boycotted. At the end of 2016, after almost twenty-five years in radio, he quit his show and went to work for the conservative, but anti-Trump, *Weekly Standard*, as well as the liberal MSNBC. Eventually ownership shuttered the *Weekly Standard* amid accusations that it was redirecting resources to a sister publication friendlier to Trump.[68] Sykes then launched the anti-Trump conservative website The Bulwark. He had been excommunicated from the tribe.[69]

Typically talk radio can't substantially affect a presidential general election, because of the sheer volume of information thrust at every American, whether or not he or she wants it. The news and campaigns are everywhere all the time, reducing the impact of niche media. But 2016 was an exception, precisely because so many conservatives, from high-profile personalities to average voters, harbored doubts about Trump. By accepting Trump anyway—voicing sincere concerns but also encouraging listeners to vote for him—hosts solidified conservatives behind a candidate they might otherwise have rejected.

It was listeners' trust that made these grudging about-faces so potent. When hosts called Trump the lesser of two evils, skeptical conservatives listened. Many hosts couldn't, in good conscience, pretend to love Trump, but they could bash Hillary Clinton, harp on the controversy surrounding her use of a private email server while serving as secretary of state, and play up the fearful ramifications of her election.[70] The other prong of talk radio's strategy was to spotlight the issues most important to conservative voters, above all immigration.

The RNC maintained its usual robust talk radio outreach operation on Trump's behalf, feeding information to hosts and monitoring national and local shows to get a sense of what was being discussed. Hosts also fed intelligence back to the RNC, especially from key battleground states in the Midwest. Hosts could tell that Trump's message was connecting with blue-collar voters.[71]

But talk radio's impact on the election went far beyond boosting Trump and flogging Clinton. That was business as usual on the medium—picking favorites and energizing the base. Talk radio didn't just stump for Trump; it created him. From his incendiary rhetoric, to his conspiracy theories, to the pithy nicknames with which he branded enemies, Trump played the role of the hosts he happily chatted with and whose style he appropriated.

Trump's election signaled that Americans now lived in the world talk radio made. That was the only world in which President Donald Trump was possible. In 1988, when George H. W. Bush learned that Trump was interested in being his running mate, the future forty-first president considered the idea "strange and unbelievable."[72] But by 2016, news, politics, and entertainment had become inextricably blurred, creating an opening for Trump. The network news era of the mid to late twentieth century was over; many Americans received their information from partisan sources more invested in pummeling the opposition than in factual niceties or newsworthiness.

Trump also tapped into the vein of the culture wars that had fueled talk radio's rise. Though voters in 2016 were awash in conservative media, and though the right had consolidated control of the Republican Party, conservatives still felt aggrieved, condescended to, and voiceless. If anything, they yearned that much more for combative figures in their corner—the America they loved was still slipping away, and they had no interest in conceding the fight. Hence the appeal of Trump's slogan, "Make America Great Again." It concisely conveyed the thesis that talk radio had been espousing for decades, as hosts rhapsodized endlessly about bedrock American values under assault and idealized the past in which those values had reigned.

Comments from Trump's adoring fans sounded eerily like those that greeted Limbaugh when talk radio burst onto the political scene. At one primary rally in Phoenix, a forty-seven-year-old machinist named Scott Lausier told a reporter, "He says what we are all talking about, what people are thinking but are too P.C. to say!" At another in South Carolina, thirty-three-year-old Nina Lewis explained, "He stands up for the blue-collar people everywhere. He speaks for us."[73] Trump's fans were thankful finally to have a champion running for office, someone who brushed aside the new norms to which they never consented. With respect to culture-war issues, he was just like their favorite hosts, except he was running for president—and he could win.

Finally, and most importantly, by 2016 talk radio had spent close to thirty years destroying the credibility of the mainstream media, at least as far as listeners were concerned. Throughout the campaign journalists would reveal Trump's objectionable and hypocritical activities, after which pundits and officials would confidently proclaim the death of his candidacy. In each case he took no more than a brief hit in the polls and then bounced back off the mat, stunning commentators. He was able to dodge disasters that would have ended virtually any other candidacy—and his own, in an earlier era—in part because his fans simply did not believe what reporters discovered about him. As one Trump backer, Lynnette Hardaway, told the *New York Times*, "All those provocative words that the media has been trying to use on him for the past nine months, I believe that they're lies."[74] Speaking of his talk radio comrades, Sykes admitted, "We bear some responsibility because we beat on the mainstream media for so long and now there are no credible sources anymore."[75]

Repeatedly during the campaign, talk radio protected Trump by attacking the messenger. One instance came in late March 2016, when Trump ignited a firestorm by asserting to MSNBC's Chris Matthews that if states outlawed abortion, women ought to face punishment for having them. This position revealed a stunning lack of understanding about the pro-life agenda, which supported punishing abortion providers but not women who got abortions. Wisconsin never-Trump host Jerry Bader shook his head. "The beef with Donald Trump is he's not real, he's not pro-life. He has no idea what a pro-life answer should be."[76]

But among hosts Bader was the exception. Limbaugh treated Trump gently while heaping scorn on Matthews. Limbaugh dismissed the anchor as a Democratic hack and "a mental midget." He observed, "Matthews and all these other left-wingers who are so consumed by their hatred for the right wing and they're so consumed by their own bias and prejudice that they think pro-life equals punishing the woman." Limbaugh appeared to be suggesting that Matthews was baiting Trump into a trap. From Limbaugh's perspective, it didn't matter that Trump fell for it. It wasn't his fault for getting his pro-life statements wrong; the fault lay with Matthews who was, as usual, attacking the Republican Party. "Yes, he's trying to trip Trump up on abortion," Limbaugh said. "My point about that is that whole interview was essentially an attack on the Republican Party, not just Trump. It set up a campaign narrative for the Democrats to use against the entire party, not just Trump."[77] What Trump said was almost incidental because he was the victim of liberal media skullduggery.

Talk radio was also there for Trump, calling out the media rather than the man, when he hit rock bottom. On October 7 the *Access Hollywood* recording leaked. Trump bragged on tape to the show's cohost, Billy Bush, about grabbing women "by the pussy." Trump could do this, he boasted, because stars "can do anything."[78] Many horrified Republicans abandoned Trump and demanded that he step aside. Instead he responded two days later with a pugnacious, circus-like performance in the second presidential debate. The spectacle included a predebate press conference with women who had accused Bill Clinton of sexual misconduct.[79]

Talk hosts handled the *Access Hollywood* revelation as they had every case during the campaign when Trump's mouth got him in trouble. Limbaugh lashed out not at Trump but at the media and Democrats for their hypocrisy.

> There is so much hypocrisy on the left when you get to the subject matter of that open-mic tape, *Access Hollywood*, Trump running around there with Billy Bush. Who are the people expressing outrage over this?
>
> The very people who applaud it and celebrated JFK, who had women trooped into the White House in droves. Bill Clinton, you go through the list of Democrats and entertainers who have made their names on the basis of infidelity and catting around and being celebrated and protected and lauded and held up as

great people. "Hey, that's sex, it's not their job. Hey, that's just private life; it doesn't matter to their leadership."

Limbaugh even spun the release of the tape as a good thing that burnished Trump's credentials as an outsider: "If you are seeking to unseat the establishment, if you are seeking to win the White House from outside the world of politics, they are going to destroy you," he said. The host who for years had gone after "the Philanderer" Ted Kennedy asked for a little sympathy on Trump's behalf. "You can take the most moral man you know . . . and there's dirt somewhere, because we're human," he advised. But then it was back to the sins of liberals and the media. His conclusion was boiling: "All these people on the left and the media running around outrageously offended? They're not offended in the slightest by what Trump said! They're capitalizing on it. They're the ones that set up this permissive society! They're the ones who have shred the boundaries."[80] Limbaugh would go on to assert that an NBC/*Wall Street Journal* poll showing Trump eleven points behind Clinton in the wake of the tape was cooked up by Democrats. "The sample is skewed," he charged. "It's all out of whack. It is classic disinformation, classic misinformation. And we find out the people who did this particular poll are working for the Clinton campaign."[81]

Even when there was a tape—Trump's words in the public's ears, impossible to dismiss—Limbaugh found a way to discredit the media. Journalists weren't objectively reporting on the tape. They were stealthy partisan operatives using the tape to try to finish Trump off.

Limbaugh's anti-media attacks over the tape went on for days. But he made time to cover another story as well, sharing the latest revelations from hacked emails related to Clinton's campaign.[82] The message to listeners was clear: Trump might be flawed, but the stench of hypocrisy wafted from Democrats and the media. They wanted to bury Trump for sins that they had long excused from their own, so that someone far worse would become president. This argument, repeated across the AM dial and conservative media generally, helped prevent Trump's support from bottoming out. It dipped, but he didn't suffer the irreparable damage that the same revelation would have done to another candidate, or even to him in a different moment.

Trump knew this page of the talk radio playbook, too. When it came to trashing the media, he gave hosts a run for their money. He routinely savaged commentators, reporters, and entire news outlets on Twitter and at his rallies. His attacks on journalists became so personal that the Secret Service had to escort one—Tur, whom Trump branded "Little Katy"—back to her car after a rally. "What a lie. Katy Tur. What a lie it was," he admonished in response to tweets of hers he didn't like. "Third. Rate. Reporter. Remember that." Nearly a year of abuse later, in the campaign's final days, Trump unloaded on Tur again while ranting about how the "dishonest" media refused to show his rally crowds. "They're not reporting it. Katy you're not reporting it, Katy. But there's something happening, Katy. There's something happening Katy." Boos and jeers rained down on Tur from the crowd.[83]

Tur was not alone in absorbing Trump's wrath. Countless outlets and journalists fell victim to Trump's offensives. CNN and the New York Times were his favorite targets, routinely degraded as "failing," "dishonest," and "low-rating."[84] Trump accused them, and the rest of the mainstream media, of being in the bag for "Crooked Hillary." His assaults could be remarkably personal and crude, not unlike what might be heard on talk radio itself. Among his favorite punching bags were MSNBC cohosts Joe Scarborough and Mika Brzezinski, former friends of his who received harsh criticism early in the campaign for their perceived pandering to the candidate.[85] After they started questioning Trump's behavior, however, he went so far as to reveal that the cohosts were a couple, tweeting, "Some day, when things calm down, I'll tell the real story of @JoeNBC and his very insecure long-time girlfriend, @morningmika. Two clowns!"[86]

These attacks delighted Trump's fans because after decades listening to talk radio, watching cable news, and reading conservative digital publications denouncing journalists, Trump's supporters saw the mainstream media not merely as flawed—a sentiment with which Americans of all ideological stripes, and journalists themselves, would likely agree—but as a genuine villain. That Trump's anger toward the mainstream media derived not just from ideology but also from insecurity and personal pique mattered little to his supporters. Here finally was a candidate taking the mainstream media to the woodshed in the way that they had hoped for, in the way that was deserved. When Trump later called journalists "the enemy of the American people," he was expressing a widely held sentiment that had flourished on talk radio long before his improbable White House run.[87]

Talk radio's long-standing feud with the Republican establishment played a similar inoculating role for Trump. Hosts had spent the better part of a decade deriding the Republican establishment, pausing only during the first two years of the Obama presidency. This practice influenced Trump's standing, blunting the impact of nonendorsements from establishment Republicans, including both former Presidents Bush. So loathed was the establishment in the minds of conservative-media consumers that when Jeb Bush attacked Trump during the primary, it arguably improved Trump's position. Anyone who provoked attacks from Bush, the epitome of an establishment figure, must have had something good to offer.[88] Trump's loudest critics—Clinton, establishment Republicans, and the mainstream press—could do nothing to convince Trump's fans that he was unworthy of office, because in the eyes of those fans, these critics were unworthy of consideration. They were, in fact, the problem that necessitated the drastic remedy that was Trump.

The distrust and disdain conservatives felt when faced with the pronouncements of mainstream political institutions may be the most important sign of talk radio's influence on the American media and electorate. That distrust and disdain underlay Trump's political success. If conservatives had not learned to see journalists, Beltway veterans, and mainstream politicians as discredited, then Trump would not have been able to overcome their expectations at every stage of his run for office. But the campaign to equate journalism and political compromise with vile liberalism—a campaign that didn't begin with Limbaugh, but which was turbocharged by talk radio and its successors—had succeeded to a degree that the so-called experts did not understand. Thus were they left with mouths agape, right up to January 20, 2017, the day Trump ascended the inaugural platform.

25

The Big Picture

THE RISE OF DONALD TRUMP confirmed that, by 2016, the Republican Party had become talk radio's party. The greater proportion of Republican voters yearned for pugnacious, fire-breathing politicians who sounded like their favorite conservative media personalities and openly expressed what they themselves thought but felt unable to say publicly. They were sick and tired of sniveling, vacillating, inoffensive elected Republicans who told them why their campaign promises weren't achievable or why compromises were necessary. Right-wing personalities on radio, television, and digital platforms egged these voters on. Together they pushed for unfiltered, ideologically extreme candidates and a party shaped in their image. Doing so meant pouncing on establishment Republicans who were insufficiently conservative, and therefore not conservative at all, in their estimation. Meeting the mark only grew harder as media figures, pressed by competition bred by new technologies and outlets, skewed farther right and brought the party with them.

Trump was the result of a steady diet of outrageous stories about Democrats and the mainstream media, of hosts and writers telling their seething fans to fight harder every day because they deserved better from the party that depended on their votes. The extinction of moderates was an outcome of talk radio's antipathy to RINOs, portrayed on air as an existential threat to the nation: by refusing to do what it took to neutralize liberals, RINOs were in league with Democrats who placed the American way of life at risk.

What Republican base voters didn't grasp was that what made for compelling radio or television didn't make for effective—or even possible—government, especially in a sharply divided country. In fact talk radio and cable news demonstrated the fundamentally incongruous goals driving pundits and elected politicians. Republican officials were motivated by the prospect of electing party members and enacting the most conservative legislation possible at any given moment. Hosts and media executives, by contrast, aimed to provide the most compelling entertainment product possible and thereby reap maximal profits. Any ideological or political agenda was secondary. The primacy of the profit motive made conservative media personalities unique among the gladiators in the political arena. Elected officials thought differently. They might eventually end up with a lucrative lobbying career, but they focused on political calculations, policy goals, ideology, and constituent whims. "He's in a very different business than I am," Republican presidential candidate Rick Santorum said of Limbaugh in 2012, distancing himself from comments the host had made about Sandra Fluke, a Georgetown University law student who testified before Congressional Democrats on the importance of access to birth control. After Limbaugh branded Fluke a "slut" and a "prostitute," Santorum responded, "He's being absurd, but that's you know, an entertainer can be absurd."[1]

Unlike politicians, hosts did not conceive of political talk programs as vehicles for changing voter preferences or driving policy. Nor did political motives shape hosts' thinking as they plotted out their shows each day. It just happens that, in chasing profits, Limbaugh had stumbled upon a segment of the population he and his successors wound up galvanizing. These were Americans who felt poorly served by the media before Limbaugh entered the national scene in 1988. Hosts provided a voice for these alienated listeners and reinforced their worldview. They created a community of like-minded people who could freely express their conservative ideology at a time when some of their viewpoints were branded taboo in society writ large.

Many observers scornfully dismissed talk radio listeners as mindless robots manipulated by hosts. Yet that characterization oversimplified and distorted the reality. Instead of manipulating fans, talkers harnessed their collective views and brought them to bear on issues, legislation, and politicians the audience otherwise might not notice. This sort of analysis, in turn, shaped listeners' perceptions and stirred their passions. Most listeners had committed themselves to conservative principles well before talk radio exerted any influence. If anything, these listeners had been hoping for something like talk radio for a long time—for media that informed and entertained in a way that reflected their values.

While hosts weren't telling listeners what to think, talk radio did demonstrate remarkable ability to mobilize voters and activists. Thus radio entertainers became something they had not intended to be: massively influential party leaders in a new Republican coalition. They embraced traditional leadership tasks such as fundraising and speaking at rallies. They usually supported the party in general elections no matter who won the nomination, as the 2016 presidential race vividly demonstrated.

Yet hosts also did something new with their leadership role. For, despite their overall support for elected Republicans, media personalities were only too ready to damage Republicans' electoral prospects and the Republican brand when doing so was expedient. Hosts weren't the party leaders of old, whose actions were driven by fealty to the team. Instead, much to the consternation of elected Republicans, hosts did what they had to do to produce good radio, no matter the consequences for the party. A classroom-style lecture on the compromises necessitated by divided government or the imperative of raising the debt ceiling was a surefire way to lose bored listeners. If being absurd, provocative, and controversial—and challenging establishment views—kept listeners tuned in, then so be it. If purity tests and RINO hunting were the only ways to maintain audiences against the pressures of the expanding conservative media landscape, then so be it. Hosts knew that failing to do so would mean being slapped with the RINO label themselves.

None of this is to say that hosts were other than sincere. Authenticity was pivotal to forging a bond with listeners, who would have seen through someone simply mouthing tropes or playing at conservatism. Hosts spoke their true convictions in a manner that would attract and hold listeners. As time went on, that meant disregarding whatever pragmatic impulses they had and sticking, or reverting, to their ideological convictions, as when Hannity reversed his "evolution" on immigration.

Hosts did become more uncompromising, but not because their views changed with the shifting political winds. As they and their fans became fed up with the seemingly tepid conservatism, both ideologically and temperamentally, of the Republicans they empowered, hosts grew bolder and more scornful of half measures or practical necessity. It wasn't hosts' opinions that changed, it was the objects and intensity of their anger. Financial

necessity and irritation at the establishment after decades of failed promises worked together to drive conservative media farther to the right.

Today there is virtually no room for disagreement in right-wing media;
free thinking earns swift, forceful repercussions. Consider the case of Tomi
Lahren, a young spitfire on conservative television and social media. In all
sorts of ways, Lahren was a perfect conservative provocateur for the Trump
era. She was an ardent supporter of the president who regularly spouted
controversial and racist ideas. Ridicule. Snark. Taking it to the "libs." Lahren
had all the boxes checked. The left hated Lahren so much that someone
threw water on her in a restaurant. Yet even Lahren was not safe from
conservative backlash. In 2017 she ventured onto *The View* and declared,
"I'm pro-choice and here's why. I am someone that loves the Constitution.
I am someone that is for limited government. So I can't sit here and be a
hypocrite and say I'm for limited government but I think that the government should decide what women do with their bodies. Stay out of my
guns, and you can stay out of my body as well."[2] Lahren's pro-choice
heresy, and the implication that pro-life conservatives were hypocrites,
sparked a fierce reaction, resulting in her firing from Glenn Beck's network,
The Blaze. While Lahren eventually landed on her feet as a Fox News personality, her experience illustrated that orthodoxy has taken over conservative
media. She would have to be chastened before she could speak again.

Enforcing purity has caused all manner of problems for elected Republicans, even those whom talk radio has not targeted directly. One serious
concern—and another indication of talk radio's influence—is that hosts'
rhetoric can ensnare politicians, forcing them to choose between unpalatable positions on topics they might otherwise safely ignore. For instance
the outcry surrounding Limbaugh's 2012 attack on Fluke—the strongest rebuke of his long career, in part because he targeted someone who wasn't
an elected official or a celebrity—created a dilemma for Republicans.[3] On
the one hand, few politicians wanted to pile on, which would anger Limbaugh and his millions of fans in an election year. On the other hand, ignoring the remarks or defending Limbaugh risked infuriating voters beyond the base. So Republicans tried to thread the needle, signaling their
dissent without coming down too hard on Limbaugh. Presidential candidate Mitt Romney timidly allowed, "It's not the language I would have
used."[4] Fellow presidential candidate Ron Paul acknowledged that the comments "sounded a little crude."[5]

Even if politicians avoided commenting, they might be tainted by the controversy. Limbaugh's stature as maybe the most powerful conservative force in politics ensured that his remarks affected perceptions of the Republican brand no matter what the party's elected officials had to say. Republicans were trapped in a similar vice in 2016 when every outrageous remark or tweet from Trump, the candidate from talk radio, came back to bite GOP politicians. Even before Trump seemed like a serious threat to win the nomination, reporters wanted others in his party on the record on his statements.

Some of the factors that made hosts and their favorite politicians so powerful were structural: the growth in gerrymandered districts; increasing voter clustering by ideology, with liberals in cities and suburbs and conservatives in exurbs and rural areas; and the crystallizing of geographic polarization, with some states unshakably red and others blue. Thanks to these changes, beginning in the 2000s, the number of states holding competitive statewide general elections dropped dramatically, and, in turn, the real action shifted from general to primary elections. Under these circumstances, the most strident voices—hosts and extremist politicians—were well placed to capture the Republican Party. To dominate the party, hosts didn't need to convince a majority of the overall electorate to embrace their perspective, only a majority of those voters who showed up in low-turnout Republican primaries. After that, partisan gravity took over in many places. Rare was the extremist politician so controversial and flawed that he or she might lose enough of the base—or inspire enough latent opposition—to falter in November. Alabama Republican Senate nominee Roy Moore, who lost a 2017 special election, is perhaps the most notable exception, but it was his purported personal conduct, not his radical views, that narrowly cost him the election.

In this primary-centric environment, hosts were the perfect spokespeople for the cause. Listeners trusted hosts' hard-right bona fides—indeed, thought of them as close friends who would never let them down—and hosts provided a platform ideally suited to insurgent candidacies. While upstarts capitalized on the name-recognition and fundraising benefits hosts offered, hosts capitalized on the opportunity to influence the party's rhetoric and policy positions.

That influence spilled over into the policymaking process itself. Talk radio's legislative power stemmed from its ability to make a bill so politically

toxic that lawmakers could not support it without inviting a primary challenge. The bill didn't have to be an especially important one, or one that
the public understood as ideologically divisive on its face. Hosts could transform a sleepy policy debate into a political war, at least in the minds of the
conservative-media consumers who held sway in primary elections. Hosts'
ample airtime—usually ten to fifteen hours per week—left them uniquely
positioned to draw attention to issues, votes, and legislative machinations
that might otherwise escape notice. This scrutiny changed what political
scientist John W. Kingdon dubbed the "political stream" in the legislative
process: the political factors that elected officials considered when weighing
how to vote on legislation. Before talk radio made its bones spotlighting
conservative apostates in the Republican Party, members could get away
with supporting legislation unpopular with the base because voter consternation was far from the only concern politically. They could also consider
how the legislation might play with the broader electorate that they'd face
in November. When it came to small, arcane matters, the posture of one's
constituents likely wasn't even a factor, because most wouldn't have an
opinion on the bill in question. But the transparency fostered by talk radio
introduced base voters into the political stream of even the most trivial votes
in Congress, making landmines out of molehills.

It was not only in the mainstream media vacuum surrounding minor
legislation that talk radio demonstrated its might. The mainstream media
focused intensively on immigration reform during the second Bush and
Obama presidencies, yet talk radio was influential in the debate. Republicans who might otherwise have compromised couldn't pay the cost of doing
so, and leadership fretted that ignoring the will of the base might prove
politically fatal. Meanwhile Republican hard-liners, even backbenchers,
had talk radio and other conservative media on their side and so had no
fear of repercussions for bucking the leadership line in favor of reform. They
knew that they could withstand an establishment-backed primary challenge
if they had to.

Conservative media's clout sometimes aided Republicans in gaining par-
tial or full control of government, but even then the result was not always
conservative policy outcomes. The extinction of moderates and promotion
of extremists has mostly generated paralysis in the 2010s. Addressing routine business, let alone national problems, became virtually impossible. By
this point, in a swing from decades prior, talk radio hindered Republicans
trying to enact an agenda more than it helped. Conservative media rou-

tinely pounded Republicans, no matter how ideologically conservative, who tried their hands at dealmaking, and derided everyone who didn't see politics as warfare. Hosts also inflated listeners' expectations as to what was achievable, especially during divided government, to such a degree that the party could not afford to focus on realistic proposals, let alone pass any. By turning the most extreme members of the Republican caucus into celebrities and bringing attention to their outlandish demands, conservative media personalities essentially compelled leadership to make moves that would never pan out or that they knew from minute one would be counterproductive.

To some extent Republicans created this mess for themselves by cultivating talk radio, lending credibility to hosts during their rise, and shamelessly adopting the bellicose, exaggerated rhetoric and demands hosts pushed. Republicans fed a beast that, over time, destroyed their party. There is of course still a Republican Party, but it is very different from the one that preceded the talk radio revolution. Today's party is trapped between politics and good governance, and, given that legislators' principal goal is reelection, the former consistently takes priority over the latter. What makes for good radio simply doesn't make for good, or even functional, government.

Republicans now are only capable of governing with unified control, and even in 2017 and 2018, when they enjoyed such control, they struggled to address major issues such as health care and immigration. Indeed, they shot themselves in the foot. In 2017 conservative media and its extremist allies in the House, such as Jordan and Meadows, pushed the caucus into supporting a health care proposal that threatened the most popular provision in the Affordable Care Act, its protections for Americans with preconditions. In 2019, newly minted Minority Leader Kevin McCarthy blamed the move for costing Republicans control of the House.[6]

When the parties share control of government, the sort of bipartisan bargaining that defined divided government as recently as the Clinton and George W. Bush administrations—and that is necessary to pass major legislation in most cases, unless the party in power controls sixty Senate seats— is nearly absent. Instead Republicans today resort to political theater such as the 2016 bill to repeal the Affordable Care Act, which President Obama was guaranteed to veto.[7]

Bipartisanship is possible only on issues that split conservative media, that conservative media personalities don't talk about, or that inspire ample conservative support. A recent example of the latter is criminal justice reform. But even in that case, reform demonstrated how wary Republicans are of infuriating their base, not a return to the dealmaking that for decades has been a prerequisite to passing most major legislation.

It is important to keep in mind that there was impressively broad support for a criminal justice reform bill in 2016, uniting Obama, Ryan, and interest groups left and right. But the politically attuned McConnell refused to allow a vote because the issue divided his caucus at a moment when Trump, on the campaign trail, was calling for "law and order." As Senate Majority Whip John Cornyn confirmed, McConnell "did not want to tee up an issue that split our caucus right before the 2016 election."[8] A full two years later an almost identical process played out as McConnell again held his ground on a narrower version of the legislation until after an another election had passed, President Trump applied significant pressure, and sponsors could garner support from a majority of Senate Republicans.[9] While the bill that eventually passed, the First Step Act, was a worthy achievement, it was hardly evidence that Republicans had shorn the yoke of conservative media and figured out how to govern in a functional manner again.

Even Republicans' most significant area of accomplishment during President Trump's first term demonstrated that the party remains well disciplined by its hard-right base. Trump and Senate Republicans proudly pushed judicial nominations through at a record pace, but in large part because the party had learned its lesson: when it came to judges, appeasing the base was nonnegotiable.[10] When George W. Bush tried to appoint White House Counsel Harriet Miers to the Supreme Court, the nomination quickly died, in part because conservative media figures, such as Ingraham, revolted. Had Trump nominated someone similar, that nominee would almost certainly have met with a similar response. Another critical factor in the GOP's judicial success was the changeover to simple majority rules for approving judges. The simple-majority threshold meant Republicans could approve judges without the need for bipartisanship, enabling them to move ahead on nominees aided by their ideologically homogeneous caucus. But, even then, the path to success proved narrow when the Senate was closely divided, and a lone senator could gum up the works. Jeff Flake's refusal to support nominees at the Judiciary Committee level stalled dozens of appointments during his final months in the Senate in 2018.[11]

Ironically, as much power as talk radio has amassed within the Republican Party—albeit a version of the party too politically unhealthy to achieve major goals—the medium's strength has eroded in the arena about which hosts and executives care most: scoring ratings and making money. In the digital age, talk radio has faced significant new challenges on the business front. As the 2000s progressed, terrestrial talk radio's advertising-based business model became more precarious. Publicly traded conglomerates with large debt loads and varied business interests now own most stations, and they have put hosts on notice lest their huge risk pools be polluted by one or two outrageous on-air comments. The advent of social media factors in here, having made it easy to publicize offensive remarks and instantaneously organize boycotts against advertisers, stations, and parent companies.

There is more material than ever for online opponents to chew on, increasing the vulnerability of hosts and their business partners. Internet archiving and streaming preserve hosts' words forever and give them new reach, often far beyond their typical audiences of fellow conservatives. Watchdog groups can monitor hosts and pounce on every ill-considered quip. Thus Lew Dickey—former CEO of Cumulus Media, which owns some of Limbaugh's affiliates—lamented that his company lost millions of dollars thanks to the social media campaign against advertisers following the Fluke comments.[12]

The influence of online boycotts extends beyond conservative talk radio, of course, suggesting that a significant counterweight even to powerhouse media figures and organizations is emerging at the grassroots. Howard Stern—who, in his own way, can be as offensive as Limbaugh—was driven to subscription-based satellite radio thanks to conflicts with the FCC and with advertisers who worried that their association with him would lose them customers. An advertiser boycott also took down O'Reilly, who at the time was perhaps the second brightest star in the conservative media firmament, after Limbaugh. The Fox anchor and his network parted ways in 2017 as advertisers fled the O'Reilly Factor, under pressure from boycott campaigns prompted by revelations that Fox had paid settlements to women who accused O'Reilly of sexual harassment.[13] His strong ratings and avid fanbase were meaningless if Fox couldn't monetize them. Moreover, O'Reilly's sullied reputation threatened to damage the broad-ranging business interests of parent company Twenty-First Century Fox.

Today there exists the possibility that AM talk radio, the medium that launched the conservative media empire, will go the way of other once-dominant media, such as the gradually receding print newspaper. Only time will tell. But most industry observers believe that the era of edgy AM political talk ushered in by Limbaugh is coming to a close.

Even so, the future of ideologically driven political infotainment is secure. Talk radio *content* will remain a vibrant part of our political discourse and a potent political force for decades to come, regardless of the delivery mechanism. People wishing to hear their favorite conservative host will simply turn to podcasts, satellite radio, or some mechanism not yet invented. There will be new challenges. For one thing, the traditional advertising model will continue to suffer. Digital audiences have at their disposal tools enabling them to block commercials, and, with so much content to select from, it is hard to believe that many audience members will choose to spend a third of their listening time imbibing advertisements. The digital world is also showing itself to be more ideologically diverse than the AM dial, which may undermine conservative talk's dominance or at least provide a political counterforce. Whereas liberal advocacy failed on radio, liberal podcasts are thriving in the age of Trump.

The success of digital liberal shows doesn't speak to any ideological leaning within the newest media, only the further erosion of gatekeepers. Conservative media flourishes alongside. New conservative digital outlets such as CRTV and Ben Shapiro's podcast are booming. Established giants such as Fox News are getting into digital streaming.[14] The digital sphere has opened space for a broader range of conservative viewpoints, from the new Bulwark, which is explicitly anti-Trump; to Shapiro, who is ambivalent about conservative populism and its practitioner-in-chief; to Breitbart, with its ceaseless cheerleading for the president's nationalist agenda. Interestingly, advertisers may exhibit less skittishness over podcast content, possibly because podcasts are not yet monitored with the same intensity as the biggest ideological radio and cable personalities.[15]

As for talk radio's king, Limbaugh's position is safe from all but father time. Conservative media personalities more publicly associated with the president, such as Hannity and Fox's Jeanine Pirro, often receive more press. But Limbaugh remains the most influential figure in conservative media and probably is the second most important kingmaker in conservative politics behind Trump. In 2018 Trump called in to commemorate Limbaugh's thirtieth year in national syndication, as both Presidents Bush had for the host's twentieth.[16] And late that year, Limbaugh's vocal opposition to a government funding deal helped precipitate a record-long government shutdown. It began after Trump reassured Limbaugh that he wouldn't cave on demands for funding for a border wall.[17] As the conservative media empire grows ever larger, making space for younger voices such as Shapiro, Limbaugh remains inescapable. Even those who don't listen to Limbaugh hear him, for he reverberates in the work of his successors. To make it as a conservative media figure, one must still embrace the model Limbaugh innovated three decades ago.

The story of U.S. politics in the late twentieth and early twenty-first centuries is one of elite polarization fueling gridlock, both of which seem to grow worse with each passing day. Talk radio is a central character in this story. The transformations it brought about created a political world in which President Donald Trump is possible. Many other factors contributed: the rise of purist political groups such as the Club for Growth, the development of social media, the Fox explosion, changes in campaign-finance regulation, and the hardening of both parties' ideological positions as a product of voter self-sorting. But these other forces do not reduce talk radio's importance. Talk radio was a prerequisite to many of these other developments.

Talk radio initiated the process through which increasing numbers of Americans came to live in echo chambers, receiving news only from sources sharing their political perspective. Hosts' influence over politics continues, even as talk listenership has dropped from its peak and other media crowd its niche. Hosts still draw attention from politicians and the mainstream media, command large audiences of voters, and influence activity in Washington. Most hosts advocate for a Republican Party that refuses to compromise in the name of governing and sticks to the principles they and their listeners find most important, regardless of the electoral consequences.

These consequences remain considerable: the difficulties talk radio poses for Republicans were not erased by 2016, when Trump defied every gloomy prediction and showed that Republicans could win the White House by appealing to conservative media personalities and their audience first and foremost—not minorities, young voters, or women. Anyone who came away from that election believing that it was 1994 all over again—that conservative media was the ticket to GOP empowerment—need only look to the 2018 midterm elections for a sobering reminder of the costs associated with being the party of talk radio. The relentless push for hard-right, populist politics, egged on by conservative media personalities, continued to narrow the party's coalition, resulting in a forty-seat gain for Democrats in the House and the end of Republican control in the chamber after eight years.

Indeed Trump's 2016 win, and his unpopularity in office, speak more to the ongoing challenge the GOP faces as the party of talk radio than to any benefits the relationship provides. It is no surprise that after dominating presidential elections from 1968 to 1988, Republicans have only captured the national popular vote once in the years since, even if they have won the Electoral College and the presidency three times. Trump lost the popular vote by nearly as many votes as George W. Bush won it in 2004, suggesting that the period of conservative media's strongest hold over Republicans has, at the very least, not been one of growing acclaim for the GOP. And while Trump's adherence to the talk radio playbook has proven wildly popular with Republican base voters, his presidential approval rating, as of this writing in early 2019, has been mired stubbornly under 45 percent.[18] The days when Richard Nixon and Ronald Reagan rode a less rigidly conservative message to vast landslides, and then maintained popularity while adopting a degree of pragmatism in order to govern, are long gone.[19] Talk radio is a big part of this transformation.

Because of talk radio's stridency—or, depending on one's perspective, commitment to principle—it is tempting to judge the medium's normative contribution to American democracy according to one's ideology. Conservatives champion talk radio for giving them a voice and counterbalancing a hopelessly biased mainstream media. Liberals write off talk radio as a bastion of bigotry.

We ought to resist this temptation and instead recognize that talk radio has been a force both for and against the ongoing American project of democratization. Talk radio invited alienated conservative Americans into the political process. Hosts encouraged political participation and interest in government, powering activism to a degree that other forms of entertainment and even broadcast news rarely did. Talk radio also increased transparency by surfacing stories that would otherwise never see the light of day, especially before the Internet took off. Talk radio provided more coverage of issues important to conservatives, stories that really were neglected by the mainstream media.

That said, talk radio also damaged the functioning of government—and democracy. For as much as hosts opened up the political process for those on the right side of the spectrum, they have sought to foreclose it in other circumstances. Right-wing personalities have pushed the argument, contradicted by facts, that voter fraud is rampant and that elections are routinely stolen by noneligible voters. This rhetoric harms democracy by needlessly undermining faith in the integrity of elections and by encouraging the adoption of voter identification laws and more restrictive voting processes that make it harder for Americans to participate in balloting.[20]

Talk radio also has harmed democracy by corrupting journalism. Hosts conflate news and entertainment, and sacrifice factual accuracy, in an effort to inflame audiences with exaggerations and misinformation. At the same time, they have labored successfully to destroy the credibility of journalists. One consequence is that a large segment of the polity now depends on entertainers for their news. With time, hosts played to this dependence, promising exclusive scoops and reporting that listeners and viewers wouldn't find elsewhere. But, in many cases, they misled rather than informed.

Talk radio also weakened journalism's contribution to democracy by creating echo chambers. The tendency only to receive information from likeminded sources plays a major role in the gridlock and polarization we now see in Washington. Echo chambers deprive Americans of a common set of basic facts necessary for fruitful, serious policy debates. Echo chambers also undermine the comity arguably necessary to a democratic society, exacerbating the sense that the "other side" does not merely disagree but is in fact an enemy hellbent on destroying the bedrock values of the nation. While it is true that hosts typically reflect the views their listeners already have, hosts cannot escape responsibility for fueling the warfare mentality in politics.

The result has been the election of Donald Trump, even though his articulation of those bedrock values is at best confused, from any ideological standpoint. He is the very type of demagogue who most concerned the founders of our system of government. He is good at creating a cult of personality, but he often appears clueless about the functioning of government and democracy and about the substance of public policy. Like many talk radio hosts, he offers up infotainment, a sometimes-toxic blend of misinformation and never-sedate packaging designed to heighten fears about change and pluralism.

So the question of talk radio's impact on democracy produces a mixed answer. The medium encouraged democratic participation. But, simultaneously, talk radio fed a process through which a smaller and smaller segment of voters dominated American politics. Abetted by the Republican

Party it eventually took over, talk radio invited uncompromising conservatives to the table but at the expense of many other voices now marginalized or no longer heard.

On the latter point, talk hosts can justifiably gloat. They slayed the hated RINO and put their avatar in the White House. But as for the complicated verdict on democratic impact? Hosts will have to leave that be. They have just simple, unambiguous messages. The effects of those messages on American democracy, however, can only be rendered in shades of gray. That would never make for good talk radio.

Notes

Acknowledgments

Index

Notes

Introduction

1. Limbaugh's average audience in 1988 was 299,000 listeners. It's hard to know how many stations aired Limbaugh's program at a given time, in part because syndicators are known to inflate numbers. Interviews suggest varying counts. North Dakota radio host and executive Scott Hennen remembered his station being one of the original forty-seven stations airing Limbaugh in 1988, whereas Tom Tradup, who picked up Limbaugh's program for WLS in Chicago in 1989, recalled being the thirty-eighth or thirty-ninth affiliate. Paul Colford, *The Rush Limbaugh Story: Talent on Loan from God an Unauthorized Biography* (New York: St Martin's Press, 1994), 94, 138; Rush Limbaugh, "Ed McLaughlin, Founder of EIB," *The Rush Limbaugh Show*, August 1, 2008, http://www.rushlimbaugh.com/daily/2008/08/01/ed_mclaughlin_founder_of_eib; Tom Tradup, interview with author, November 13, 2012; Scott Hennen, interview with author, December 18, 2012.

2. Frank Ahrens, "Chat to the Future; Can Talk Radio Change with the Times?" *Washington Post*, February 2, 1999; Louis Bolce, Gerald De Maio, and Douglas Muzzio, "Dial in Democracy: Talk Radio and the 1994 Election," *Political Science Quarterly* 111, no. 3 (1996): 459. Sources differ as to how many talk stations existed in the early to mid-1980s. A 1995 *Nation* article claimed that there were 300 all-talk stations in 1985, while a 1995 *Time* piece placed that number at 200 stations. In *Listening In*, Susan Douglas cited 238 such stations in 1987. These numbers suggest that the rapid increase in the number of talk stations occurred earlier than is usually assumed; the disagreement among estimates may result from differing definitions of what constituted a talk station. Talk grew as a format throughout the 1980s, but probably not quickly

enough to produce these totals in 1985 and 1987. The smaller number I cite, from Ahrens's article and credited to radio consultant Walter Sabo, is most likely to be correct, given the history of talk radio's development. Sheryl James, "AM Turning to Talk Radio," *St. Petersburg Times*, November 24, 1987; Peter Viles, "Talk Radio Riding High," *Broadcasting and Cable*, June 15, 1992, 24; Jim Cooper, "Talkers Brace for 'Fairness' Assault," *Broadcasting and Cable*, September 6, 1993, 44; Richard Corliss and John F. Dickerson, "Look Who Is Talking," *Time*, January 23, 1995, 22–25; Micah L. Sifry and Marc Cooper, "Americans Talk Back to Power," *The Nation*, April 10, 1995, 482; Susan Douglas, *Listening In: Radio and the American Imagination* (Minneapolis: University of Minnesota Press, 2004), 300.

3. See, for example, Bill Press, *Toxic Talk: How the Radical Right Has Poisoned America's Airwaves* (New York: Thomas Dunne Books, 2010), 245–249; Eric Klineberg, *Fighting for Air: The Battle to Control America's Media* (New York: Metropolitan Books, 2007), 76–79.

4. There is a third thread, not addressed in this book, which chronicles liberal opinion radio's commercial struggles. See Brian Rosenwald, "Mount Rushmore: The Rise of Talk Radio and Its Impact on Politics and Public Policy" (Ph.D. diss., University of Virginia, 2015).

5. See Kathleen Hall Jamieson and Joseph Cappella, *Echo Chamber: Rush Limbaugh and the Conservative Media Establishment* (New York: Oxford University Press, 2008). Ample evidence shows that many Americans consume news only from ideologically likeminded sources. See, for example, Natalie Jomini Stroud, *Niche News: The Politics of News Choice* (New York: Oxford University Press, 2012). But a nascent literature argues that the case for echo chambers is overstated and that most Americans either abstain from ideological news sources or receive a more balanced news diet than previously believed. See, for example, Kevin Arceneaux and Martin Johnson, *Changing Minds or Changing Channels? Partisan News in an Age of Choice* (Chicago: University of Chicago Press, 2013). See also Matthew Gentzkow and Jesse M. Shapiro, "Ideological Segregation Online and Offline," *Quarterly Journal of Economics* 126 (2011): 1799–1839.

6. See Matthew Levendusky, *How Partisan Media Polarize America* (Chicago: University of Chicago Press, 2013).

7. See, among others, David C. Barker, *Rushed to Judgment: Talk Radio, Persuasion, and American Political Behavior* (New York: Columbia University Press, 2002); Barker, "Rushed Decisions, Political Talk Radio and Voter Choice, 1994–1996," *Journal of Politics* 61, no. 2 (1999): 532–535; Barker and Kathleen Knight, "Political Talk Radio and Public Opinion," *Public Opinion Quarterly* 64, no. 2 (2000): 149–170; Bolce, De Maio, and Muzzio, "Dial in

Democracy," 461–464, 466, 469; David A. Jones, "Political Talk Radio: The Limbaugh Effect on Primary Voters," *Political Communication* 15, no. 3 (1998): 367–381; R. Lance Holbert, "Political Talk Radio, Perceived Fairness, and the Establishment of President George W. Bush's Political Legitimacy," *Harvard International Journal of Press / Politics* 9, no. 3 (2004): 12–27; Diana Owen, "Talk Radio and Evaluations of President Clinton," *Political Communication* 14, no. 3 (1997): 333–353; Barry A. Hollander, "Political Talk Radio in the '90s: A Panel Study," *Journal of Radio Studies* 6, no. 2 (1999): 236–245; Hollander, "Talk Radio: Predictors of Use and Effects on Attitudes about Government," *Journalism and Mass Communication Quarterly* 73, no. 1 (1997): 102–113.

8. See especially Jeffrey M. Berry and Sarah Sobieraj, *The Outrage Industry: Political Opinion Media and the New Incivility* (New York: Oxford University Press, 2014), 128, 142.

9. A chapter of Susan Douglas's *Listening In* covers the rise of Limbaugh, Don Imus, and other hosts. But Douglas misinterprets the disjunction within talk radio represented by Limbaugh's rise nationally, failing to account for Limbaugh's revolutionary show and its differences from the milquetoast talk programming dominant before 1988. Nicole Hemmer and Heather Hendershot explore the rise and fall of an earlier generation of conservative broadcasters and media impresarios, who shared little with today's conservative entertainers outside of their political philosophy. Several scholars, including Jeffrey Berry, Sarah Sobieraj, and William Mayer, have refuted the idea that political bias explains the imbalance between conservatives and liberals in talk radio. Berry and Sobieraj capably depict the second half of talk radio's rise during the 2000s, but their portrayal does not offer much on the first half of this process, during which most of the transformation occurred. See Mayer, "Why Talk Radio Is Conservative," *Public Interest* 156: 86–103; Berry and Sobieraj, "Understanding the Rise of Talk Radio," *PS: Political Science and Politics* 44, no. 4 (2011): 762–767; Douglas, *Listening In*, 283–318; Berry and Sobieraj, *Outrage Industry*; Nicole Hemmer, *Messengers of the Right: Conservative Media and the Transformation of American Politics* (Philadelphia: University of Pennsylvania Press, 2016); Heather Hendershot, *What's Fair on the Air? Cold War Right-Wing Broadcasting and the Public Interest* (Chicago: University of Chicago Press, 2011).

10. Limbaugh's audience ebbs and flows, but for three decades he has consistently had the largest audience in talk radio. While Limbaugh rarely speaks about the size of his audience, he did assert in 2018 that his cumulative weekly audience was almost twice an estimated 13.75 million. Rush Limbaugh, "Kimmel's Ignorance and Our Audience Size," *The Rush Limbaugh Show*, February 5, 2018, https://www.rushlimbaugh.com/daily/2018/02/05/kimmels -ignorance-and-the-eib-audience.

11. Ron Bonjean, interview with author, January 11, 2013.

12. In referencing John Aldrich's depictions of the role of activists in the nomination process, Marty Cohen and colleagues write, "Activists . . . provide helpful electoral resources, but the resources come at the cost of pressure that limits the flexibility of candidates to take the policy positions that will most please voters." This discussion is limited to elections, but it also accurately describes the role talk radio's activist hosts play in the Republican coalition generally. Marty Cohen, David Karol, Hans Noel, and John Zaller, *The Party Decides: Presidential Nominations Before and After Reform* (Chicago: University of Chicago Press, 2008), 28.

1. The Colossus Rises

1. Susan Douglas traces talk radio's ascent to the troubles facing AM radio, the impact of new technologies, cultural alienation, and deregulation. She fails, however, to recognize Rush Limbaugh's effect on the style of talk radio. Instead Douglas places Limbaugh in the tradition of earlier talk radio. This contention rests on a misreading of the earlier landscape. Hosts who exhibited similarities to Limbaugh and Stern were exceptions to the more staid norm and could only be heard in select markets. She also does not cover the process by which AM talk became almost entirely conservative as this book does. See Susan Douglas, *Listening In: Radio and the American Imagination* (Minneapolis: University of Minnesota Press, 2004), 283–318.

2. In discussing the rise of "outrage media"—concentrated in cable news, talk radio, and blogs—Jeffrey M. Berry and Sarah Sobieraj emphasize the role of technological change in the rise of talk radio and the politics it fosters. But many of the developments they discuss, such as voice-tracking technology and music streaming, came long after talk radio ascended. They focus on growth during the 2000s, but this was a second round of expansion. Jeffrey M. Berry and Sarah Sobieraj, *The Outrage Industry: Political Opinion Media and the New Incivility* (New York: Oxford University Press, 2014), 66–94.

3. See Andrew Hartman, *A War for the Soul of America: A History of the Culture Wars* (Chicago: University of Chicago Press, 2015), for a full history of the culture wars.

4. On the fierce anti-feminist uprising in defense of the traditional nuclear family, see Robert Self, *All in the Family: The Realignment of American Democracy since the 1960s* (New York: Hill and Wang, 2012); and Stacie Taranto, *Kitchen Table Politics: Conservative Women and Family Values in New York* (Philadelphia: University of Pennsylvania Press, 2017).

5. Richard Harrington, "The Capitol Hill Rock War," *Washington Post*, September 20, 1985; Anita Manning, "Teens and Sex in the Age of AIDS," *USA*

Today, October 3, 1988; Curt Suplee, "Sex in the 90s," *Washington Post,* January 8, 1989; Irene Sege, "Teen-Age Pregnancy: An American Problem," *Dallas Morning News,* December 5, 1986; Stuart Elliot, "Advertisers in the Line of Fire: 'New Puritans' Launch Attack on 'Trash' TV," *USA Today,* March 29, 1989; "Do We Value Our Children Growing Up in a Changing World?" *Record* (Bergen County, NJ), March 29, 1987.

6. See Natalia Mehlman Petrzela, *Classroom Wars: Language, Sex, and the Making of Modern Political Culture* (New York: Oxford University Press, 2015); Trey Kay, Deborah George, and Stan Bumgardner, "The Great Textbook Wars," American Radioworks, http://americanradioworks.publicradio.org/features /textbooks; Adam Laats, *The Other School Reformers: Conservative Activism in American Education* (Cambridge, MA: Harvard University Press, 2015), 186–237; and Gary Nash, Charlotte Crabtree, and Ross Dunn, *History on Trial: Culture Wars and the Teaching of the Past* (New York: Vintage Books, 2000).

7. Jonathan Kaufman, "The Color Line a Generation after the Civil Rights Movement," *Boston Globe,* June 18, 1989. See also Murray B. Levin, *Talk Radio and the American Dream* (Lexington, MA: Lexington Books, 1987), xiv.

8. James Davison Hunter, *Culture Wars: The Struggle to Define America* (New York: Basic Books, 1991); James Davison Hunter and Alan Wolfe, *Is There a Culture War: A Dialogue on Values and American Public Life* (Washington, DC: Pew Forum/Brookings Institution Press, 2006), 2, 14. See also Jonathan Haidt, *The Righteous Mind: Why Good People Are Divided by Politics and Religion* (New York: Vintage Books, 2012), 150–216.

9. T. R. Reid, "Robertson Faded, but Born-Again Christians Remain Potent Force," *Washington Post,* August 16, 1988.

10. Jan Norman, "Too Hot to Handle? Outraged Viewers Carry Protests to TV Program Advertisers," *Orange County Register,* April 23, 1989.

11. Douglas, *Listening In,* 291–293; Berry and Sobieraj, *Outrage Industry,* 146–148.

12. Berry and Sobieraj, *Outrage Industry,* 147. They also write that outrage media is "most easily recognizable by the rhetoric that defines it, with its hallmark venom, vilification of opponents, and hyperbolic reinterpretations of current events," 4.

13. Jason Zengerle, "Talking Back," *New Republic,* February 16, 2004, 19–25.

14. Dave Elswick, interview with author, November 27, 2012.

15. Roger Hedgecock, interview with author, January 9, 2013.

16. Howard Kurtz, "Party Poopers: Conservative Pundits Who Break Ranks Find Themselves on the Wrong Side of the Right," *Washington Post,* July 22, 1997, B1.

17. Hugh Hewitt, interview with author, November 5, 2012; Lars Larson, interview with author, November 16, 2012.

18. Hewitt, interview; Larson, interview.

19. Elswick, interview.

20. J. D. Hayworth, interview with author, September 26, 2012. Dan Balz, "Carter-Baker Panel to Call for Voting Fixes," *Washington Post*, September 19, 2005.

21. Hayworth, interview.

22. Rush Limbaugh, "Discussion on Budget Cuts at the City University of New York, Animal Rights Protesters or PETA, the Republican Contract with America, Democratic Views on Social Issues and the Republican Tax Cut," *Rush Limbaugh*, produced by Roger Ailes, aired April 5, 1995 (Multimedia Entertainment).

23. Rush Limbaugh, "Discussion of Homosexuals and Gays Visiting the White House; Michael Jackson and Lisa Marie Presley's Interview; and President Clinton's Announcement on How He Plans to Balance the Budget," *Rush Limbaugh*, produced by Roger Ailes, aired June 15, 1995 (Multimedia Entertainment); Jill Zuckman and John Aloysius Farrell, "Democrats in Uproar at Budget Plan," *Boston Globe*, June 15, 1995.

24. Patrick Joseph Buchanan, "Culture Wars Speech: Address to the Republican National Convention," August 17, 1992, available at Voices of Democracy: The U.S. Oratory Project, http://voicesofdemocracy.uimd.edu/buchanan-culture-war-speech-speech-text.

25. Greg Stevens, "Cybercampaigning: Why It Promises More than Just Geek Votes," *Roll Call*, August 3, 1995.

26. See Douglas, *Listening In*, 255–282, for a complete description of the rise of FM radio.

27. "The Trend Continues," *Broadcasting*, July 4, 1988, 40; "Can AM Radio Be Saved?" *Broadcasting and Cable*, July 3, 1989, 20; Robert Unmacht, interview with author, January 25, 2013.

28. "AM Radio: Survival of the Fittest—AM Fights Back," *Broadcasting and Cable*, August 14, 1989, 54; David Kinney, "Will AM Radio Fade Out as Force in Broadcasting?" *Business North Carolina*, July 1, 1986, 6.

29. Deborah Mesce, "Troubled Times for AM Radio," Associated Press, April 10, 1988; Paul Fiddick, interview with author, December 21, 2012.

30. Barry Farber, interview with author, November 29, 2012; Tom Leykis, interview with author, August 19, 2014; Maurice Tunick, interview with author, November 17, 2014.

31. John Burgess, "AM Radio Fights against Decline," *Houston Chronicle*, April 3, 1988; Janet DeStefano, "Yakity-Yak: AM Radio Talks Back to Compete," *Record* (Bergen County, NJ), May 24, 1987.

32. Kinney, "Will AM Radio Fade Out?"

33. Douglas, *Listening In*, 288.

34. For a history of the FCC's battle against the Fairness Doctrine between 1981 and 1987 see Donald Jung, *The Federal Communications Commission, the Broadcast Industry, and the Fairness Doctrine 1981–1987* (Lanham, MD: University Press of America, 1996). For the Fairness Doctrine's pre-1981 history see Steven J. Simmons, *The Fairness Doctrine and the Media* (Berkeley: University of California Press, 1978), especially 16–71. See also Peter Boyer, "FCC Struggled with Itself Six Years before Reversing a Policy It Opposed," *New York Times*, August 6, 1987; Martin Tolchin, "How Fair Is the Fairness Doctrine?" *New York Times*, April 5, 1987; Ernest Holsendoph, "FCC Asks End of Fairness Doctrine," *New York Times*, September 18, 1981; Tom Shales, "Danger Signs: The FCC Homes In on the Fairness Doctrine," *Washington Post*, October 8, 1981; Ernest Holsendoph, "FCC Chief Assails 'Fairness' Policy," *New York Times*, April 8, 1982; "Q&A: Mark S. Fowler; An F.C.C. for the Common Man," *New York Times*, May 25, 1985; Reginald Stuart, "The Fowler Years," *Broadcasting*, March 2, 1987, 51–54; Reginald Stuart, "Fairness Doctrine Assailed by FCC," *New York Times*, August 8, 1985.

35. Ronald Reagan, Message to the Senate Returning S. 742 Without Approval, 23 Weekly Comp. Pres. Doc. 715 (June 19, 1987).

36. According to Tyler Cox, KFBK had another host who often delved into opposing viewpoints during that period, satisfying the Fairness Doctrine; Tyler Cox, email message to author, March 5, 2015.

37. Neal Boortz, "Boortz Bio: Neal Boortz, aka: The Talkmaster, Mighty Whitey and the High Priest of the Church of the Painful Truth," February 28, 2001, accessible via the Wayback Machine at https://web.archive.org/web /20130402024342/http://www.boortz.com/news/entertainment/personalities /boortz-bio/n8Lt.

38. Gary Burns, interview with author, September 13, 2012; Unmacht, interview; Randall Bloomquist, interview with author, August 27, 2012; Gabe Hobbs, email message to author, February 25, 2019. See Douglas, *Listening In*, 287–288 and 293–295, for more detail on technical changes that propelled talk radio.

39. Gil Troy, *Morning in America: How Ronald Reagan Invented the 1980s* (Princeton: Princeton University Press, 2005), 115–146, 276–280.

40. Arlene Rodda, "Talk Radio: The Phenomenon and Some of Its Personalities," *Alert Collector* 35, no 1 (September 1, 1995), 19; Cindy Richards, "Taking Back Talk Radio," *Chicago Sun-Times*, November 20, 1994; Arlene Levinson, "America's Yakking It Up," *Pittsburgh Post-Gazette*, September 4, 1994; Associated Press, "Talk Radio Is a Favorite Forum for GOP Presidential Hopefuls," November 26, 1995; Michael Harrison, interview with author, November 9, 2010; Martin Walker, "Patriotism in the Roar of Talk Radio," *The Guardian*, March 23, 1991; Alan W. Bock, "Yakety, Yak! And You Can Talk

Back!" *Orange County Register*, March 12, 1989; Fraser Smith, "Big Talk: Radio Host Alan Christian Was on a Crusade to Save America," *Regardie's The Business of Washington*, October 1, 1990; Scott Hennen, interview with author, December 18, 2012.

41. Bruce Webber, "A Loud Angry World on the Dial," *New York Times*, June 7, 1992, 31.

42. For more on the intimacy of radio, see Roland Marchand, *Advertising the American Dream: Making Way for Modernity, 1920–1940* (Berkeley: University of California Press, 1985), 88: "Radio surpassed all others in its capacity to deny its own status as a *mass* medium . . . listeners might readily imagine that the speaker was talking personally to them."

43. Thom Hartmann, interview with author, November 3, 2012.

44. Vincent Coppola, "Neal Boortz: Have Mouth, Will Talk," *Atlanta Magazine*, July 1, 1998, http://www.atlantamagazine.com/features/1998/07/01/neal-boortz-have-mouth-will-talk.

45. Hayworth, interview.

46. Berry and Sobieraj, *Outrage Industry*, 132–135; Ron Hartenbaum, interview with author, December 11, 2012.

47. Tom Becka, interview with author, December 19, 2012; Tom Taylor, interview with author, January 11, 2013.

48. Doug McIntyre, interview with author, November 1, 2012.

49. Dave Elswick, interview with author, November 27, 2012.

50. Lisa Liddane, "Hundreds Join KFI Cash Mob to Keep Toy Shop Afloat," *Orange County Register*, August 1, 2012; Amy Senk, "Cash Mob Infusion Keeps O.C. Toy Store Open for Now," *Orange County Register*, August 5, 2012.

2. With Talent on Loan from God

1. Greg Hamilton, "Minister Longs to Wrestle for Rush," *St. Petersburg Times*, March 21, 1994; Scott Hennen, interview with author, December 18, 2012; Steve Goldstein, interview with author, November 6, 2012; Jon Sinton, email message to author, April 25, 2012.

2. Heather Hendershot, "Introduction," *Cinema Journal* 51, no. 4 (2012): 160–165; Jeffrey M. Berry and Sarah Sobieraj, "Understanding the Rise of Talk Radio," *PS: Political Science and Politics* 44, no. 4 (2011): 762–767; Frank Ahrens, "Chat to the Future: Can Talk Radio Change with the Times?" *Washington Post*, February 2, 1999; Louis Bolce, Gerald De Maio, and Douglas Muzzio, "Dial-In Democracy: Talk Radio and the 1994 Election," *Political Science Quarterly* 111, no. 3 (1996): 457–481; Sheryl James, "AM Turning to Talk Radio," *St. Petersburg Times*, November 24, 1987; Peter Viles, "Talk Radio Riding High: Both Ratings and Influence Are on the Rise; Can

Respect Be Far Behind?" *Broadcasting and Cable*, June 15, 1992, 24; Jim Cooper, "Talkers Brace for 'Fairness' Assault," *Broadcasting and Cable*, September 6, 1993, 44.

3. Paul D. Colford, *The Rush Limbaugh Story: Talent on Loan from God, an Unauthorized Biography* (New York: St. Martin's Press, 1994), 28.

4. Rush Limbaugh, "Ed McLaughlin, Founder of EIB," *The Rush Limbaugh Show*, August 1, 2008, http://www.rushlimbaugh.com/daily/2008/08/01/ed _mclaughlin_founder_of_eib; Bill McMahon, interview with author, January 23, 2013; Colford, *The Rush Limbaugh Story*, 50–84; Museum of Television and Radio Seminar Series, "The First Annual Radio Festival: Rush Limbaugh and the Talk Radio Revolution," October 24, 1995, catalog number T:40932, Paley Center's New York branch; Bruce Marr, interview with author, October 11, 2014; Tyler Cox, interview with author, October 24, 2014; Kathryn Cramer Brownell, *Showbiz Politics: Hollywood in American Political Life* (Chapel Hill: University of North Carolina Press, 2014).

5. Colford, *Rush Limbaugh Story*, 72–88.

6. Tim Grieve, "On the Road with America's Most-Listened-To Talk-Show Host," *Sacramento Bee*, December 17, 1989.

7. Limbaugh, "Ed McLaughlin, Founder of EIB."

8. Hennen, interview; Hennen, email message to author, February 1, 2013.

9. For the history of this earlier period of conservative radio, see Alan Brinkley, *Voices of Protest: Huey Long, Father Coughlin and the Great Depression* (New York: Vintage Books, 1982); Heather Hendershot, *What's Fair on the Air: Cold War Right-Wing Broadcasting and the Public Interest* (Chicago: University of Chicago Press, 2011); Nicole Hemmer, "Messengers of the Right" (Ph.D. diss., Columbia University, 2010); Nicole Hemmer, *Messengers of the Right: Conservative Media and the Transformation of American Politics* (Philadelphia: University of Pennsylvania Press, 2016).

10. Robert P. Laurence, "Still Awake after 'Late Night'? Now There's 'Later,'" *San Diego Union*, August 22, 1988.

11. Barry Farber, interview with author, November 29, 2012.

12. Richard Lacayo, Elaine Dutka, and Marilyn Alva, "Audiences Love to Hate Them," *Time*, July 9, 1984, 86; Mickey Luckoff, interview with author, August 27, 2014; Tom Leykis, interview with author, August 29, 2014; John Mainelli, email messages to author, October 20 and November 21, 2010.

13. At its peak, Coughlin's "Golden Hour of the Little Flower" had at least 10 million listeners weekly; Brinkley, *Voices of Protest*, 119–120.

14. Hendershot, *What's Fair on the Air?* 26–102.

15. Hendershot, *What's Fair on the Air?* Kindle Edition, 99–100; Hemmer, *Messengers of the Right*, 68.

16. Rush Limbaugh, "The Original Gorbasm," *The Rush Limbaugh Show*, February 2, 2005, http://www.rushlimbaugh.com/daily/2005/02/02/the_original_gorbasm2.

17. Colford, *Rush Limbaugh Story*, 141.

18. Maurice Tunick, interviews with author, November 17 and 19, 2014.

19. Bob Rose, "Kook-Baiting Pyne Likes Controversy," *Washington Post*, July 29, 1967.

20. Don Page, "Pyne Newest Figure to Stir the Natives," *Los Angeles Times*, April 22, 1962.

21. Doug McIntyre, interview with author, November 1, 2012.

22. This broadcast occurred at Jacque Demers Bar in the Embassy Suites in Southfield, Michigan, likely on February 23, 1990; I received a copy of it from Art Vuolo.

23. John Mainelli, email message to author, October 20, 2010.

24. Eric Morgenthaler, "A Common Touch: 'Dittoheads' All Over Make Rush Limbaugh Superstar of the Right," *Wall Street Journal*, June 28, 1993.

25. Rush Limbaugh, "The Animal Rights Update Theme in Honor of the Late, Great Andy Williams," *The Rush Limbaugh Show*, September 26, 2012, https://www.rushlimbaugh.com/daily/2012/09/26/the_animal_rights_update_theme_in_honor_of_the_late_great_andy_williams.

26. Peter Boyer, "Bull Rush," *Vanity Fair*, May 1992, 158; Rush Limbaugh, "We're Not Your Problem, Barney," *The Rush Limbaugh Show*, September 30, 2010, https://www.rushlimbaugh.com/daily/2010/09/30/we_re_not_your_problem_barney; "The Philanderer: Teddy the Swimmer," http://www.youtube.com/watch?v=f4huqCCBcSI; "Barney Frank, Banking Queen," https://www.youtube.com/watch?v=a5NrqqK6oOI.

27. "Rush Limbaugh's America," *Frontline*, season 13, episode 11, directed by Marian Marzynski, produced by Steve Talbot, aired February 28, 1995, https://www.youtube.com/watch?v=tWD_F6sZ5dE.

28. George Oliva, interview with author, November 26, 2012; Valerie Geller, interview with author, January 14, 2013.

29. Tom Tradup, interview with author, November 13, 2012; Oliva, interview.

30. Peter Viles, "AM Radio's One Man Comeback (Talk Show Host Rush Limbaugh)," *Broadcasting and Cable*, May 4, 1992, 55; Peter Viles, "Talk Explodes in National Syndication," *Broadcasting and Cable*, May 17, 1993, 34; Henry Allen, "Media to the Left! Media to the Right!" *Washington Post*, August 20, 1992; Morgenthaler, "A Common Touch"; Lewis Grossberger, "The Rush Hours," *New York Times*, December 16, 1990.

31. Carrie Borzillo, "Fans Rush for Lunch Listening; NPR, Denon Team for Promo," *Billboard*, July 31, 1993, 68; Steven V. Roberts, "What a Rush," *U.S. News & World Report*, August 16, 1993, 26.

32. Geller, interview; David Rimmer, interview with author, September 6, 2012; Gary Burns, interview with author, September 13, 2012; John McConnell, interview with author, December 2, 2012; Robin Bertolucci, interview with author, October 17, 2012; Dave Elswick, interview with author, November 27, 2012; Tom Becka, interview with author, December 19, 2012; Jeffrey M. Berry and Sarah Sobieraj, *The Outrage Industry: Political Opinion Media and the New Incivility* (New York: Oxford University Press, 2014), 114–116.

33. Sam Howe Verhovek, "Out of Politics, but Still Talking, Radio Style," *New York Times*, March 13, 1995.

34. Grossberger, "The Rush Hours"; Sam Howe Verhovek, "The Media Business: Talk Radio Gets a Spirited New Voice from the Left," *New York Times*, May 9, 1994.

35. Howe Verhovek, "Out of Politics."

36. Michael Harrison, "The Importance of Air America," *Talkers Magazine*, April 2004, 43, 46.

37. Some sources, including Limbaugh at times, style the title "Gulf War I."

38. In many ways, Limbaugh epitomized the rise of entertainment politics chronicled by Brownell, *Showbiz Politics*.

39. Rush Limbaugh, "The Gulf War Retrospective," January 16, 1992, Paley Center catalog number R:8373, Paley Center's New York branch.

40. Laura Ingraham, *The Laura Ingraham Show*, February 11, 2005, Library of Congress's Web Radio Recording Project, which can be accessed only in the Library.

41. Michael Medved, *The Michael Medved Show*, September 22, 2006, Library of Congress's Web Radio Recording Project, which can be accessed only in the Library.

3. Media That Sounds Like Us

1. Steven V. Roberts, "What a Rush," *U.S. News and World Report*, August 16, 1993, 26.

2. Museum of Television and Radio Seminar Series, "The First Annual Radio Festival: Rush Limbaugh and the Talk Radio Revolution," October 24, 1995, catalog number T:40932, accessed at the Paley Center's New York branch.

3. For example, Gary Burns, interview with author, September 13, 2012; Doug McIntyre, interview with author, November 1, 2012; David Hall, interview with author, September 25, 2012; Gabe Hobbs, interview with author, August 29, 2012; Doug Stephan, interview with author, December 10, 2012.

4. Henry Allen, "Media to the Left! Media to the Right!" *Washington Post*, August 20, 1992.

5. Berry and Sobieraj label hosts "supportive cheerleaders for and defenders of the values that fans hold dear." Jeffrey M. Berry and Sarah Sobieraj, *The Outrage Industry: Political Opinion Media and the New Incivility* (New York: Oxford University Press, 2014), 141; Amy Bernstein, "Show Time in the Rush Room," *U.S. News and World Report*, August 16, 1993, 36.

6. *The Rush Limbaugh Show*, "The Segment," Paley Center for the Media, catalog number 12583R.

7. Eric Morgenthaler, "A Common Touch," *Wall Street Journal*, June 28, 1993.

8. Roberts, "What a Rush."

9. Vincent Coppola, "Neal Boortz: Have Mouth, Will Talk," *Atlanta Magazine*, July 1, 1998, https://www.atlantamagazine.com/great-reads/neal-boortz-have-mouth-will-talk.

10. Neal Boortz, *Maybe I Should Just Shut Up and Go Away* (Franklin, TN: Carpenter's Son Publishing, 2012), Kindle location 2401.

11. Howard Kurtz, "Talk Radio Hosts Waking Up on the Right Side of the Bed," *Washington Post*, November 10, 1994.

12. Tom Becka, interview with author, December 19, 2012; Susan Douglas, *Listening In: Radio and the American Imagination* (Minneapolis: University of Minnesota Press, 2004), 292, 310–312.

13. Berry and Sobieraj, *Outrage Industry*, 127; Howard Kurtz, "Radio Daze: A Day with the Country's Masters of Gab," *Washington Post*, October 24, 1994, B01; Arlene Levinson, "America's Yakking It Up," *Pittsburgh Post-Gazette*, September 4, 1994.

14. John McGuire, "The Loudest Limb on the Family Tree," *St. Louis Post-Dispatch*, September 27, 1992.

15. Anonymous radio producer 1, interview with author, August 12, 2016; anonymous radio producer 2, interview with author, December 20, 2016.

16. Joe Getty, interview with author, February 13, 2013; Jack Armstrong, interview with author, February 25, 2013.

17. David G. Hall, interview with author, September 25, 2012; Morgenthaler, "A Common Touch."

18. Even before Limbaugh's show began to air nationally in 1988, Murray Levin described talk radio as the province of proletarian discontent and the only mass medium available to the underclass; Murray B. Levin, *Talk Radio and the American Dream* (Lexington, MA: Lexington Books, 1987), xiii.

19. Allison Perlman details how Limbaugh appropriated the mantle of civil rights for conservatives, in part by conflating race consciousness with racism and color blindness with racial progress. See Allison Perlman, "Rush Limbaugh and the Problem of the Color Line," *Cinema Journal* 51, no. 4 (2012): 198–204; Larry Letich, "Why White Men Jump," *Washington Post*, October 30, 1994. For an explanation of the roots of this sentiment, see Thomas Byrne Edsall and

Mary D. Edsall, *Chain Reaction: The Impact of Race, Rights, and Taxes on American Politics* (New York: W. W. Norton, 1992); and Rick Perlstein, *Nixonland: The Rise of a President and the Fracturing of America* (New York: Scribner, 2008).

20. Jack Armstrong, interview with author; Douglas, *Listening In*, 288–292, 302–307.

21. Kathleen Hall Jamieson and Joseph Cappella, *Echo Chamber: Rush Limbaugh and the Conservative Media Establishment* (New York: Oxford University Press, 2008), 90–104.

22. G. Gordon Liddy, *The G. Gordon Liddy Show*, July 5, 1994, C-Span, http://www.c-spanvideo.org/program/58461-1.

23. Neal Boortz, *The Neal Boortz Show*, May 31, 2005, Library of Congress's Web Radio Recording Project, which can be accessed only in the Library.

24. Bill Cunningham, *The Big Show with Bill Cunningham*, December 20, 2005, Library of Congress's Web Radio Recording Project, which can be accessed only in the Library.

25. Rush Limbaugh, *Rush Limbaugh*, produced by Roger Ailes, aired October 23, 1992 (Multimedia Entertainment).

26. *G. Gordon Liddy Show*, July 5, 1994.

27. Levinson, "America's Yakking It Up"; Donna Petrozzello, "Clinton Criticizes Media for Message," *Broadcasting and Cable*, July 4, 1994.

28. Jamieson and Cappella, *Echo Chamber*, 77; Howard Kurtz, "Radio's New Right Fielder," *Washington Post*, January 14, 2002.

29. Bill Lambrecht, "Radio Activity: In a Big Rush," *St. Louis Post-Dispatch*, November 13, 1994.

30. For analysis of the development of Sunbelt conservatism, see Lisa McGirr, *Suburban Warriors: The Origins of the New American Right* (Princeton: Princeton University Press, 2001); Matthew Lassiter, *The Silent Majority: Suburban Politics in the Sunbelt South* (Princeton: Princeton University Press, 2006); Kevin Kruse, *White Flight: Atlanta and the Making of Modern Conservatism* (Princeton: Princeton University Press, 2005).

31. Rush Limbaugh, "Discussion about Students from Different Colleges Joining the Program; How Sam Donaldson Is in the Hot Seat; Higher Taxes for the Wealthy," *Rush Limbaugh*, aired April 3, 1995; Rush Limbaugh, *Rush Limbaugh*, aired October 14, 1992.

32. Jamieson and Cappella, *Echo Chamber*, 90–104.

33. David Remnick, "Day of the Dittohead," *Washington Post*, February 20, 1994.

34. Paul D. Colford, *The Rush Limbaugh Story: Talent on Loan from God, an Unauthorized Biography* (New York: St. Martin's Press, 1994), 2–13.

35. David Barker offers evidence that Limbaugh affects his listeners' attitudes toward the issues. Barker, *Rushed to Judgment: Talk Radio, Persuasion, and American Political Behavior* (New York: Columbia University Press, 2002), 30–74.

36. Sean Hannity and Alan Colmes, "Interview with Rush Limbaugh; Bush Responds to DUI Charge from 1976," *Hannity & Colmes*, Fox News Channel, November 3, 2000, TV transcript.

37. Bill McMahon, interview with author, January 23, 2013; Thom Hartmann, interview with author, November 3, 2012; George Oliva, interview with author, November 26, 2012; Valerie Geller, interview with author, January 14, 2013.

38. Juan Williams, "Interview with Rush Limbaugh," *Special Report with Brit Hume*, Fox News Channel, February 25, 1999, Federal Document Clearing House, TV transcript.

39. Jim Rutenberg, "Despite Other Voices, Limbaugh's Is Still Strong," *New York Times*, April 24, 2000. This claim fits with the findings of Daniel Hopkins and Jonathan Ladd, whose research on Fox News shows that "access to an ideologically distinctive media source reinforces the loyalty of co-partisans without influencing out-partisans." Daniel J. Hopkins and Jonathan McDonald Ladd, "The Consequences of Broader Media Choice: Evidence from the Expansion of Fox News," *Quarterly Journal of Political Science* 9, no. 1 (2014): 115–135.

40. Bernstein, "Show Time in the Rush Room."

4. Necessity, Mother of Invention

1. Robert Walker, interview with author, October 10, 2013.

2. Danielle Herubin, "Appearance as Radio Talk-Show Host Tempers Dornan's Disappointment," *Orange County Register*, December 21, 1991; "The Buzz: This Week—Politics," *Orange County Register*, September 6, 1993.

3. Marlin Fitzwater, "Phone Call to Representative Dornan Hosting The Rush Limbaugh Talk Radio Show," Memo to President Bush, Bush Presidential Library, email to author from Cody McMillian, February 15, 2019.

4. Bill Himpler, interview with author, October 23, 2012; Ed Gillespie, interview with author, July 31, 2013.

5. Michael S. Johnson, interview with author, October 8, 2013; Dick Armey, interview with author, March 7, 2013; John Feehery, interview with author, May 2, 2013.

6. Missi Tessier, interview with author, October 22, 2013.

7. Dan Balz and Ron Brownstein, *Storming the Gates: Protest Politics and the Republican Revival* (Boston: Little Brown, 1996), 172.

8. Paul Luthringer, interview with author, October 29, 2013.

9. Dorrance Smith, interview with author, October 23, 2013.

10. Barrie Tron, interview with author, October 10, 2013.

11. Tron, interview.

12. Some of this focus owed to timing: only in the second or third year of Bush's term did talk radio, spurred by Limbaugh's rapidly blossoming stardom, truly

emerge nationally as a combatant in the political arena. By this point, however, Bush's team had already established their communications strategy, which directed their focus to other media; Tron, interview.

13. This perspective fit with Smith's charge, which was to optimize use of all the television tools available to the White House during the last two years of Bush's term. Smith also oversaw regional media.

14. Smith, interview.

15. "Remarks by the President in Interview with Gene Burns of WOR Radio," US Newswire, August 24, 1994.

16. Richard Strauss, interview with author, November 30, 2012.

17. Luthringer, interview; Steve Rabinowitz, interview with author, June 7, 2013.

18. Strauss, interview; Jeff Eller, interview with author, January 16, 2013.

19. Strauss, interview.

20. "Politics Unusual," *Nightline*, ABC News, aired September 29, 2004; Mandy Grunwald, email message to author, February 25, 2019.

21. Strauss, interview.

22. Mark Gearan, interview with author, November 6, 2013.

23. Rabinowitz, interview.

24. Will Feltus, interview with author, October 23, 2013.

25. Balz and Brownstein, *Storming the Gates*, 172.

26. Associated Press, "Limbaugh a Guest at White House," June 11, 1992.

27. "Interview: Rush Limbaugh Talks about His Stay at the White House," *The Today Show*, NBC News, June 8, 1992.

28. Correspondence, Bush Presidential Library, no. 345747 ME001, email to author from Cody McMillian, February 15, 2019.

29. Documents, Bush Presidential Library, no. 367693 ME001, email to author from Cody McMillian, February 15, 2019.

30. Jerry Hagstrom, "Campaign Sideshow," *National Journal*, September 5, 1992.

31. Elizabeth Long, email message to author, April 18, 2013.

32. Long, email; Balz and Brownstein, *Storming the Gates*, 172; Mary Matalin and James Carville with Peter Knobler, *All's Fair: Love, War and Running for President* (New York: Touchstone and Random House, 1995), 284–285; Associated Press, "Quayle Invites Limbaugh to Be Debate Moderator," October 2, 1992; "Candidate George Bush Visited Rush Limbaugh's Radio Show," *St. Louis Post-Dispatch*, September 27, 1992; Michael Wines, "The 1992 Campaign: White House; Quayle Says Character Will Be Big Issue in Fall," *New York Times*, July 8, 1992; Rush Limbaugh, "Quayle Campaign Appearance," *The Rush Limbaugh Show*, July 7, 1992, http://www.c-span.org/video/?27000-1 /QuayleCampaignApp; Feltus, interview.

33. Long, email.

34. Clinton's appearance on MTV spawned a debate in the White House over whether Bush, too, should appear on the network. Eventually Bush's advisers decided he wouldn't be comfortable in such a venue. Smith, interview; Feltus, interview.

35. Walt Riker, interview with author, November 14, 2013.

36. Clarkson Hine, interview with author, November 23, 2013; Bob Grant, *The Bob Grant Show*, WABC Radio, April 8, 1994, http://www.c-span.org/video/?55911-1 /BobGr.

37. Hine, interview.

38. Mark Updegrove, *The Last Republicans: Inside the Extraordinary Relationship between George H. W. Bush and George W. Bush* (New York: HarperCollins 2017), 239.

39. Jim Cooper, "Talkers Brace for 'Fairness' Assault," *Broadcasting and Cable*, September 6, 1993, 44.

40. Times Mirror Center for the People and the Press, "The Vocal Minority in American Politics," July 16, 1993, 2, 14–15, http://people-press.org/report /19930716/the-vocal-minority-in-american-politics.

41. Peter Viles, "Only in America: Liddy Goes National," *Broadcasting and Cable*, May 3, 1993, 43.

42. Gabe Hobbs, interview with author, August 29, 2012; Randall Bloomquist, interview with author, August 27, 2012; Holland Cooke, interview with author, October 4, 2012; Brian Jennings, interview with author, October 29, 2012.

43. G. Gordon Liddy, "Interview with Rich Noyes," *The G. Gordon Liddy Program*, March 21, 2006, Library of Congress's Web Radio Recording Project, which can be accessed only in the Library.

44. Joel Oxley and Jim Farley, who worked for Washington all-news station WTOP, conveyed that only eleven markets had such stations. By contrast, the Pew Research Center's 2015 State of the Media Report put the number of all-news stations at thirty-one (in twenty-seven markets) in 2014, down from thirty-seven in 2012. This discrepancy may owe to differing definitions of what constituted all-news stations. Jim Farley, email message to author, August 30, 2014; Joel Oxley, interview with author, January 14, 2013.

45. Hobbs, interview; Michael Smerconish, interview with author, October 5, 2012. Finding data to support this theory would be difficult because many stations, including a lot of the small ones that aired Limbaugh's program at the time, were unrated. Additionally, Arbitron measured by daypart, including a midday slot of 10 a.m. to 3 p.m., and Limbaugh's show only aired for two or three hours of that block, depending on the market.

46. Shannon Sweatte, interview with author, April 15, 2013; Jennings, interview.

47. Susan Douglas calls Clinton's election "arguably one of the best things that happened to Limbaugh." Susan Douglas, *Listening In: Radio and the American Imagination* (Minneapolis: University of Minnesota Press, 2004), 315.

48. Tom Taylor, interview with author, January 11, 2013.

49. "Playboy Interview: Rush Limbaugh," *Playboy Magazine*, December 1993, 59.

5. The New Republican King

1. James Bowman, "Rush: The Leader of the Opposition," *National Review*, September 6, 1993.

2. "Convention Tidbits: The Last in a Series," *National Journal* "Hotline," August 21, 1992; Karl Vick, "GOP Youth Seen but Mostly Heard," *St. Petersburg Times*, August 22, 1992; John Carmody, "The TV Column," *Washington Post*, September 10, 1992.

3. "Candidate George Bush Visited Rush Limbaugh's Radio Show," *St. Louis Post-Dispatch*, September 27, 1992.

4. "White House '96—New Hampshire: Campbell, Gramm, and Perot Check the Foliage," *National Journal* "Hotline," October 25, 1993; "Poll Update—Harris: Dole Maintains Lead in GOPstakes," *National Journal* "Hotline," January 3, 1995.

5. Rush Limbaugh, "Tribute to Ronald Reagan," *Rush Limbaugh*, produced by Roger Ailes, aired September 5, 1996 (Multimedia Entertainment).

6. Kathleen Hall Jamieson and Joseph Cappella note that Limbaugh is a party leader, and that conservative media figures fulfill functions once associated with party leaders. They do not, however, explore the leadership function beyond messaging and rhetoric. More broadly the literature on political parties fails to mention this leadership role. Kathleen Hall Jamieson and Joseph Cappella, *Echo Chamber: Rush Limbaugh and the Conservative Media Establishment* (New York: Oxford University Press, 2008), xiii, 46.

7. Scholarship on the 1990s Republican Party tends to ignore the impact of talk radio on the party. Among the many works on the rise of the new Republican Party are Douglas L. Koopman, *Hostile Takeover: The House Republican Party 1980–1995* (Lanham, MD: Rowman and Littlefield, 1996); Dan Balz and Ronald Brownstein, *Storming the Gates: Protest Politics and the Republican Revival* (Boston: Little Brown, 1996); William F. Connelly Jr. and John J. Pitney Jr., *Congress' Permanent Minority: Republicans in the U.S. House* (Lanham, MD: Rowman and Littlefield, 1994); Nicol C. Rae, *Conservative Reformers: The Republican Freshmen and the Lessons of the 104th Congress* (Armonk, NY: M. E. Sharpe, 1998); James G. Gimpel, *Legislating the Revolution: The Contract with America in Its First Hundred Days* (Boston: Allyn and Bacon, 1996). Of these authors only Balz and Brownstein cover Republicans'

use of talk radio, but they do not explore ways in which radio hosts constrained the party, partly because the period they discuss featured less such constraint. Elsewhere David Brock oversimplifies the relationship between Republicans and talk radio hosts, portraying hosts as mere conduits. David Brock, *The Republican Noise Machine: Right-Wing Media and How It Corrupts Democracy* (New York: Crown Publishers, 2004), 261–291.

8. "Parties in the United States are best understood as coalitions of interest groups and activists seeking to capture and use government for their particular goals, which range from material self-interest to high-minded idealism. The coalition of policy-demanding groups develops an agenda of mutually acceptable policies, insists on the nomination of candidates with a demonstrated commitment to its program, and works to elect these candidates to office." Kathleen Bawn, Martin Cohen, David Karol, Seth Masket, Hans Noel, and John Zaller, "A Theory of Political Parties: Groups, Policy Demands and Nominations in American Politics," *Perspectives on Politics* 10, no. 3 (2012): 571–597.

9. Charles Walston, "Center's Limo Offers Voters a Taste of Gingrich Lifestyle," *Atlanta Journal Constitution*, October 24, 1992.

10. Rush Limbaugh, *Rush Limbaugh*, aired November 2, 1992 (Multimedia Entertainment); Paul J. Hendrie, "Stumping through New Jersey: Ridgewood Roars 20,000 Supporters Greet Bush at Rally," *Record* (Bergen County, NJ), October 23, 1992; Terry Mutchler, "Bush Swings through NJ Urging Voters to Ignore Polls, Trust Him," Associated Press, October 22, 1992.

11. George H. W. Bush, "Remarks to the Community in Madison, New Jersey," November 2, 1992, the American Presidency Project, http://www.presidency .ucsb.edu/ws/?pid=21726.

12. This argument builds on recent literature explaining that the political parties are not weak, as scholars once argued, but rather, when employing a broader definition of party appropriate for the twenty-first century, quite strong. However, these arguments eschew ideological media personalities from even the more expansive notion of party, thereby omitting a critical segment of contemporary party leadership. Seth E. Masket, *No Middle Ground: How Informal Party Organizations Control Nominations and Polarize Legislatures* (Ann Arbor: University of Michigan Press, 2009); Marty Cohen, David Karol, Hans Noel, and John Zaller, *The Party Decides: Presidential Nominations Before and After Reform* (Chicago: University of Chicago Press, 2008); John H. Aldrich, *Why Parties? A Second Look* (Chicago: University of Chicago Press, 2011), especially 286–292.

13. Michael S. Johnson, interview with author, October 8, 2013.

14. Anonymous campaign staffer 2, interview with author, September 14, 2016.

15. "Election Hot Sheet," *Atlanta Journal Constitution,* October 30, 2004; Neal Boortz, *Maybe I Should Just Shut Up and Go Away* (Franklin, TN: Carpenter's Son Publishing, 2012), Kindle location 802–803.

16. Mark Mellman, interview with author, October 11, 2013.

17. Rush Limbaugh, "Comments on the New Jersey Senate Race, The Homework Issue at Cabrillo Unified School, Debate between Senator Kennedy and Mitt Romney and Estimates What a Candidate Spends per Vote They Receive," *Rush Limbaugh,* produced by Roger Ailes, aired October 26, 1994 (Multimedia Entertainment).

18. Ruth Marcus, "Bush Takes Up Draft Cry; Clinton Accused of Failing to Level with Public," *Washington Post,* September 22, 1992; John W. Mashek, "Bush Accuses Clinton of Failure to Come Clean on Vietnam," *Boston Globe,* September 22, 1992; Frank J. Murray, "Bush Tells Foe to 'Come Clean' First Direct Jab on Draft Issue," *Washington Times,* September 22, 1992; Rush Limbaugh, *Rush Limbaugh,* produced by Roger Ailes, aired September 21, 1992 (Multimedia Entertainment).

19. Rush Limbaugh, *Rush Limbaugh,* produced by Roger Ailes, aired November 6, 1992 (Multimedia Entertainment).

6. Bill Clinton, Talk Radio Innovator

1. Benjamin Page and Jason Tannenbaum note that callers, more than hosts, drove the discussion on talk radio. "Zoe Baird, Nannies, and Talk Radio," in *Who Deliberates: Mass Media in Modern Democracy,* ed. Benjamin Page, 77–105 (Chicago: University of Chicago Press, 1996); "Radio Talk Shows Increasing Influence on Policy," *Morning Edition,* 1130, segment no. 14 (July 16, 1993); Tom Hamburger, "Attorney General Search Says Much about Politics and Washington in '90s," *Minneapolis Star Tribune,* February 9, 1993; Bob Dart, "Dial-tone Democracy Born of Technology, Talk Shows," *Austin American Statesman,* February 6, 1993; Elizabeth Kolbert, "The People Are Heard, at Least Those Who Call Talk Radio," *New York Times,* January 29, 1993; Rod McQueen, "Baird Fiasco Showed Clinton Is Listening to Public," *Financial Times,* January 27, 1993; Jill Lawrence, "Baird Galvanized America," *Austin American Statesman,* January 24, 1993; Howard Kurtz, "Talk Radio's Early Word on Zoe Baird," *Washington Post,* January 23, 1993; John Aloysius Farrell, "Baird: Reminder of Populist Outrage," *Boston Globe,* January 23, 1993; Lynne Duke and Michael Isikoff, "Baird's Illegal Hiring Raises Sharp Debate," *Washington Post,* January 21, 1993.

2. Howard Fineman, Mark Miller, and Ann McDaniel, "Hillary's Role," *Newsweek,* February 15, 1993, 18.

3. Mark Gearan, interview with author, November 6, 2013.

4. Michael Harrison, "George Stephanopoulos Interviewed," *Talkers Magazine*, June 1994, 1, 10.

5. Richard Strauss, interview with author, November 30, 2012.

6. Strauss, interview.

7. Jeff Eller, interview with author, January 16, 2013.

8. Strauss, interview; Gearan, interview.

9. "Remarks by President Clinton on 'Imus in the Morning' Radio Show," U.S. Newswire, February 17, 1994.

10. Strauss, interview.

11. Michael Harrison, "Chief Executive Reaches Out to Talk Radio," *Talkers Magazine*, no. 53 (1994), 6, 13.

12. Howard Kurtz, "Talking Back: Radio Hosts Stir Up Fires and Bask in Newfound Glow," *Washington Post*, June 22, 1996.

13. Eller, interview.

14. Terrance Hunt, "Radio Show Hosts Flock to D.C.," *New Orleans Times Picayune*, September 22, 1993.

15. Rush Limbaugh, *The Rush Limbaugh Show*, February 18, 1994, accessible via the C-SPAN library at https://www.c-span.org/video/?54681-1/rush-limbaugh -radio-talk-show.

16. Clinton Presidential Records, Subject Files OA/ID number 100676, Scan ID 046960, Folder Title FG006-01, Stack S, Row 88, Section 6, Shelf 6, Position 7, Clinton Presidential Library, Little Rock, AR.

17. Ron Fournier, "Gab Gonzos Take over White House Lawn," Associated Press, September 23, 1993; Howard Kurtz, "Radio Free America: White House Troops Deliver Health-Care Air Blitz," *Washington Post*, September 24, 1993; Hunt, "Radio Show Hosts Flock to D.C."; "Washington Reacts to President Clinton's Speech on Health Care," *NBC News*, September 23, 1993; Thomas Friedman, "Clinton's Health Plan," *New York Times*, September 24, 1993; Elizabeth Kolbert, "An Open Mike, a Loudmouth Live, and Thou," *New York Times*, September 26, 1993; Frank J. Murray, "Radio Hosts Pitch Tents as White House Pitches Plan," *Washington Times*, September 24, 1993; Ann Devroy, "It's Show Time under Clinton's Big Top," *Washington Post*, September 24, 1993.

18. Gearan, interview.

19. Kurtz, "Talking Back."

20. Gearan, interview.

21. All interviews made available online by Gerhard Peters and John T. Woolley, The American Presidency Project: William J. Clinton, interview with Bruce Newbury of WPRO Radio, Providence, RI, https://www.presidency.ucsb.edu /node/218043; William J. Clinton, interview with Mike Siegel of KVI Radio,

Seattle, WA, https://www.presidency.ucsb.edu/node/218204; William J. Clinton, interview with John Watson of WILM Radio, Wilmington, DE, https://www.presidency.ucsb.edu/node/218215; William J. Clinton, interview with John Gambling of WOR Radio, New York City, https://www.presidency.ucsb.edu/node/218346; William J. Clinton, interview with Paul W. Smith of WWDB Radio, Philadelphia, PA, https://www.presidency.ucsb.edu/node/218351.

7. Stopping Legislation in Its Tracks

1. For more on the rise of cloture, see Barbara Sinclair, *Party Wars: Polarization and the Politics of National Policy Making* (Norman: University of Oklahoma Press, 2006), 185–233; and Sean M. Theriault, *The Gingrich Senators: The Roots of Partisan Warfare in Congress* (New York: Oxford University Press, 2013), especially 124.
2. R. Douglas Arnold, *The Logic of Congressional Action* (New Haven: Yale University Press, 1990), 5.
3. To put talk radio into Arnold's model, hosts served as instigators, who activated what might otherwise be an inattentive public. See Arnold, *Logic of Congressional Action*, 17–87, especially 30 and 68–69.
4. See, generally, John W. Kingdon, *Agendas, Alternatives and Public Policies*, updated 2nd ed. (Boston: Longman, 2011), 66.
5. Rush Limbaugh, *The Rush Limbaugh Show*, at 38:00, November 3, 1992, http://c-spanvideo.org/program/Limb.
6. Arnold, *Logic of Congressional Action*, 100–101.
7. Berry and Sobieraj note the effectiveness of "outrage media" at "enhancing the traceability of actions by legislators." Jeffrey M. Berry and Sarah Sobieraj, *The Outrage Industry: Political Opinion Media and the New Incivility* (New York: Oxford University Press, 2014), 195.
8. Frank R. Baumgartner and Bryan Jones, *Agendas and Instabilities in American Politics*, 2nd ed. (Chicago: University of Chicago Press, 2009), 103–126.
9. Berry and Sobieraj offer evidence that "outrage media" could introduce new frames into public policy debates; Berry and Sobieraj, *Outrage Industry*, 198–199. See also Frank R. Baumgartner et al., *Lobbying and Policy Change: Who Wins, Who Loses, and Why* (Chicago: University of Chicago Press, 1993), 173–187.
10. Candi Wolff, interview with author, January 22, 2015.
11. E. J. Dionne, Jr., "Washington Talk: Radio and Politics," *New York Times*, February 15, 1989; Jeffrey York, "On the Dial: Tea but No Sympathy," *Washington Post*, February 14, 1989; "Hill Steamed over Radio's Tea Time," *Broadcasting and Cable*, February 13, 1989; Bruce McCabe, "AM Radio Heating Up the Airwaves," *Boston Globe*, February 10, 1989.

12. Anonymous House staffer 1, interview with author, March 12, 2015.

13. Brian Williams, "President's Lobbying Reform Proposal Killed by Republicans," *NBC Nightly News*, October 6, 1994.

14. Paul Brubaker, interview with author, December 4, 2014.

15. Senate Roll Call Vote 116, on S. 349, Lobbying Disclosure Act of 1994, 103rd Cong. 1st. sess., May 6, 1993, http://www.senate.gov/legislative/LIS/roll _call_lists/roll_call_vote_cfm.cfm?congress=103&session=1&vote=00116.

16. House Roll Call Vote 90, on S. 349, Lobbying Disclosure Act of 1994, 103rd Cong. 2nd sess., March 24, 1994, http://clerk.house.gov/evs/1994/roll090 .xml.

17. Linda Gustitus, email message to author, quoting anonymous Senate staffer 1, February 25, 2014.

18. Christopher Drew, "Pro-GOP Calls Help Kill Lobbying Bill," *Orange County Register*, October 7, 1994.

19. Database searches for "lobbying disclosure" from August 28 to September 29, 1994, the day the House passed the conference report on the bill, find few instances: a Factiva search finds only four newspaper articles on the topic and no network television segments; a Nexus Uni search finds just two newspaper articles and one CNN mention, by Senate Majority Leader George Mitchell.

20. Drew, "Pro-GOP Calls"; Jim Drinkard, "Grassroots Groups Fire Up Faxes, Phones and Airwaves," Associated Press, October 6, 1994; Katharine Q. Seelye, "All-Out Strategy Hobbled Lobby Bill," *New York Times*, October 7, 1994.

21. Representative Bryant, 140 Cong. Rec. (September 29, 1994) H26756.

22. Representative Bryant, 140 Cong. Rec. (September 29, 1994) H26759.

23. House Roll Call Vote 449, on H. Res. 550, Waiving Points of Order against the Conference Report to Accompany S. 349; Lobbying Disclosure Act, On Agreeing to the Resolution, 103rd Cong. 2nd sess., September 29, 1994, http://clerk.house.gov/evs/1994/roll449.xml; House Roll Call Vote 450, on S. 349, Lobbying Disclosure Act, On Motion to Recommit the Conference Report, 103rd Cong. 2nd sess., September 29, 1994, http://clerk.house.gov/evs /1994/roll450.xml; House Roll Call Vote 451, on S. 349, Lobbying Disclosure Act, On Agreeing to the Conference Report, 103rd Cong. 2nd sess., September 29, 1994, http://clerk.house.gov/evs/1994/roll451.xml.

24. Rush Limbaugh, *Rush Limbaugh*, produced by Roger Ailes, aired September 29, 1994 (Multimedia Entertainment).

25. Anonymous House staffer 1, interview.

26. Gustitus, email; anonymous Senate staffer 1, interview with author, November 25, 2014.

27. Brubaker, interview.

28. According to Limbaugh's longtime Chief of Staff Kit Carson, Levin was the most "prolific" Democrat ever to appear on Limbaugh's program. Drew, "Pro-GOP Calls"; Kit Carson, email message to author, December 5, 2013.

29. Drew, "Pro-GOP Calls"; anonymous Senate staffer 1, interview.

30. Editorial, *Washington Post*, October 9, 1994; Senate Roll Call Vote 325, S. 349, Lobbying Disclosure Act, 103rd Cong. 2nd sess., October 7, 1994, On the Cloture Motion, http://www.senate.gov/legislative/LIS/roll_call_lists/roll_call _vote_cfm.cfm?congress=103&session=2&vote=00325.

31. Jim Drinkard, "Hi-Tech E-Lobbying Swamps Reform Bill," *Charleston Gazette*, October 7, 1994.

32. Linda Gustitus, interview with author, February 10, 2014; anonymous House staffer 1, interview; Senate Roll Call Vote 328, S. 1060, Lobbying Disclosure Act of 1995, On Passage of the Bill, 104th Cong. 1st sess., July 25, 1995, http://www.senate.gov/legislative/LIS/roll_call_lists/roll_call_vote_cfm.cfm ?congress=104&session=1&vote=00328; House Roll Call Vote 828, H.R. 2564, Lobbying Disclosure Act, 104th Cong. 1st. sess., November 29, 1995, http://clerk .house.gov/evs/1995/roll828.xml; Candi Wolff, interview with author, January 22, 2015; "Lawmakers Enact Lobbying Reforms," in *CQ Almanac 1995*, 51st ed., 1-38-1-41. Washington, DC: Congressional Quarterly, 1996, http:// library.cqpress.com/cqalmanac/cqal95-1099505.

33. Scott Hogenson, interview with author, September 7, 2012.

34. Lisa Nelson, interview with author, September 22, 2015.

35. Patricia Schroeder, interview with author, March 24, 2014.

36. David Leach, interview with author, January 23, 2014.

37. Mike Mills, "How an Editorial and an Ad Changed the GATT Debate," *Washington Post*, November 25, 1994.

38. Mills, "How an Editorial"; Leach, interview; "Campaign Bombshell Dropped on Incumbents," Business Wire, October 4, 1994.

39. Leach, interview.

40. David Leach provided me with a copy of this fact sheet from his personal files, along with a cover letter dated October 7, 1994, from Chairman Dingell, Ranking Member Carlos Moorhead, and a bipartisan group of five other senior members of the committee and relevant subcommittees. "Pioneer's Preference Financing Defended at Extraordinary Hearing," *Communications Daily*, October 6, 1994; Jeannine Aversa, "Republicans Back Price Break Plan at Special House Hearing," Associated Press, October 5, 1994.

41. Mills, "How an Editorial."

42. Leach, interview.

43. Tom Davis, interview with author, September 10, 2013.

44. Brett Shogren, interview with author, February 23, 2015.

8. The Political Earthquake

1. Sam Howe Verhovek, "The Media Business," *New York Times*, May 9, 1994; Tim Jones, "Talk, Talk, Talk on the Radio," *Buffalo News*, July 21, 1994; Katharine Q. Seelye, "Talk Radio Hosts Answer a Political Call," *New York Times*, April 16, 1994.

2. Jack Swanson, interview with author, September 19, 2012.

3. Mickey Luckoff, interviews with author, November 27, 2012, and August 27, 2014; Swanson, interview.

4. Jim Farley, interview with author, December 20, 2012.

5. John Herndon, "Talk Radio Fans Defy Expectation," *Austin American Statesman*, May 19, 1994.

6. Douglas Turner, "Paxon Makes Mark Heading GOP Panel," *Buffalo News*, February 27, 1994.

7. Political professionals and scholars are skeptical that talk radio can have a decisive impact on electoral outcomes. Yet 1994 was a year in which talk radio played a substantial role in electoral outcomes because several unique factors enabled the medium to have a greater impact than it would subsequently have. These factors included many Republican-leaning districts with veteran Democratic incumbents; Limbaugh, who had only recently become a cultural phenomenon; and the purity of talk radio support for House Republicans, who had yet to anger hosts with the decisions demanded by governing. Without talk radio, Republican congressional candidates would have had greater difficulty defeating Democratic incumbents simply because they would have struggled to get their message out thanks to being substantially outspent in paid media, and because the mainstream media paid minimal attention to most individual House races because journalists considered it unlikely that Republicans could capture control of the House.

8. Adam Clymer, "Michel, G.O.P. House Leader, to Retire," *New York Times*, October 5, 1993.

9. Lisa Nelson, interview with author, September 22, 2015; Kevin Schweers, interview with author, January 25, 2013; Dick Armey, interview with author, March 7, 2013; Robert Walker, interview with author, October 10, 2013.

10. Bill Paxon, interview with author, September 20, 2012.

11. Dan Horn, "Chabot Battles the Clock," *Cincinnati Post*, October 31, 1994.

12. Leslie Phillips, "Talk Radio Hosts Crank Up the Political Volume," *USA Today*, October 26, 1994.

13. Federal Election Commission Campaign Summary Report Index L through December 31, 1994, for Thomas S. Foley, Candidate ID H6WA05023 and George R. Nethercutt, Candidate ID H4WA05028. Obtained via email from Matthew Rowley on February 4, 2017.

14. George Nethercutt, interview with author, February 24, 2014.

15. Ken Lisaius, interview with author, October 12, 2012.

16. Jeffrey R. Biggs and Thomas S. Foley, *Honor in the House* (Pullman: Washington State University Press, 1999), 252–253; Jim Camden, interview with author, September 16, 2013; Bob Shrum, interview with author, October 7, 2013.

17. Mark Souder, email message to author, September 26, 2013.

18. Saxby Chambliss, interview with author, May 14, 2015.

19. "Rush Limbaugh's America," *Frontline*, season 13, episode 11, directed by Marian Marzynski, produced by Steve Talbot, aired February 28, 1995, https://www.youtube.com/watch?v=tWD_F6sZ5dE.

20. "Rush Limbaugh's America"; Rush Limbaugh, "Views of CBS News / *New York Times* Poll Dealing with Voter Sentiment, Alienation, Outlook, Trust in Government and Government's Response to Populace," *Rush Limbaugh*, produced by Roger Ailes, aired November 4, 1994 (Multimedia Entertainment).

21. Rush Limbaugh, "Discussion on Barbara Streisand, President Clinton and Political Ads for Democratic Candidates," *Rush Limbaugh*, produced by Roger Ailes, aired October 4, 1994 (Multimedia Entertainment).

22. Rush Limbaugh, "Comments on Roseanne Barr; Household Contributions to Organizations Are Down; Advertisements Regarding the Congressional Elections; and the Use of Morphing to Create Ads for the Congressional Elections," *Rush Limbaugh*, produced by Roger Ailes, aired October 19, 1994 (Multimedia Entertainment).

23. Rush Limbaugh, "Discusses Mario Cuomo's Election Strategy, Ross Perot's and Rudolph Giuliani's '94 Endorsements, Texas Opinion Poll of Perot, and Research Study Showing Link between Abortions and Breast-Cancer Risks," *Rush Limbaugh*, aired November 2, 1994 (Multimedia Entertainment).

24. Rush Limbaugh, "Discussion on Electing Republicans to the House of Representatives; the Attempt to Ban Assault Weapons; and Alice Revlon's Memo That Suggests How to Deal With the Budget," *Rush Limbaugh*, produced by Roger Ailes, aired October 24, 1994 (Multimedia Entertainment).

25. Rush Limbaugh, "Look at the Upcoming Election and How Republicans Can Do Better," *Rush Limbaugh*, produced by Roger Ailes, aired October 31, 1994 (Multimedia Entertainment).

26. Rush Limbaugh, "Satirical Analysis of the Day's Political News," *Rush Limbaugh*, aired October 3, 1994 (Multimedia Entertainment).

27. Associated Press, "Cynical Public Blasts Bush on Taxes," *Record* (Bergen County, NJ), June 28, 1990; Gerry Yandel, "'Read My Lips,' Too: Talk Radio Callers Sound Off in Disgust," *Atlanta Journal Constitution*, June 28, 1990; Robert Dvorchak, "For Lip Readers, Bush's Turnabout Flops—Even in Peoria," Associated Press, June 27, 1990.

28. George H. W. Bush, "Address Accepting the Presidential Nomination at the Republican National Convention in New Orleans," August 18, 1988, available at the American Presidency Project, https://www.presidency.ucsb.edu/documents /address-accepting-the-presidential-nomination-the-republican-national -convention-new.

29. Limbaugh answered this question during the 1990 segment he did with Detroit host Denny McClain. I received a copy of this broadcast from Art Vuolo's collection.

30. Rush Limbaugh, *Rush Limbaugh*, produced by Roger Ailes, aired October 27, 1994 (Multimedia Entertainment).

31. *Rush Limbaugh*, October 27, 1994; *Rush Limbaugh*, October 31, 1994.

32. *Rush Limbaugh*, October 27, 1994; *Rush Limbaugh*, October 31, 1994. Limbaugh also told the Zschau story on his June 1, 1990, radio show, which C-SPAN recorded, http://www.c-span.org/video/?12584-1/Rush, at 1:21:50.

33. Walker, interview; Nelson, interview.

9. Everything Changes

1. "Rush Limbaugh Highlights," catalog number 12568R, accessed at the Paley Center's New York branch.

2. "Rush Limbaugh's America," *Frontline*, PBS, February 28, 1995; Linda Killian, *The Freshmen* (Boulder, CO: Westview Press, 1998), 26; Rush Limbaugh, "Address to Republican Freshman Orientation," December 10, 1994, at 14:45 and 1:12:50, https://www.c-span.org/video/?62105-1/republican-freshmen -orientation. See also Steve Kornacki, *The Red and the Blue: The 1990s and the Birth of Political Tribalism* (New York: HarperCollins, 2018), 292.

3. Howard Kurtz, "The Talkmeisters: Saying All of the Right Things," *Washington Post*, January 5, 1995; Dick Armey, interview with author, March 7, 2013; "Rush Limbaugh's America," *Frontline*.

4. Kevin Merida, "Rush Limbaugh Saluted as Majority Maker," *Washington Post*, December 11, 1994; Katharine Q. Steele, "Republicans Get a Pep Talk from Rush Limbaugh," *New York Times*, December 12, 1994; Jim Rutenberg, "Despite Other Voices, Limbaugh Still Strong," *New York Times*, April 20, 2000.

5. The *Washington Post*'s Howard Kurtz observed in 1994 that approximately 70 percent of talk radio hosts were conservative. Yet "right of center" better describes hosts' ideological views at the time, which were less doctrinaire than they would be later. Howard Kurtz, "Radio Daze: A Day with the Country's Masters of Gab," *Washington Post*, October 24, 1994; Joe Logan, "Tuning In to More Than Disaffection," *Philadelphia Inquirer*, May 7, 1995.

6. Alexandra Marks, "Talk Radio's Voice Booms across America," *Christian Science Monitor*, November 1, 1995.

7. Joseph N. Cappella, Joseph Turow, and Kathleen Hall Jamieson, "Call-In Political Talk Radio: Background, Content, Audiences, Portrayal in Mainstream Media," Report Series, no. 5, Annenberg Public Policy Center, University of Pennsylvania, August 7, 1996, 5.

8. Cappella et al., "Call-In Political Talk Radio," 14.

9. David Rimmer, interview with author, September 6, 2012.

10. Limbaugh, "Address to Republican Freshman Orientation," at 25:15.

11. Phil Kuntz and Jackie Calmes, "With Some Pomp and Circumstance, Gingrich Assumes Role as House Speaker," *Wall Street Journal*, January 5, 1995; Kurtz, "Talkmeisters."

12. Chad Kolton, interview with author, August 1, 2012.

13. Bill Paxon, interview with author, September 20, 2012.

14. Benjamin Sheffner, "GOP Hosts Talk Radio," *Roll Call*, March 20, 1995.

15. Armey, interview.

16. Andrew Weinstein, interview with author, June 3, 2013.

17. John King, "Gingrich Again Considers Running for President," *Austin American Statesman*, June 3, 1995.

18. Weinstein, interview; Christina Martin, interview with author, May 8, 2013; Kevin Schweers, interview with author, January 25, 2013; Lauren Maddox, interview with author, November 25, 2013; Leigh Ann Pusey, interview with author, December 10, 2013; Rachel Robinson, interview with author, January 13, 2014.

19. Kornacki, *The Red and the Blue*, 296.

20. Limbaugh, "Address to Republican Freshman Orientation," at 34:48.

21. Rush Limbaugh, "Insufficient Ammunition for US Military Going to Haiti," *Rush Limbaugh*, produced by Roger Ailes, aired September 22, 1994 (Multimedia Entertainment).

22. Deroy Murdock, "A Republican Leader," *Washington Times*, April 9, 1997; Tara Meyer, "Gingrich Says He Still Wants a Tax Cut This Year," *New Orleans Times-Picayune*, April 5, 1997; Greg Hitt, "Gingrich Vows to Kill New Rule Taxing Business Partnerships," Dow Jones News Services, April 3, 1997; Katharine Q. Seelye, "Gingrich Moves to Turn Back Any Challenge to Leadership," *New York Times*, April 4, 1997.

23. "Transcript of Newt Gingrich Appearance on the Rush Limbaugh Program on March 20, 1997," Newt Gingrich Collection, Box 2231, Folder 27, University of West Georgia, Carrollton, GA.

24. Kyle Downey, interview with author, December 12, 2012.

25. "Museum of Television and Radio Seminar Series, The First Annual Radio Festival: Rush Limbaugh and the Talk Radio Revolution," October 24, 1995, Catalog number T:40932, accessed at the Paley Center's New York branch; Mary Jacoby, "Aftershocks," *Roll Call*, January 5, 1995.

26. Mike Stokke, interview with author, July 2, 2014; J. Dennis Hastert, interview with author, June 11, 2014.

27. Mark Souder, email message to author, September 26, 2013.

28. Souder, email; Jack Kingston, interview with author, January 8, 2016; John Linder, interview with author, January 15, 2016.

29. Linder, interview; Kingston, interview.

30. Robert Bennett, interview with author, January 4, 2013; Downey, interview.

31. Dave Hodgden, interview with author, October 23, 2013; Downey, interview.

32. Jon Kyl, interview with author, October 15, 2015.

33. Chris Paulitz, interview with author, January 9, 2013.

34. Trent Lott, interview with author, September 16, 2013.

35. Lott, interview.

36. Armey, interview.

37. Killian, *The Freshmen*, 32–62.

38. Robert Walker, interview with author, October 10, 2013; House Roll Call Vote 276, on H.J. Res. 73, On Agreeing to the Substitute Amendment, 104th Cong. 1st sess., March 29, 1995, http://clerk.house.gov/evs/1995/roll276.xml; House Roll Call Vote 277, on H.J. Res. 73, Term Limits Constitutional Amendment, 104th Cong. 1st sess., March 29, 1995, http://clerk.house.gov/evs/1995/roll277.xml.

39. Wesley Pruden, "What a Difference a Subpoena Makes," *Washington Times*, March 11, 1994; Howard Kurtz, "Whitewater Weirdness," *Washington Post*, April 23, 1994; John Aloysius Farrell, "White House Cleared in Death of Aide Foster," *Boston Globe*, July 1, 1994; Susan Schmidt, "Foster's Family Pleads for End of Public Scrutiny," *Buffalo News*, July 21, 1994; Anthony Lewis, "Abroad at Home: The Grassy Knoll," *New York Times*, August 5, 1994; David L. Michelmore, "Right Wingers Claim Clinton Lawyer's Death Is a Cover-Up," *Pittsburgh Post-Gazette*, April 30, 1995; John Yemma, "Object of Disaffection Mrs. Clinton Suffers Slings and Arrows of Radio Outrage," *Boston Globe*, January 26, 1996; Michael Isikoff and Mark Miller, "Road to a Subpoena," *Newsweek*, February 5, 1996, 32; David Brock, *The Republican Noise Machine: Right-Wing Media and How It Corrupts Democracy* (New York: Crown Publishers, 2004), 286.

40. Kornacki, *The Red and the Blue*, 261.

41. Steve M. Gillon, *The Pact: Bill Clinton, Newt Gingrich, and the Rivalry That Defined a Generation* (New York: Oxford University Press, 2008).

42. Conservative media criticism of moderate Republicans predates talk radio. For example, *Human Events, National Review*, and other conservative publications routinely eviscerated the Dewey-Eisenhower moderate faction within the Republican Party in the 1940s and 1950s. Michael Bowen, *The Roots of Modern Conservatism* (Chapel Hill: University of North Carolina Press, 2011). See also

Nicole Hemmer, *Messengers of the Right: Conservative Media and the Transformation of American Politics* (Philadelphia: University of Pennsylvania Press, 2016).

43. "50 State Report—Oregon: Hatfield Faces '96 Wrath of BBA Vote, If He Runs," *National Journal* "Hotline," March 3, 1995.

44. Connie Morella, interview with author, August 22, 2013; Chet Lunner, interview with author, September 5, 2013.

45. Peter Blute, interview with author, May 3, 2013.

46. Nancy Johnson, interview with author, August 1, 2013; Mike Castle, interview with author, February 7, 2013; James Walsh, interview with author, March 6, 2013.

47. "House Leaders Beware: A Loaded Gun," *National Journal*, October 2, 1993; Mary Jacoby, "Discharge Bill May Be Gutted," *Roll Call*, September 13, 1993; Jack Quinn, interview with author, February 20, 2013.

48. Steve LaTourette, interview with author, February 12, 2013; Castle, interview.

49. Steve Nousen, interview with author, August 7, 2013.

50. Of the 600 respondents to a primary poll conducted by Specter's 2004 campaign, 32 percent identified as very conservative and another 35 percent identified as somewhat conservative. Glen Bolger, email message to author, September 16, 2013.

51. Scott Hoeflich, interview with author, August 13, 2013.

52. Rush Limbaugh, "Boston Herald Article on Liberals; Atlanta's Crime Rate; Troubles within the Republican Party; Liberal Media; Menendez Attorney Leslie Abramson," *Rush Limbaugh*, produced by Roger Ailes, aired August 29, 1996 (Multimedia Entertainment).

10. The Democrats Wake Up

1. Gabriel Kahn, "Like GOP, Democrats Now Turn to Talk Radio," *Roll Call*, January 26, 1995; Jennifer Senior, "With More Time Now at Their Disposal, Democrats Take to the Airwaves," *The Hill*, March 8, 1995.

2. Paul Starobin, "Politics: Be There or Be Square," *National Journal*, August 3, 1996.

3. Tom O'Donnell, interview with author, November 13, 2013; Laura Nichols, interview with author, January 8, 2014; Dan Sallick, interview with author, December 9, 2013.

4. Fred Clarke, interview with author, October 30, 2012.

5. Clarke, interview.

6. Clarke, interview.

7. Howard Kurtz, "Mario Cuomo, the Limbaugh of the Left?" *Washington Post*, June 20, 1995; Jennifer Senior, "Dems Mount Talk Show Offensive," *The Hill*, April 10, 1996.

8. Nichols, interview.

9. David Bonior, interview with author, February 24, 2014.

10. Tom O'Donnell, interview with author, November 13, 2013.

11. Rosa DeLauro, interview with author, February 7, 2014.

12. DeLauro, interview; O'Donnell, interview; Bonior, interview; "Congressional Democrats Discuss Medicare Cuts on Talk Radio," news release from office of Richard Gephardt, May 17, 1995.

13. Sallick, interview; Julianne Corbett Waldron, interview with author, November 29, 2012.

14. Waldron, interview.

15. Micha L Sifry, "A Kick-Ass Liberal (Tom Leykis)," *The Nation*, April 10, 1995.

16. Nichols, interview.

17. Kimberlin Love, interview with author, February 26, 2013; Waldron, interview.

18. DeLauro, interview.

19. Bonior, interview; Patricia Schroeder, interview with author, March 24, 2014; DeLauro, interview.

20. Schroeder, interview.

21. Tom Daschle, interview with author, April 19, 2013; Laura Quinn, interview with author, December 12, 2012.

22. Quinn, interview; Roger Lotz, interview with author, September 18, 2012.

23. Byron Dorgan, interview with author, May 13, 2013.

24. Lotz, interview; Quinn, interview; Daschle, interview.

25. Jim Kennedy, interview with author, December 27, 2013; Jano Cabrera, interview with author, November 12, 2013; Kathie Scarrah, interview with author, January 20, 2014.

26. Starobin, "Politics: Be There or Be Square."

27. Scarrah, interview; Kennedy, interview.

28. More than other liberals, Lieberman had support from across the political spectrum; Scarrah, interview; Kennedy, interview.

29. Quinn, interview.

30. Waldron, interview.

31. Clinton Presidential Records, Harold Ickes Files, OA/ID 9298, Stack S, Row 22, Section 5, Shelf 3, Position 1, FOIA# 2011-1067-F, 80–85, Clinton Presidential Library, Little Rock, AR.

32. Clinton Presidential Records, Harold Ickes Files, OA/ID 9298, folder title "Talk Radio-White House [1]," 114.

33. Megan Moloney, interview with author, February 11, 2013; Mike McCurry, interview with author, October 21, 2013; Joe Lockhart, interview with author, December 10, 2013; Don Baer, interview with author, November 15, 2013; Loretta Ucelli, interview with author, February 28, 2013.

34. "Clinton Blasts Negative Media Coverage," *Washington Times*, June 25, 1994; Cheryl Wetzstein and Ralph Z. Hallow, "Clinton Lashes Out at Religious Conservatives," *Washington Times*, June 25, 1994; Harry Levins, "Clinton, Limbaugh Swap Slaps on KMOX," *St. Louis Post-Dispatch*, June 25, 1994; Douglas Jehl, "Clinton Calls Show to Assail Press, Falwell and Limbaugh," Associated Press, June 25, 1994; Ann Devroy and Kevin Merida, "Angry President Assails Radio Talk Shows, Press," *Washington Post*, June 25, 1994.

35. Dan Balz and Howard Kurtz, "Clinton Assails Spread of Hate through Media," *Washington Post*, April 25, 1995; J. Jennings Moss and George Archibald, "Clinton Lashes Out at 'Angry Voices,'" *Washington Times*, April 25, 1995; Bill Nichols, "Aides Soft-Pedal President's 'Hate' Remarks," *USA Today*, April 25, 1995; Todd S. Purdum, "Clinton Blames 'Loud and Angry' Voices in Media for Spreading Hate," *Los Angeles Daily News*, April 25, 1995; Michael K. Frisby and Joe Davidson, "Clinton Continues Attack on Hate Speech as Hunt for Bombing Suspect Intensifies," *Wall Street Journal*, April 25, 1995; John Aloysius Farrell, "Clinton Decries Hate Spread on Airwaves," *Boston Globe*, April 25, 1995; Mike Feinsliber, "A New Round of Angry Talk over Hate Talk and Its Consequences," Associated Press, April 25, 1995; "Radio Talk Show Hosts Take Offense at President Clinton's Criticism of Hatred on the Airwaves," NBC *Nightly News*, aired April 25, 1995.

11. Talk Radio Takes Over Television

1. Gabriel Sherman, *Loudest Voice in the Room: How the Brilliant, Bombastic Roger Ailes Built Fox News—and Divided a Country* (New York: Random House, 2014), 214.

2. Sherman, *Loudest Voice*, 226.

3. Rush Limbaugh, "Direct Read Ad for Fox News," *The Rush Limbaugh Show*, July 23, 1997, provided by the Missouri History Museum, St. Louis, MO.

4. Sherman, *Loudest Voice*, 178.

5. For a description of how early conservative media spread the concept of liberal media bias, see Nicole Hemmer, *Messengers of the Right: Conservative Media and the Transformation of American Politics* (Philadelphia: University of Pennsylvania Press, 2016).

6. Jim Rutenberg, "The Right Strategy for Fox," *New York Times*, September 18, 2000.

7. Sherman, *Loudest Voice*, 198.

8. Paul Fahri, "Is Sean Hannity a Journalist or Not? Here's Why It Matters," *Washington Post*, April 18, 2018; Brendan Karet, "'I'm Not a Journalist': Sean Hannity Attacks Critics," Media Matters for America blog, April 13, 2016,

https://www.mediamatters.org/blog/2016/04/13/im-not-journalist-sean-hannity
-attacks-critics-calling-out-his-softball-interviews-trump/209912.

9. Sarah Ellison, "Will Fox News Survive as a House United?" *Washington Post*,
   November 11, 2018; Daniel D'Addario, "Shep Smith Has the Hardest Job on
   Fox News," *Time Magazine*, March 15, 2018; Rob Tornoe, "Fox News Anchor
   Martha MacCallum: We're Not Trump's State-run TV," *Philadelphia Inquirer*,
   November 5, 2018; Susan B. Glasser, "Is Trump the Second Coming of
   Reagan?" *New Yorker*, May 18, 2018.

10. Joe Lockhart, interview with author, December 10, 2013.

11. Megan Moloney, interview with author, February 11, 2013.

12. Lockhart, interview.

13. Kandie Stroud, interview with author, April 8, 2013.

14. Jerry Zremsky, "Houghton Hounded by Critics, Media," *Buffalo News*,
    December 10, 1998; Robert J. McCarthy, "Houghton's 'No' Decision Spawns
    2000 Opponent, Voter Complaints," *Buffalo News*, December 12, 1998; Rachel
    Van Dongan, "Colleagues, Constituents Lead Souder to Rethink Vote," *Roll
    Call*, December 17, 1998; Brian Fitzpatrick, interview with author, August 29,
    2013; Chet Lunner, interview with author, September 5, 2013; "Clinton
    Accused: The Impeachment Vote," *Washington Post*, http://www
    .washingtonpost.com/wp-srv/politics/special/clinton/housevote/in.htm; Mark
    Souder, email messages to author, September 26 and October 12, 2013.

15. Christopher Shays, interview with author, August 11, 2013.

16. Princeton Survey Research Associates/*Newsweek* Poll, December 1998, USP-
    SRNEW.121298.R09A; CBS News/*New York Times* Poll, December 1998,
    USCBSNYT.122198.R24; Gallup Poll, December 1998, USGALLUP.98DC16
    .R02; ABC News/*Washington Post* Poll, December 1998, USABCWP.121498.R04.

17. Geoffrey Skelley, "How Crazy Is It That the Senate and House Might Move in
    Opposite Directions This Year?" FiveThirtyEight, October 8, 2018, https://
    fivethirtyeight.com/features/how-crazy-is-it-that-the-senate-and-house-might
    -move-in-opposite-directions-this-year.

18. Chris Murphy, "Musser's Abortion Stand Assailed; GOP Pledges Support
    amid Call for Fund Cut," *Capital Times* (Madison, WI), October 16, 1998.

19. Jamieson and Cappella write, "Limbaugh is ultimately interested in electing
    Republicans rather than Democrats. He is pragmatic about ensuring the
    election of those of as like mind as the electoral process permits." However,
    this became less true over time, as Limbaugh's stance toward moderates grew
    less tolerant. Kathleen Hall Jamieson and Joseph N. Cappella, *Echo Chamber:
    Rush Limbaugh and the Conservative Media Establishment* (New York: Oxford
    University Press, 2008), 118.

20. James Greenwood, interview with author, May 26, 2015.

21. Gary W. Cox and Mathew D. McCubbins, *Setting the Agenda: Responsible Party Government in the U.S. House of Representatives* (New York: Cambridge University Press, 2005), 29–30; Barbara Sinclair, *Party Wars: Polarization and the Politics of National Policy Making* (Norman: University of Oklahoma Press, 2006), 166–168.

12. Money Propels Talk Radio to the Right

1. House Roll Call Vote 25 on S. 652, Telecommunications Reform Act, 104th Cong. 2nd sess., February 1, 1996, http://clerk.house.gov/evs/1996/roll025 .xml; Senate Roll Call Vote 8 on S. 652, Telecommunications Reform Act, 104th Cong. 2nd sess., February 1, 1996, https://www.senate.gov/legislative/LIS /roll_call_lists/roll_call_vote_cfm.cfm?congress=104&session=2&vote=00008.

2. Josh Hyatt, "Radio Waves to the Future," *Boston Globe*, January 23, 1994; Eric Klineberg, *Fighting for Air: The Battle to Control America's Media* (New York: Metropolitan Books / Henry Holt, 2007), 26–27.

3. Other sources of consolidation included another deregulatory move—the suspension of the so-called anti-trafficking rule, which had previously forced companies to own a station for three years before reselling it—and the advantages of scale economies. Small owners sold to big companies that paid twelve or fifteen times the station's cashflow. Former station owner Chuck Schwartz, who sold his stations during the intense period of consolidation in the mid- to late 1990s, confirmed that he felt like his company had two choices: get big or sell. Susan Douglas, *Listening In: Radio and the American Imagination* (Minneapolis: University of Minnesota Press, 2004), 296, 298; Klineberg, *Fighting for Air*, 57–61; Holland Cooke, interview with author, October 4, 2012; Tom Taylor, interview with author, January 11, 2013; Chuck Schwartz, interview with author, September 18, 2015; Walter Sabo, interview with author, November 7, 2012.

4. The precise number of stations owned by these companies at any one moment fluctuated. Taylor, interview; Christopher Stern, "Blocked Radio Deals Approved: Chairman of FCC Uses Administrative Power," *Washington Post*, March 13, 2001; Tim Jones, "Fall of Milwaukee-Based Media Empire Shows Perilous Flip Side of Buying Frenzy," *Chicago Tribune*, May 20, 2000; Katherine Yung, "Merger Creates World's Largest Radio, Billboard Company," *Dallas Morning News*, October 5, 1999.

5. Klineberg, *Fighting for Air*, 62. Others calculate the proportion differently. A 2001 op-ed by Senators Ernest Hollings and Byron Dorgan claimed the top four companies controlled 90 percent of the industry's advertising revenue. Ernest F. Hollings and Byron Dorgan, "Your Local Station, Signing Off," *Washington Post*, June 20, 2001.

6. Harry A. Jessell, "Telecom Bill; a Deal, but Not Done," *Broadcasting and Cable*, January 1, 1996.

7. Bill Handel, interview with author, November 20, 2012.

8. John Kobylt, interview with author, February 8, 2013; Jeremy Coleman, interview with author, January 18, 2013.

9. Dan Collins, "DJs Dumped over Church Sex Stunt," CBS News, August 21, 2002, https://www.cbsnews.com/news/djs-dumped-over-church-sex-stunt; "Radio Show Canned after Sex Stunt," CNN, August 22, 2002; Stephen Battaglio with Maki Becker, "Racy L.A. Host Replaces WNEW's Shock Jerks," *New York Daily News*, August 24, 2002; Gayle Ronan Sims, "Radio Show Is Canceled over Sex Stunt," *Philadelphia Inquirer*, August 23, 2002; William K. Rashbaum, "Radio Station Cancels a Show after Complaints of Indecency," *New York Times*, August 23, 2002; Dareh Gregorian and Michael Star, "Fired & Brimstone: Radio Jerks Axed for Church Sex Stunt," *New York Post*, August 23, 2002.

10. Talk radio had to manage some advertiser tensions as well. After three years of allowing ABC Radio to sell Limbaugh's show as part of larger advertising packages, Ed McLaughlin contracted another company to sell the show as a stand-alone entity. McLaughlin felt that Limbaugh needed advertisers who knew what they were signing up for. Limbaugh has slowly dropped many of the most controversial elements of his show, such as the updates, at least in part because advertisers did not like them. Ron Hartenbaum, email message to author, January 28, 2013; David Hall, interview with author, September 25, 2012; Gabe Hobbs, interview with author, August 29, 2012; Doug Stephan, interview with author, December 10, 2012; Randall Bloomquist, interviews with author, August 27, 2012, and January 28, 2013.

11. Kobylt, interview; Hobbs, email message to author, March 18, 2013.

12. Tom Leykis, interview with author, August 19, 2014.

13. See "Buckley Radio," http://buckleyradio.com; and "Richard D. Buckley," http://web.archive.org/web/20130627131407/http://www.buckleyradio.com/pages/15818922.php; Neil MacFarquhar, "WOR Hires Bob Grant to Be Host of Program," *New York Times*, April 28, 1996; Lawrie Mifflin, "Bob Grant Is Off Air Following Remarks on Brown's Death," *New York Times*, April 18, 1996.

13. Talk Radio in the 2000s

1. Jane L. Levere, "The Fox News Channel Tops CNN's Audience," *New York Times*, January 30, 2002; Pradnya Joshi, "How Fox News's Influence Grew under Roger Ailes," *New York Times*, July 22, 2016.

2. John McConnell, interview with author, December 2, 2012; Jack Swanson, interview with author, September 19, 2012; Elisha Krauss, interview with author, May 18, 2018.

3. "Radio Networks," *Mediaweek*, September 3, 2001.

4. McConnell, interview.

5. Pamela Davis, "Beck Muscles Out Dr. Laura at WFLA," *St. Petersburg Times*, September 18, 2001; "Westwood One and Fox News' The Radio Factor with Bill O'Reilly Is the Biggest Launch in the History of Talk Radio," Business Wire, May 6, 2002; Miriam Longino, "On Radio WSB Taking Boortz and Howard National," *Atlanta Constitution*, December 16, 1998; David Hinckley, "Gallagher: 'Going Back to What I Enjoy and Do Best,'" *New York Daily News*, October 26, 1998; "Inside Media," *Mediaweek*, May 21, 2001; David Hinckley, "Twin Cities Show Gets Gotham Dancing to a Brand-New Beat," *New York Daily News*, February 26, 1998.

6. *Editorializing by Broadcast Licensees*, 13 FCC 1246 (1949), 1250.

7. See, for example, Rush Limbaugh, "Mr. President, Keep the Airwaves Free," *Wall Street Journal*, February 20, 2009; Keach Hagey, "Fairness Doctrine Fight Goes On," Politico, January 16, 2011, https://www.politico.com/story/2011/01/fairness-doctrine-fight-goes-on-047669; John Hudson, "Talk Radio's Long War on the Fairness Doctrine Is Over," *The Atlantic*, June 8, 2011, https://www.theatlantic.com/business/archive/2011/06/talk-radios-long-war-fairness-doctrine-over/351566.

8. Marin Cogan, "Bum Rush," *New Republic*, December 3, 2008, 8–10.

9. John Mainelli, email message to author, October 20, 2010; Michael Harrison, interview with author, November 9, 2010; Jon Sinton, email message to author, April 25, 2012.

10. Scott Herman, interview with author, December 26, 2012.

11. Many programmers believed that, at least under some circumstances, liberals and conservatives could succeed on the same station. David Hall, interview with author, September 25, 2012; Mickey Luckoff, interviews with author, November 27, 2012, and August 27, 2014; Mickey Luckoff, email message to author, January 29, 2013; Robert Unmacht, email message to author, January 26, 2013; Holland Cooke, interview with author, October 4, 2012; Gabe Hobbs, interview with author, August 29, 2012; Paula Span, "Radio Waves: Talk-Show Host Randi Rhodes Joined a New Liberal Network," *Washington Post*, September 12, 2004.

12. Laurie Cantillo, email message to author, January 21, 2013.

13. Phil Boyce, interview with author, October 15, 2014.

14. Walter Sabo, interview with author, November 7, 2012; Steve Goldstein, interview with author, November 6, 2012; Robert Unmacht, interview with author, January 25, 2013; Hall, interview; Jim Farley, interview with author, December 20, 2012. See also Jeffrey M. Berry and Sarah Sobieraj, *The Outrage Industry: Political Opinion Media and the New Incivility* (New York: Oxford University Press, 2014), 100.

15. Farley, interview.

16. See Brian Rosenwald, "Mount Rushmore: The Rise of Talk Radio and Its Impact on Politics and Public Policy" (Ph.D. diss., University of Virginia, 2015), 109–166, for a more extensive discussion of factors involved in liberal talk radio's failure to take off.

17. Bill Weston, email message to author, May 15, 2013; Steve Goldstein, email message to author, May 23, 2013; Kraig Kitchin, interview with author, February 13, 2013; Harrison, interview.

18. Berry and Sobieraj also argue that alternative programming fragmented the potential audience for liberal talk radio, though they do not mention morning zoo–style programs. See Jeffrey M. Berry and Sarah Sobieraj, "Understanding the Rise of Talk Radio," *PS: Political Science and Politics* 44, no. 4 (2011): 762–767, 766.

14. The Parties Go Their Own Ways

1. Mark Pfeifle, interview with author, January 16, 2013; Chris Paulitz, interview with author, January 9, 2013.

2. Susan Phalen, interview with author, April 1, 2013.

3. "Interview of the Vice President by Sean Hannity," January 11, 2006, https:// georgewbush-whitehouse.archives.gov/news/releases/2006/01/20060111-9.html; "Interview of the Vice President by Rush Limbaugh," February 1, 2006, https://georgewbush-whitehouse.archives.gov/news/releases/2006/02/20060201-7 .html; "Interview of the Vice President by Laura Ingraham," February 3, 2006, https://georgewbush-whitehouse.archives.gov/news/releases/2006/02/20060203-5 .html; all from the George W. Bush White House Archives.

4. See Peter Baker, *Days of Fire: Bush and Cheney in the White House* (New York: Doubleday, 2013), 421, 495.

5. Trey Bohn, interview with author, October 31, 2012; Taylor Gross, interview with author, March 13, 2013; Nick Piatek, interview with author, January 2, 2017.

6. Gross, interview.

7. Susan Russ, interview with author, August 16, 2013; James Jeffords, *My Declaration of Independence* (New York: Simon and Schuster, 2001).

8. Paul Kane, "How Jim Jeffords Single-Handedly Bent the Arc of Politics," *Washington Post*, August 18, 2014.

9. Bohn, interview; Brian Walton, interview with author, February 20, 2013; Scott Hogenson, interview with author, September 7, 2012.

10. Sandra Sobieraj, "Radio Hosts Descend on White House for Political Talk," Associated Press, October 30, 2002.

11. Michelle Grasso, interview with author, October 2, 2013.

12. Gene Ulm, interview with author, August 6, 2013.

13. Saxby Chambliss, interview with author, May 14, 2015.

14. Grasso, interview; Paige Perdue, interview with author, October 9, 2013.

15. Kathleen Hall Jamieson and Joseph N. Cappella, *Echo Chamber: Rush Limbaugh and the Conservative Media Establishment* (New York: Oxford University Press, 2008), 20–41.

16. Joe Holley, "Sen. Robert Byrd Dead at 92," *Washington Post*, June 28, 2010.

17. Howard Kurtz, "Dan Rather to Step Down at CBS," *Washington Post*, November 24, 2004; Alex Weprin, "The Untold Story behind Dan Rather's Departure from CBS," *Adweek*, April 16, 2012, https://www.adweek.com /tvnewser/the-untold-story-behind-dan-rathers-departure-from-cbs.

18. Sean Hannity, *The Sean Hannity Show*, March 11, 2005, Library of Congress's Web Radio Recording Project, which can be accessed only in the Library; "Sen. Robert Byrd Talks with Alan Colmes," *Hannity and Colmes*, Fox News, March 10, 2005, http://www.foxnews.com/story/2005/03/11/sen-robert-byrd-talks -with-alan-colmes.

19. Randall Bloomquist, interview with author, August 27, 2012; anonymous Republican staffer, interview with author, November 16, 2016; Piatek, interview; Elisha Krauss, interview with author, May 18, 2018.

20. Ample evidence shows that many Americans consume news only from ideologically likeminded sources; see, for example, Natalie Jomini Stroud, *Niche News: The Politics of News Choice* (New York: Oxford University Press, 2012). However, a nascent literature argues that the case for echo chambers is overstated, and most Americans either abstain from ideological news sources or receive a much more balanced news diet than previously believed. See, for example, Kevin Arceneaux and Martin Johnson, *Changing Minds or Changing Channels? Partisan News in an Age of Choice* (Chicago: University of Chicago Press, 2013).

21. Jamieson and Cappella, *Echo Chamber*, especially 62–76.

22. Jamieson and Cappella, *Echo Chamber*, 126–140.

23. Jamieson and Cappella, *Echo Chamber*, 184–185.

24. Hannity, *Sean Hannity Show*, March 11, 2005.

25. Jamieson and Cappella, *Echo Chamber*, 82, 141.

26. Jamieson and Cappella, *Echo Chamber*, 142.

27. For a description of this activism between the 1940s and the 1970s, see Nicole Hemmer, *Messengers of the Right: Conservative Media and the Transformation of American Politics* (Philadelphia: University of Pennsylvania Press, 2016).

28. Rush Limbaugh, "Discussion of Prosecutor Marcia Clark, Mario Cuomo and the Upcoming Congressional Elections," aired October 6, 1994; Rush Limbaugh, "Comments on the Limbaugh Ad for the *New York Times* and the NOW Boycott; Ordinary Citizens Stopping Crime in the City; Mainstream

Media's Complaints of Not Being as Powerful as They Used to Be," aired
October 21, 1994; Rush Limbaugh, "Discussed Mario Cuomo's Election
Strategy, Ross Perot's and Rudolph Giuliani's '94 Endorsements, Texas Opinion
Poll of Perot, and Research Study Showing Link between Abortions and
Breast-Cancer Risks," aired November 2, 1994; all *Rush Limbaugh*, produced
by Roger Ailes (Multimedia Entertainment). For additional examples of the
unflattering nicknames Limbaugh gave to prominent journalists, see Jamieson
and Cappella, *Echo Chamber*, 147.

29. Jamieson and Cappella, *Echo Chamber*, 39, 71, 125.

30. Rush Limbaugh, "Florida Orange Juice Sales Rose in July Despite NOW
Boycott; Abe Lincoln's Wife Abused Him Physically; Democrats Up for
Re-Election Avoid Link with Clinton; Environmental Wacko Communes with
Trees," aired September 5, 1994; Rush Limbaugh, "Discusses Upcoming
Elections and Various Campaigns; The Clinton Administration and the Labor
Department's Job Corps Program," aired October 7, 1994; Rush Limbaugh,
"Talks about a Personal Letter from Former President Ronald Reagan and
Does a Presentation of Various Campaigns around the Country," aired
October 17, 1994; Rush Limbaugh, "Discussion of Senatorial Election Races in
Massachusetts and Virginia, Fashion and Its Effect on Feminism, the *New
York Times* and Lack of Credit Perceived by Democrats for Improvement in the
Economy," aired October 18, 1994; Rush Limbaugh, "Comments on the
Limbaugh Ad for the *New York Times* and the NOW Boycott; Ordinary
Citizens Stopping Crime in the City; Mainstream Media's Complaints of Not
Being as Powerful as They Used to Be," aired October 21, 1994; Rush Lim-
baugh, "Comments on the New Jersey Senate Race, the Homework Issue at
Cabrillo Unified School, Debate between Senator Kennedy and Mitt Romney,
and Estimates What a Candidate Spends per Vote They Receive," aired
October 26, 1994; Rush Limbaugh, [episode title unavailable], aired
November 1, 1994; all *Rush Limbaugh*, produced by Roger Ailes (Multimedia
Entertainment). Jamieson and Cappella, *Echo Chamber*, 169.

31. Jamieson and Cappella offer evidence that regular Limbaugh listeners during
the 1996 presidential campaign believed that President Clinton's positions on
Medicare spending and missile defense deviated further from their own
stances than was actually the case. Limbaugh's listeners also experienced more
negative feelings toward Clinton and more positive feelings toward Bob Dole
than did respondents who eschewed talk radio or who listened to liberal or
other conservative hosts. Further research indicates that listening to talk radio
was associated with increased likelihood of voting Republican in 1994 and of
shifting support from Democrats to Republicans between 1992 and 1994 and
between 1994 and 1996. One weakness of this research is that cause cannot

always be disentangled from effect. Did talk radio change listeners' votes, or did it attract people otherwise inclined to vote Republican? Jamieson and Cappella, *Echo Chamber*, 134–139, 195–210, 232; David C. Barker, *Rushed to Judgment: Talk Radio, Persuasion, and American Political Behavior* (New York: Columbia University Press, 2002); David Barker, "Rushed Decisions, Political Talk Radio and Voter Choice, 1994–1996," *Journal of Politics* 61, no. 2 (1999): 527–539, 532–535; Barker and Kathleen Knight, "Political Talk Radio and Public Opinion," *Public Opinion Quarterly* 64, no. 2 (2000): 149–170; Louis Bolce, Gerald De Maio, and Douglas Muzzio, "Dial in Democracy: Talk Radio and the 1994 Election," *Political Science Quarterly* 111, no. 3 (1996): 461–464, 466, 469.

32. Randi Rhodes, "The Randi Rhodes Show Part 4/5" Youtube video, May 4, 2004, posted on January 18, 2013, https://www.youtube.com/watch?v=f_uoI _qbLwk.

33. Byron Dorgan, interview with author, May 13, 2013; Tom Daschle, interview with author, April 19, 2013; Russ Kelley, interviews with author, May 1 and May 3, 2013; Howard Kurtz, "A Voice from Above, and to the Left," *Washington Post*, January 10, 2005.

34. Daschle, interview; Eric Burns, interview with author, May 28, 2013; Mike Papantonio, interview with author, June 11, 2013; Janet Robert, interview with author, December 3, 2012.

35. Bill Press, *Toxic Talk: How the Radical Right Has Poisoned America's Airwaves* (New York: Thomas Dunne Books, 2010), 255; Mark Walsh, interview with author, April 22, 2013.

36. See Brian Rosenwald, "Mount Rushmore: The Rise of Talk Radio and Its Impact on Politics and Public Policy" (Ph.D. diss., University of Virginia, 2015), 139–157, for a detailed discussion of the failure of Air America.

37. Jamal Simmons, interview with author, November 25, 2013.

38. Laura Nichols, interview with author, January 8, 2014.

39. Brendan Daly, interview with author, April 24, 2013; Kelley, interviews; Andrea Purse, interview with author, May 9, 2013; Jim Manley, interview with author, July 22, 2013; Rodell Mollineau, interview with author, October 24, 2013.

40. "Pelosi: House Democrats Hit the Airwaves for New Direction Radio Day," November 1, 2006, news release from the office of the Democratic leader, https://votesmart.org/public-statement/225601/pelosi-house-democrats-hit-the -airwaves-for-new-direction-radio-day.

41. Loretta Ucelli, interview with author, February 28, 2013; Josh Gottheimer, interview with author, May 31, 2013.

42. Don Baer, interview with author, November 15, 2013.

43. Karina Newton, interview with author, April 30, 2013.

44. Gail Hoffman, interview with author, July 10, 2013.
45. Ari Rabin-Havt, interview with author, June 13, 2013.
46. Hoffman, interview; Rabin-Havt, interview. For a description of the Dean campaign's Internet operation and how it contributed to later Democratic efforts online, see Daniel Kreiss, *Taking Our Country Back: The Crafting of Networked Politics from Howard Dean to Barack Obama* (New York: Oxford University Press, 2012).
47. For more on the role the Internet played in liberal grassroots organizing, see David Karpf, *The MoveOn Effect: The Unexpected Transformation of American Political Advocacy* (New York: Oxford University Press, 2012).
48. Bill Richardson, interview with author, February 13, 2013.
49. David DiMartino, interview with author, June 21, 2016.
50. Rosa DeLauro, interview with author, February 7, 2014.
51. Jano Cabrera, interview with author, November 12, 2013.
52. American Conservative Union, "Federal Legislative Ratings," http://acuratings .conservative.org/acu-federal-legislative-ratings/?year1=2004&chamber =13&state1=0&sortable=1; Senate roster, 107th Congress, Voteview, UCLA Department of Political Science, https://voteview.com/congress/senate/107/text.
53. Sean Hannity, "The Sean Hannity Show," August 4, 2006, Library of Congress's Web Radio Recording Project.
54. Hannity, *Sean Hannity Show*, August 4, 2006.
55. "DW-NOMINATE Scores, 107th Congress, House of Representatives," Voteview, UCLA Department of Political Science, https://voteview.com /congress/house/107/text; American Conservative Union, "Federal Legislative Ratings," http://acuratings.conservative.org/acu-federal-legislative-ratings/ ?year1=2002&chamber=12&state1=45&sortable=1.
56. Sean Hannity, *The Sean Hannity Show*, August 20, 2002, Paley Center for the Media, catalog number RB:26220, Paley Center's New York branch.
57. Patricia Schroeder, interview with author, March 24, 2014.
58. Clarke, interview; Schroeder, interview; Paul Starobin, "Politics: Be There or Be Square," *National Journal*, August 3, 1996.
59. Dorgan, interview.
60. DeLauro, interview; David Bonior, interview with author, February 24, 2014.

15. Disgruntled but Still Loyal

1. Brian Walton, interview with author, February 20, 2013.
2. Jim Rutenberg, "Bush's Campaign Finds Outlet on Local Radio," *New York Times*, December 29, 2003.
3. Kevin Madden, interview with author, August 26, 2013. Between 1960 and 2000, West Virginia had voted for Republican presidential nominees just

twice, during the landslide years of 1972 and 1984. The state backed Jimmy Carter in 1980 and Michael Dukakis in 1988, even as both Democrats were crushed nationally.

4. Elisha Krauss, interview with author, May 18, 2018.

5. Tom Davis, interview with author, September 10, 2013.

6. Christopher Shays, interview with author, August 11, 2013.

7. "Senate Roster, 108th Congress," Voteview, UCLA Department of Political Science https://voteview.com/congress/senate/108/text.

8. Shanin Specter, email message to author, November 7, 2016.

9. Specter later became a Democrat and lost his 2010 primary run.

10. Federal Elections Commission, "Federal Elections 2004, Election Results for the U.S. President, the U.S. Senate and the U.S. House of Representatives," May 2005, https://transition.fec.gov/pubrec/fe2004/federalelections2004.pdf.

11. Mark Dion, interview with author, September 17, 2013.

12. Chris Nicholas, interview with author, August 27, 2013; Chris Mottola, interview with author, August 23, 2013.

13. Deroy Murdock, "The Bush-Soros Pick," *National Review*, April 19, 2004.

14. Rush Limbaugh, "Specter: No Soros Connection," *The Rush Limbaugh Show*, April 14, 2004, http://www.rushlimbaugh.com/daily/2004/04/14/specter_no _soros_connection.

15. Dion, interview.

16. Lars Larson, email message to author, August 7, 2013; Dion, interview.

17. Nicholas, interview; Mottola, interview; Dion, interview.

18. Michael Smerconish, email message to author, July 30, 2013.

19. Carl Hulse, "Specter Switches Parties," *New York Times*, April 28, 2009.

20. Rush Limbaugh, "Moderate RINOS Undermine the GOP," *The Rush Limbaugh Show*, November 11, 2005, http://www.rushlimbaugh.com/daily/2005 /11/11/moderate_rinos_undermine_the_gop2.

21. Howard Kurtz, "Radio Hosts Get Closer to the White House—If Only Physically," *Washington Post*, October 25, 2006; Jim Rutenberg, "As Talk Radio Wavers, Bush Moves to Firm Up Support," *New York Times*, October 17, 2006.

22. Anonymous radio producer 2, interview with author, December 20, 2016.

23. Charlie Cook, "Midterm Elections Could Be a Wave," *National Journal*, July 29, 2013, http://www.nationaljournal.com/columns/off-to-the-races /midterm-elections-could-be-a-wave-but-who-s-going-to-drown-20130729; Kyle Trygstad, "History Shows Midterm Elections a Hard Slog for President's Party," *Roll Call*, January 21, 2013, http://www.rollcall.com/news/history_shows _midterm_elections_a_hard_slog_for_presidents_party-220970-1.html.

24. Peter Baker made a similar observation: "When the red light on the camera came on that night, January 10, Bush as he often did, looked uncomfortable,

stiff, and small, 'wound tightly,' as J.D. Crouch put it, not the robust figure his advisers saw in private." Peter Baker, *Days of Fire: Bush and Cheney in the White House* (New York: Doubleday, 2013), 525; Trey Bohn, interview with author, October 31, 2012.

25. Mike Gallagher, "My Meeting with President Bush," *Talkers Magazine*, October 2006, 15–16; Boortz, "Today's Nuze," September 18, 2006, Internet Archive Wayback Machine, https://web.archive.org/web/20151204001803 /http://www.wsbradio.com/weblogs/nealz-nuze/2006/sep/18/2006-09-18; Michael Medved, *The Michael Medved Show*, September 18, September 19, and September 22, 2006, all at the Library of Congress's Web Radio Recording Project, which can be accessed only in the Library.

26. Kurtz, "Radio Hosts Get Closer."

27. David Callender, "Gov Race Brings Out the Stars," *Capital Times & Wisconsin State Journal*, November 4, 2006; Dave Pidgeon, "Santorum on Casey: 'He has no ideas,'" *Lancaster New Era / Intelligencer Journal / Sunday News*, October 30, 2006; Ann E. Marimow, "GOP Heavyweights Help with Steele's Fundraising," *Washington Post*, October 25, 2006; "The 21st Century Version of 'This Is Your Life,'" *National Journal* "Hotline," September 29, 2006; "Overlooked," *National Journal* "Hotline," September 29, 2006; Michael D. Shear and Tim Craig, "Allen Calls Webb Aide, Apologizes for Remark," *Washington Post*, August 24, 2006; David Jackson and Richard Benedetto, "Bush Tries to Regain His Footing on Once-Rock-Solid Conservative Base," *USA Today*, June 2, 2006; "A New York State of Mind," *National Journal* "Hotline," May 9, 2006; Anita Kumar, Adam C. Smith, and Bill Adair, "Harris Race Is Grist For Rumor Mill in Capital," *St. Petersburg* Times, March 9, 2006; Kurtz, "Radio Hosts Get Closer."

28. Sean Hannity, *The Sean Hannity Show*, August 4, 2006, Library of Congress's Web Radio Recording Project, which can be accessed only in the Library.

29. Paige Perdue, interview with author, October 9, 2013.

30. Jamieson and Cappella demonstrate how conservative talkers employed these techniques during presidential campaigns. But they don't focus on congressional elections, which presented an even more fertile setting for this sort of leadership. Kathleen Hall Jamieson and Joseph Cappella, *Echo Chamber: Rush Limbaugh and the Conservative Media Establishment* (New York: Oxford University Press, 2008); Kurtz, "Radio Hosts Get Closer."

31. *The Michael Medved Show*, September 22, 2006.

32. Sean Hannity, *The Sean Hannity Show*, July 31, 2006, Library of Congress's Web Radio Recording Project.

33. *The Sean Hannity Show*, August 4, 2006.

34. Kurtz, "Radio Hosts Get Closer."

35. Howard Kurtz, "Party Poopers: Conservative Pundits Who Break Ranks Find Themselves on the Wrong Side of the Right," *Washington Post*, July 22, 1997; "Analysis: New Revelations in the Paula Jones-Bill Clinton Sexual Harassment Case," *Meet the Press*, June 22, 1997; Katharine Q. Seelye, "Gingrich Moves to Turn Back Any Challenge to Leadership," *New York Times*, April 4, 1997; "House GOP Conservatives Warn Leadership on Agenda," *Congress Daily*, March 21, 1997; Laurie Kellman, "Term-limits Supporters Shift Focus to White House," *Washington Times*, March 21, 1995.

36. For another example see Michael D. Shear and Tim Craig, "Allen Calls Webb Aide, Apologizes for Remark," *Washington Post*, August 24, 2006; John Feehery, interview with author, May 2, 2013.

37. Matt Zapotosky, "Judge Sentences Former U.S. House Speaker Dennis Hastert," *Washington Post*, April 27, 2016.

38. Jeff Zeleny, "Hastert, a Political Survivor, Vows to Overcome Scandal," *New York Times*, October 6, 2006; Dana Milbank, "A Few Conservative Voices Still Speak for the Speaker," *Washington Post*, October 4, 2006; "Denny, But Not Out," *National Journal* "Hotline," October 4, 2006.

39. Ron Bonjean, interview with author, January 11, 2013.

40. Peter Baker and Jim VandeHei, "Kerry Offers Apology to Troops," *Washington Post*, November 2, 2006.

41. John Ziegler, "How the John Kerry Gaffe Story Really Broke," *Talkers Magazine*, November 2006, 1, 29.

42. Kate Zernike, "Flubbed Joke Makes Kerry a Political Punching Bag, Again," *New York Times*, November 2, 2006.

43. "Troops Respond to 'Jon Carry' with Plea for 'Halp,'" CNN, November 2, 2006.

44. Bob von Sternberg, "Minnesota Unit behind 'Irak' Sign," *Minneapolis Star-Tribune*, November 3, 2006; Niles Lathem and Todd Venezia, "Genius GIs' Joy at Last Laugh," *New York Post*, November 3, 2006.

45. Rush Limbaugh, "Rush's Interview with President George W. Bush," *The Rush Limbaugh Show*, November 1, 2006; "Kerry Apologizes for Clumsy Attempt at Joke," *The Situation Room*, CNN, November 1, 2006.

46. Sean Hannity, *The Sean Hannity Show*, November 6, 2006; the first thirty minutes of this show are available on the Library of Congress's Web Radio Recording Project.

47. Rush Limbaugh, *The Rush Limbaugh Show*, November 6, 2006, Library of Congress's Web Recording Project.

48. See David Leip, "United States Presidential Elections Results: Rhode Island," http://uselectionatlas.org/RESULTS; "Senate roster, 109th Congress," Voteview, UCLA Department of Political Science, https://voteview.com/congress /senate/109/text.

49. See Katherine Gregg and Mark Arsenault, "Senate Candidates Go One-on-One," *Providence Journal*, August 18, 2006; Ottoe, "Rush vs. Chafee and SCLM Hypocrisy," Daily Kos (blog), July 20, 2006, http://www.dailykos.com /story/2006/07/20/229184/-Rush-vs-Chafee-and-SCLM-Hypocrisy#.

50. Rush Limbaugh, "Matthews Remark Exposes Left-Wing Anti-Semitism," *The Rush Limbaugh Show*, August 9, 2006, http://www.rushlimbaugh.com/daily /2006/08/09/matthews_remark_exposes_left_wing_anti_semitism.

51. Hugh Hewitt, interview with author, November 5, 2012; "Guess Who's Coming to Lunch?" *National Journal* "Hotline," September 13, 2006.

52. "McCain at the New School: Day 4," *National Journal* "Hotline," May 23, 2006; "It's '08 Already," *National Journal* "Hotline," July 24, 2006.

53. It is impossible to determine what percentage of Laffey's out-of-state fundraising was driven by talk radio as opposed to national conservative groups, but it is reasonable to assume that talk radio contributed. The percentage is calculated using Laffey's FEC reports for the 2006 election cycle, http://www .fec.gov/fecviewer/CandidateCommitteeDetail.do. Gene Ulm, interview with author, August 26, 2013; Mottola, interview.

54. Sherwood Boehlert, interview with author, February 5, 2013.

55. In 2006 Hagel, Graham, and McCain had respective DW-NOMINATE scores of 0.344, 0.408, and 0.381. See "Senate roster, 109th Congress," Voteview, UCLA Department of Political Science, https://voteview.com/congress/senate /109/text.

56. *The Sean Hannity Show*, August 4, 2006.

16. The Titans of Talk 1 - Bipartisanship 0

1. *How Democracy Works Now*, episode 3, "Sam in the Snow," produced and directed by Michael Cammerini and Shari Robertson, at 32:15.

2. *How Democracy Works Now*, episode 1, "The Game Is On," produced and directed by Michael Cammerini and Shari Robertson.

3. *How Democracy Works Now*, episode 1; Marshall Fitz, interview with author, February 21, 2014.

4. Frank Sharry, interview with author, February 24, 2014.

5. Roger Hedgecock, interview with author, January 9, 2013.

6. Adam Sharon, "Hosts and Their Listeners Hold Politicians' Feet to the Fire," *Talkers Magazine*, May 2005, 46–47.

7. House Roll Call Vote 661, H.R. 4437, Border Protection, Antiterrorism, and Illegal Immigration Control Act, On Passage, 109th Cong. 1st. Sess., December 16, 2005, http://clerk.house.gov/evs/2005/roll661.xml; National Conference of State Legislatures, "Border Protection, Antiterrorism and Illegal Immigration Control Act," H.R. 4437 Co-Sponsors: Representative James

Sensenbrenner (R-WI) and Representative Peter King (R-NY), Immigrant Policy Project, accessed May 29, 2015, http://www.ncsl.org/research /immigration/summary-of-the-sensenbrenner-immigration-bill.aspx; The Border Protection, Antiterrorism and Illegal Immigration Control Act of 2005, H.R. 4437, 109th Cong., http://www.gpo.gov/fdsys/pkg/BILLS-109hr4437rfs/pdf /BILLS-109hr4437rfs.pdf; Patrick O'Connor, "DeLay Must Bridge Gap with Bush," *The Hill*, September 20, 2005; Emily Heil, "White House Huddles with Congress on Immigration Plan, *CongressDaily/P.M*, September 19, 2005; Doug Rivlin, interview with author, November 2, 2017; Patrick O'Connor, "Lawmakers, Rove Talk Immigration," *The Hill*, September 15, 2005.

8. Laura Burton Capps, interview with author, February 21, 2014; Fitz, interview.

9. G. Gordon Liddy, *The G. Gordon Liddy Program*, March 23, 2006, Library of Congress's Web Radio Recording Project, which can be accessed only in the Library. The Library of Congress happened to record Liddy's March 23, 2006, program from his Manchester, Tennessee, affiliate. If groups opposing immigration reform purchased advertisements on this station, they probably also placed them on stations in other states home to key senators.

10. Rush Limbaugh, "Republicans Abandon Principle Out of Fear," *The Rush Limbaugh Show*, April 3, 2006, http://www.rushlimbaugh.com/daily/2006/04/03 /republicans_abandon_principle_out_of_fear.

11. Rush Limbaugh, "Democrats Ripe for Political Embarrassment, but Gutless GOP Would Rather Pander," *The Rush Limbaugh Show*, April 4, 2006, http://www.rushlimbaugh.com/daily/2006/04/06/democrats_ripe_for_political _embarrassment_but_gutless_gop_would_rather_pander. Emphasis in original.

12. Senate Roll Call Vote 157, S. 2611, Comprehensive Immigration Reform Act of 2006, On Passage of the Bill, 109th Cong. 2nd Sess., May 25, 2006, http://www .senate.gov/legislative/LIS/roll_call_lists/roll_call_vote_cfm.cfm?congress =109&session=2&vote=00157.

13. Fitz, interview; Rivlin, interview.

14. Joel Kaplan, interview with author, October 1, 2014.

15. Fitz, interview.

16. Jon Kyl, interview with author, October 15, 2014.

17. Lars Larson, interview with author, November 16, 2012.

18. Kyl, interview.

19. Rush Limbaugh, "Immigration Bill Must Be Defeated," *The Rush Limbaugh Show*, May 21, 2007, http://www.rushlimbaugh.com/daily/2007/05/21 /immigration_bill_must_be_defeated.

20. Anonymous Senate staffer 2, interview with author, April 3, 2014.

21. Becky Talent, interview with author, February 13, 2017.

22. Trent Lott, interview with author, September 16, 2013; Saxby Chambliss, interview with author, May 14, 2015; Kyl, interview; Robert Bennett, interview with author, January 4, 2013; Jonathan Weisman and Shailagh Murray, "Republicans Hearing Static from Conservative Radio Hosts," *Washington Post*, June 20, 2007.

23. Hedgecock, interview; Larson, interview.

24. Pew Research Center, "Will Conservative Talkers Take on Immigration Reform," Pew Research Center, February 1, 2013, http://www.journalism.org /2013/02/01/will-conservative-talkers-take-immigration-reform; "Did Talk Radio Hosts Help Derail the Immigration Bill?" Pew Research Center, June 14, 2007, http://www.journalism.org/2007/06/14/pej-talk-show-index-june-3-8-2007. More broadly, Berry and Sobieraj mention that hosts devoted 16 percent of their airtime to the immigration debate during the entire second quarter of 2007; Jeffrey M. Berry and Sarah Sobieraj, *The Outrage Industry: Political Opinion Media and the New Incivility* (New York: Oxford University Press, 2014), 205.

25. Kaplan, interview.

26. Chambliss, interview; Stephen Dinan, "Georgia Senators at Center of Battle," *Washington Times*, June 20, 2007.

27. Charles Babington, "Talk Shows Influence Immigration Debate," Associated Press, June 23, 2007.

28. Kyl, interview.

29. Mara Liasson, "Republicans Lash Back at Talk Radio's Criticism," *All Things Considered*, National Public Radio, June 27, 2007.

30. Tony Fratto, interview with author, July 2, 2013; Bennett, interview; Lott, interview; Kyl, interview; Ed Gillespie, interview with author, July 31, 2013.

31. Dinan, "Georgia Senators at Center of Battle"; Dinan, "Bloggers, Radio Reshaping Bill on Immigration," *Washington Times*, June 23, 2007; Gail Russell Chaddock, "Fury Grows over US Immigration Bill," *Christian Science Monitor*, May 25, 2007; N. C. Aizenman, "Small-Town Resistance Helped to Seal Defeat," *Washington Post*, June 29, 2007.

32. Rush Limbaugh, "What Do We Do about Trent Lott?" *The Rush Limbaugh Show*, June 15, 2007, http://www.rushlimbaugh.com/daily/2007/06/15/what_do _we_do_about_trent_lott.

33. Rush Limbaugh, "The List: GOP Senators Who Voted for Cloture," *The Rush Limbaugh Show*, June 26, 2007, http://www.rushlimbaugh.com/daily/2007/06 /26/the_list_gop_senators_who_voted_for_cloture.

34. Bennett, interview; Kaplan, interview.

35. Senate Roll Call Vote 235, S. 1639, A Bill to Provide for Comprehensive Immigration Reform and for Other Purposes, On the Cloture Motion, 110th Cong. 1st Sess., June 28, 2007, http://www.senate.gov/legislative/LIS/roll _call_lists/roll_call_vote_cfm.cfm?congress=110&session=1&vote=00235.

36. Federation for American Immigration Reform, "Feet to the Fire 2013"; FAIR has subsequently redesigned its website and removed this page. It can be accessed using the Internet Archive Wayback Machine, http://web.archive.org /web/20130425024008/http://www.fairus.org/action/feet-to-the-fire-2013.

37. Sharry, interview; Senate Roll Call Vote 235, S. 1639; Senate Roll Call Vote 157, S. 2611.

38. John Kobylt, interview with author, February 13, 2013; Hugh Halpern, interview with author, August 20, 2014.

39. Kobylt, interview; Valerie Richardson, "Dreier Targeted on Immigration," *Washington Times*, October 31, 2004.

40. John Fund, "Rush for the Border; Rush Limbaugh Issues a Warning to President Bush," *Wall Street Journal*, January 31, 2005; Richardson, "Dreier Targeted on Immigration."

41. Federal Elections Commission, "Federal Elections 2004 Election Results for the U.S. President, the U.S. Senate and the U.S. House of Representatives," May 2005, https://transition.fec.gov/pubrec/fe2004/federalelections2004.pdf; Federal Elections Commission, "Federal Elections 2006 Election Results for the U.S. President, the U.S. Senate and the U.S. House of Representatives," June 2007, https://transition.fec.gov/pubrec/fe2006/federalelections2006.pdf.

42. Kaplan, interview.

43. Theda Skocpol and Vanessa Williamson reveal the large emphasis Tea Party members placed on combating illegal immigration. While the fiscal views of the Tea Party have garnered more attention, the members interviewed by Skocpol and Williamson passionately opposed immigration reform. They considered illegal immigration such a problem that they supported greater government spending and police power to combat it. Berry and Sobieraj support this analysis, citing data from Gary C. Jacobson to argue that Tea Party support was highly correlated with anti-immigration attitudes; Skocpol and Williamson, *The Tea Party and the Remaking of Republican Conservatism* (New York: Oxford University Press, 2013), 57; Berry and Sobieraj, *Outrage Industry*, 205.

17. Never a Republican Puppet

1. Nick Piatek, interview with author, January 2, 2017; Trey Bohn, interview with author, October 31, 2012; Kevin Sullivan, interview with author, December 19, 2016; Ed Gillespie, interview with author, July 31, 2013.

2. Lars Larson, "Orators in the Oval Office," *Talkers Magazine*, September 2007, 34; George W. Bush Library, "Appointments and Scheduling, White House Office of Presidential Daily Diary Backup," Stack W, Row 16, Section 28, Shelf 9, Position 6, FRC ID 13658, Location or Hollinger ID, 26521, NARA Number 13716, OA Number 13695.

3. Piatek, interview.

4. Rush Limbaugh, "Rush Meets with President Bush," *The Rush Limbaugh Show*, August 3, 2007, https://www.rushlimbaugh.com/daily/2007/08/03/rush _meets_with_president_bush.

5. Rush Limbaugh, "The Bush Family Calls Rush," *The Rush Limbaugh Show*, July 31, 2008, http://www.rushlimbaugh.com/daily/2008/08/01/the_bush_family _calls_rush2.

6. Michael Steel, interview with author, July 6, 2016; anonymous House staffer 2, interview with author, December 15, 2016; Mike Sommers, interview with author, November 14, 2016.

7. Anonymous Senate staffer 3, interview with author, November 16, 2016; anonymous Senate staffer 4, interview with author, January 11, 2017; Josh Holmes, interview with author, February 23, 2016.

8. Amanda Isaacson, interview with author, January 13, 2017; anonymous Senate staffer 3, interview.

9. Rush Limbaugh, "Rush Upstages Obama's Dinner with Washingtonian Republicans," *The Rush Limbaugh Show*, January 14, 2009, https://www .rushlimbaugh.com/daily/2009/01/14/rush_upstages_obama_s_dinner_with _washingtonian_republicans.

10. Hugh Hewitt, @hughhewitt, "On the last Wednesday of his presidency, W met with conservative talk show hosts to urge them to give new guy a chance," Twitter, January 15, 2009, 8:43 p.m., https://twitter.com/hughhewitt/status /820854055488536577; George W. Bush Library, President's Daily Diary, January 13, 2009, FRC ID 13597; White House Office of Records Management, "Subject Files FG001-07," January 13, 2009, FRC ID 13124.

11. Rush Limbaugh, "I Hope Obama Fails," *The Rush Limbaugh Show*, January 16, 2009, https://www.rushlimbaugh.com/daily/2009/01/16/limbaugh_i_hope _obama_fails.

12. Robert Walker, interview with author, October 10, 2013.

13. Gillespie, interview.

14. Taylor Gross, interview with author, March 13, 2013.

15. Scott Hennen, interview with author, December 18, 2012.

16. John Feehery, interview with author, May 2, 2013; Kevin Schweers, interview with author, January 25, 2013; Mark Pfiefle, interviews with author, January 16 and January 30, 2013; anonymous Senate staffer 5, interview with author, March 22, 2016.

17. Feehery, interview.

18. Hennen, interview; Lars Larson, interview with author, November 16, 2012.

19. Anonymous radio producer 2, interview with author, December 20, 2016.

20. Isaacson, interview.

21. Larson, interview.

22. Chad Kolton, interview with author, August 1, 2012; "Did Talk Radio Hosts Help Derail the Immigration Bill?" PEJ Talk Show Index, June 3–8, 2007, Pew Research Center, June 14, 2007, http://www.journalism.org/2007/06/14/pej-talk -show-index-june-3-8-2007.

23. Feehery, interview.

24. Gross, interview.

25. Evan Smith, "Dan Bartlett on Life in the White House," *Texas Monthly*, January 2008.

26. The piece admitted that the hosts only sometimes used the talking points. Dave Zweifel, "What's Wrong with Right-Wing Radio," *Capital Times & Wisconsin State Journal*, December 1, 2008; Dan Shelley, "Secrets of Talk Radio, *Milwaukee Magazine*, November 17, 2008.

27. Anonymous radio producer 2, interview.

28. Hosts' power complicates Donald Critchlow's claim that President Reagan "failed to impose a permanent conservative regime within the Republican party itself." By following his deregulatory philosophy and abolishing the Fairness Doctrine, Reagan unintentionally paved the way for the rise of conservative talk radio, which in turn contributed significantly to the long-term consolidation of conservative control over the Republican Party. Critchlow, *The Conservative Ascendancy: How the Republican Right Rose to Power in Modern America* (Lawrence: University Press of Kansas, 2011), 186.

29. Jonathan Martin, "Gingrey Apologizes over Limbaugh," Politico, January 28, 2009, https://www.politico.com/story/2009/01/gingrey-apologizes-over-limbaugh -018067; Jim Galloway, "Political Insider: Phil Gingrey to Rush Limbaugh: 'I Regret Those Stupid Comments,'" *Atlanta Journal Constitution*, January 28, 2009; Rush Limbaugh, "Congressman Phil Gingrey to Rush: 'I Regret Those Stupid Comments,'" *The Rush Limbaugh Show*, January 28, 2009, https://www .rushlimbaugh.com/daily/2011/05/19/congressman_phil_gingrey_to_rush_i _regret_those_stupid_comments.

30. Rush Limbaugh, "A Few Words for Michael Steele," *The Rush Limbaugh Show*, March 2, 2009; Mike Allen, "Steele to Rush: I'm Sorry," Politico, March 2, 2009, https://www.politico.com/story/2009/03/steele-to-rush-im-sorry-019517.

31. David Callender, "Thompson's Plans Add to State of Indecision," *Capital Times & Wisconsin State Journal*, April 14, 2006; John Nichols, "The Courage, Conscience of Dale Schultz," *Capital Times & Wisconsin State Journal*, March 6, 2013.

32. Kathleen Hall Jamieson and Joseph N. Cappella, *Echo Chamber: Rush Limbaugh and the Conservative Media Establishment* (New York: Oxford University Press, 2008), 115–120; "Schwarzenegger Sold Out," *The Rush*

Limbaugh Show, March 20, 2007, http://www.rushlimbaugh.com/daily/2007/03
/20/schwarzenegger_sold_out.

33. "EIB Interview: Governor Schwarzenegger Calls Rush," *The Rush Limbaugh Show,* March 21, 2007, http://www.rushlimbaugh.com/daily/2007/03/21/eib _interview_governor_schwarzenegger_calls_rush2.

34. Jamieson and Cappella, *Echo Chamber,* 113–115; David Barker, *Rushed to Judgment: Talk Radio, Persuasion, and American Political Behavior* (New York: Columbia University Press, 2002), 87.

35. Anonymous campaign staffer 1, interview with author, March 22, 2016.

36. Anonymous campaign staffer 1, interview; Crystal Benton, interview with author, July 28, 2016; anonymous Republican consultant 1, interview with author, March 27, 2017.

37. Anonymous campaign staffer 2, interview with author, September 14, 2016; Benton, interview.

38. Andy Polesovsky, interview with author, August 11, 2016; Benton, interview; anonymous campaign staffer 2, interview.

18. The Conservative Media Empire

1. John Randall, interview with author, March 29, 2016; Ben Shapiro, interview with author, May 4, 2017.

2. The same pattern existed in liberal opinion media. Ed Schultz, one of the most significant liberal radio hosts during the 2000s, hosted a daily MSNBC program from 2009 to 2015. Rachel Maddow broadcast on both MSNBC and Air America.

3. Mike Gallagher, *The Mike Gallagher Show,* November 10, 2000, http://c -spanvideo.org/program/ElectionReactio.

4. Douglas Wilson, email message to author, May 30, 2013; Hugh Hewitt, email message to author, May 20, 2013; Genevieve Wood, email message to author, May 20, 2013.

5. Molly Ball, "Is the Most Powerful Conservative in America Losing His Edge?" *The Atlantic,* January / February 2015.

6. Joshua Green, *Devil's Bargain: Steve Bannon, Donald Trump, and the Storming of the Presidency* (New York: Penguin Press, 2017), 109.

7. Elisha Krauss, interview with author, May 18, 2018.

8. Robin Abcarian, "Andrew Breitbart: The Man behind the Shirley Sherrod Affair," *Los Angeles Times,* September 2, 2010; James Rainey, "Breitbart.com Sets Sights on Ruling the Conservative Conversation," *Los Angeles Times,* August 1, 2012.

9. Andrew Breitbart, *Righteous Indignation: Excuse Me While I Save the World* (New York: Grand Central Publishing, 2012), 33–44.

10. Green, *Devil's Bargain*, 143–145.

11. These personalities served as what Benkler and colleagues dub "attention backbones." They define attention backbones as more-trafficked websites that "amplify less-visible individual voices on a specific subject," though the term could apply as well to popular talk radio and cable news programs. Yochai Benkler, Hal Roberts, Robert Faris, Alicia Solow-Niederman, and Bruce Etling, "Social Mobilization and the Networked Public Sphere: Mapping the SOPA-PIPA Debate," Berkman Center for Internet & Society Research Publication Series no. 2013-16, Berkman Klein Center, Harvard University, July 2013, http://cyber.law.harvard.edu/publications/2013/social_mobilization _and_the_networked_public_sphere.

12. Oliver Darcy, "Glenn Beck's TheBlaze and CRTV Merge," CNN, December 3, 2018, https://www.cnn.com/2018/12/03/media/crtv-blaze-merger/index .html; Chris Crane, interview with author, April 11, 2017.

13. Green, *Devil's, Bargain*, 108, 124, 140, 172.

14. Dave Hodgden, interview with author, October 23, 2013.

15. Anonymous House staffer 3, interview with author, December 20, 2016; David Popp, interview with author, November 10, 2015; Randall, interview.

19. I Hope He Fails

1. See Daniel Kreiss, *Taking Our Country Back: The Crafting of Networked Politics from Howard Dean to Barack Obama* (New York: Oxford University Press, 2012), 121–202.

2. Zach Galifianakis, "President Barack Obama: Between Two Ferns with Zach Galifianakis," March 13, 2014, https://www.youtube.com/watch?v =UnW3xkHxIEQ; Kory Grow, "10 Most Fascinating Quotes from Obama's 'WTF' Chat with Marc Maron," *Rolling Stone*, June 22, 2015; Amy Kaufman, "Podcaster in Chief: How Marc Maron Landed the Obama Interview," *Los Angeles Times*, June 20, 2015; Barack Obama, "I Am Barack Obama, President of the United States—AMA," Reddit, August 29, 2012, https://www.reddit.com/r /IAmA/comments/z1c9z/i_am_barack_obama_president_of_the_united_states.

3. Bill Burton, interview with author, May 19, 2016; Dag Vega, interview with author, June 9, 2015; Jen Psaki, interview with author, February 22, 2017; Jay Carney, interview with author, March 3, 2016.

4. David Bonior, interview with author, February 24, 2014.

5. Laura Quinn, interview with author, December 12, 2012; Kimberlin Love, interview with author, February 26, 2013; Julianne Corbett Waldron, interview with author, November 29, 2012.

6. Most major cities had robust talk radio stations, but they also had many more media options.

7. David DiMartino, interview with author, June 21, 2016.

8. Bill Richardson, interview with author, February 13, 2013.

9. Debra DeShong, interview with author, June 19, 2013. On the development of targeting and microtargeting, see Sasha Issenberg, *The Victory Lab: The Secret Science of Winning Campaigns* (New York: Broadway Books, 2013).

10. Psaki, interview.

11. Kathleen Hall Jamieson and Joseph N. Cappella, *Echo Chamber: Rush Limbaugh and the Conservative Media Establishment* (New York: Oxford University Press, 2008), 136–137.

12. See Jamieson and Cappella, *Echo Chamber*, 190–236, for findings that indicate why this would be likely.

20. The Relationship Sours

1. Anonymous Senate staffer 3, interview with author, November 16, 2016.

2. Robert G. Kaiser, *Act of Congress: How America's Essential Institution Works, and How It Doesn't* (New York: Vintage Books, 2013).

3. Kaiser, *Act of Congress*, 248–249.

4. For rule changes that shifted the center of power in Congress, see also Julian Zelizer, *On Capitol Hill: The Struggles to Reform Congress and Its Consequences* (New York: Cambridge University Press, 2004); and Barbara Sinclair, *Party Wars* (Norman: University of Oklahoma Press, 2006).

5. Kaiser, *Act of Congress*, 249, 265–266.

6. Dick Armey, interview with author, March 7, 2013.

7. Ben Shapiro, interview with author, May 4, 2017.

8. Charlie Dent, interview with author, January 9, 2017; Neil Bradley, interview with author, June 20, 2017.

9. Sean Hannity, *The Sean Hannity Show*, August 4, 2006, Library of Congress's Web Radio Recording Project, which can be accessed only in the Library.

10. Skocpol and Williamson see conservative media as one of the three pillars of the Tea Party movement. Berry and Sobieraj observe that talk radio, more than the other outrage media, influenced Tea Party priorities. Theda Skocpol and Vanessa Williamson, *The Tea Party and the Remaking of Republican Conservatism* (New York: Oxford University Press, 2012), 12–13; Jeffrey M. Berry and Sarah Sobieraj, *The Outrage Industry: Political Opinion Media and the New Incivility* (New York: Oxford University Press, 2014), 165.

11. Anonymous House staffer 2, interview with author, December 15, 2016.

12. Rush Limbaugh, "Madoff Sentenced to 150 Years, Waxman and Markey Remain Free," *The Rush Limbaugh Show*, June 29, 2009, http://www.rushlimbaugh.com/daily/2009/06/29/madoff_sentenced_to_150_years_waxman_and_markey_remain_free.

13. "Delaware," 270 to Win website, http://www.270towin.com/states/Delaware.

14. Don Surber, "Fighting for the Soul of the Republican Party," *Charleston Gazette*, October 29, 2009.

15. Sean Hannity, "Conservatives Taking the GOP; Interview with Dick Morris," *Hannity*, Fox News, aired November 2, 2009; Sean Hannity, "Independents Vote for GOP Candidates; Videos Surfaced of Kids Praising Obama in School," *Hannity*, Fox News, aired November 4, 2009.

16. Rush Limbaugh, "Why NY-23 Isn't a Third-Party Race," *The Rush Limbaugh Show*, October 27, 2009, http://www.rushlimbaugh.com/daily/2009/10/27/why _ny_23_isn_t_a_third_party_race.

17. Rush Limbaugh, "Dede Scozzafava Screws RINOs," *The Rush Limbaugh Show*, November 2, 2009, http://www.rushlimbaugh.com/daily/2009/11/02/dede _scozzafava_screws_rinos.

18. "Massachusetts," 270 to Win website, https://www.270towin.com/states /Massachusetts

19. Scott Brown, email message to author, July 16, 2013.

20. Rob Willington, interview with author, September 19, 2013.

21. Patrick Ruffini, "Scott Brown's Online Fundraising Machine," Engage (blog), January 28, 2010, https://enga.ge/scott-browns-online-fundraising-machine -inside-the-numbers.

22. Willington, interview. A Brown consultant put this number at $2.3 million, but others indicate $1.3 million.

23. Ruffini, "Scott Brown's Online Fundraising Machine."

24. American Conservative Union, "Federal Legislative Ratings," http://acuratings .conservative.org/acu-federal-legislative-ratings/?year1=2002&chamber =12&state1=45&sortable=1; "DW-NOMINATE Scores, 111th Congress, House of Representatives," Voteview, UCLA Department of Political Science, https://voteview.com/congress/house/111/text.

25. Chris Good, "Tea Party Express's Delaware Ads," *The Atlantic*, September 1, 2010; David Eldridge, "In Delaware, GOP Insurgent Storms Castle," *Washington Times*, September 3, 2010; Chris Matthews, "Obama's News Conference; Quran Burning; 'Don't Ask, Don't Tell' Is Unconstitutional; 9/11 No Longer a Day Free of Politics," *Hardball*, MSNBC, September 10, 2010; Howard Kurtz, "Media Notes: Conservative Pundits on 'Suicide' Watch," *Washington Post*, September 15, 2010.

26. Sean Hannity, "Interview with Michelle Malkin," *Hannity*, Fox News, aired September 8, 2010.

27. Sean Hannity, "The Great American Panel," *Hannity*, Fox News, aired September 14, 2010.

28. Rush Limbaugh, "The Limbaugh Rule: Vote for Most Conservative Candidate in Primary," *The Rush Limbaugh Show*, September 14, 2010, http://www

.rushlimbaugh.com/daily/2010/09/14/the_limbaugh_rule_vote_for_most
_conservative_candidate_in_primary.

29. Michael Medved, interview with author, January 18, 2017.

30. Rush Limbaugh, "What If Everyone in This Audience Sent Christine
O'Donnell a Buck," *The Rush Limbaugh Show*, September 15, 2010, http://www
.rushlimbaugh.com/daily/2010/09/15/what_if_everyone_in_this_audience_sent
_christine_o_donnell_a_buck; Rush Limbaugh, "Can Christine O'Donnell
Raise Another Million in Next 24 Hours," *The Rush Limbaugh Show*, September 16, 2010, http://www.rushlimbaugh.com/daily/2010/09/16/can_christine
_o_donnell_raise_another_million_in_next_24_hours2.

31. "DW Nominate Scores for the United States Senate for the 107th Congress,"
Voteview, UCLA Department of Political Science, https://voteview.com
/congress/senate/107/text.

32. See "Incumbent Senators Who Lost in Their Party's Primary," produced by
the Senate Historian's Office via email from Mary Baumann on October 18,
2013. See also Robert KC Johnson, "Not Many Senators Have Found Themselves in Joe Lieberman's Predicament," History News Network, George
Washington University, n.d., http://hnn.us/article/28947.

21. Hunting RINOs

1. There is much scholarly debate about whether and how talk radio affects
elections. Some scholars find evidence of substantial electoral impact. But the
claim that listening to talk radio motivated someone to vote for a Republican
in a general election is difficult to prove because causation cannot be inferred
from correlation. Are listeners more likely to vote Republican because talk
radio content affects their opinions? Or are they predisposed to vote Republican and indicating that predisposition by listening to talk radio? Diana Owen
found that, although talk radio listeners were more disapproving of President
Clinton than were nonlisteners, talk radio did not generate these negative
sentiments. Owen hypothesized that talk radio might have intensified negative
feelings toward Clinton but did not create these feelings. Similarly, R. Lance
Holbert found no direct relationship between talk radio listenership and
perceptions of fairness regarding the outcome of the 2000 election. David C.
Barker, *Rushed to Judgment: Talk Radio, Persuasion, and American Political
Behavior* (New York: Columbia University Press, 2002); Barker, "Rushed
Decisions, Political Talk Radio and Voter Choice, 1994–1996," *Journal of
Politics* 61, no. 2 (1999): 527–539, 532–535; Barker and Kathleen Knight,
"Political Talk Radio and Public Opinion," *Public Opinion Quarterly* 64, no. 2
(2000): 149–170; Louis Bolce, Gerald De Maio, and Douglas Muzzio, "Dial in
Democracy: Talk Radio and the 1994 Election," *Political Science Quarterly* 111,

no. 3 (1996): 457–481, 461–464, 466, 469; R. Lance Holbert, "Political Talk Radio, Perceived Fairness, and the Establishment of President George W. Bush's Political Legitimacy," *Harvard International Journal of Press/Politics* 9, no. 3 (2004): 12–27; Diana Owen, "Talk Radio and Evaluations of President Clinton," *Political Communication* 14, no. 3 (1997): 333–353; Kathleen Hall Jamieson and Joseph N. Cappella, *Echo Chamber: Rush Limbaugh and the Conservative Media Establishment* (New York: Oxford University Press, 2008), 123.

2. See Jamieson and Cappella, *Echo Chamber*, 134–139, 195–210.

3. Jamieson and Cappella, *Echo Chamber*, 123. See also Sean Wilenz and Julian E. Zelizer, "A Rotten Way to Pick a President," *Washington Post*, February 17, 2008. Even John Aldrich, who has argued that political parties are top-down creations of politicians that exist to benefit those politicians, noted that, in primaries, activists pressure politicians to take their extreme views; John Aldrich, *Why Parties? A Second Look* (Chicago: University of Chicago Press, 2011), Kindle location 449; Jeff Roe, interview with author, April 7, 2017.

4. Chris Mottola, interview with author, August 23, 2013.

5. Public Opinion Strategies, "Pennsylvania Statewide March Brushfire Study," 277–282, 287–294. Poll conducted for Specter campaign, provided by Glen Bolger in email message to author, September 16, 2013. Bolger was the campaign's pollster.

6. Mottola, interview; Mark Dion, interview with author, September 17, 2013.

7. Robert Bennett, interview with author, January 4, 2013.

8. This was true of local bloggers as well. Theda Skocpol and Vanessa Williamson, *The Tea Party and the Remaking of Republican Conservatism* (New York: Oxford University Press, 2012), 176.

9. Berry and Sobieraj quote programmer Robin Bertolucci analogizing hosts endorsing a product and someone's brother or sister telling them about it. There can be a similar effect with respect to candidates for office. Jeffrey M. Berry and Sarah Sobieraj, *The Outrage Industry: Political Opinion Media and the New Incivility* (New York: Oxford University Press, 2014), 109; Paul Begala, interview with author, November 29, 2012.

10. Phillip Bump, "The Remarkable Recent Decline of Split-ticket Voting," *Washington Post*, November 10, 2014; Bump (@pbump), "@brianros1 Looks like 103 in 1992 and 100 in 1994"; Twitter, November 10, 2014, 2:38 p.m., https://twitter.com/pbump/status/531938987166810112; Bob Shrum, interview with author, October 7, 2013.

11. Jamieson and Cappella, *Echo Chamber*, 113–115; Barker, *Rushed to Judgment*, 87. Some presidential-level evidence is in conflict. Jamieson and Cappella found that during the 1996 primary Limbaugh listeners had a reduced opinion

of Pat Buchanan, who came in for criticism on the show. David A. Jones found no such effect. Jamieson and Cappella, *Echo Chamber*, 111–113; David A. Jones, "Political Talk Radio: The Limbaugh Effect on Primary Voters," *Political Communication* 15, no. 3 (1998): 367–381.

12. Zev Chafets, *Rush Limbaugh: An Army of One* (New York: Sentinel, 2010), 193–196.

13. Office of the State Election Commissioner, "State of Delaware Elections System Official Election Results Primary Elections," September 14, 2010, http://elections.delaware.gov/archive/elect10/elect10_Primary/html/stwoff _kwns.shtml.

14. Jan Van Lohuizen, email messages to author, June 8 and July 31, 2013.

15. Sherwood Boehlert, interview with author, February 5, 2013; Steve LaTourette, interview with author, February 12, 2013; Wayne Gilchrest, interview with author, June 8, 2015.

16. R. Douglas Arnold, *The Logic of Congressional Action* (New Haven: Yale University Press, 1990), 5.

17. The theories of political parties offered by Masket and by Bawn and colleagues focus on the critical importance of primaries as the mechanism through which ideological activists, interest groups, and new-style party leaders control political parties. As Bawn and colleagues write, upstarts "do not fight with bare knuckles. They need money, door knockers, pollsters, admakers, and much else. Where do they get these resources? Usually from the coalition of interest groups and activists associated with a party in a particular community." Talk radio was an essential player in this coalition. Kathleen Bawn, Martin Cohen, David Karol, Seth Masket, Hans Noel, and John Zaller, "A Theory of Political Parties," *Perspectives on Politics* 10, no. 3 (2013): 571–597, 585; Seth E. Masket, *No Middle Ground: How Informal Party Organizations Control Nominations and Polarize Legislatures* (Ann Arbor: University of Michigan Press, 2011).

18. Andrew B. Hall, "How the Public Funding of Elections Increases Candidate Polarization" (unpublished manuscript, August 13, 2014), http://www .andrewbenjaminhall.com/Hall_publicfunding.pdf. Ansolabehere and Snyder also demonstrated that more powerful incumbents receive more PAC money; Stephen Ansolabehere and James M. Snyder Jr., "Money and Institutional Power," *Texas Law Review* 77, no. 7 (1999): 1673–1704.

19. Jordan Gehrke, interview with author, August 28, 2013; Gene Ulm, interview with author, August 6, 2013.

20. Charlie Dent, interview with author, January 9, 2017.

21. "Little Voter Discomfort with Romney's Mormon Religion," Pew Research Center, July 26, 2012, http://www.pewforum.org/2012/07/26/2012-romney -mormonism-obamas-religion; Jennifer Agiesta, "Misperceptions Persist about

Obama's Faith," CNN, September 14, 2015, http://www.cnn.com/2015/09/13/politics/barack-obama-religion-christian-misperceptions/index.html; Sarah Pulliam Bailey, "A Startling Number of Americans Still Believe President Obama Is a Muslim," *Washington Post*, September 14, 2015; Louis Jacobson, "Do 59 Percent of Americans Believe Barack Obama Is Muslim?" Punditfact, November 23, 2015, http://www.politifact.com/punditfact/statements/2015/nov/23/arsalan-iftikhar/do-59-percent-americans-believe-barack-obama-musli.

22. Bob Inglis, interview with author, June 7, 2016.

23. Inglis, interview.

24. Phillip Bump, "Kerry Bentivolio's Loss Was the 8th Worst for an Incumbent since 1968," *Washington Post*, August 6, 2014.

25. Inglis, interview.

22. Trying (and Failing) to Govern

1. Anonymous House staffer 2, interview with author, December 15, 2016; anonymous House staffer 3, interview with author, December 20, 2016; anonymous House staffer 4, interview with author, December 20, 2016; Michael Steel, interview with author, July 6, 2016; Mike Sommers, interview with author, November 14, 2016; Tim Alberta, "John Boehner Unchained," Politico Magazine, November/December 2017, https://www.politico.com/magazine/story/2017/10/29/john-boehner-trump-house-republican-party-retirement-profile-feature-215741.

2. Nate Hodson, interview with author, October 14, 2015; anonymous House staffer 5, interview with author, November 10, 2015.

3. Hodson, interview; anonymous House staffer 5, interview.

4. Josh Holmes, interview with author, February 23, 2016; Amanda Isaacson, interview with author, January 13, 2017; anonymous Senate staffer 3, interview with author, November 16, 2016.

5. Aldo Beckman, "Won't Oppose Percy Bid for Now, Says Nixon," *Chicago Tribune*, October 4, 1973; Michael Kilian, "Expect Bayh, Lugar in Faceoff for Senate," *Chicago Tribune*, February 3, 1974; Michael Kilian, "Indianapolis Mayor Ready to Go It Alone," *Chicago Tribune*, February 3, 1974.

6. David Willkie, interviews with author, February 10 and 11, 2016.

7. See 116th Congress Senators, DW-NOMINATE plot, VoteView, UCLA Department of Political Science, https://voteview.com/congress/senate/text; Richard Lugar, interview with author, January 28, 2016.

8. Andrew Prokop, "Losing Obama's Favorite Republican," *New Yorker*, May 8, 2012; Ken Strickland, "Barack Obama's Favorite Republican," NBC News, October 17, 2008, http://www.nbcnews.com/id/27241356/ns/politics-decision_08/t/barack-obamas-favorite-republican.

9. Laura Ingraham, "Interview with Richard Mourdock," *The Laura Ingraham Show*, May 7, 2012, http://www.lauraingraham.com/mediabits.

10. Jim Holden, interview with author, June 2, 2016; Richard Mourdock, interview with author, June 6, 2016; Greg Garrison, interview with author, April 11, 2016; Audrey Mullen, interview with author, June 15, 2016.

11. Mark Levin, *The Mark Levin Show*, August 11, 2011, http://www.marklevinshow .com/2011-podcast-archive; Mark Levin, *The Mark Levin Show*, March 28 and May 7, 2012, http://www.marklevinshow.com/2012-podcast-archive.

12. Rush Limbaugh, "Tea Party Fights for Conservatism in Indiana," *The Rush Limbaugh Show*, May 8, 2012, https://www.rushlimbaugh.com/daily/2012/05/08 /tea_party_fights_for_conservatism_in_indiana; Rush Limbaugh, "Life in Obamaville: "My Employer Is Going Out of Business," *The Rush Limbaugh Show*, May 4, 2012, https://www.rushlimbaugh.com/daily/2012/05/04/life_in _obamaville_my_employer_is_going_out_of_business.

13. Erick Erickson, "Ah . . . Dick Lugar," RedState, November 18, 2010, https://www.redstate.com/diary/Erick/2010/11/18/ah-dick-lugar; Erickson, "Dick Lugar's Voting Record," RedState, April 30, 2012, http://www.redstate .com/erick/2012/04/30/dick-lugars-voting-record; Erickson, "Tomorrow, Retire Dick Lugar," RedState, May 7, 2012, http://www.redstate.com/erick/2012/05/07 /tomorrow-retire-dick-lugar; Chris Chocola, "It's Time to Bring Lugar Home," RedState, February 14, 2012, http://www.redstate.com/diary/chris _chocola_cfg/2012/02/14/its-time-to-bring-lugar-home; Leon H. Wolf, "Richard Lugar Calls TEA Party Voters Morons," RedState, February 24, 2012, http://www.redstate.com/leon_h_wolf/2012/02/24/richard-lugar-calls-tea -party-voters-morons.

14. Steve Southerland, interview with author, December 14, 2017.

15. Michael Medved, "Why the Right Hates Mitt Romney and His 2012 Presidential Bid," Daily Beast, November 10, 2011, https://www.thedailybeast.com/why -the-right-hates-mitt-romney-and-his-2012-presidential-bid.

16. Rush Limbaugh, "I'll Endorse When I Decide, Folks," *The Rush Limbaugh Show*, October 12, 2011, https://www.rushlimbaugh.com/daily/2011/10/12/i_ll _endorse_when_i_decide_folks.

17. Anonymous campaign staffer 3, interview with author, December 28, 2016; Anna Sugg, interview with author, February 6, 2016.

18. Noah Rothman, "Laura Ingraham Tears into Romney Campaign," Mediaite, August 10, 2012, https://www.mediaite.com/online/laura-ingraham-tears-into -romney-campaign-he-needs-new-communications-team-strategy; Alexander Burns, "Laura Ingraham: 'Romney's Losing,'" Politico, August 10, 2012, https://www.politico.com/blogs/burns-haberman/2012/08/laura-ingraham -romneys-losing-131662; "Laura Ingraham to GOP: 'If You Can't Beat Obama,'"

Huffington Post, September 10, 2012, https://www.huffingtonpost.com/entry
/laura-ingraham-gop-obama-shut-down-party_n_1871911.

19. Karen Tumulty, "Romney Shifts to More Moderate Stances," *Washington Post*,
October 10, 2012.

20. Lori Montgomery, "Boehner, House GOP Leaders Offer 'Fiscal Cliff'
Counterproposal," *Washington Post*, December 3, 2012.

21. Zachary A. Goldfarb and Scott Wilson, "Obama Calls for Immediate Freeze
on Middle-class Tax Rates," *Washington Post*, November 9, 2012; Barack
Obama, "Remarks on the National Economy," November 9, 2012, American
Presidency Project, University of California, Santa Barbara, https://www
.presidency.ucsb.edu/documents/remarks-the-national-economy-30.

22. Rush Limbaugh, "There's No Common Ground on the Cliff," *The Rush
Limbaugh Show*, December 6, 2012, https://www.rushlimbaugh.com/daily/2012/12
/06/there_s_no_common_ground_on_the_cliff; Rush Limbaugh, "The GOP
Seminar in Surrender," *The Rush Limbaugh Show*, December 5, 2012,
https://www.rushlimbaugh.com/daily/2012/12/05/the_gop_seminar_in_surrender.

23. Alberta, "John Boehner Unchained."

24. For a history of the Heritage Foundation, see Jason Stahl, *Right Moves: The
Conservative Think Tank in American Political Culture since 1945* (Chapel Hill:
University of North Carolina Press, 2016), 47–134.

25. Ed O'Keefe and Rosalind S. Helderman, "Club for Growth Comes Out
against 'Plan B,'" *Washington Post*, December 19, 2012; Natalie Jennings,
"'Plan B' Vote Won't Violate Norquist Pledge," *Washington Post*,
December 20, 2012; Rachel Weiner, "FreedomWorks Flips, Now Opposes
'Plan B,'" *Washington Post*, December 20, 2012.

26. Doug Heye, interview with author, November 21, 2016; Alberta, "John Boehner
Unchained"; Ed O'Keefe, "As 'Plan B' Vote Nears, John Boehner Seen
Whipping Votes," *Washington Post*, December 20, 2012; Paul Kane, Ed
O'Keefe, and Lori Montgomery, "How Boehner's Plan B for the 'Fiscal Cliff'
Began and Fell Apart," *Washington Post*, December 20, 2012.

27. Lori Montgomery and Paul Kane, "Obama, Senate Republicans Reach
Agreement on 'Fiscal Cliff,'" *Washington Post*, January 1, 2013; Jennifer
Steinhauer, "Divided House Passes Tax Deal," *New York Times*, January 1, 2013.

28. House Roll Call Vote 659 on H.R. 8, To extend certain tax relief provisions
enacted in 2001 and 2003, and to provide for expedited consideration of a bill
providing for comprehensive tax reform, and for other purposes, 112th Cong.
2nd Sess., January 1, 2013, http://clerk.house.gov/evs/2012/roll659.xml.

29. Rush Limbaugh, "Don't Blame Me for Plan B Debacle," *The Rush Limbaugh
Show*, December 21, 2012, https://www.rushlimbaugh.com/daily/2012/12/21/don
_t_blame_me_for_plan_b_debacle.

30. Sommers, interview; Rory Cooper, interview with author, May 29, 2015.

31. Southerland, interview; Charlie Dent, interview with author, January 9, 2017; Neil Bradley, interview with author, June 20, 2017.

32. For more on the Tea Party's opposition to immigration reform, see Theda Skocpol and Vanessa Williamson, *The Tea Party and the Remaking of Republican Conservatism* (New York: Oxford University Press, 2012).

33. Henry Barbour, Sally Bradshaw, Ari Fleischer, Zori Fonalledas, and Glenn McCall, The Growth and Opportunity Project, https://gop.com/growth-and -opportunity-project.

34. "Immigration Battle," *Frontline*, Season 33, episode 16, produced by Michael Camerini and Shari Robertson, at 1:18, http://www.pbs.org/wgbh/frontline/film /immigration-battle.

35. "Immigration Battle," *Frontline*, at 1:21; Elspeth Reeve, "Steve King Wants to Protect the Border from Cantaloupe-Sized Calves," *The Atlantic*, July 23, 2013.

36. MacKenzie Weinger, "Hannity: I've 'Evolved' on Immigration and Support a 'Pathway to Citizenship,'" Politico, November 8, 2012, http://www.politico.com /blogs/media/2012/11/hannity-ive-evolved-on-immigration-and-support-a -pathway-to-citizenship-149078.

37. Kerri Sherlock Talbot, interview with author, April 21, 2017; Mark Delich, interview with author, April 28, 2017; Cesar Conda, interview with author, May 4, 2017.

38. Jason Horowitz, "Marco Rubio Pushed for Immigration Reform with Conservative Media," *New York Times*, February 27, 2016; anonymous Senate staffer 6, interview with author, June 6, 2017.

39. Rush Limbaugh, "Senator Rubio Makes His Case," *The Rush Limbaugh Show*, January 29, 2013, https://www.rushlimbaugh.com/daily/2013/01/29/senator_rubio _makes_his_case; Conda, interview; Jon Baselice, interview with author, June 21, 2017; anonymous Senate staffer 7, interview with author, July 8, 2016.

40. Rush Limbaugh, "The Limbaugh Amnesty Proposal," *The Rush Limbaugh Show*, January 29, 2013, https://www.rushlimbaugh.com/daily/2013/01/29/the _limbaugh_amnesty_proposal.

41. Joshua Green, *Devil's Bargain: Steve Bannon, Donald Trump, and the Storming of the Presidency* (New York: Penguin Press, 2017), 108–109; Todd Schulte, interview with author, March 16, 2017.

42. Anonymous Senate staffer 7, interview.

43. Green, *Devil's Bargain*, especially 108–109 and 145.

44. Matthew Boyle, "Senate Passes Amnesty by Vote of 68-32," Breitbart, June 27, 2013, http://www.breitbart.com/big-government/2013/06/27/senate-passes -amnesty-68-32; Mike Flynn, "The 'Angry Birds': GOP Senators Voting for Amnesty over Security," Breitbart, June 27, 2013, http://www.breitbart.com/big

-government/2013/06/27/the-angry-birds-gop-senators-voting-for-amnesty-over-security.

45. Baselice, interview; Becky Tallent, interview with author, February 13, 2017.

46. Micah Cohen, "Which G.O.P. House Members Might Support Immigration Reform?" *New York Times*, February 3, 2013.

47. Delich, interview; anonymous House staffer 6, interview with author, May 19, 2017.

48. David Bier, interview with author, July 13, 2017.

49. Tallent, interview; Bier, interview.

50. Bier, interview; Bradley, interview.

51. "Sam Johnson: An Unlikely Immigration Negotiator," *Roll Call*, April 29, 2013; Alec MacGillis, "How Republicans Lost Their Best Shot at the Hispanic Vote," *New York Times Magazine*, September 15, 2016; Doug Rivlin, interview with author, November 3, 2017.

52. Deidre Walsh, "Key Republican in Immigration Debate," CNN, February 5, 2013, http://politicalticker.blogs.cnn.com/2013/02/05/key-republican-in-immigration-debate-says-undocumented-immigrants-not-clamoring-for-citizenship; Ashley Parker, "A Bipartisan House Group Works to Present Its Own Immigration Proposal," *New York Times*, February 2, 2013.

53. Sara Murray, "Focus of Immigration Debate Shifts to House," *Wall Street Journal*, July 10, 2013; Alan Gomez, "House Group Reaches Deal on Immigration Bill," *USA Today*, May 16, 2013; Kristina Peterson and Corey Boles, "Bipartisan House Group Reaches Broad Immigration Deal," *Wall Street Journal*, May 16, 2013; MacGillis, "How Republicans Lost"; Rebecca Kaplan, "Raul Labrador Quits House Immigration Group, Bipartisan Effort in Jeopardy," *National Journal*, June 5, 2013; Bier, interview; Rivlin, interview; anonymous House staffer 7, interview with author, August 9, 2017.

54. Ed O'Keefe, "Two Republicans Drop Out of House 'Group of Seven' Immigration Talks," *Washington Post*, September 20, 2013; Alan Gomez, "House Immigration Group Collapses," *USA Today*, September 20, 2013.

55. Rivlin, interview.

56. "Immigration Battle," *Frontline*.

57. Tony Lee, "Boehner Hires Adviser Who Helped McCain Push Amnesty," Breitbart, December 3, 2013, http://www.breitbart.com/big-government/2013/12/03/boehner-hires-adviser-who-helped-mccain-push-amnesty.

58. Anonymous Senate staffer 7, interview.

59. Alberta, "John Boehner Unchained."

60. Rush Limbaugh, "Amnesty Is Suicide for GOP—and America," *The Rush Limbaugh Show*, January 31, 2014, https://www.rushlimbaugh.com/daily/2014/01/31/amnesty_is_suicide_for_gop_and_america.

61. Laura Ingraham, "Does Rep. Renee Ellmers (R-NC) Want to Flood Labor Market?" *The Laura Ingraham Show,* March 13, 2014, http://www .lauraingraham.com/b/Does-Rep.-Renee-Ellmers-R-NC-want-to-flood-labor -market-to-help-her-big-money-backers-Explosive-interview/17705.html.

62. Laura Ingraham, "Frank Roche: Rep. Ellmers Is 'Not the Voice of Republicans, Let Alone Conservatives,'" *The Laura Ingraham Show,* March 14, 2014, http://www.lauraingraham.com/b/Frank-Roche:-Rep.-Ellmers-is-not-the-voice -of-Republicans,-let-alone-conservatives/17723.html.

63. Tal Kopan, "Ellmers: Ingraham's 'Ignorant' Stand," Politico, March 13, 2014, https://www.politico.com/story/2014/03/renee-ellmers-laura-ingraham-104632.

64. Anonymous House staffer 7, interview with author, August 9, 2017.

65. "Immigration Battle," *Frontline,* at 1:31; MacGillis, "How Republicans Lost"; Heye, interview; Cooper, interview; Bradley, interview; Dylan Byers, "Right-wing Radio's Win," Politico, June 11, 2014, https://www.politico.com/story/2014 /06/eric-cantor-laura-ingraham-107743.

66. Southerland, interview.

67. Dent, interview.

23. Turning the Power Structure Upside Down

1. Molly Ball, "Is the Most Powerful Conservative in America Losing His Edge?" *The Atlantic,* January/February 2015.

2. Josh Holmes, interview with author, February 23, 2016; Amanda Carpenter, interview with author, September 8, 2016; anonymous House staffer 4, interview with author, December 20, 2016; Mike Sommers, interview with author, November 14, 2016; anonymous House staffer 8, interview with author, August 12, 2016; Nate Hodson, interview with author, October 14, 2015; anonymous House staffer 6, interview with author, May 19, 2017; Andrew Rosenthal, "No Comment Necessary: Drug Mules," *New York Times,* July 24, 2013.

3. Anonymous House staffer 8, interview; Aaron Blake, "Here Are the Republicans Who Voted against John Boehner for Speaker," *Washington Post,* January 6, 2015.

4. Laura Ingraham, "Interview with Ted Cruz," *The Laura Ingraham Show,* October 21, 2015, under October 2015 at http://www.lauraingraham.com/mediabits.

5. Laura Ingraham, "Interview with Jim Jordan," *The Laura Ingraham Show,* April 29, 2015, under April 2015 at http://www.lauraingraham.com/mediabits.

6. Daniel Newhauser, Lauren Fox, and National Journal, "GOP Leaders Pull Abortion Bill after Revolt by Women, Moderates," *The Atlantic,* January 21, 2015.

7. Tim Alberta, "John Boehner Unchained," Politico Magazine, November /December 2017, https://www.politico.com/magazine/story/2017/10/29/john

-boehner-trump-house-republican-party-retirement-profile-feature-215741;
Sarah Ferris, "House GOP Mulls Lifting a Ban on Earmarks," Politico,
January 9, 2018, https://www.politico.com/story/2018/01/09/republican-lifting
-earmark-ban-271491; Devin Dwyer and Matthew Jaffe, "Senate Republicans
Ban Earmarks; Will Democrats Follow?" ABC News, November 16, 2010,
https://abcnews.go.com/Politics/earmark-moratorium-republicans-poised-ban
-pork-barrel-spending/story?id=12155964.

8. Sommers, interview.

9. Jim Gerlach, interview with author, February 5, 2016.

10. Matt Fuller, "Rule Vote Retribution Continues; Chaffetz Takes Away Subcommittee Gavel," Roll Call, June 20, 2015; Alberta, "John Boehner Unchained."

11. "To my knowledge, nobody has been shot or killed at this point. But there is a
whole lot of backroom deals that get done on a regular basis," Meadows said.
Elise Viebeck, "Mark Meadows' House of Cards Moment," Washington Post,
June 25, 2015; anonymous House staffer 6, interview; anonymous House staffer
2, interview with author, December 15, 2016; Alberta, "John Boehner Unchained"; Sommers, interview.

12. Lauren French, "9 Republicans Launch House Freedom Caucus," Politico,
January 26, 2015, http://www.politico.com/story/2015/01/house-freedom-caucus
-conservative-legislation-114593.

13. Emma Dumain and Matt Fuller, "Conservatives Fume over Leadership's
Crackdown on Rebels," Roll Call, June 22, 2015; Elise Viebeck, "Defiant
Meadows Responds to Leadership Swipe," Washington Post, June 22, 2015;
Mark Levin, The Mark Levin Show, June 22, 2015, http://www.marklevinshow
.com/2015-podcast-archive; anonymous House staffer 8, interview; Viebeck,
"Mark Meadows' House of Cards Moment."

14. Laura Ingraham, The Laura Ingraham Show, June 22, 2015, under June 2015 at
http://www.lauraingraham.com/mediabits.

15. Neil Cavuto, "Interview with Utah Congressman Jason Chaffetz," Your World
with Neil Cavuto, Fox News, June 24, 2015.

16. Alex Swoyer, "Huckabee Applauds Rep. Mark Meadows for Voting against
ObamaTrade," Breitbart, June 22, 2015, http://www.breitbart.com/big
-government/2015/06/22/huckabee-applauds-rep-mark-meadows-for-voting
-against-obamatrade; Robert Wilde, "'Courageous Conservative' Axed by GOP
Leadership for 'Voting His Conscience,'" Breitbart, June 22, 2015, http://www
.breitbart.com/big-government/2015/06/22/courageous-conservative-axed-by
-gop-leadership-for-voting-his-conscience; Alex Swoyer, "Cruz versus Team
Boehner-Obama: Slams 'Washington Cartel' on Obamatrade and Ex-Import
Bank," Breitbart, June 24, 2015, http://www.breitbart.com/big-government/2015
/06/24/cruz-versus-team-boehner-obama-slams-washington-cartel-on

-obamatrade-and-ex-import-bank; "Sarah Palin: GOP Establishment Failed to Heed Stunning Grassroots Victory against Eric Cantor," Breitbart, June 22, 2015, http://www.breitbart.com/big-government/2015/06/22/sarah-palin-gop -establishment-failed-to-heed-stunning-grassroots-victory-against-eric-cantor.

17. Anonymous House staffer 8, interview.

18. Alberta, "John Boehner Unchained."

19. Elise Viebeck, "He's Back: Mark Meadows Regains Subcommittee Gavel," *Washington Post,* June 25, 2015; Joint Statement on Meadows' Reinstatement as Chair of Government Operations, Rep. Mark Meadows (R-NC) News Release, Congressional Documents and Publications, June 25, 2015; Matt Fuller, "Meadows Gets Subcommittee Gavel Back," *Roll Call,* June 25, 2015; Jake Sherman and Anna Palmer, "GOP Leaders Reverse Punishment for Dissenter," Politico, June 25, 2015, https://www.politico.com/story/2015/06/gop-leaders -reverse-punishment-mark-meadows-jason-chaffetz-119422; anonymous House staffer 6, interview; anonymous House staffer 4, interview; Sommers, interview.

20. Anonymous House staffer 8, interview.

21. Alberta, "John Boehner Unchained."

22. Heather Caygle, "Boehner's Successor Joins Freedom Caucus," Politico, June 9, 2016, https://www.politico.com/story/2016/06/warren-davidson-freedom -caucus-224145.

23. Charlie Dent, interview with author, January 9, 2017; Gerlach, interview.

24. Laura Ingraham, "Interview with Ken Cuccinelli," *The Laura Ingraham Show,* September 28, 2015, under April 2015 at http://www.lauraingraham.com/mediabits.

25. Laura Ingraham, "Interview with Mo Brooks," *The Laura Ingraham Show,* October 22, 2015, accessible via the free clips under October 2015 at http://www .lauraingraham.com/mediabits.

26. Anonymous House staffer 3, interview with author, December 20, 2016; Kristina Peterson, email message to author, February 1, 2016; Jenna Sakwa, email message to author, November 3, 2017.

24. The President That Talk Radio Made

1. Alexander Burns, "Donald Trump, Pushing Someone Rich, Offers Himself," *New York Times,* June 17, 2015.

2. Rush Limbaugh, "Trump's Message Will Resonate," *The Rush Limbaugh Show,* June 16, 2015, https://www.rushlimbaugh.com/daily/2015/06/16/trump_s _message_will_resonate.

3. Alex Swoyer, "Donald Trump Wants to Make America Great Again, An-nounces 2016 Campaign," Breitbart, June 16, 2015, http://www.breitbart.com /big-government/2015/06/16/donald-trump-wants-to-make-america-great-again -announces-2016-campaign.

4. Rush Limbaugh, "The Orders to Take Out Trump Must Have Gone to Fox, Not the Other Candidates," *The Rush Limbaugh Show*, August 7, 2015, https://www.rushlimbaugh.com/daily/2015/08/07/the_orders_to_take_out _trump_must_have_gone_to_fox_not_the_other_candidates/.

5. NBC News / *Wall Street Journal* Poll, July 2015, USNBCWSJ.080315.R29, indexed by iPOLL, Roper Center for Public Opinion Research, Cornell University.

6. Fox News Poll, July 2015, USASFOX.071615.R36; Suffolk University / *USA Today* Poll, July 2015, USSUFF.071415.R32, indexed by iPOLL, Roper Center for Public Opinion Research, Cornell University.

7. Joshua Green, *Devil's Bargain: Steve Bannon, Donald Trump, and the Storming of the Presidency* (New York: Penguin Press, 2017), 109.

8. Laura Ingraham, "Interview with Donald Trump," *The Laura Ingraham Show*, June 12, 2012, under June 2012 at http://www.lauraingraham.com/mediabits.

9. Laura Ingraham, "Interview with Donald Trump," *The Laura Ingraham Show*, April 1, 2015, under April 2015 at http://www.lauraingraham.com/mediabits.

10. Ben Schreckinger, "Trump Attacks McCain: 'I Like People Who Weren't Captured,'" Politico, July 18, 2015, http://www.politico.com/story/2015/07/trump -attacks-mccain-i-like-people-who-werent-captured-120317.

11. Rush Limbaugh, "The Drive-Bys Missed My Point on Trump," *The Rush Limbaugh Show*, July 21, 2015, https://www.rushlimbaugh.com/daily/2015/07/21 /the_drive_bys_missed_my_point_on_trump. The transcript reads "politically correct," but this is almost certainly in error.

12. NBC News / *Wall Street Journal* Poll, July 2015, USNBCWSJ.080315.R17; Fox News Poll, July 2015, USASFOX.080315.R07; Bloomberg Poll, July 2015, USSELZER.080415.R01; CBS News Poll, July, 2015, USCBS.080415.R17; ABC News / *Washington Post* Poll, July 2015, USABCWP.072015A.R05; Fox News Poll, June 2015, USASFOX.062415.R29, all indexed by iPOLL, Roper Center for Public Opinion Research, Cornell University.

13. Alan Rappeport, "Conservative Airwaves Grapple with Donald Trump, Aiding His Rise," *New York Times*, July 23, 2015.

14. John Kobylt, interview with author, April 10, 2016.

15. Hal Shapiro and Lael Brainard, "Fast Track Trade Promotion Authority," Brookings Policy Briefing Series, December 1, 2001, https://www.brookings.edu /research/fast-track-trade-promotion-authority.

16. Paul Teller, interview with author, August 14, 2017.

17. Rush Limbaugh, "The Rare EIB Interview: Senator Ted Cruz on Why He Called His Leader a Liar," *The Rush Limbaugh Show*, July 24, 2015, https:// origin-www.rushlimbaugh.com/daily/2015/07/24/the_rare_eib_interview _senator_ted_cruz_on_why_he_called_his_leader_a_liar; Rush Limbaugh,

"Cruz Calls McConnell a Liar," *The Rush Limbaugh Show*, July 24, 2015, https://www.rushlimbaugh.com/daily/2015/07/24/cruz_calls_mcconnell_a_liar; Mike DeBonis, "Ted Cruz Calls Mitch McConnell a Liar on the Senate Floor," *Washington Post*, July 24, 2015.

18. Teller, interview; Amanda Carpenter, Twitter direct message to author, November 14, 2017.

19. *The Mark Levin Show*, July 24, 2015, http://www.marklevinshow.com/2015 -podcast-archive.

20. "GOP Candidates Debate," Fox News, August 6, 2015.

21. Donald Trump (@RealDonaldTrump), "I really enjoyed the debate tonight even though the @FoxNews trio, especially @megynkelly, was not very good or professional!" Twitter, August 7, 2015, 12:53 a.m., https://twitter.com /realDonaldTrump/status/629561051982495744.

22. Phillip Rucker, "Trump Says Fox's Megyn Kelly Had 'Blood Coming Out of Her Wherever,'" *Washington Post*, August 8, 2015; Brian Stelter and Tom Kludt, "Fox Moderators Get Applause for Tough Debate Questions," CNN, August 7, 2015, http://money.cnn.com/2015/08/06/media/republican-debate-fox/index.html.

23. Carly Fiorina (@CarolyFiorina), "Mr. Trump: There. Is. No. Excuse.," Twitter, August 7, 2015, 8:41 p.m., https://twitter.com/CarlyFiorina/status /629860026916716545.

24. Jonathan Martin and Maggie Haberman, "Hand-Wringing in G.O.P. after Donald Trump's Remarks on Megyn Kelly," *New York Times*, August 9, 2015.

25. Rush Limbaugh, "Trump Resonates Because Millions of People Are Sick of Political Correctness, Phony Outrage and Phony Apologies," *The Rush Limbaugh Show*, August 10, 2015, https://www.rushlimbaugh.com/daily/2015/08 /10/trump_resonates_because_millions_of_people_are_sick_of_political _correctness_phony_outrage_and_phony_apologies.

26. Josh Feldman, "Fox's Krauthammer: This Debate Was 'The Collapse of Trump,'" Mediaite, August 6, 2015, https://www.mediaite.com/tv/foxs -krauthammer-this-debate-was-the-collapse-of-trump.

27. Rush Limbaugh, "Fox Backlash across the Fruited Plain," *The Rush Limbaugh Show*, August 7, 2015, https://www.rushlimbaugh.com/daily/2015/08/07/fox _backlash_across_the_fruited_plain.

28. Robert Wilde, "Mark Levin: Fox News, Megyn Kelly 'Hosted a National Enquirer Debate, Not a Republican Debate—Owe American People an Apology,'" Breitbart, August 9, 2015, http://www.breitbart.com/big-journalism /2015/08/09/mark-levin-fox-news-megyn-kelly-hosted-a-national-enquirer -debate-not-a-republican-debate-owe-american-people-an-apology.

29. Donald Trump (@realDonaldTrump), "The hatred that clown @krauthammer has for me is unbelievable—causes him to lie when many others say Trump

easily won debate," Twitter, August 7, 2015, 1:36 p.m., https://twitter.com
/realDonaldTrump/status/629753109481422848; Donald Trump (@real
DonaldTrump), ". . . . Dopey @krauthammer should be fired. @FoxNews,"
Twitter, August 7, 2015, 1:35 p.m., https://twitter.com/realDonaldTrump/status
/629752759009583104.

30. Donald Trump (@realDonaldTrump), "So many 'politically correct' fools in
    our country. We have to all get back to work and stop wasting time and energy
    on nonsense!" Twitter, August 8, 2015, 5:29 a.m., https://twitter.com
    /realDonaldTrump/status/629992743788523520; Donald Trump (@real
    DonaldTrump), "@redstate I miss you all, and thanks for all of your support.
    Political correctness is killing our country. 'weakness.'" Twitter, August 8, 2015,
    6:26 a.m., https://twitter.com/realDonaldTrump/status/630007166129303552.

31. Rush Limbaugh, "Why I Don't Endorse in Primaries," *The Rush Limbaugh
    Show*, February 12, 2016, https://www.rushlimbaugh.com/daily/2016/02/12/why_i
    _don_t_endorse_in_primaries; Rush Limbaugh, "If Conservatism Is Your
    Only Priority, There Is No Choice Other than Ted Cruz," *The Rush Lim-
    baugh Show*, February 10, 2016, https://www.rushlimbaugh.com/daily/2016/02
    /10/if_conservatism_is_your_only_priority_there_is_no_choice_other_than
    _ted_cruz.

32. Judd Legum, "How Sean Hannity Managed to Interview Trump 41 Times and
    Never Once Made News," Think Progress, April 11, 2016, https://thinkprogress
    .org/how-sean-hannity-managed-to-interview-trump-41-times-and-never-once
    -made-news-3a762a1fe170.

33. streiff, "Who Has Sean Hannity Interviewed 41 Times without Making News?
    Can You Guess?" RedState, April 12, 2016, http://www.redstate.com/streiff/2016
    /04/12/sean-hannity-interviewed-41-times-without-making-news-can-guess.

34. Lynda McLaughlin, "Candidate Time on The Sean Hannity Radio and TV
    Shows," *The Sean Hannity Show*, April 13, 2016, accessible via the Internet
    Archive Wayback Machine, https://web.archive.org/web/20160415194837
    /http://www.hannity.com/articles/election-493995/candidate-time-on-the-sean
    -hannity-14601203.

35. Leon H. Wolf, "Sean Hannity Is Not Happy with Redstate," RedState, April 13,
    2016, http://www.redstate.com/leon_h_wolf/2016/04/13/sean-hannity-happy
    -redstate.

36. Josh Feldman, "'You Gotta Stop!' Hannity Loses His Cool with Ted Cruz over
    Delegates," Mediaite, April 19, 2016, http://www.mediaite.com/online/you-gotta
    -stop-hannity-loses-his-cool-with-ted-cruz-over-delegates.

37. Rush Limbaugh, "The Day Is Finally Here," *The Rush Limbaugh Show*,
    November 8, 2016, https://www.rushlimbaugh.com/daily/2016/11/08/the_day_is
    _finally_here.

38. Donald Trump (@realDonaldTrump), "@Don_Vito_08: 'A picture is worth a thousand words' @realDonaldTrump #LyingTed #NeverCruz @MELANIA-TRUMP," Twitter, March 23, 2016, 8:55 p.m., https://twitter.com /realDonaldTrump/status/712850174838771712; Theodore Schleifer and Julia Manchester, "Donald Trump Makes Wild Threat to 'Spill the Beans' on Ted Cruz's Wife," March 22, 2016, CNN, http://www.cnn.com/2016/03/22/politics /ted-cruz-melania-trump-twitter-donald-trump-heidi/index.html.

39. Nolan D. McCaskill, "Trump Walks into #NeverTrump Radio Buzzsaw," Politico, March 28, 2016, http://www.politico.com/blogs/2016-gop-primary-live -updates-and-results/2016/03/trump-charlie-sykes-interview-221289; Charlie Sykes interviews Donald Trump, WTMJ, posted on Soundcloud, https:// soundcloud.com/620-wtmj/charlie-sykes-interviews-donald-trump; "Wisconsin Radio Host Charlie Sykes Batters Donald Trump in Contentious Interview," March 28, 2016, https://www.youtube.com/watch?v=UOif2C3jPr8; Kevin Bohn, "Conservative Radio Hosts' Influence Seen in Trump's Wisconsin Loss," CNN, April 6, 2016, http://www.cnn.com/2016/04/05/politics/wisconsin-radio-host -donald-trump-primary/index.html; Mark Sommerhauser, "Talk Radio Hosts Hammer Trump on Views, Ideas," *Capital Times & Wisconsin State Journal*, March 29, 2016.

40. Ashley Parker and Nick Corasanti, "6 Talk Radio Hosts, on a Mission to Stop Donald Trump in Wisconsin," *New York Times*, April 4, 2016; Jonathan Lemire, "Trump Grilled by Dean of Wisconsin Conservative Talk Radio," Associated Press, March 28, 2016; Bohn, "Conservative Radio Hosts' Influence"; John Fund, "Trump Steps into Wisconsin Talk-Radio Buzzsaw," *National Review*, March 29, 2016.

41. Kobylt, interview.

42. Greg Garrison, interview with author, April 11, 2016.

43. Chris Stigall, email messages to author, April 14, 2016, and October 19, 2017.

44. Jones was a regular guest of Stern's. The host also mocked and parodied him. "Glenn Beck Mocks Alex Jones," posted by ulaghchi to Youtube on July 29, 2014, https://www.youtube.com/watch?v=VfrGYb_uVjk; "Alex Jones," *Last Week Tonight*, July 30, 2017; Stern Show (@sternshow), "Alex Jones joined the #SternShow this week via satellite to protect his identity from @HowardStern, plug a few products, and sing a new song," Twitter, February 7, 2019, 1:18 p.m., https://twitter.com/sternshow/status/1093620050542710791.

45. Eric Hananoki, "A Guide to Donald Trump's Relationship with Alex Jones," Media Matters for America, May 3, 2007, https://www.mediamatters.org /research/2017/05/03/guide-donald-trump-s-relationship-alex-jones/216263; Manuel Roig-Franzia, "How Alex Jones, Conspiracy Theorist Extraordinaire, Got Donald Trump's Ear," *Washington Post*, November 17, 2016; William

Finnegan, "Donald Trump and the 'Amazing' Alex Jones," *New Yorker,* June 23, 2016; Callum Borchers, "Donald Trump Just Appeared with a Leading 9/11 Conspiracy Theorist," *Washington Post,* December 2, 2015.

46. Andrew Marantz, "Trolls for Trump," *New Yorker,* October 31, 2016; Liam Stack, "Who Is Mike Cernovich? A Guide," *New York Times,* April 5, 2017.

47. Charle Warzel, "How Bill Mitchell Owned the Liberal Media," Buzzfeed, November 13, 2016, https://www.buzzfeed.com/charliewarzel/bill-mitchells -revenge; Charle Warzel, "FiveThirtyHate: Meet the Trump Movement's Post-Truth, Post-Math Anti-Nate Silver," Buzzfeed, October 18, 2016, https://www.buzzfeed.com/charliewarzel/meet-the-trump-movements-post -truth-post-math-anti-nate-silv.

48. See the Trump twitter archive, http://www.trumptwitterarchive.com/archive. The tweets, sometimes twice in one day, occurred on July 24, October 16, November 10, and December 27, 2015; January 28 and February 22, 2016; and March 22, 2017.

49. Yochai Benkler, Robert Faris, Hal Roberts, and Ethan Zuckerman, "Study: Breitbart-led Right-wing Media Ecosystem Altered Broader Media Agenda," *Columbia Journalism Review,* March 3, 2017, https://www.cjr.org/analysis /breitbart-media-trump-harvard-study.php.

50. Sean Spicer, interview with author, June 28, 2018.

51. Ryan Lovelace, "Inside RNC's Stealth Push for Talk Radio to Save GOP," *Washington Examiner,* June 3, 2016.

52. Lloyd Grove, "Breitbart Rolls Over after Reporter 'Grabbed' by Trump Aide," *Daily Beast,* March 9, 2016, http://www.thedailybeast.com/breitbart-rolls-over -after-reporter-grabbed-by-trump-aide; Eric Levitz, "Breitbart Sides with Trump Campaign over Its Own Reporter in Assault Dispute," *New York Magazine,* March 11, 2016; Rosie Gray and McKay Coppins, "Michelle Fields, Ben Shapiro Resign from Breitbart," Buzzfeed, March 14, 2016, https://www.buzzfeed.com/rosiegray/michelle-fields-ben-shapiro-resign-from -breitbart.

53. Robert Costa, Jose A. DelReal, and Jenna Johnson, "Trump Shakes Up Campaign, Demotes Top Adviser," *Washington Post,* August 17, 2016; Jonathan Martin, Jim Rutenberg, and Maggie Haberman, "Donald Trump Appoints Media Firebrand to Run Campaign," *New York Times,* August 17, 2016; Green, *Devil's Bargain,* 208–209.

54. Katy Tur, *Unbelievable: My Front-Row Seat to the Craziest Campaign in American History* (New York: Dey St., 2017), 244.

55. Dylan Byers, "Sean Hannity Participates in Trump Promotional Video," CNN, September 21, 2016, http://money.cnn.com/2016/09/20/media/hannity-trump /index.html.

56. Phil Shiver, "Levin: I'm Voting for Trump . . . Here's Why," *Conservative Review*, September 6, 2016, https://www.conservativereview.com/articles/levin -im-voting-for-trump.

57. Shiver, "Levin: I'm Voting for Trump"; LevinTV, "Decision Time," Facebook, September 7, 2016, https://www.facebook.com/LevinTV/videos/vb .1546815202270918/1786065018345934.

58. Rush Limbaugh, "We're beyond Ideology, Folks," *The Rush Limbaugh Show*, September 15, 2016, https://www.rushlimbaugh.com/daily/2016/09/15/we_re _beyond_ideology_folks.

59. Rush Limbaugh, "The Day Is Finally Here."

60. Amanda Carpenter, interview with author, September 8, 2016.

61. Tim Miller, interview with author, September 8, 2016.

62. Kobylt, interview; Brett Winterble, interview with author, January 23, 2017.

63. Hadas Gold, "Michael Medved Suffers for His Anti-Trump Stance," Politico, November 6, 2016, http://www.politico.com/story/2016/11/michael-medved -salem-radio-donald-trump-230810; Michael Medved, interview with author, January 18, 2017; Charlie J. Sykes, "Charlie Sykes on Where the Right Went Wrong," *New York Times*, December 15, 2016; Charlie Sykes, interview with author, December 12, 2016.

64. Nicole Pinto, "Cancer Survivor Medved Signs Salem Contract Extension," *San Fernando Valley Business Journal*, November 18, 2015, http://www.sfvbj .com/news/2015/nov/18/cancer-survivor-medved-signs-salem-contract-extens; Asawin Suebsaeng, Maxwell Tani, and Andrew Kirell, "Seb Gorka in Talks to Be Salem Radio's New Host," Daily Beast, July 20, 2018, https://www .thedailybeast.com/seb-gorka-in-talks-to-be-salem-radios-new-host-as-network -plots-a-coup-against-its-trump-critics; "Sebastian Gorka to Replace Michael Medved in Salem Radio Network Lineup," All Access Music Group, November 8, 2018, https://www.allaccess.com/net-news/archive/story/181574 /sebastian-gorka-to-replace-michael-medved-in-salem.

65. Brian Stelter, "'Mass Firing' at Conservative Site RedState," CNN, April 27, 2018, https://money.cnn.com/2018/04/27/media/redstate-blog-salem-media /index.html.

66. Hadas Gold and Oliver Darcy, "Salem Executives Pressured Radio Hosts to Cover Trump More Positively, Emails Show," CNN, May 9, 2018, http:// money.cnn.com/2018/05/09/media/salem-radio-executives-trump/index .html.

67. Elisha Krauss, interview with author, May 18, 2018; Ben Shapiro, interview with author, May 4, 2017; Hadas Gold, "Michelle Fields, Ben Shapiro Resign from Breitbart," Politico, March 14, 2016, https://www.politico.com/blogs/on -media/2016/03/michelle-fields-ben-shapiro-resign-from-breitbart-220709.

68. Michael M. Grynbaum and Jim Rutenberg, "The *Weekly Standard*, Pugnacious to the End, Will Cease Publication," *New York Times*, December 14, 2018.

69. Sykes, "Charlie Sykes on Where the Right Went Wrong"; Sykes, interview.

70. Steve Guest, interview with author, December 5, 2016; anonymous Republican staffer, interview with author, November 16, 2016; Scott Hogensen, interview with author, July 18, 2018.

71. Hogensen, interview; Spicer, interview.

72. Jon Meacham, *Destiny and Power: The American Odyssey of George Herbert Walker Bush* (New York: Random House, 2015), 326.

73. For discussion of conservative appeals to blue-collar whites, see Timothy Lombardo, *Blue-Collar Conservatism: Frank Rizzo's Philadelphia and Populist Politics* (Philadelphia: University of Pennsylvania Press, 2018); Stephanie McCrummen, "Cheers, a Punch, a Slur: What It's Like in the Crowd at a Donald Trump Rally," *Washington Post*, December 17, 2015; Molly Ball, "The Ecstasy of Donald Trump," *The Atlantic*, November 26, 2015.

74. Emma Roller, "The Women Who Like Donald Trump," *New York Times*, May 10, 2016; Melinda Henneberger, "What Trump Supporters Talk about When They Talk about Trump," *Roll Call*, June 13, 2016.

75. Eli Stokols, "Why Wisconsin's 'Never Trump' Movement Is Different," Politico, March 30, 2016, https://www.politico.com/story/2016/03/why-wisconsins-never-trump-movement-is-different-221407.

76. Gregory Krieg and Martin Savidge, "Why Wisconsin Hasn't Warmed to Donald Trump," CNN, April 4, 2016, http://www.cnn.com/2016/04/04/politics/donald-trump-wisconsin-problems-scott-walker/index.html.

77. These comments came from Limbaugh's March 31, 2016, and April 1, 2016, shows. I took the quotes from the transcripts accessible on Limbaugh's website at the time. Subsequently his website underwent a redesign, and all of the transcripts from that week are unavailable as of this writing.

78. David Fahrenthold, "Trump Recorded Having Extremely Lewd Conversation about Women in 2005," *Washington Post*, October 8, 2016.

79. Jose A. DelReal, "Ahead of Debate, Trump Holds News Conference with Bill Clinton Accusers," *Washington Post*, October 9, 2016.

80. Rush Limbaugh, "This Is What It Looks Like When You Take on the Establishment," *The Rush Limbaugh Show*, October 10, 2016, https://www.rushlimbaugh.com/daily/2016/10/10/this_is_what_it_looks_like_when_you_take_on_the_establishment.

81. Rush Limbaugh, "John Harwood, Democrat Operative," *The Rush Limbaugh Show*, October 11, 2016, https://www.rushlimbaugh.com/daily/2016/10/11/john_harwood_democrat_operative.

82. Rush Limbaugh, "The Bombshells in Hillary's Wall Street Speeches," *The Rush Limbaugh Show,* October 10, 2016, https://www.rushlimbaugh.com/daily /2016/10/10/the_bombshells_in_hillary_s_wall_street_speeches; Rush Limbaugh, "More Jaw-Dropping Revelations in the WikiLeaks Clinton Email Dump," *The Rush Limbaugh Show,* October 11, 2016, https://www .rushlimbaugh.com/daily/2016/10/11/more_jaw_dropping_revelations_in_the _wikileaks_clinton_email_dump.

83. Tur, *Unbelievable,* 172–173, 272–273; Callum Borchers, "'Hide of a Rhinoceros' Helps NBC's Katy Tur Withstand Donald Trump's Taunts," *Washington Post,* November 3, 2016; Dylan Byers, "Donald Trump Singles Out NBC's Katy Tur, Again," CNN, November 2, 2016, https://money.cnn.com/2016/11/02/media /donald-trump-katy-tur/index.html; Katy Tur, "My Crazy Year with Trump," *Marie Claire,* September 1, 2016.

84. See the Trump Twitter archive under the category of "Media Disdain" for a list of Trump's Twitter assaults on media figures and journalists, http://www .trumptwitterarchive.com.

85. Matt Taibbi, "Morning Blow: How Joe and Mika Became Trump's Lapdogs," *Rolling Stone,* February 23, 2016; Eliza Relman, "The Rise and Fall of Trump's Relationship with Mika Brezinski," Business Insider, June 30, 2017, http://www .businessinsider.com/who-is-mika-brzezinski-trump-feud-face-lift-2017-6; Lloyd Grove, "Is 'Morning Joe' Too Close to Donald Trump?" Daily Beast, February 17, 2016, https://www.thedailybeast.com/is-morning-joe-too-close-to -donald-trump; Sarah Quinlan, "Joe Scarborough, Anti-Trumper?" *National Review,* July 21, 2017.

86. Donald Trump (@realdonaldtrump), Twitter, August 22, 2016, 4:29 A.M., https://twitter.com/realdonaldtrump/status/767685048703279104?lang=en.

87. Michael M. Grynbaum, "Trump Calls the News Media 'the Enemy of the American People,'" *New York Times,* February 17, 2017.

88. Miller, interview.

25. The Big Picture

1. "Santorum Calls Limbaugh Comments 'Absurd,'" CNN, March 2, 2012, http://politicalticker.blogs.cnn.com/2012/03/02/santorum-calls-limbaugh -comments-absurd.

2. Kayla Webley Adler, "'I Was Fired for Being Pro-Choice,'" *Marie Claire,* June 23, 2017; "Watch: Tomi Lahren Joins 'The View,' Explains Why She's Pro-Choice," Fox News, May 17, 2017, http://insider.foxnews.com/2017/03/17 /tomi-lahren-explains-why-shes-pro-choice-view-interview; Amy Zimmerman, "Tomi Lahren Is Terrible. Period," Daily Beast, December 9, 2016, https://www .thedailybeast.com/tomi-lahren-is-terrible-period; Jonah Engel Bromwich,

"Tomi Lahren: Young, Vocal and the Right's Rising Media Star," *New York Times*, December 4, 2016; Ashley May, "Fox Contributor Tomi Lahren Said Diner Threw Water on Her; Trump Tweeted His Support," *USA Today*, May 24, 2018.

3. Jeffrey M. Berry and Sarah Sobieraj, *The Outrage Industry: Political Opinion Media and the New Incivility* (New York: Oxford University Press, 2014), 3–4.

4. Sarah B. Boxer, "Romney: Limbaugh Remarks 'Not Language I Would Have Used,'" CBS, March 3, 2012, http://www.cbsnews.com/news/romney-limbaugh -remarks-not-language-i-would-have-used.

5. Gregory Wallace, "Paul Calls Limbaugh Comments 'Crude,'" CNN, March 3, 2012, http://politicalticker.blogs.cnn.com/2012/03/03/paul-calls-limbaugh -comments-crude.

6. Mike DeBonis, "McCarthy Blames Republican Loss of House Majority on GOP Health Care Bill," *Washington Post*, February 12, 2019.

7. Jennifer Haberkorn, "Obama Vetoes Obamacare Repeal Bill," Politico, January 8, 2016, https://www.politico.com/story/2016/01/obama-vetoes -obamacare-repeal-bill-217505; Mike DeBonis, "Obama Vetoes Republican Repeal of Health-care Law," *Washington Post*, January 8, 2016.

8. Carl Hulse, "Why the Senate Couldn't Pass a Crime Bill Both Parties Backed," *New York Times*, September 16, 2016.

9. Carl Hulse, "It Took Quite a Push, but McConnell Finally Allows Criminal Justice Vote," *New York Times*, December 13, 2018; Kolby Itkowitz, "Why Isn't Mitch McConnell Bringing Up Criminal Justice Reform?" *Washington Post*, November 30, 2018.

10. Jason Zengerle, "How the Trump Administration Is Remaking the Court," *New York Times Magazine*, August 22, 2018.

11. Manu Raju, "Senate Judiciary Committee Scraps Votes on Judges Because of Flake," CNN, December 5, 2018, https://www.cnn.com/2018/12/05/politics /senate-judiciary-committee-jeff-flake/index.html.

12. David Hinckley, "Rush Limbaugh Did Cost Our Company Millions, Says Cumulus CEO," *New York Daily News*, May 7, 2013.

13. Emily Steel and Michael S. Schmidt, "Bill O'Reilly Is Forced Out at Fox News," *New York Times*, April 19, 2017; "Bill O'Reilly Thrives at Fox News, Even as Harassment Settlements Add Up," *New York Times*, April 1, 2017; "Bill O'Reilly Settled New Harassment Claim, Then Fox Renewed His Contract," *New York Times*, October 21, 2017.

14. Stephen Battaglio, "Fox News Launches 'Fox Nation' as News Networks Try to Catch the Streaming Wave," *Los Angeles Times*, November 26, 2018.

15. Gabe Hobbs, email message to author, February 11, 2019.

16. Rush Limbaugh, "President Trump Calls the Show!" *The Rush Limbaugh Show*, August 1, 2018, https://www.rushlimbaugh.com/daily/2018/08/01/president -trump-calls-the-show.

17. Rush Limbaugh, "A Great Day for the Swamp: Dems Get Everything, Trump Gets Less than Nothing," *The Rush Limbaugh Show*, December 19, 2018, https://www.rushlimbaugh.com/daily/2018/12/19/a-great-day-for-the-swamp -dems-get-everything-trump-gets-less-than-nothing; Rush Limbaugh, "The President Tells Me It's Money or Nothing," *The Rush Limbaugh Show*, December 20, 2018, https://www.rushlimbaugh.com/daily/2018/12/20/my -sources-say-trump-wont-sign-a-bill-without-real-money-for-the-wall; Jason Schwartz, "Rush Limbaugh Roars Back," Politico, December 21, 2018, https://www.politico.com/story/2018/12/21/rush-limbaugh-trump-comeback -1073726.

18. "Trump: Favorable / Unfavorable," RealClear Politics, https://www .realclearpolitics.com/epolls/other/trump_favorableunfavorable-5493.html.

19. Nixon and Reagan did at times suffer large approval dips, but their ratings floor was close to Trump's ceiling—except when the anomaly of Watergate turned the country against Nixon.

20. Rush Limbaugh, "Non-Citizen Voting Confirmed in Texas and Pennsylvania," *The Rush Limbaugh Show*, January 31, 2019, https://www.rushlimbaugh.com /daily/2019/01/31/non-citizen-voting-confirmed-in-texas-and-pennsylvania; "Caravan Arrives, Dems Steal Elections—and GOP Holds a Press Conference on Leadership Elections!" *The Rush Limbaugh Show*, November 14, 2018, https://www.rushlimbaugh.com/daily/2018/11/14/caravan-arrives-dems-steal -elections-and-gop-holds-a-press-conference-on-leadership-elections.

Acknowledgments

I am deeply indebted to the many people without whom this project would not have been possible.

First, a huge thank you to the more than three hundred people from the radio and political worlds who graciously took time from their busy schedules to answer my questions and mostly went on the record. Some of them put up with repeated follow-ups and nagging emails as I developed an understanding of the talk radio business and its political implications, which would not have been possible without their participation. When I began this project, I never imagined that I would interview anywhere near this many people, but now, almost nine years later, I cannot imagine the book without their input. For the many who contributed but don't see their names in the notes: rest assured that you, too, helped shape this book.

I have been fortunate to receive fellowships from the Fox Leadership Program at the University of Pennsylvania and the Corcoran Department of History at the University of Virginia over the past nine years, which made it far easier to complete this book. I am grateful to have been a part of the Fox family, both because of the great work the program does and because of the terrific people who work at Fox, especially Joe Tierney, who sets the tone for everything. Special thanks to Chuck Brutsche, Laura Thornton, Euria Chung, and Wendy Jensen, who have provided so much assistance through the years on matters big and small.

My professors deserve much credit for all that is good in this book. The fantastic teaching of Rogers Smith, Walter McDougall, Tom Childers, Kathleen Hall Jamieson, and the late Rick Beeman and Sheldon Hackney inspired me to head down a scholarly path and showed me that good scholarship can and should involve good storytelling. In many ways this project is the culmination of a journey that began in their college classrooms. In graduate school, the tutelage of Mel Leffler and Gary Gallagher, especially on the craft of writing, was invaluable. I had few more demanding teachers, but I am a far better scholar for having studied with Mel and Gary.

I also owe a debt of gratitude to the many scholars whose contributions enriched this work. These include members of my dissertation committee—Bernie Carlson, Sarah Milov, and Bruce Williams. David Greenberg and Allison Perlman provided astute comments that benefited the manuscript. Tom Sugrue, Matt Levendusky, Alison Dagnes, Dannagal Young, Jim Snyder, Frank Baumgartner, Tim Lombardo, Andrew Hall, and the late Jim Baughman all generously shared advice, insight, and expertise. I have also been fortunate to have students who had real interest in this research, asked fantastic questions, and in several cases, generously used their connections to put me in touch with potential interview subjects. For that I am thankful.

Lauren Turek's questions might have occasionally exasperated me in the moment, but all of her pushing made this book better. Without Lauren, I am not sure that I would have made it through the last nine years of research and writing.

Alyssa MacMillan, Julianne Huegel, Matt and Alexandra Sklar, Andy Wilkowski, Tom Mullen, deMauri Mackie, Andy Poenicke, Erin O'Brien, Rich Eisenberg, Stephen Danley, Alec Hickmott, and so many other friends must have wondered why it was taking so long for me to finish this book, but they never once asked the question. Instead they offered good company, reassurance, support, and most importantly, friendship. You guys mean the world to me.

I wish to thank Michael Smerconish, who started out as an interview subject and has become a friend and collaborator. Talking with Michael and coauthoring a piece with him that explored the themes of this book helped hone the ideas in the preceding pages. Michael has also been a champion of this project, offering a platform to share and develop these ideas with his radio and television audiences. Every time I'm on Michael's show, I am reminded of how he provides a model for all of us commenting on public affairs. He is thoughtful and measured, without being dull or boring, proving that one can do great radio and television without extremism or hyperbole.

To John Dickerson, working with you the last four years has been a great joy. Your zest for historical understanding has enriched my outlook and my quest for answers. Your magnificent storytelling ability has helped push me to tell a story in the preceding pages, complete with those little dashes of color that so enrich every episode of the *Whistlestop* podcast we produce together. Your encouragement has meant the world, and your kindness and willingness to share credit provide an example for all of us who want to treat people well. I spend every day in amazement at how you manage to pull off so many different things at such a high level.

Thanks to Thomas LeBien, Simon Waxman, and all of the other men and women at Harvard University Press who have made this final product so much better. Thomas and Harvard took a chance on this manuscript, and I hope the end product has met, or even exceeded, their expectations. From jacket design, to cogent editing that is evident on every page of the book, to patient encouragement as I struggled with deadlines—without their tireless work, this book simply wouldn't have been possible. They've also been a joy to work with and made what could have been an extremely painful process far less so. I also thank the two anonymous peer reviewers whose comments and ideas so enriched this final version of the manuscript.

Working with Niki Hemmer and Katie Cramer Brownell every day has provided immense inspiration and fellowship. I have been truly blessed over the last two years to have such wonderful, understanding, supportive colleagues. Without their support and encouragement, this book would never have gotten finished. Katie also offered wise feedback on the entire manuscript, and Niki lent her expertise to several parts as well.

I would never have gotten to this point without Brian Balogh. Brian's suggestion spawned this project, and he patiently read draft after draft of each chapter. Brian's probing questions slowly and steadily shaped and improved the book. Thanks to his efforts, the final product is far more readable. During my graduate school years, Brian provided ample encouragement and sound advice, while giving me the freedom to explore and experiment. He taught me to see the big picture, encouraged creativity, and treated me like a colleague. I am grateful for his support and encouragement.

Simply put, no one has ever been a better mentor and sounding board than John DiIulio. For seventeen years John has been a sage, cheerleader, friend, and booster. John's belief in me and my work often exceeds my own. I can honestly say that I would never have made it through graduate school and through this project without John's support. He taught me to root my work in the world beyond academia and to think about the practical implications of scholarly topics. He has always had my back, for which I am perpetually grateful. John has also served as a model of what a scholar, a college teacher, and, most importantly, a person ought to be. There is no one with a bigger heart than John. I can only hope to reach the high bar he has set.

I owe my parents everything. They deserve the credit for my strengths and none of the blame for my weaknesses. Without their sacrifices, support, and encouragement, none of my achievements would have been possible. They cultivated and nurtured my curiosity and my interest in reading, thinking, and public affairs. They have also patiently tolerated my moodiness, frustration, occasional radio silence, and all of the other ups and downs, while always remaining my biggest cheerleaders. My mom especially has taken on tasks and borne the brunt of my stress-induced short fuse with kindness, patience, and love. Even when I've been down on myself, she continued to believe and tout my accomplishments. Mom and Dad, I love you and I hope that this book makes you proud.

Finally, I must note that, in spite of the many contributions cited above and my own best efforts, there are inevitably mistakes and imperfections in the preceding pages. Those, of course, are my responsibility alone. So I thank you, the reader, for your forbearance, and for understanding that those stem from human imperfections, not intent.

Index